The **FAST** Plan for Tax Reform

The **FAST** Plan for Tax Reform

A **F**air, **A**ccountable, and **S**imple **T**ax Plan
to Chop Away the Federal Tax Thicket

Donald E. Phillipson

iUniverse LLC
Bloomington

THE FAST PLAN FOR TAX REFORM
A FAIR, ACCOUNTABLE, AND SIMPLE TAX PLAN TO
CHOP AWAY THE FEDERAL TAX THICKET

iUniverse books may be ordered through booksellers or by contacting:

iUniverse
1663 Liberty Drive
Bloomington, IN 47403
www.iuniverse.com
1-800-Authors (1-800-288-4677)

Because of the dynamic nature of the Internet, any web addresses or links contained in this book may have changed since publication and may no longer be valid. The views expressed in this work are solely those of the author and do not necessarily reflect the views of the publisher, and the publisher hereby disclaims any responsibility for them.

Any people depicted in stock imagery provided by Thinkstock are models, and such images are being used for illustrative purposes only.

Certain stock imagery © Thinkstock

ISBN: 978-1-4759-9741-5 (sc)
ISBN: 978-1-4759-9742-2 (e)

Library of Congress Control Number: 2013912109

Printed in the United States of America.

iUniverse rev. date: 11/11/2013

Contents

List of Tables and Figures xvi

Preface xvii

Acknowledgments xix

Introduction 1
    Barriers to Real Tax Reform 1
    How Do We Overcome the Barriers to Tax Reform? 2
    We Should Reform Federal Taxes Now 3

Part I: Setting the Stage 5

1   Why Do We Have Federal Taxes? 7
    Purposes of Federal Taxes 7
    How Much Is Enough? 8

2   The Impacts of Deficit Spending 10
    The Annual Federal Deficit 10
        Federal Deficit 10
        Federal Surplus 10
        Public Debt 11
    The National Debt 11
        Federal Government Accounts Debt 12
        Alternative Deficit Figures 12
        Alternative Deficit Figures 2001–2008 .13
        Recent Evolution of the National Debt .14
        National Debt up to September 2008 14
        National Debt after September 2008 15

The National Debt's Impact on Historic Budgets 15
    Fiscal Year 2008 Example. 16
    Alternate Portrayals of Interest Paid. 16
The National Debt's Impact on Future Taxes 18
    Net Interest on the Public Debt 18
    Interest on Borrowings from Federal Trust Funds 20
Deficit Spending Recap 21

3 Borrowings from Federal Trust Funds. 22
  Adequacy of Dedicated Taxes 22
  Fate of Dedicated Tax Money 23
  The Impacts of Borrowings on Trust Fund Beneficiaries 23
  Dealing with the Impacts of Borrowings 25
  Consequences of Unpaid Borrowings 25

4 Criteria for Judging All Federal Taxes. 27
  What Is Fairness? 27
  What Is Accountability? 28
  What Is Simplicity? 28
  Applying the Criteria 30

5 Choices from Potential Tax Alternatives 31
  A Philosophical Issue. 31
  Practical Tax Considerations 32
    Taxes on Individual Income 32
    Taxes on Corporation Income 34
    Taxes on a Deceased's Estate 34
    Taxes on Gifts 35
    Excise Taxes 35
    Tariffs 35
    Taxes on Sales. 36
    Taxes on Real Property 37
    Taxes on Personal Property 37
    Taxes on Value Added. 37
  Decisions on the Tax Alternatives 38
    Choices from the Six Current Federal Taxes. 38
    Choices from the Four Other Potential Federal Taxes 39
  Moving Forward with the Choices 41

6 Basic Tax Concepts 42

    Tax Rates 42

        Standard-Rate Tax 42

        Graduated Tax Rates 42

        Marginal Tax Rate 43

    Subsidies 43

        Direct Subsidies 43

        Tax Subsidies 43

        Impacts of Direct and Tax Subsidies 45

    Using Tax Concepts 46

7 What Makes Current Federal Taxes So Complicated? 47

    Complicating Features of Taxes on Individual Income 47

        Using Different Tax Rates for Different Kinds of Income 48

        Phasing Out or Phasing In Tax Provisions Application 48

        Providing Elective Tax Subsidies in Multiple Ways 49

        Applying an Alternative Minimum Tax 50

    Complicating Features of the Corporation Income Tax 50

    Complicating Features of the Tax on Deceased's Estates 51

    Addressing These Complicating Features .52

8 The FAST Plan's Bottom Line 53

    The FAST Plan Overview 54

    The FAST Plan for Individual Income, Social Security, and Medicare Taxes 55

    The FAST Plan for Corporation Income Tax 57

    The FAST Plan for Estate and Gift Taxes 57

    Using the FAST Plan's Bottom Line 58

Part II: Reforming Taxes on Individual Income .59

9 How Individual Income Is Taxed Today 61

    Social Security and Medicare Taxes 61

    Individual Income Tax 62

        Taxable Income 62

        Income Tax 62

        Tax Credits 63

    What Is Coming Up 63

    Meeting the Most Difficult Reform Challenge 63

10 Should We Retain Graduated Income Tax Rates? 64

    Historic Effects of Graduated Income Tax Rates 64

        Filing Categories 64

        Capital Gains 65

        Tax Discrimination 65

        Marginal Total Federal Tax Rate 65

    Say Good-Bye to Graduated Tax Rates 67

        Flaws in Flat-Tax Proposals 67

        The Standard-Rate Tax of the FAST Plan 68

    The Amount of the Standard Rate 69

    What Should Be the Target for Tax Receipts? 70

    Testing an Alternative Approach with Facts 72

    Applying the Standard-Rate Tax 72

11 Solving the Social Security and Medicare Taxes Dilemma 74

    Solving the Add-On Dilemma 74

    Solving the Different Applications Dilemma .74

    Important Features of Social Security and Medicare Taxes 75

        Social Security and Medicare Taxes on Employees 76

        Social Security and Medicare Taxes on Self-Employed Individuals 77

    Social Security and Medicare Taxes in Context 79

    Marginal Total Federal Tax Rates 80

        Under Current Law 80

        Under a Standard-Rate Tax within Current Law 82

    The Parity Challenge: Employees and Self-Employed Individuals 83

    Equalizing Credits for Employees and Self-Employed Individuals 83

        Adjustments for Employees 84

        Adjustments for Self-Employed Individuals 85

    The Dilemma Recap 86

12 What Income Should Be Taxed? 88

    What Is Income? 88

    What Is Taxable Income? 89

    The Most Important Kinds of Individual Income 89

13 Historic Ordinary Income 92

    Wages 92

        Tax Withholding on Wages 92

        A Contentious Wages Issue 93

    Personal Business Income 94

    Partnership and S Corporation Income 95

        Partnerships 95

        S Corporations 95

    Interest 95

        Should Interest Have Special Tax Rates? 96

        Municipal Bonds Interest 96

    Miscellaneous Income 96

    Historic Ordinary Income Recap 97

14 Capital Gains 99

    What Is a "Capital Gain"? 99

        Current Tax Treatment of Capital Gains 100

        Current Tax-Law Consequences 100

    Who Has Significant Capital Gains Income? 101

    How Does Capital Gains Income Affect Tax Owed? 102

        Example Comparison of Tax Owed 102

        Primary Beneficiaries of Less Tax Owed 102

        Conclusions from the Data 103

    Do Rationales for Lower Capital Gains Taxes Have Merit? 104

        To Minimize Income "Bunching" Disadvantages 104

        To Encourage Investment 105

        To Benefit Society 107

        The Rationales Fail Their Burden of Proof 107

    What Other Capital Gains Issues Should We Consider? 108

        Dealing with Inflation 109

        Capital Gain on the Sale of a Principal Residence 111

    Capital Gains Recap 111

15 Dividends. 113

   Arguments for Special Treatment of Dividends Income. 113

     The Corporation's Perspective. 113

     The Shareholder's Perspective. 114

     Other Proponents' Arguments 114

   Arguments for Treating Dividends as Ordinary Income 114

   Changing the Tax Framework for Dividends Income 115

16 Social Security Benefits. 117

   Competing Taxation Philosophies. 117

   Historic and Current Taxation of Social Security Benefits 118

   Flaws in Section 86 119

     Excess Complexity. 119

     Inadequate Thresholds. 119

   FAST Plan Treatment of Social Security Benefits .120

   Social Security Benefits Recap. 121

17 Pension Payments and Retirement-Plan Distributions 122

   A Non-Taxation Advantage 122

   Removing the Non-Taxation Advantage 123

18 Tax-Exempt Income. 125

   Categorizing Exclusions from Gross Income 125

     Personal Benefits. 125

     Healthy Life Necessities 126

     Miscellaneous Exclusions. 126

     Tax Subsidies 126

   The Tax Subsidy Exclusion of State and Local Bond Interest 126

     Fairness Issues. 127

     Accountability Issues 127

     Accountability Using the FAST Plan 128

   On to Taxable Income. 128

19 Evaluating Current Reductions from Income 129

   Determining Taxable Income 129

   Structural Problems with Current Reductions from Income 130

     Problems Inherent with Many Current Reductions 130

     Problems Inherent with Above-the-Line Reductions 131

Ripple Effects of Reductions on Many State Governments 131

Congress's Attempts at Reductions Fairness. 132

Should Itemized Deductions as a Whole Be Limited? 133

Should Exemptions Be Limited?. 133

Categorizing Reductions from Income 134

20 Appropriate Reductions Above the Line 136

Limiting the Types of Reductions Placed Above the Line 136

Business Reductions for Determining Individual Business Income 137

Reductions for Business-Related Activities. 137

Income Transfers That Ultimately Will Be Taxable 138

Money Transfers That Only Postpone Income Tax Liability 138

Money Transfers That Are Taxable to Another Person 139

Above-the-Line Recap 140

21 Reductions for Payments Necessary for a Healthy Life. 141

Exemptions 141

Standard Deduction 142

Tax Treatment of Medical Expenses 142

Current Law 143

A Better Way 144

The Only Below-the-Line Reductions 145

22 Reductions for Elective Payments. 147

Payments That Benefit Oneself 147

Payments That Benefit Others (Gifts to Charity) 148

23 Reductions for Nonelective Payments 150

Reductions for Payment of State and Local Taxes 150

Which States and Local Taxes Are Favored as Reductions?. 150

Competing Schools of Thought 151

The FAST Plan Solution. 152

Reductions for Payment of Federal Self-Employment Taxes. 153

Reductions for Uncompensated Losses 154

Uniqueness of the Uncompensated Losses Deduction 154

The Uncompensated Losses Deduction in Practice 154

The FAST Plan Approach 155

Nonelective Payments Recap. 155

24 Expanded Role of Tax Credits for Subsidies 156

Problems with Current Tax and Direct Subsidies 156

The FAST Plan Solution 157

The Way Tax Credits Work Today. 157

Practical Merits of Using Only Tax Credits for All Subsidies. 158

Tax Credits for Tax Subsidies 158

Tax Credits for Direct Subsidies. 160

Tax Credits Recap. 160

25 Current Individual Income Tax Credits. 162

The Earned Income Credit 162

The EIC's Mixture of Two Ideas 163

Future Fate of the EIC 163

Improving the EIC 164

Business-Related Income Tax Credits 164

Upcoming Issues. 165

26 Two Special Cases: Investors and Retirees. 166

Investors 166

The Potential Inequity 167

Addressing the Potential Inequity. 167

Retirees. 168

Reliance on Social Security, Pensions, and Retirement Plans 168

Reliance on Investment Income 169

How Long Is "Temporary"? 170

27 The "Marriage Penalty" (and "Marriage Bonus"). 171

Origin of Different Sets of Tax Rates. 172

The Bonus Effect of the Joint Return 172

Perceived Unfairness of the Joint Return. 173

Structural Flaws in the Different Sets of Tax Rates 173

The Separate Returns Penalty 173

The Equal Incomes Penalty 173

How to Remove the Tax Inequities 174

28 The Alternative Minimum Tax on Individuals 176

How the AMT Works in Practice 177

Targeted Tax Subsidies 177

Ending the Alternative Minimum Tax 178

Moving On 178

Part III: Reforming Related Taxes 179

29 Reforming the Corporation Income Tax 181

The Code's Approach to Taxing Corporations 181

Challenging the Code's Historic Underpinning 182

Personal Business Features 182

Corporate Business Features 183

Conclusion from Comparative Business Features 184

Flaws in the Earnings Tax Base 184

A New Taxable Income Base for Corporations 185

Advantages of Using Corporation Revenue as the Tax Base 186

Dealing with Corporation Tax History 188

Corporations with Small Earnings 188

International Treaties 188

Foreign Tax Credits 188

Taxable Business Income Symmetry 189

Tax-Exempt Nonprofit Corporations 189

S Corporations 189

Appropriate New Tax Rate on Corporation Revenue 189

A Potential Tweak to Taxable Revenue 190

Adjustments in Tax Credits Available to Corporations 190

When to Treat Noncorporate Business Entities as Corporations 190

Corporation-Like Attributes 191

Closing a Potential Loophole 192

Fairness for All Noncorporate Business Entities 192

30 New Rules for Estates and Gifts 194

The Current Estate Tax 195

Comparison to the Individual Income Tax 195

Recent Estate Tax History 195

The "Stepped-Up Basis" Rule of Federal Income Tax Law 196
    Congress's Short-Term Reform 196
    Future Fate of the Stepped-Up Basis Rule 197
    Answering Critics of a No Stepped-Up Basis Rule 198
    An Option for Heirs 198
To Have or Not to Have Federal Estate and Gift Taxes 199
    Arguments Against an Estate Tax 199
    Arguments For an Estate Tax 199
    The FAST Plan Approach 200

Part IV: Making Change Happen 203

31 The First Step 205

32 Transition 209
Transition to a Standard-Rate Individual Income Tax 209
    Social Security and Medicare Tax Credits Equality 210
    A Fairly Determined Standard Tax Rate 210
    Using Only Tax Credits for Subsidies 210
    Standard-Rate Universal Application 211
Transition to a Standard-Rate Income Tax on All Capital Gains 211
Transition to a Standard-Rate Income Tax on Dividends 212
Transition to a Corporation Revenue Tax 212
Three Potential Changes within Current Law 213
Transition Reality 214

33 Tax Payment Impacts of the FAST Plan 215
Decreased Compliance Costs for Everyone 215
Individuals Who Will Likely Pay More Federal Taxes 216
Individuals Who Will Likely Pay Less Federal Taxes 217
Individuals with Significant Dividends Income 217
The Corporate World 218
Reform Reality 218

34 Are We Ready? 219

Appendixes 221
    Introduction 223
    List of Appendixes. 225
    Tables and Figures in the Appendixes 229
    Appendixes 237

Notes 409

Glossary 449

Bibliography 455

Index 461

List of Tables and Figures

Table 2.1.   Comparing federal debt at the end of selected fiscal years (billions of current dollars). 14

Table 2.2.   Comparing fiscal year 2008 net interest payments to receipts and outlays (billions of current dollars) 17

Table 2.3.   Comparing fiscal year 2008 gross interest obligations to receipts and outlays (billions of current dollars) 17

Table 11.1.   Comparing 2009 Social Security and Medicare tax rates paid by employees and employers 77

Table 12.1.   Major kinds of reported individual income, tax year 2007 90

Figure 24.1.   Example form for income tax credits with limits (29 percent standard rate) 159

Table 32.1.   Potential staged transition to a new corporation revenue tax. 213

Preface

I have had an odd curiosity about federal tax policy for many years. Maybe my curiosity is an outgrowth of having prepared multiple personal tax returns as a self-employed individual. The usual 1040 form with its schedules and worksheets have been complicated enough to deal with, but sometimes I also created spreadsheets of data just to get the numbers correct for estimated tax payments. Or maybe my curiosity is an outgrowth of having to make sense of business financial information that was relevant to the commercial lawsuits that I handled for many years as a trial lawyer.

Whatever the underlying cause of this curiosity, more than a decade ago, I began writing down ideas about how federal taxes work in practice and how they could be made simpler and less discriminatory. In early 2009, a few new ideas came to me that removed barriers to simplifying the often-conflicting taxation approaches that are found in the current Internal Revenue Code. These ideas also solved important problems with some proposals for tax reform that have found their way into the political arena. So I decided to write a pamphlet as a way to get these ideas into public discussion.

The process of writing a pamphlet spawned more ideas to try to fit everything together. Some of the ideas that I had written down years ago also proved to have merit. This endeavor soon expanded far beyond a pamphlet.

Four decades of experience in federal court litigation, first as a partner in the Denver law firm Davis, Graham & Stubbs and later as a consultant, then became useful. That experience included investigating facts, assembling evidence, researching and analyzing relevant law, writing briefs for courts and advisory memoranda for clients, and presenting cases in court. Using skills learned from that experience, I conducted extensive research so that my descriptions of tax history, current law, and the impacts of federal taxes on different groups of people would be legally and factually accurate. Fortunately, three public sources provide a huge amount of useful information: the Internal Revenue Code, the budgets of the US government, especially their Historical Tables, and the Statistics of Income (SOI) Tax Stats compiled by the Internal Revenue Service. These efforts have created *The FAST Plan for Tax Reform.*

The FAST Plan for Tax Reform is not as daunting as first appears because it has two very different segments of nearly equal length. The first segment is written for anyone who has an interest in federal tax policy. This main text sets the stage for and presents the FAST Plan. The second segment is written for that smaller group of people who may want detailed proof for statements in the first segment. This segment includes multiple appendixes with data, calculations, and other facts that support the statements in the main text.

Writing *The FAST Plan for Tax Reform* is an endeavor that I could not have predicted when I obtained my Juris Doctor from Stanford Law School way back in 1968. At that time, my legal interests were focused on natural resources. Two wonderful mentors at Davis, Graham & Stubbs—Robert H. Harry and John M. Sayre—encouraged me to go far beyond those interests. They showed me that rigorous factual investigation and analysis applies to any subject and can be fun no matter what the subject. That lesson has remained with me all these years. I hope that you will find that it has been applied well in *The FAST Plan for Tax Reform*.

Acknowledgments

As with any written effort of this magnitude, I owe thanks to a number of people. Four people were particularly important in my development of the ideas reflected in *The FAST Plan for Tax Reform*.

First, thanks to my wife Barbara for giving me the space needed to create this book and also for putting up with my grumpiness when my writing was not going so well. Second, thanks to Laurence E. Nemirow, my former law partner at Davis, Graham & Stubbs and a real expert in tax law, who early on checked the accuracy of many of my descriptions of current law and economic theories. Third, thanks to my friend Jock Jacober, who read an early version of my manuscript and provided encouragement for me to continue writing and to try to get my ideas into the political arena. Fourth, thanks to Professor Joseph Bankman of the Stanford Law School, a tax policy expert who encouraged me to continue developing and publicizing my ideas to see what ideas might generate political or public support.

On a less personal level, thanks also to those unsung people in federal agencies who collect, organize, and report data, without which sensible economic analyses would be impossible. My analyses in *The FAST Plan for Tax Reform* rely particularly on data assembled by the Internal Revenue Service and the Office of Management and Budget, with important but somewhat less reliance on data assembled by the US Census Bureau and the Bureau of Labor Statistics.

Finally, thanks to the editors and staff at iUniverse for bringing my manuscript to the public. I particularly thank editors Claire Matze and Cheri Madison, whose constructive criticism, perceptive questions, recommended changes, and specific edits significantly improved the presentation of my ideas about tax reform.

Introduction

Simplify federal taxes!

How often have many of us thought, muttered, or even shouted this idea?

We are not alone.

Economists support simplifying federal taxes so that the effort and money now spent complying with tax laws can be used for more productive purposes. Businesses support this idea as a way to reduce their compliance costs. Politicians support this idea so that they can discern the actual cost of existing or proposed tax subsidies that support a wide range of policies. Federal tax collectors support this idea because excess complexity causes more errors by honest taxpayers and allows greater manipulation by tax cheaters, all of which reduces tax receipts. Individuals support this idea so that they can spend less time on what has become an increasingly aggravating process to fill out tax forms and worksheets.

So why is such an appealing idea so hard to achieve?

Barriers to Real Tax Reform

Human inertia may be the biggest barrier to simplifying federal taxes. We may not like how complicated these taxes have become, especially individual income taxes, but many of their basic features are familiar. Some of the complexity that now exists arises from special provisions that are designed to address particular situations, sometimes to increase taxes because of those situations but more often to decrease them. People have become used to these provisions. Independently, many of these special provisions may have made good sense at the time that they were adopted. Collectively, they are a mess. Unraveling this mess will require people to step outside their comfort zones to consider sometimes greatly different alternatives.

The sheer volume of the Internal Revenue Code and its regulations creates another barrier. The code and its regulations reflect many years of Congress adding concepts, incorporating changed philosophies, and creating tax subsidies. Only real experts understand their intricacies. Often a change in one provision can have a ripple effect on another provision that alters what

1

is taxable and in what way. Federal taxes form an interconnected thicket, and the total thicket determines how much each taxpayer pays to the United States each year. Where to start in this thicket and whether that start will simplify the thicket or make it even more dense are questions that do not have easy answers.

A third barrier can best be described as vested interests. Over the years, Congress has adopted special tax provisions designed to promote a variety of policies. Often these provisions give discriminatory tax advantages to selected groups. Some individuals or corporations pay much less federal taxes than other individuals or corporations that have the same real income. Tax complexity hides many of these provisions from public scrutiny. Vested interests have little desire to lessen tax complexity and thus bring these discriminatory advantages into the light.

How Do We Overcome the Barriers to Tax Reform?

If the barriers to reforming federal taxes are so formidable, should they be circumvented by replacing federal taxes with something entirely different, or should current federal taxes be modified despite the difficulty in trying to do so?

The first segment of this book, which I call the "main text," begins by focusing on this question. Because federal taxes do not exist in a vacuum, part 1 of the main text examines the broad role of federal taxes, along with hidden facts about deficit spending and the national debt. Although simplicity is a worthy and primary goal, it cannot be the only criterion used to judge a federal tax system, or the American people will or at least should reject the system.

Part 1 of the main text defines not only simplicity, but also accountability and fairness as criteria to use in judging any tax system. Part 1 then examines alternative tax approaches, some of which have been ardently advanced by some politicians, economists, or pundits. These approaches have their own flaws when judged against the three criteria. The examination concludes that the current federal tax system, which relies primarily on taxes on income, should be modified significantly but not wholly replaced. You may not initially agree with this conclusion, but after reading part 1, at least you will see how this conclusion is reached. Part 1 ends with a summary of the FAST Plan, a name that invokes the three criteria by standing for Fair, Accountable, and Simple Tax Plan.

The lengthy part 2 of the main text addresses in detail federal taxes on individual income, while part 3 addresses the related taxes on corporations and on estates and gifts. No existing tax feature is considered sacrosanct. Tax provisions that have been around for decades receive as much scrutiny as newer or proposed tax provisions. In the process of reform, one necessarily bumps against policies and philosophies that underlie current federal tax approaches. These are not ignored but identified, discussed, and assessed. Often, different and simpler ways to promote the same policies are possible and part of the FAST Plan's proposed changes. Among the new ideas found in the FAST Plan are a standard-rate individual income tax with tax credits for payment of Social Security and Medicare taxes (this is *not* a flat tax), tax subsidies only via tax credits, and a small corporation revenue tax in place of the current corporation income tax.

Some of the ideas in the FAST Plan will not be new, although their total context may be. Some new ideas will seem heretical or even crazy. Examined in isolation, they may be both. Examined in the context of other ideas, however, their logic and consistency with the fairness, accountability, and simplicity criteria hopefully will become apparent. At the very least, you will know why the idea is presented. Again, the combined effect of all federal tax provisions is what matters.

Part 4 of the main text concludes with realistic ideas about making the FAST Plan reforms a reality. These ideas show that the FAST Plan can provide real federal tax reform without having to create new tax collection structures.

The second segment of this book includes thirty-four appendixes, notes, a glossary, and a bibliography. The appendixes provide details, data, and facts that support the statements in the main text. Some appendixes also present data in new ways that can be helpful to politicians, economists, and others in considering future tax and budgetary policies. The glossary has ninety terms, each of which is highlighted with bold print when first used in the text. The bibliography contains references to my source documents, so that those who wish can check facts or do research in the originals.

We Should Reform Federal Taxes Now

We should reform federal taxes now because recent developments show that the next few years present a unique time for reform.

The significant tax changes that Congress made in 2001 and 2003 were scheduled to expire automatically at the end of 2010.[1] Congress reached a compromise in December 2010 that extended many of these tax changes and modified others, but this compromise covered only 2011 and 2012.[2] In addition, in 2010 President Obama appointed a fiscal commission to study and make recommendations on how the United States can stop incurring so much debt. The National Commission on Fiscal Responsibility and Reform (Fiscal Commission) issued its report *The Moment of Truth* in December 2010. Comprehensive tax reform is one of the six major components of the report's recommended plan.[3]

At the end of 2012, Congress reached yet another tax compromise that extended the 2001 and 2003 tax changes for most individuals, but reinstated prior rates for individual incomes exceeding designated threshold amounts.[4] Although this fiscal cliff tax compromise adopted permanent tax provisions, it was not even close to making tax reforms at the broad levels recommended in the Fiscal Commission's report.

These developments show that federal taxes will continue to be part of upcoming political agendas even though Congress and the president may not like having to deal with real federal tax reform.

How can we achieve real tax reform today?

We all approach this task with a set of expectations or frustrations based on our own experiences with federal taxes. These taxes have been complex for a long time. Multiple exceptions and special provisions can easily create a belief that one's own tax obligation is somehow unfair compared to the tax obligations of others. This belief can then lead to a desire for and even active promotion of special tax provisions designed to reduce that perceived unfairness. Taxpayers may blame "special interests" and politicians for the complicated mess that exists today, but closer to the truth is that much of the current complexity results from what large segments of the American population have wanted for themselves. A tax break here, a tax incentive there, a special program somewhere else, and before long complexity takes over.

Eliminating this thicket will not be possible unless we taxpayers can look beyond our own narrow situations to judge how well a whole system can function with changes. The FAST Plan shows that current federal taxes can be reformed so that they are fair, accountable, and simple without having to create new tax collection structures. As you journey through the main text, I ask that you keep an open mind to new ideas and new perspectives on old ideas on how to improve the federal tax system.

This journey will begin with basics. We will start with an overview of the need for federal taxes generally and will then examine the impacts of deficit spending. Meaningful tax reform cannot occur outside the context of these current realities.

As you start this journey, I have another request that arises from my creation of *The FAST Plan for Tax Reform*. Although my original intent was just to get new ideas into public discussion, tax reform is so important that mere dialogue is not enough. Action is needed now to reform the federal tax code. If you agree with the ideas and proposals of the FAST Plan (or at least most of them), I urge you to get involved in the political arena so that your elected representatives will take the steps necessary to adopt the FAST Plan to improve our federal tax system.

Part I:

Setting the Stage

Chapter 1

Why Do We Have Federal Taxes?

The US government cannot function without money. Government operations, programs, and services cannot occur without paying people to do work, purchasing materials that support such work, and providing facilities for those people or for other purposes that support the operations, programs, and services. These basic and obvious facts sometimes get lost when people demand that the federal government do X or Y. Neither X nor Y is free.

How best to raise money to pay for US government operations, programs, and services and just what those operations, programs, and services should be have been contentious issues for many years. This is the context in which we have to start our reform of federal taxes.

Purposes of Federal Taxes

The vast majority of federal government operations, programs, and services have historically relied upon tax receipts for their funding. Obvious examples are national defense, general government operations, basic scientific research, and Social Security. A major purpose of federal taxes then is to raise money to pay for federal government operations, programs, and services.

Sometimes suggestions are made that money to fund many government programs and services can be obtained without federal taxes. To be sure, other methods to raise money also exist. Money to support part or all of some federal government services can come from fees charged to those who benefit directly from the service. One example is fees for patent applications, which can be used to offset the cost of running the United States Patent and Trademark Office. Another example is fees to enter national parks, which can be used to offset the cost of maintaining all of the national parks. History has shown, however, that this and other methods to raise money have limited application and make no sense in the context of major programs like national defense.

Raising money to pay for federal government operations, programs, and services is not the only potential purpose of federal taxes.

For example, sometimes federal taxes are proposed and even enacted to discourage particular kinds of activities. Some existing alcohol and tobacco taxes arguably fit this description. They are designed in part to discourage excessive use of alcohol and tobacco, which may lead to serious health problems. The recently proposed carbon tax also fits this description. The carbon tax would impose a tax on the burning of fossil fuels to discourage that activity and thereby reduce carbon dioxide emissions into the atmosphere.

Although some of these other purposes may be worthy, in this book, I will view the purpose of federal taxes solely as a way to raise the money needed for US operations, programs, and services. This limited view allows us to focus only on potential reforms that might affect this major purpose.

How Much Is Enough?

So what should be the federal government operations, programs, and services that need funding through federal taxes?

Different people have different visions about what the federal government should or should not do. Those different visions are influenced by different philosophies about how much taxation in different forms or in total is too much to be tolerated. The political resolution of these different visions each year is what determines the scope of federal government operations, programs, and services for that year and the amount of tax receipts needed to pay for them. A recent example of that resolution will provide perspective on the amount of federal tax receipts needed each year.

Let's take fiscal year 2008 as an example of how the political resolution determined the scope of federal government operations, programs, and services for that fiscal year. The **federal fiscal year** for the United States runs from October 1 through September 30. When people refer to government expenses in a year like 2008, they mean the fiscal year that ended on September 30, 2008. I chose the year 2008 because decisions for that year were made before the financial crisis in September 2008, which severely deepened a worldwide recession that had begun nine months earlier. Remember that the federal budget for fiscal year 2008 was adopted in 2007 and that most of the money for that budget came from 2007 federal income taxes that were due on April 15, 2008. In government reports, the term **outlays** is used for money spent by the federal government. The total federal outlays in fiscal year 2008 were $2,983 billion.[5] Six "superfunction" categories comprised this total. They were:

- National defense ($616 billion)
- Human resources ($1,896 billion)
- Physical resources ($162 billion)
- Net interest ($253 billion)
- Other functions ($142 billion)
- Undistributed offsetting receipts (*credit* of $86 billion)

Because "human resources" was so large, further breakdown by function is appropriate. Human resources included:

- Social Security ($617 billion)
- Medicare ($391 billion)
- Income security ($431 billion) [e.g., federal employee retirement and disability ($109 billion)]
- Health ($281 billion) [mostly health care services]
- Education, training, employment, and social services ($91 billion)
- Veterans' benefits and services ($85 billion)

At least for fiscal year 2008, $2,983 billion was a target amount for federal receipts from all federal taxes and other income sources. Actual federal receipts for fiscal year 2008 were considerably less at $2,524 billion.

I offer no opinion in this book on the appropriate scope of federal government operations, programs, and services. However, we cannot ignore the fact that the first decade of the twenty-first century witnessed a steady increase in total federal outlays per person in the United States after those outlays remained essentially constant during the previous decade. In constant dollars, total outlays per person rose from $7,270 in fiscal year 2001 to $8,895 in fiscal year 2008, an increase of 22 percent.[6] And these increases preceded even larger outlays that occurred after the September 2008 fiscal crisis.

Real tax reform should include ways to achieve total tax receipts that are adequate to fund all politically determined US government operations, programs, and services. And what is "adequate" has to take into consideration the issues of deficit spending and US government borrowing generally. The next two chapters consider these issues in depth because they impact the amount of tax receipts that will have to be achieved in the future by the current or any modified or new federal tax system.

Chapter 2

——◆•◆•◆——

The Impacts of Deficit Spending

Two recent books have described in laymen's terms some of the problems created by federal **deficit spending**. In *I.O.U.S.A.* and *Where Does the Money Go?* the authors show that deficit spending has already created and will continue to create a long-term demand on federal tax **receipts**.[7] We need to understand the nature, scope, and consequences of deficit spending as a prelude to proposing tax reforms that will have to deal with this current reality.

In this chapter, we will examine the annual federal deficit, the national debt with its components and recent evolution, and the historic and future impacts of the national debt on federal taxes.

The Annual Federal Deficit

To understand the nature and scope of deficit spending requires some background, including a few descriptions of terms.

Federal Deficit

A **federal deficit** occurs when the United States spends more money in a fiscal year than it receives from all federal taxes and other revenue sources. The federal deficit for that fiscal year is the difference between the total amount of money spent (**federal outlays**) and the total amount of money received (**federal receipts**). Government data tables often label this number the "total" figure.

Federal Surplus

Although rarely in the last thirty years, sometimes the United States spends less money in a fiscal year than it receives. This creates what is called a **federal surplus** for that fiscal year. The term "surplus" is misleading because it implies that all US fiscal requirements have been met even when the United States has significant national debt commitments at the end of the fiscal year. Using the term "surplus" thus creates an incorrect impression that the United States has received more tax and other receipts than it can use in that fiscal year.

Public Debt

Contrary to what some people believe, the United States does not just print more money to cover an annual federal deficit. Instead, the United States issues **treasury securities** in a variety of forms, such as "bills" and "notes" that are bought by the public. Each treasury security includes a promise by the United States to pay a specified rate of interest on the principal amount of the security. The United States thus creates a **public debt** by borrowing from the public the money needed to cover the federal deficit and incurs obligations to pay interest on that money.

To meet those obligations, a portion of all annual federal tax receipts must be allocated to paying the interest on these treasury securities held by the public. Obviously the greater the total interest obligation on this public debt, the greater the amount of federal tax receipts that have to be devoted to this purpose. If this total obligation becomes large enough, federal taxes will have to be increased for the sole purpose of paying this obligation.

This simple logic reveals only part of the demand on federal tax receipts caused by deficit spending. Unfortunately, it understates the tax risks posed by the full scope of deficit spending endemic for all but a few of the last thirty years.

Welcome now to the world of the "national debt."

The National Debt

The **national debt** is the sum of all of the US treasury securities issued over time that have not been paid back. The national debt at the end of each fiscal year has increased every year since 1970, albeit not at a steady rate.[8] With treasury securities being sold to the public to cover the annual federal deficit, we would expect that these increases in the national debt each fiscal year would be close to the amount of the federal deficit that year. The facts are otherwise.

Especially in the last thirty years, these increases in the national debt have been greater than the annual federal deficit, sometimes by large amounts. How can this be?

Simply put, the federal deficit as described above, which is what usually is discussed in the media, tells an incomplete and even misleading story of the relationships among federal tax receipts, spending, and borrowing. Let's now examine why this is so.

Federal Government Accounts Debt

Note that the annual federal deficit is the difference between the *total* outlays and the *total* receipts.

Significant portions of the total receipts come from taxes that are dedicated to specific purposes. Money collected from dedicated taxes is allocated initially to federal **trust funds**. Money in trust funds is to be spent only for the purposes of the dedicated taxes. Although benefits paid for these purposes also are included in the total amount of money spent, the total annual receipts from dedicated taxes in the last thirty years have exceeded total annual payments for their dedicated purposes.[9] That excess money has been used for general government expenditures and has reduced the amount of the federal deficit each year. In four years, that excess money even created a federal surplus (1998 to 2001).[10]

The United States has not surreptitiously taken the excess money raised by dedicated taxes. Instead, it has borrowed that excess money from the trust funds for which the dedicated tax money was intended. These extra borrowings are included in the national debt and are designated as the debt held by federal government accounts. In addition, the excess money raised by dedicated taxes has allowed the United States to postpone making actual payments of interest owed on previous borrowings from some trust funds. Actual payments of interest have not been needed because the annual dedicated tax receipts have covered all annual payments from those trust funds. The postponed interest payments have been added to the government accounts portion of the national debt.

These borrowings and postponed interest payments account for most of the differences between an annual federal deficit and an increase in the national debt by the end of that year.[11]

The national debt thus comprises two parts: the **public debt** and the **federal government accounts debt**.

Alternative Deficit Figures

So if the annual federal deficit tells an incomplete and even misleading story of the relationships among federal tax receipts, spending, and borrowing, what data would be more revealing?

To answer this question, we again need a few descriptions of terms.[12]

The annual **federal deficit** has already been described as the difference between total federal outlays and total federal receipts when outlays exceed receipts.

The annual **on-budget deficit** is a comparison between **on-budget outlays** and **on-budget receipts** when those outlays exceed receipts. These are all outlays and receipts other than those allocated to the Social Security trust funds and (in much smaller amounts) to the United States Postal Service.

The annual **federal funds deficit** is a comparison between **federal funds outlays** and **federal funds receipts** when those outlays exceed receipts. These are all outlays and receipts other than those allocated to *all* federal trust funds (including the Social Security trust funds). Other examples of these federal trust funds are the highway trust fund and the Medicare hospital insurance trust fund.[13]

Now we are ready to use these terms and their underlying concepts to see more clearly the relationships among federal tax receipts, spending, and borrowing.

Alternative Deficit Figures 2001–2008

Let's consider what occurred in the eight years beginning with fiscal year 2001, the last year when there was a federal surplus, and ending with fiscal year 2008, the last budget year before Congress had to create budgets in the full context of what has become known as the Great Recession. We have to look at the numbers to see the scope of different perceptions revealed by using alternative deficit figures.

Federal deficits from 2001 to 2008 averaged $251 billion in current dollars. Without the excess money from Social Security taxes and deferred interest payments owed to the Social Security trust funds, the federal on-budget deficits in that same time period averaged $421 billion. And without the excess money from *all* dedicated taxes and deferred payments to their related trust funds, the federal funds deficit (which I will also call the federal **true discretionary deficit**) averaged $481 billion, almost twice the amount of the commonly reported federal deficit.[14]

When compared against average total federal tax receipts of $2,145 billion in current dollars during this same eight-year time period, these three numbers create very different perceptions of how well the US government is living within its means. As a percentage of total federal tax receipts, the respective deficit figures were

- Federal deficit = 12 percent,
- On-budget deficit = 20 percent, and
- True discretionary deficit = 22 percent.

Perceptions created by a 12 percent deficit rather than a 22 percent deficit can and probably did impact decisions about the proper scope of federal government operations, programs, and services and the corresponding need for federal taxes from 2001 to 2008.[15]

Recent Evolution of the National Debt

Having now seen that different deficit figures tell very different stories about federal deficit spending, we are ready to examine what the national debt tells us about deficit spending generally and especially recent deficit spending. This examination will give us background for considering the national debt's consequences for future federal taxes.

Bluntly stated, the national debt figures tell the truth about how much the US government has lived beyond its annual tax receipts. The numbers are huge. The historic perspective shown in table 2.1 helps to place them in context.[16]

Table 2.1. Comparing federal debt at the end of selected fiscal years (billions of current dollars)

Federal fiscal year	Gross federal debt	Less debt held by federal government accounts	Equals debt held by the public
1980	909	197	712
*1990	3,206	795	2,412
2000	5,629	2,219	3,410
2008	9,986	4,183	5,803
2009	11,876	4,331	7,545
2010	13,529	4,510	9,019
2011	14,764	4,636	10,128
2012	16,051	4,770	11,281

*Rounding causes numeric discrepancy

National Debt up to September 2008

The figures in table 2.1 show that within the national debt of $9,986 billion at the end of fiscal year 2008, a surprising amount of $4,183 billion was owed to federal government accounts. As noted above, these are federal trust funds for designated purposes from which the United States has borrowed money to pay for general government expenditures. This large federal accounts figure reflects the way that money had been borrowed extensively from federal trust funds before 2008, which reduced the federal deficit figures.

National Debt after September 2008

Fiscal year 2009 was in a new category altogether. A double whammy increased the total national debt by $1,890 billion in just one year.

Most of that increase occurred in the public debt. The United States spent huge amounts of money to avoid a meltdown of the American and global financial systems and to try to jump-start new economic activity to minimize a deepening recession. These decisions were made to avoid repeating the unemployment and diminished capital catastrophe of the Great Depression in the 1930s.[17]

At the same time, the Great Recession also diminished federal tax receipts.[18] Similar but less severe circumstances occurred in fiscal years 2010, 2011, and 2012. The figures in table 2.1 show not only a greatly increased gross federal debt after fiscal year 2008, but also a change in the components of that debt. Public debt accounted for nearly all of the national debt increase, so public debt was a much higher proportion of the national debt at the end of fiscal year 2012 than at the end of fiscal year 2008.

Although the extra spending that occurred after September 2008 has received a lot of political attention, the decrease in federal tax receipts has not. That decrease has been huge. Using current dollars, just two comparisons will illustrate this fact. [19]

- Total federal receipts in fiscal year 2009 were $463 billion dollars *less* than total federal receipts in fiscal year 2007, a decline of 18 percent.
- Even more shocking, the on-budget receipts in fiscal year 2009 that exclude Social Security tax receipts were $482 billion *less* than in fiscal year 2007, a decline of 25 percent for those receipts.

We can use fiscal year 2009 to put the impact of these numbers in context. If we add the on-budget receipts shortfall of $482 billion in 2009 to the average $421 billion on-budget deficit that occurred in preceding years as noted above (current dollars), we get $903 billion as a built-in on-budget deficit for fiscal year 2009. This built-in on-budget deficit would have occurred in fiscal year 2009 even if there had been no increased recession-related spending for economic stimulus, emergency federal loans, or other purposes and if the US economy had performed exactly as it did perform in that fiscal year.

The National Debt's Impact on Historic Budgets

One fact alone makes the huge numbers associated with the national debt a problem for taxpayers: this borrowed money does not come for free. The United States owes interest on the treasury securities that comprise the national debt. The annual amounts of that interest are staggering.

Fiscal Year 2008 Example

Because the Great Recession makes fiscal years 2009 and later unique, I will use fiscal year 2008 as a more typical year during the past decade for most data comparisons. Just three numbers from federal outlays in that fiscal year translate the interest problem into a reality check:

> Net interest = $253 billion
> Federal accounts interest = $198 billion
> Gross interest (total interest) = $451 billion

By anyone's standards, this is serious money for a single fiscal year.[20]

Net interest is the amount paid on the public debt and is money actually paid out from federal tax receipts.

Federal accounts interest is money credited to all government accounts (mostly trust funds) but does not always have to be money actually paid from federal tax receipts. Because the receipts from dedicated taxes in fiscal year 2008 that were allocated to most of those trust funds were greater than payments from those funds, actual money from general federal tax receipts was not needed to pay federal account interest in that fiscal year.

Gross interest, of course, is the sum of the figures for net interest and federal accounts interest.

Alternate Portrayals of Interest Paid

As with the federal deficit numbers for annual expenditures, the full impact of the national debt interest and its demand on federal tax receipts tends to be understated in most statistics about federal government spending.

The most common comparison uses only the net interest figure and compares it to total federal outlays.[21] Total outlays, however, include spending that is paid by incurring more national debt.

A more revealing comparison uses the net interest figure and compares it to total federal tax receipts.

A more disturbing comparison uses the net interest figure and compares it to total federal tax receipts excluding social insurance and retirement receipts (mostly receipts from Social Security and Medicare taxes) because these taxes are firmly dedicated to purposes that do not include paying interest on the national debt.

The most grim picture is revealed if gross interest obligations rather than net interest payments are compared against the same three figures, namely total federal outlays, total federal tax receipts, and total federal tax receipts excluding social insurance and retirement receipts.

All of these figures for fiscal year 2008 are shown in tables 2.2 and 2.3.[22]

Table 2.2. Comparing fiscal year 2008 net interest payments to receipts and outlays (billions of current dollars)

Description of compared amount	Compared amount	Net interest payments	Net interest payments as % of compared amount
Total federal outlays	2,983	253	8.5%
Total federal receipts	2,524	253	10%
Total federal receipts less social insurance and retirement receipts	1,624	253	16%

Table 2.3. Comparing fiscal year 2008 gross interest obligations to receipts and outlays (billions of current dollars)

Description of compared amount	Compared amount	Gross interest obligations	Gross interest obligations as % of compared amount
Total federal outlays	2,983	451	15%
Total federal receipts	2,524	451	18%
Total federal receipts less social insurance and retirement receipts	1,624	451	28%

In fiscal year 2008, net interest payments on only the public debt portion of the national debt siphoned off 16 percent of all federal tax receipts other than those receipts from dedicated Social Security, Medicare, and related taxes. Even worse, the gross interest obligations on the full national debt were nearly double that amount. They would have commandeered 28 percent of those receipts if all interest had been paid as owed to the federal trust funds, rather than most of that interest being rolled into the national debt.[23] No wonder no one wants to talk about the real demand of the national debt on federal tax receipts.

These figures are a snapshot of time in fiscal year 2008. What about the future?

The National Debt's Impact on Future Taxes

The United States needs tax receipts in order to pay its interest obligations on the treasury securities that comprise the national debt. The United States also needs tax receipts in order to pay the principal of any treasury securities it decides or needs to pay off to reduce the national debt. Reducing the national debt in the foreseeable future is very unlikely, so we will focus on the potential ways that national debt interest obligations will impact future taxes. Interest obligations differ somewhat in practice between the public debt and the government accounts debt components of the national debt.

The public debt component of the national debt is the less flexible portion of the national debt, so it will be considered first.

Net Interest on the Public Debt

The public debt is unique because it permanently commits a portion of future taxes to a single nonproductive purpose—paying interest to public owners of treasury securities. Decisions already made by Congress and presidents that have created the national debt are forcing a transfer of wealth from future American taxpayers to those owners. Because today's Americans, not future taxpaying Americans, are the direct beneficiaries of many expenditures that have increased the national debt, a form of taxation without representation has already occurred when large deficit spending greatly increased the national debt.

How big will this commitment be in the future?

Simple mathematics dictates that two factors will determine that commitment: the interest rates on outstanding treasury securities and the total amount of those securities as represented by the public debt portion of the national debt.

Interest rates on the public debt

Interest rates on existing treasury securities are not locked in forever. The current average maturity of treasury securities is about five years.[24] This means that half the public debt will have to be refinanced within five years. The treasury securities that have recently been sold have carried historically low or sometimes even zero interest rates. Indeed, the federal net interest paid in fiscal year 2009 was less than in 2008 even though the public debt increased by large amounts in 2009.[25]

If global investment market forces cause interest rates generally to increase, eventually the average rates on outstanding treasury securities could also increase. This has occurred in the past. For example, one measure of average interest rates on the public debt shows that in 1990 those rates were 1.7 times the rates in 2008 and 2.9 times the rates in 2009. Even higher rates occurred in the early and mid 1980s.[26]

In addition, so far US treasury securities have enjoyed market favor as a sound investment. A variety of decisions or events could adversely affect that favor, and thus cause an increase in average rates on outstanding treasury securities.

Whatever the cause, an increase in the average interest rates paid on treasury securities will increase the total amount of interest that has to be paid on the public debt. General inflation often leads to higher interest rates, so understandably the Federal Reserve will be forced into whatever actions it can take to avoid inflation just to protect the American public from having to pay more taxes solely to cover net interest on the public debt.[27]

Amount of the public debt

Like interest, the amount of the public debt portion of the national debt is not static, especially under current federal spending policies. The historic willingness to engage in deficit spending has relied on a general assumption that even an increasing public debt can continually roll over so that only interest will ever have to be paid. Thus far, that assumption has proven to be valid. Will it continue to be valid in the future?

The US **gross domestic product (GDP)** is one measure of the size of the US economy. A statistic that has been devised to provide some comfort level for the amount of the public debt each year is its comparison to the US GDP. That comfort level is now diminishing as the public debt's percentage of GDP in 2012 reached a level even higher than experienced in the mid-1990s and surpassed only by the percentages reached in the decade following World War II.[28]

This measure, and perhaps other indirect measures, avoids the most immediate problem posed by the public debt—the amount of net interest that has to be paid from federal tax receipts in a fiscal year.

Net interest amount

What can be done if the annual amount of net interest gets uncomfortably large?

Sadly, maybe nothing without significant pain.

The interest commitment caused by the public debt can only be reduced by (1) paying back some of this portion of the national debt or (2) replacing some treasury securities with ones that have lower interest rates.

The first method requires either increased tax receipts or removing money from government operations, programs, and services. Whether and how that can be done will affect all future citizens. They will have to pay more taxes, experience diminished federal government operations, programs, and services, or both.

The second method requires an investment market that will accept reduced interest rates from treasury securities. Given the extremely low interest rates of the last five years, this requirement will be almost impossible to meet in the future.

So the public debt portion of the national debt is a time bomb that potentially could siphon off a much larger portion of federal tax receipts than historically has been the case. Any reformed system of federal taxes should be flexible to be able to meet this challenge should it occur.

Other public debt risks

Beyond potentially requiring huge interest payments, a very large public debt has other dangers as well. In *The Moment of Truth*, the Fiscal Commission has identified some of these dangers in this sobering language (at page 11):[29]

> Rising debt will also hamstring the government, depriving it of the resources needed to respond to future crises and invest in other priorities. Deficit spending is often used to respond to short-term financial "emergency" needs such as wars or recessions. If our national debt grows higher, the federal government may even have difficulty borrowing funds at an affordable interest rate, preventing it from effectively responding.
>
> Large debt will put America at risk by exposing it to foreign creditors. They currently own more than half our public debt, and the interest we pay them reduces our own standard of living. The single largest foreign holder of our debt is China, a nation that may not share our country's aspirations and strategic interests. In a worst-case scenario, investors could lose confidence that our nation is able or willing to repay its loans—possibly triggering a debt crisis that would force the government to implement the most stringent of austerity measures.

Interest on Borrowings from Federal Trust Funds

Our discussion so far has centered on the public debt portion of the national debt. What about the more than $4,770 billion owed to federal government accounts at the end of fiscal year 2012?

The portion of the national debt owed to federal government accounts, which consists primarily of borrowings from federal trust funds like the **Social Security trust funds**, is different than the public debt portion in two important ways.

Unlike the public debt, although interest has been paid to these trust funds in an accounting sense, few general tax receipts have been transferred to these trust funds for that purpose. As noted previously, these transfers have not been required because the dedicated tax receipts that are allocated to these funds have historically been more than adequate to cover payments from those funds. Thus, the interest owed annually to federal trust funds on borrowings from those funds has not yet fiscally impacted other federal spending. That fiscal impact will begin if dedicated tax receipts are inadequate to cover payments from the fund to which receipts are dedicated. If that occurs, cash interest payments will have to be made to add to a trust fund's dedicated tax receipts, and that cash will have to come from general tax receipts.

The second important difference between the public debt and borrowings from federal trust funds lies with the nature of these borrowings. Unlike the public debt, the debt owed to federal trust funds will not roll over so that only interest has to be paid. At some point, the United States will be obligated to start paying back the principal borrowed from the trust funds. That will occur if or when payments from a federal trust fund exceed the combination of dedicated tax receipts that pour into the trust fund and cash payments of interest on prior borrowings from that fund. Without these paybacks, the trust fund will not be solvent and able to make promised payments to support the purposes of the trust fund. These paybacks will put a new demand on other general tax receipts.

Deficit Spending Recap

This chapter has revealed candid facts about deficit spending, has shown how endemic deficit spending has created the national debt with its public and government accounts debt components, and has illustrated the national debt's impact on the need for present federal taxes and potentially for future federal taxes.

We are now ready in the next chapter to take a closer look at the national debt obligations to federal trust funds and what those obligations mean for federal taxes generally.

Chapter 3

———◆·◆·◆———

Borrowings from Federal Trust Funds

Chapter 2 has already looked at borrowings from federal trust funds from the perspective of the national debt. In this chapter, we will examine those borrowings from the perspective of the federal trust funds and their intended beneficiaries. This examination will lead us to an important conclusion about the relationship between dedicated taxes and other federal taxes when proposing tax reform.

The most well-known and talked-about trust funds with dedicated taxes are the Social Security trust funds and the Medicare hospital insurance trust fund. The Social Security trust funds will be used as the primary example here, with some analogous references to the Medicare hospital insurance trust fund. The basic principles also apply to the other trust funds that have dedicated taxes as their revenue source.[30] Remember that the money collected from dedicated taxes like the Social Security and Medicare taxes is supposed to be used only for the purposes for which the dedicated taxes were imposed.

Adequacy of Dedicated Taxes

Social Security taxes are paid into two trust funds that collectively pay all Social Security benefits, whether for retirement or disability. Medicare taxes, on the other hand, are paid only into the Medicare hospital insurance trust fund. The Medicare supplementary medical insurance trust fund receives its money from premiums and other sources.[31]

Faced with a looming shortfall in funds from Social Security taxes to pay current Social Security benefits, in the early 1980s Congress passed laws that increased those taxes. The increases occurred in steps up to 1990, when they reached their current level. In all of the years since 1990 up to fiscal year 2010, the total receipts from the Social Security taxes each year were greater than the total payments made for Social Security benefits during the same year.[32]

In other words, the payment of Social Security benefits during that time period contributed *zero* to the national debt. Those who claim that the Social Security "entitlement" is somehow partly responsible for the national debt up to 2010 are just plain wrong.[33]

Faced with a similar shortfall in funds from Medicare taxes, Congress also increased Medicare taxes to their current level as of 1986. In the years since 1986 up to fiscal year 2003, the annual receipts from the Medicare tax were sometimes more and sometimes less than the payment of Medicare hospital insurance benefits. Since 2003, Medicare tax receipts have been less in amount than the payments of those benefits, but other receipts kept the fund in annual balance until fiscal year 2009. So far, total annual receipts surpluses have exceeded total annual payments deficits.[34]

Fate of Dedicated Tax Money

But what has actually happened to this extra money in the Social Security and **Medicare trust funds**?

It has been spent on other federal government programs and services.

Without this extra money during the many years when this extra money was available, the scope of government operations, programs, and services would have been less, other taxes would have been greater to provide adequate tax receipts for those functions, or federal deficits would have been greater to cover the extra need for money (closer to the on-budget deficits described in chapter 2).

To be sure, as described in chapter 2, the United States has treated its use of this extra money as a loan from each trust fund. The actual numbers show the large size of these borrowings, especially those from the Social Security trust funds.

- The sum of these borrowings from the two Social Security trust funds at the end of fiscal year 2009 was $2,504 billion in current dollars, reflecting an increase of $1,649 billion in the decade from 2000 to 2009.[35] These total borrowings include a sizable amount of interest on prior borrowings that was not paid when due.
- The sum of borrowings from the Medicare hospital insurance trust fund at the end of fiscal year 2009 was $310 billion, reflecting an increase of $156 billion in the decade from 2000 to 2009.[36]

The Impacts of Borrowings on Trust Fund Beneficiaries

When current financial commitments to Social Security and Medicare beneficiaries are examined, the future fiscal problem they can create is often expressed in terms of when each trust fund "runs out." We will use Social Security as the example.

Many people regard "runs out" as the time when the annual receipts from Social Security taxes are inadequate to pay current Social Security benefits *and* when all borrowings by the United States from the Social Security trust funds have been paid back. Even the Fiscal Commission's 2010 report used this measurement of "runs out" when estimating the year 2037 as the time when the major Social Security solvency crisis will occur if nothing is done now to adjust Social Security commitments and taxes.[37] In my opinion, the first crisis in Social Security commitments will come long before this "runs out" scenario.

The first Social Security crisis will occur when the annual receipts from Social Security taxes are regularly inadequate to pay annual Social Security benefits. A crisis will exist even if the Social Security trust funds have lots of money owed to them by the United States. This is so because the money to pay both the interest on and the principal of these borrowings will have to come from somewhere. To pay all Social Security benefits when this crisis occurs, the United States will have four major action options, none of which is very palatable:

(1) Increase general tax receipts by raising taxes in an amount necessary to pay back borrowings from the Social Security trust funds as needed.
(2) Cut or reduce other federal government operations, programs, and services to free up money to pay back borrowings from the Social Security trust funds as needed.
(3) Increase the national debt by issuing more public treasury securities to replace the treasury securities held by the Social Security trust funds.
(4) Reduce Social Security benefits so that part or all of the borrowings from the Social Security trust funds will not have to be paid back.

There is, of course, a fifth possibility. We can hope that the US economy expands enough to generate the increased general tax receipts needed without having to take any action specifically directed at having adequate money to pay all Social Security benefits.

The same analysis applies to the Medicare hospital insurance trust fund, although the amounts of money involved are much smaller.

This first crisis is not theoretical for a future day. In fiscal year 2010, the money received from Social Security taxes was less than the amount of benefits paid out.[38] The United States actually had to pay some of the interest owed on its borrowings from the Social Security trust funds to cover Social Security benefits. This circumstance is widely regarded as a temporary result of two features of the Great Recession: increased unemployment diminished the total receipts from the Social Security taxes and more people than normal who were eligible to retire early did so because they could not find jobs.[39] These temporary features also meant that excess Social Security tax receipts no longer helped to mask the true extent of deficit spending as represented by on-budget deficits.

Although the US economy is expected to improve enough to reverse these temporary features, even the Fiscal Commission's 2010 report projects that the shortfall in Social Security tax receipts that occurred in 2010 will reoccur as early as 2015, this time as an ongoing condition.[40] Fiscal year 2010 is a warning that now—not later—is the time to figure out how to deal with the borrowings from trust funds.

Dealing with the Impacts of Borrowings

If the US economy does not expand enough for the needed general tax receipts to materialize automatically, which one or combination of the four action options is the most probable response to this first crisis when it occurs for Social Security? Social Security is singled out here because the borrowings from the Social Security trust funds are by far the largest total borrowings from any group of trust funds (57 percent of all debt to federal government accounts).[41]

These borrowings are so large that immense political pressures will exist to avoid the options of tax increases, diminished government operations, programs, and services, and public debt increases. Therefore, the most probable response will be to adjust Social Security benefits so that the borrowings from the Social Security trust funds will never have to be paid back.

Congress has the legal power to make this response. Indeed, the following statement in the 2014 US budget documents illustrates the fragility of the Social Security trust funds and all federal trust funds when facing competing political and economic pressures:[42]

> The term trust fund as used in Federal budget accounting is frequently misunderstood. In the private sector, "trust" refers to funds of one party held by a second party (the trustee) in a fiduciary capacity. In the Federal budget, the term "trust fund" means only that the law requires the funds be accounted for separately and used only for specified purposes and that the account in which the funds are deposited is designated as a "trust fund." A change in law may change the future receipts and the terms under which the fund's resources are spent. The determining factor as to whether a particular fund is designated as a "Federal" fund or "trust" fund is the designation specified in the law governing the fund.

Consequences of Unpaid Borrowings

If, in fact, the borrowings from the Social Security trust funds are never paid back, look at what this means. Money that was supposed to have been used for Social Security benefits will finally have been used for general governmental purposes in all the years when the borrowings occurred and never for Social Security benefits.

A few numbers will help to put in perspective this transfer of Social Security money for general governmental use.

> During the decade from 2000 to 2009, when most of the borrowings from the Social Security trust funds occurred, approximately 8 percent of the Social Security tax *receipts* were diverted to general governmental expenditures.[43] That modest figure ignores the failure of the United States to pay interest into the Social Security trust funds on prior borrowings from those funds.
>
> When those unpaid (but credited) interest obligations are included in the cash income of the Social Security trust funds, an astounding 24 percent of the cash income to the Social Security trust funds during the decade 2000 to 2009 was diverted to general governmental expenditures.[44] That is why the borrowings from the Social Security trust fund increased $1,649 billion during that decade.

Particularly in the years of the 2000–2009 decade when federal deficit spending occurred (every fiscal year except 2000 and 2001), without the extra money generated by Social Security taxes, the federal deficit in each year would have been even greater than it was. That fact would have created political pressure to increase taxes, reduce spending, or both.

In blunt terms, the excess money from Social Security taxes paid for a major part of the shortfall in federal tax receipts that resulted from a combination of the decreased income taxes passed by Congress in 2001 and 2003[45] and concurrent federal government spending decisions after 2000. Yet that excess Social Security tax money was initially paid by or on behalf of every individual who had earned income above minuscule amounts, without any subtractions even for personal survival expenses.[46]

This potential, or even likelihood, that the United States will never pay back borrowings from the Social Security trust funds is why treating Social Security (and Medicare) taxes as completely independent from federal individual income or other federal taxes is a misleading fiction.

For this reason, we will address all federal tax interrelationships, including those involving the Social Security and Medicare taxes, in proposing federal tax reforms. This basic conclusion allows us now to begin setting up our framework for that reform.

Chapter 4

————◆·◆·◆————

Criteria for Judging All Federal Taxes

When federal taxes are needed to provide money to pay for government operations, programs, and services, we need some way to choose what taxes to adopt. Clearly stated criteria allow us to make those choices by assessing how each kind of tax and potential combinations of taxes meet those criteria.

For some people, the only good federal taxes are no taxes, so their only criterion for assessing these taxes is how to eliminate them. At least that criterion is clearly stated, albeit not realistic in today's society.

The criteria used in this book are fairness, accountability, and simplicity. These criteria are not always self-evident or complementary. Also, judging each tax individually is only the beginning of a proper evaluation. The combination of all federal taxes also affects people and entities, so federal taxes should be judged in their combined form as well as separately.

By consistently applying the same criteria, it is possible to create a new federal tax system that reflects logical balances among the criteria.

What Is Fairness?

Fairness is the most subjective criterion for federal taxes because what is "fair" depends largely upon a person's philosophies and prejudices. To some people, of course, there is no such thing as a fair tax because the whole idea of taxation is unfair. Assuming that federal taxes are needed, though, fairness questions inevitably arise when comparing the amounts of taxes owed by different people and when considering the total amount of taxes owed by an individual.

We will use just two standards here to judge whether particular federal taxes are fair. By setting forth these standards, you will know how various tax proposals will be analyzed for fairness in this book. Change these standards, and the conclusions about fairness may also change.

One standard we will use is based on nondiscrimination. Namely, in an income-based tax system, individuals who receive the same cash or cash-equivalent benefits in a year should owe the same total amount of federal taxes before the calculation of defined and accountable federal subsidies that may be applicable. This nondiscrimination standard is based on the notion that the value of cash is the same regardless of its source. Therefore, the initial responsibility to pay tax on that cash should also be the same. A similar standard to judge "fairness" can be used in a consumption-based tax system such as one using **sales taxes**. Namely, individuals who spend the same amounts in a year should owe the same amount of federal taxes before the calculation of applicable defined and accountable subsidies.

A second standard we will use to judge fairness is that every person should be able to use without taxation an amount of money that is necessary to maintain a healthy life, whether for food, water, clothing, shelter, or medical care. This standard is considered at length in chapter 21, which examines reductions from income for payments necessary for a healthy life.

What Is Accountability?

The criterion of **accountability** as used here is the ability to ascertain easily the total monetary impacts on federal tax receipts of every federal tax provision.

Current federal taxes have a complex structure. This structure has a mixture of different tax rates for different total incomes and multiple subsidies that are found sometimes as income reductions, sometimes as tax credits, and sometimes as lower tax rates for selected kinds of income.

This mixture makes it nearly impossible to determine the total monetary impact of many tax provisions. Today, those impacts have to be estimated by reliance on a variety of well-intentioned assumptions. The true costs of policies that Congress intended to advance with many of those provisions are thus uncertain at best and unknown at worst. A better system would have federal tax returns revealing directly any tax policy's impact on taxpayers and federal tax receipts.

Accountability is an appropriate goal for one primary reason. If elected officials and the public knew the real monetary impact on federal tax receipts created by each tax provision, maybe that knowledge alone would cause many provisions to be reexamined on a regular basis. Regular scrutiny is particularly important for those tax provisions that were intended to provide subsidies to promote certain policies. Over time, those policies or the cost of supporting those policies may no longer be appropriate.

What Is Simplicity?

Simplicity is not so simple. As a criterion here, simplicity has three dimensions:

- Calculations should be mathematically easy.
- Few calculations should be needed to determine the amount of taxes owed.
- The policies that underlie the calculations should be readily apparent and understandable, whether or not one agrees with them.

An example of a provision in current federal income tax law that involves both a simple calculation and an understandable policy is the reduction from income called an "exemption" that is allowed for each dependent child. The reduction is an easy subtraction of a fixed amount. It reflects a policy not to tax money deemed essential for a dependent's survival, such as paying for water, food, clothing, and shelter.

Even with exemptions, however, simplicity suffers when other policies are superimposed on the exemption provision. Again using tax year 2009 as the benchmark, that is what occurred with the phase-out of exemptions for individuals with larger incomes. The phase-out diminished exemptions via a ten-step formula when adjusted gross income exceeded certain amounts.[47]

Greater simplicity in federal taxes has several significant benefits.

Most obvious, greater simplicity can reduce the enormous amount of time now spent by individuals, tax preparers, corporations, and other entities in collecting necessary data and documents, filling out numerous forms, and performing calculations just to file required tax returns (notwithstanding computer software now available to ease this process). If a revised system of federal tax laws could trim this time even by half, that time could be used for many productive or personal purposes.

Greater simplicity also has the potential to reduce errors and to make cheating more difficult, thus increasing tax receipts and partially closing the "tax gap" between what taxpayers should have paid and what they actually paid.[48] The tax gap represents a burden of increased federal taxes, increased national debt, or decreased federal government services imposed by individuals who do not pay their full taxes on those who do.

Greater simplicity is desirable as well to protect the integrity of the federal tax system. Simplicity's opposite, excessive complexity, breeds frustration and mistrust. Frustration follows from having to spend a lot of time filling out tax forms and from inadequate explanations about or lack of understanding why some calculations are required. Mistrust creeps in when complex forms appear to have exceptions for or special application to some people but not others. People sensibly ask: why are some people singled out, whether for reduced or increased taxes? Any federal tax system will ultimately crumble if frustration and mistrust erode the confidence of too many citizens in the system's fairness.

Although simplifying federal taxes can reduce these four effects, no tax system can totally avoid some questions that may require complex consideration. For example, applying a tax on an individual's income will require decisions about what is "income." As another example, a national sales tax will require decisions about what sales are taxable and even what is a "sale." These kinds of questions are manageable if limited in number and if limited to basic questions that everyone can understand need answering.

Applying the Criteria

Now that we have identified fairness, accountability, and simplicity as criteria for judging federal taxes, we are ready to consider potential tax alternatives in our quest for real tax reform. Our discussion of tax alternatives and tax provisions in later chapters will emphasize the criterion that is most important to the topic at hand, rather than using the three criteria as a continual rigid checklist.

Chapter 5

✦•✦•✦

Choices from Potential Tax Alternatives

Over history, just about every conceivable form of taxation has been used by governments to raise revenue. In the United States alone, taxes have been and are today levied by one government or another on such diverse items as individual incomes, corporation net profits, estates of deceased people, general sales of goods, fuel sales, real property (land and buildings), personal property (such as cars), imported goods (in the form of tariffs), alcoholic beverages, tobacco, extraction of minerals and petroleum, and telephone services. Outside the United States, a major form of taxation is the value-added tax.

Among this array of potential or actual taxes, the vast majority of federal tax receipts currently come from taxes on individual incomes (income tax, Social Security tax, and Medicare tax) and on corporation net profit (the "corporation income tax"). These two categories alone comprised 91 percent of all federal receipts in fiscal year 2008.[49]

This chapter will critique a wide variety of potential federal taxes. This critique will include all major forms of taxes now used by the federal government, as well as very different alternative taxes advocated by some proponents of major federal tax reform. Examination will begin by touching upon a philosophical issue that permeates major tax reform. Summaries of potential federal taxes will follow to illustrate some of their advantages or disadvantages if used at the federal level. Finally, choices will be made from those potential taxes. Those choices will then dictate the framework of the FAST Plan.

A Philosophical Issue

Some economists and scholars look at idealized tax systems to determine their merits. Published materials have taken an expansive view of taxes on individuals by considering the relative merits of an income tax as compared to a "consumption tax." A **consumption tax** is a tax on spending for goods and services. In the economics model, an "ideal" consumption tax is a tax on *all* spending for goods and services but not on savings (investments).[50] In this model, by excluding savings from taxation, total returns can be realized without initial or annual diminution by taxes, thus maximizing society's use of its capital. According to Edward J. McCaffery in his excellent book *Fair Not Flat*, "there are two forms of consumption tax—one that is imposed when the money is first earned and another that is imposed later, when the money is spent."[51] A tax on income that systematically deducts savings from taxable income is a consumption tax imposed when money is first earned. It is a consumption tax because, by definition, any use of money other than for savings is a consumption use. A national sales tax and a European-style value-added tax would be forms of a consumption tax that is imposed when money is spent.

Practical Tax Considerations

For tax reform, my proposals assume that we do not live in an ideal world. Instead, proposals will be based on the practical application of potential taxes, including an individual income tax and consumption taxes, such as sales and value-added taxes. To choose which taxes have the best practical merit at the federal level, this chapter will consider the ten most common forms of historic taxes. These are taxes on (1) individual income, (2) corporation income, (3) a deceased's estate, (4) gifts, (5) specific commodities or activities (excise taxes), (6) imported goods (tariffs), (7) sales, (8) real property, (9) personal property, and (10) "value added."

Taxes on Individual Income
More than 79 percent of all federal receipts in fiscal year 2008 came from taxes on individual income (combined totals from the income tax, Social Security tax, and Medicare tax).[52]

Practical advantages
All of these taxes on individual income are applied only on income when received. This feature has the practical advantage that money is then available to pay the tax without having to use other assets. This availability makes payment easier and less disruptive to other activities. Also, the vast majority of people have income of one kind or another, so a tax on individual income means that nearly everyone is in a potential position to pay some tax to help pay for federal government operations, programs, and services.

Fairness issues

The most widespread complaints about taxes on individual income arise from the way that the current income tax is applied, not the way that Social Security and Medicare taxes are applied. Fairness complaints have a variety of dimensions.

Some people, for example, assert that the current individual income tax system is skewered and unfair because a small portion of the population pays a large portion of the total income tax money collected. This assertion ignores the fact that a major reason this small portion of the population pays a relatively large amount of total income taxes is that this portion of the population also has a relatively large portion of the total income received by all individuals. Real numbers, rather than some of the numbers that are bandied around by some people who assert this unfairness, demonstrate this fact.

For example, in tax year 2007, before the Great Recession, individual tax returns that reported adjusted gross incomes of $500,000 or more comprised only 0.73 percent of all returns filed, but accounted for 21.1 percent of all reported adjusted gross income, 27.3 percent of all reported taxable income, and 36.9 percent of all individual income taxes paid.[53] When all taxes on individual income are counted (the sum of income, Social Security, and Medicare taxes), this same group of individuals accounted for less than 24 percent of all federal taxes paid on individual income in tax year 2007, a figure that is close to this group's 21.1 percent of all reported adjusted gross income.[54]

Other people complain that a large portion of the population pays no individual income tax at all. Many factors account for this result, ranging from individuals having little income in the first place to individuals taking advantage of multiple tax subsidies to avoid paying any income tax on substantial incomes. With respect to income tax avoidance through tax subsidies, simplifying federal taxes on individual income will reveal how each subsidy impacts total tax receipts and should place each subsidy under renewed scrutiny. That scrutiny should minimize tax avoidance. As a cautionary note, the people who make these complaints often ignore the total tax contribution by this same portion of the population via Social Security and Medicare taxes. As described in chapter 3, especially in the first decade of the twenty-first century, an important part of the receipts from these taxes has been used for general US government expenditures that theoretically are supposed to be paid for by other taxes.

Many complaints about the current way that the individual income tax is applied focus on the definition and therefore calculation of *taxable* income. Political decisions about what constitutes income and what amounts can be subtracted from income to determine taxable income have real effects on the fairness of any individual income tax. Changing historic decisions on these questions can create a greatly simplified income tax as opposed to what individuals have experienced in the past. Changing some of these decisions can even turn an individual income tax into one form of a true consumption tax that is imposed when the money is first earned.[55]

Taxes on Corporation Income

As stated in chapter 7 on what makes other federal taxes so complicated, the commonly used term "corporation income tax" for what is really a tax only on corporation net profit improperly makes this tax analogous to the individual income tax. A more accurate term is the "corporation net profit tax." For corporations, extensive subtractions from revenue for business expenses are available to reduce or even eliminate the net profit that is subject to the federal corporation net profit tax. Some huge corporations that enjoy the benefits of many federal government programs and services end up paying no corporation net profit tax at all. In contrast, for wage earners with at least modest incomes, a large portion of their incomes is subject to tax because the reductions from income that are allowed to determine taxable income are relatively small (minuscule with respect to payment of Social Security and Medicare taxes). To make taxes on corporations more analogous to the individual income tax, an alternative tax on corporations could use an income base different from net profit as currently defined or even net profit at all.

Taxes on a Deceased's Estate

The federal estate tax is a tax on the value of a deceased's estate, meaning property owned by the decedent at the time of death. "Property" includes everything that the decedent owned. Items as different as cash, land, houses, securities, cars, jewelry, and artwork are all swept into an estate. Even though all property is included in an estate, federal estate tax law typically has excluded a certain total value of this property from the estate tax. As for the property that exceeds that total value, the estate tax rates can be steep (45 percent being the maximum rate in 2009).[56] Because property includes more than cash, some estate property may have to be sold to generate enough cash to pay the federal estate tax.

Estate planning is used to minimize the application of the federal estate tax to an estate or to minimize the probability of having to pay any federal estate tax at all. This planning can be very complicated. The creation of trusts, asset transfers among spouses, and other techniques are available to postpone and sometimes avoid estate taxes altogether where the total property is close to or just above the trigger amount for the tax. Estate planning has been made particularly complicated since 2001 because rules have changed almost from year to year regarding the amount of estate property that is excluded from the estate tax.

Taxes on Gifts

The federal gift tax exists as a necessary complement to the federal estate tax and uses the same tax rates.[57] Without the gift tax, a person could avoid the estate tax merely by giving property to intended heirs before dying.

Excise Taxes

Excise taxes are taxes on the manufacture, sale, or use of commodities or on identified activities. Historically, excise taxes have been limited to specifically defined commodities or activities, although Congress has imposed excise taxes on a great variety of commodities and activities. Despite this great variety, some categorization of excise taxes is possible.

Some excise taxes can be considered as ways to reimburse the United States for funds spent on federal services that directly benefit the activity taxed. Examples include:

- *Excise taxes on the sale of gasoline, diesel fuel, tires, and heavy trucks and trailers.* These taxes are designed to obtain funds that will be used primarily for construction of highways. The federal highway trust fund is the accounting setup that attempts to assure this result.[58]
- *Excise tax on "transportation by air."* This tax helps to pay for the Federal Aviation Agency, federal air traffic control operators, and federal subsidies for the construction of new airports because these receipts are designated to a trust fund for those and other purposes.[59]
- *Excise tax on telephone services.* This tax helps to offset the cost of regulation by the Federal Communications Commission, without which electronic communications could become jumbled nonsense.[60]

Some excise taxes can be considered an indirect way to reimburse the United States for general expenditures that are greater than they would be in the absence of the taxed commodity or activity. The so-called "sin taxes" on tobacco and alcohol ("distilled spirits, wines, and beer") may fit this category because these products arguably cause increased poor health (tobacco and alcohol) or traffic accidents (alcohol) that require increased federal expenditures for medical care for some of the affected people.[61]

Other excise taxes seem to have no rationale beyond raising more money for the US treasury. Examples are the excise taxes on luxury passenger automobiles, on wagers, on sport fishing equipment, and on bows and arrows.[62]

Tariffs

A **tariff** is a tax on the import or export of an item. During the last thirty years, expanded treaties, free-trade policies, and communications and transportation technologies have created economic interdependence among nations in ways never seen before on a global scale. An important part of this interdependence is low or nonexistent tariffs on goods imported into or exported from the United States. Rejecting this development, some groups claim that tariffs (and some excise taxes) could supply enough revenues to fund all proper federal government operations.[63] Their vision of what constitutes proper federal government operations is a tiny fraction of what exists today. Even if their calculations were to be correct about federal revenues and expenses under their vision, changing the current international free-trade regime in the near future does not seem possible without huge unknown economic and political impacts.

Taxes on Sales

To provide money for their services and programs, many states and local governments tax general sales of goods and services that occur in their jurisdictions. Both the tax rates applied to sales and what sales are subject to a general sales tax vary widely from place to place. For example, sales taxes typically do not apply to food bought in a grocery store but do apply to food bought at a restaurant. What is classified as "food" also varies from time to time, with some items like soft drinks or candy sometimes being classified as "food" and sometimes not. Like the receipt of income, a sale normally involves a cash transfer, so cash is on hand to pay the tax. General sales taxes are consumption taxes because they are paid by the buyer (although collected by the seller), and they have been applied historically only to consumer goods and services, not to sales of real property, stocks, and other property that can be considered investments.

Proponents of a national sales tax dub it the "**fair tax**."[64] But "fair" to whom? Some analysts regard general sales taxes as regressive. That is, they impact relatively poor people disproportionately compared to relatively rich people. This may be true because general sales taxes historically have applied to sales of many items that relatively poor people can buy, such as televisions, bicycles, and cars, but have not applied to sales of some large items that relatively poor people cannot buy, such as houses or resort condominiums. Many sales taxes also historically have not applied to most services, whether those services are more likely to be used by everyone (such as haircuts) or more likely to be used by more wealthy people (such as home decor consulting). Any national sales tax that is designed to replace other federal taxes should remove these discrepancies, or relatively poor people will end up paying a larger portion of their incomes as federal taxes than will relatively rich people.

An extension of a national sales tax to cover *all* transactions also has been suggested, although to my knowledge this very broad form of sales tax has not been tried anywhere in the United States. Duard Lawley, the author of this idea in his book *Common Sense Tax Reform*, calls this extension a "Uniform Transaction Tax."[65] Under this idea, no transaction would be exempt from the tax, no matter what the subject of the transaction or who participates in the transaction.

For example, every purchase or exchange of stock on the New York Stock Exchange would be taxed, as would every purchase by a nonprofit organization. As with historic sales taxes, the buyer would pay the transaction tax, but the seller would collect it. The uniform transaction tax would not be a consumption tax because it applies to transactions that most economists would classify as "savings" (investments) as well as to transactions that would be classified as spending. By applying to an extremely broad base, the tax rate for a uniform transaction tax could presumably be much lower than the rates generally proposed for a national sales tax.

Taxes on Real Property

Many states and local governments impose a tax on the assessed value of **real property** (land and structures attached to the land) to provide money for their programs and services. Rates vary from jurisdiction to jurisdiction and also according to the classification of the real property (such as agricultural, business, or residential). Unlike a tax on sales or income, money to pay a real property tax is not automatically on hand but must come from some other source. At the probable tax levels required to fund the federal government, this fact could impose serious burdens on such property owners as retirees with low incomes. In addition, if a federal tax were to be imposed on real property, federal involvement in both its valuation and classification for tax purposes would be inevitable.

Taxes on Personal Property

Some states impose taxes on a variety of **personal property**, which is all property other than real property. Most commonly these taxes are on motor vehicles, such as cars and trucks. In just the realm of motor vehicles, a personal property tax can be imposed in many different ways. For example, vehicle taxes can be a flat amount on each vehicle, a percentage of a vehicle's assessed value, or an amount calculated from a formula based on the original purchase price and age of the vehicle. Like a tax on real property, money to pay a personal property tax is not automatically on hand and must come from some other source. Used on a national level, personal property taxes would have problems similar to those encountered when imposing a real property tax, although the tax amounts per item would be smaller. Federal involvement would also be inevitable in the classification of personal property for tax purposes and the valuation of the personal property if the tax were to be based on value.

Taxes on Value Added

The typical **value-added tax** is a tax on the market value added to a consumer item at each stage of its creation and distribution. An example of a value-added tax in action can be provided by an idealized version of the stages in the creation and sale of an automobile.

The total value-added tax on an automobile could be the sum of (1) the tax on the value added by the production of steel from iron ore and the production of all other materials used in its manufacture (upon sale of these materials to fabricators), (2) the tax on the value added by fabricating steel into axles, engines, chassis, and other parts, and by fabricating other materials into other parts (upon sale of these parts to a manufacturer/assembler), (3) the tax on the value added by assembling all of the parts into a complete automobile (upon sale of the automobile to a dealer), and (4) the tax on the value added by the dealer that purchases the automobile (upon sale to the ultimate consumer).

Much like they do for sales taxes, businesses collect the value-added tax for the government. Logistically, the value-added tax is applied to the sale price of the product received by each business in the supply chain, but upon its sale of the same or enhanced product, each business can recover the value-added tax that it paid when it purchased the product from the previous business in the supply chain. In that way, the total value-added tax remains a constant percentage of the market value of the final item taxed. The ultimate consumer, of course, ends up paying the total value-added tax for the item he or she purchases. For items that remain unpurchased, including products in different stages of the supply chain, businesses in the supply chain will end up paying the value-added tax up to that point.

As with a national sales tax, a critical question in considering a national value-added tax is what items or transactions would be subject to the tax. If the tax applies only to consumer goods, it would be as regressive as a national sales tax. A value-added tax may not be expandable to cover other items or kinds of transactions like sales of real estate that would help prevent it from being regressive.

Decisions on the Tax Alternatives

Having now summarized ten historic forms of taxes that are realistic candidates for federal taxes, which taxes have the best practical merit at the federal level?

Current federal taxes include six of these potential taxes. The United States imposes taxes on individual income, corporation income (in the form of net profit), deceased's estates, gifts, commodities and activities (excise taxes), and imported goods (tariffs). We will consider these six current taxes first and will then consider the other four potential taxes.

Choices from the Six Current Federal Taxes

The taxes on individual income (income tax, Social Security tax, and Medicare tax) are by far the most important current source of federal tax receipts. These should remain as the most important source of tax receipts, albeit with significant changes in the individual income tax to meet the criteria of fairness, accountability, and simplicity. The FAST Plan's proposed changes to meet these criteria do not turn the individual income tax into a consumption tax imposed when money is first earned (as proposed by McCaffery).[66] Using taxes on individual income has two advantages over some other potential taxes. First, the receipt of income provides money on hand to pay a tax without having to draw on other assets (as compared to a property tax). Second, the amount of tax paid has a logical relationship to an individual's ability to pay a tax.

As the second most important current source of federal tax receipts, a tax on corporation income also should remain, but not in its current form. In chapter 29, I describe the problems inherent in the current corporation net profit tax and propose a different form of corporation income tax to eliminate those problems.

The current federal tax on deceased's estates and its complementary tax on gifts achieve only a very small part of current federal receipts (1.1 percent of total federal receipts in fiscal year 2008).[67] The law relating to estate taxes, however, has some features that directly impact potential income tax receipts. Those features should be modified. They are addressed in chapter 30 on estate and gift taxes. As for the taxes themselves, maybe someone can figure out a way to make them simple, but I am unable to see how. Even without taking a position on the arguments for and against these taxes, simplicity dictates repeal of federal estate and gift taxes, but only if the FAST Plan's related income tax modifications are adopted.

Federal excise taxes exist in great variety, making them impossible to summarize adequately, although as shown above, some categorization is possible. This variety also provides fodder to those who oppose federal taxes altogether and like to list all federal taxes to show how the federal government has impinged on personal liberties through pervasive taxation.[68] In sheer number, most of the taxes in these lists are excise taxes. Despite their number, tax receipts from all federal excise taxes are modest compared to receipts from other federal taxes (2.7 percent of federal receipts in fiscal year 2008).[69] Excise taxes cannot generate enough receipts to be considered a contender to replace federal income taxes. They also generally have no interrelation with the individual income tax or corporation income tax. They will not be considered further in the context of federal tax reform.

Tariffs also are a modest source of additional federal receipts (1.1 percent of total federal receipts in fiscal year 2008).[70] Like excise taxes, tariffs do not have the potential in today's global market and free-trade climate to provide a major portion of needed federal receipts. They will also not be considered further.

Choices from the Four Other Potential Federal Taxes

What about the four other potential federal taxes?

Substituting any or all of these other taxes for the individual income tax or corporation income tax will not accomplish fairness, accountability, or simplicity in federal taxes despite what some of their proponents claim. Furthermore, without changes from their historic applications, these other potential taxes would be worse than existing federal taxes if imposed on a national level. Building on their summary descriptions in this chapter, I reject all of them for a variety of respective reasons.

Potential federal sales tax

A federal sales tax would be an unfair regressive tax unless the kinds of sales that are subject to the tax were to be expanded significantly from current sales tax models. That expansion would be outside the normal history and experience of these taxes. Expansion would thus require a significant reevaluation of what sales and services should be subject to a sales tax. An even greater reevaluation would have to occur under the further expansion of a national sales tax to a uniform transaction tax. Many Americans are likely to rebel against both expansions.

These expansions would also create a much more complicated tax collection structure than summarily envisioned by the proponents of a federal sales tax or uniform transaction tax. In addition, a national sales tax would impinge upon an important tax revenue source of many state and local governments. Proposals to use national sales tax receipts to replace those revenues underestimate the contentious difficulty of allocating these receipts to different states.

Potential federal tax on real property

A federal tax on real property would greatly increase existing real property taxes if it were to produce worthwhile tax receipts. This tax would require owners to pay substantial amounts of money to the United States when money to do so may not be available. In addition, historically, real property taxes have been based on property values, with different rates applying to different classifications of real property. A federal real property tax would likely encourage efforts to create many new classifications of real property with special lower tax rates as property owners try to minimize their property taxes. Multiple classifications would greatly complicate the tax structure.

The most problematic feature of a federal real property tax would be property valuations. Reliance on state and local value assessments carries a huge risk of biased taxes based not only on local pressures to reduce taxes but also on potentially inadequate funding for assessors to perform competent valuations. In addition, real property values vary tremendously across the United States, resulting in tax disparities that likely would create public dissension.

Potential federal tax on personal property

A federal tax on personal property would have the same problems as a federal tax on real property if it were to be based on value. If not based on value, some fair measure of the tax would have to be created. That would be difficult because different kinds of personal property can have very different characteristics. What personal property should be subject to the tax would also be an ongoing issue. Questions of privacy are inherent with personal property taxes on almost anything other than motor vehicles. Yet taxes on motor vehicles alone cannot raise significant revenues unless the taxes are huge relative to the value of the vehicles.

Potential value-added tax

The value-added tax ardently promoted by some people is outside taxing traditions in the United States. Entirely new mechanisms would have to be created to determine and collect the tax. These features should not automatically cause their rejection, but they do make adoption more difficult. Unless a value-added tax applies to more than consumer goods, a value-added tax would also be regressive, like current general sales taxes. Trying to expand what would be covered by a federal value-added tax would be as contentious as trying to expand what would be covered by a federal sales tax. All of these issues make a value-added tax just too much to take on at this juncture in our history.

Moving Forward with the Choices

In this chapter, we examined ten potential taxes as candidates for consideration in federal tax reform. Our examination reaffirmed six existing federal taxes as viable candidates for retention but rejected the other four potential taxes. Among the six existing federal taxes, our examination also concluded that excise taxes and tariffs need not be the subject of overall reform at this time. This examination leaves taxes on individual income, corporation income (potentially redefined), and estates and gifts as the subjects for reform.

How should those taxes be modified to achieve the goals of fairness, accountability, and simplicity?

The remainder of this book proposes answers to this question. To begin those answers, chapter 6 first sets forth important tax concepts that will permeate future discussion. Chapter 7 then identifies structural problems that cause current versions of the federal taxes on individual income, corporation income, and estates and gifts to fail the simplicity criterion. Chapter 8, the last chapter in part 1 of the main text, sets forth a summary version of the FAST Plan for tax reform, with guides to the detailed examinations that follow in parts 2 and 3.

Chapter 6

---◆·◆·◆---

Basic Tax Concepts

Discussions about tax reform often assume that everyone already knows the meaning of tax jargon used in the discussion. Tax jargon is simply shorthand for basic tax concepts. This chapter describes two sets of jargon that I will use in evaluating and proposing changes to current federal taxes. The first set has terms about tax rates, and the second set has terms about subsidies.

Tax Rates

Historically, federal tax rates on income, estates, and gifts have been in the form of percentages applied against taxable amounts. That is the limited meaning of "tax rate" that will be used throughout this book. Within this meaning, three additional terms require description: standard-rate tax, graduated tax rates, and marginal tax rate.

Standard-Rate Tax

As used in this book, a **standard-rate tax** is a tax that uses a single rate for all taxable amounts. A typical example of a standard-rate tax is a general sales tax of 3 percent applied against the sales price of goods sold in a state.

Graduated Tax Rates

Graduated tax rates apply a lower tax rate to the first amount of taxable income received in a year, a higher tax rate to the second amount of taxable income, a yet higher tax rate to the third amount of taxable income, and so on until a maximum rate is reached that applies to all taxable income above a certain amount. In other words, different tax rates apply to different segments of taxable income. These segments are known as **tax brackets**. When an individual or entity is said to be in a certain tax bracket, the tax bracket referred to is the one with the highest rate that applies to that individual's or entity's taxable income. The current individual income tax, corporation income tax, and estate and gift taxes all feature graduated tax rates.

Marginal Tax Rate

The **marginal tax rate** is the rate applied to the last additional dollar of income that is subject to a tax.

Subsidies

The common meaning of subsidy—a pecuniary aid to an individual or entity provided by a government—applies also to subsidies in the tax realm.[71] There are, however, two very different kinds of subsidies in that realm: direct subsidies and tax subsidies. Both kinds of subsidies permeate federal tax law.

Direct Subsidies

In the tax realm, a **direct subsidy** exists if a tax provision *can* require the United States to pay an individual or entity money that is not otherwise held by the United States on behalf of the individual.

Congress chose to provide payment of the subsidy through the tax system, but it could have chosen a number of other ways to make that payment. For example, Congress could have required an individual to apply to a federal agency for the subsidy.

A common form of direct subsidy in tax law is a "refundable" credit that is based on some action by the individual, such as buying a qualified energy-efficient home furnace. For this credit, the United States first applies the credit to the income tax owed by the individual, but if the credit exceeds the income tax, the United States will pay the excess to the individual. These kinds of tax provisions provide direct subsidies even though for many individuals the credit will be less than the income tax owed and the United States will not have to make a payment to the individual. Direct subsidies to individuals are normally in the form of credits and thus are easily recognizable and often accountable.

Tax Subsidies

One reason why federal individual income taxes are so complicated is the scattering of tax subsidies among different kinds of tax provisions. So, what is a "tax subsidy" anyway?

Tax subsidies for individuals

A broad way to identify a **tax subsidy** in the realm of individual income taxes is to create a standard individual taxpayer who pays the maximum total tax on all income received.

Any tax provision that allows a greater reduction of a taxpayer's income before taxes apply, a monetary credit against taxes otherwise due, or a lower or zero tax rate on certain kinds of income can be considered a tax subsidy because the tax provision reduces the amount of taxes due compared to this standard taxpayer.

This broad description is a useful yardstick for identifying a tax subsidy provided that two exceptions are recognized.

First, a tax provision that provides a direct subsidy will not be considered to be a tax subsidy, but instead will be labeled what it is—a "direct subsidy."

Second, tax provisions that fit an overall policy not to tax income that is necessary for the healthy life of the individual or the individual's dependents will not be considered tax subsidies. Under current tax law, these provisions would include standard deductions, personal exemptions, and itemized deductions for payments for medical expenses (reasonably defined).

Under this broad definition of a tax subsidy, individual tax subsidies fall into two general categories. These are tax subsidies for payments or actions that benefit the taxpayer and tax subsidies for payments or actions that benefit someone else. Many individual tax subsidies, of course, benefit both the taxpayer and someone else, at least in a general way. Some tax subsidies are called "tax incentives" because their stated purposes are to encourage an individual's actions to promote some politically determined goals, even though those actions also benefit the individual.

A few examples of individual tax subsidies in current law will illustrate these subsidies in action.

A well-known example of an individual tax subsidy for payments that primarily provide a benefit to the individual taxpayer is the itemized deduction for home mortgage interest payments.[72] That is, these interest payments are subtracted from income to reduce the amount of income that is subject to the income tax. This tax subsidy also arguably benefits industries like the home-building industry because it encourages more people to buy homes than would do so without the subsidy. This tax subsidy can even promote a societal goal to increase the number of people owning property.

An example of an individual tax subsidy for payments that provide a benefit to someone other than the individual taxpayer is the itemized deduction for gifts to charities, including qualified educational and religious organizations.[73] The individual gives this money (or property) to someone else to be used for what Congress has deemed to be good societal purposes, but the donation nevertheless reduces taxable income and thus federal tax receipts.

A final example of a current individual tax subsidy is the income tax credit for qualified adoption expenses.[74] This tax subsidy provides a monetary benefit to the individual taxpayer, but also arguably benefits children whose lives may be improved by being adopted because it encourages more people to adopt children than would do so without the subsidy.

Tax subsidies for entities

Of course, individuals are not the only beneficiaries of federal tax and direct subsidies. Corporations and other legal entities also have their share of these subsidies. Most of these entities are business enterprises. A broad way to identify a current tax subsidy for a business entity is to create a model business enterprise that determines net profit from actual fiscal year income and expenses, with expenses including depreciation of capital assets only as determined using a simple straight-line method. This model can be created hypothetically for each type of business entity. If a tax on these entities is imposed on the entity's net profit (such as the current corporation income tax), the basic federal tax on the net profit, if any, can be computed for that model. Whatever accounting or other permitted maneuver that reduces the basic federal tax for entities of that type can then be identified as a tax subsidy. Like direct subsidies for individuals, direct subsidies for a business entity can be identified by their refundability.

Impacts of Direct and Tax Subsidies

The Fiscal Commission's 2010 report uses the broad term "income tax expenditures" for all special tax provisions that constitute "spending by another name."[75] By the examples given in that report, a person may be able to construct a definition of "tax expenditure," but defining criteria are not found in the report. I think that the report uses "tax expenditures" to mean both direct and tax subsidies. Throughout this book, I will use the terms "direct subsidy" and "tax subsidy" rather than "tax expenditure" as more precise terms and to avoid confusion with the Fiscal Commission's report.

However described, direct and tax subsidies have two important effects. They allow some taxpayers to pay less taxes than other taxpayers with the same total real income, and they reduce total federal tax receipts, thus requiring higher overall tax rates to secure enough tax receipts to pay for all federal government operations, programs, and services.

By identifying or discussing direct and tax subsidies as benefiting certain taxpayers or reducing tax receipts, I am not suggesting that all direct and tax subsidies are bad or that the policies behind all of them are misdirected. My criticism of tax subsidies in particular is based mostly on the multiple ways that these subsidies occur within the federal tax system. These multiple ways greatly complicate federal taxes and also reduce the accountability of tax subsidies. My definitions of tax subsidies allow us to look at many tax provisions in a new light. In later chapters, I will show that some tax provisions that are not generally thought of as providing subsidies are indeed tax subsidies and should be analyzed as such. I will also suggest alternative ways to provide some current tax subsidies that will meet our fairness, accountability, and simplicity goals.

Using Tax Concepts

Armed with basic tax concepts relating to subsidies and tax rates, we are ready to begin identifying structural tax features that have contributed to making the current federal tax thicket.

Chapter 7

------◆·◆·◆------

What Makes Current Federal Taxes So Complicated?

Most Americans pay directly some form of tax on individual income, whether designated as income, Social Security, or Medicare tax. These taxes account for most federal tax receipts, but other taxes also contribute important revenues. Among these other taxes, the corporation income tax contributes the most revenue. Federal estate and gift taxes also play their roles.[76] Efforts to meet the simplicity goal for federal taxes must start with identifying the predominant features of those taxes that make them complicated to apply in practice.

Complicating Features of Taxes on Individual Income

Social Security and Medicare taxes are easily calculated from an individual's earned income, and earned income is readily known from wages or from net profit of a personal business. For individuals, current federal tax complexity thus occurs mostly in the individual income tax law and regulations.

Four features of the individual income tax cause much of this complexity:

(1) Using different tax rates for different kinds of income
(2) Phasing out or phasing in the application of tax provisions
(3) Providing subsidies in multiple ways
(4) Applying an alternative minimum tax

Undoubtedly other people could point to other features that frustrate them and create additional complexity.

The provisions that make up these four numbered features were supported by rationales that Congress thought from time to time had merit. The combination of all of these provisions, however, is a mess. And the combination of all of these provisions also fails the fairness criterion by permitting significant tax discrimination whereby individuals with the same real income and family circumstances can end up paying very different amounts of income taxes or total federal taxes (adding income, Social Security, and Medicare taxes).

Let's look briefly at each of these four features to provide a framework for later discussion about how to accomplish simplicity while also addressing the rationales that led to the provisions that comprise these features. Tax year 2009 will be used as the benchmark. Special one-year provisions were effective in 2010 and later extended through 2011 and 2012 as part of the December 2010 tax compromise. However, the 2012 fiscal cliff tax compromise reintroduced many 2009 provisions.[77]

Using Different Tax Rates for Different Kinds of Income

Here we will consider the graduated tax rates and marginal tax rate concepts described in chapter 6. Current individual income tax law not only uses graduated tax rates, but also applies different sets of tax rates to different *kinds* of income. Rules exist to determine which set of rates apply based on both the classification of the income and a variety of calculations. Some of these different sets of rates can be illustrated by considering the 2009 rates on ordinary income, capital gains, and qualified dividends.

> In 2009, ordinary individual income, such as wages and self-employed business income, was taxed at marginal rates ranging from 10 percent to a maximum 35 percent.[78] Within this range, different rates applied to different segments of income depending upon the filing status of the taxpayer (e.g., married filing jointly or unmarried individual). Most long-term capital gains income, however, was taxed at special rates ranging from 0 percent to a maximum 15 percent, although other maximum rates applied to some types of long-term capital gains.[79] Qualified dividends income from corporate stocks was taxed like long-term capital gains, at special rates that could not exceed 15 percent.[80]

Phasing Out or Phasing In Tax Provisions Application

The idea of phasing out or phasing in the application of particular tax provisions appears to come mostly from decisions about who should be eligible to take advantage of those provisions. Eligibility has often been determined by how much income an individual has received in the tax year. Accordingly, Congress has adopted formulas that use income and some other factors to reduce gradually the availability of selected tax provisions to some taxpayers. These formulas are often found in "worksheets" that have to be used in figuring taxes. Worksheets have become a significant feature of tax-return filing in the last decade.[81]

Two examples will illustrate the phasing-in or phasing-out approach that is designed to limit the application of some tax provisions to some taxpayers.

Under current federal tax law, all individuals have a choice between using a standard deduction or using itemized deductions to reduce the amount of their income that is subject to tax. People who have larger incomes often choose itemized deductions because they are more likely to have deductible expenses that collectively exceed the standard deduction (such as deductions for state income taxes, state property taxes, and mortgage interest payments). In the early 1990s, Congress decided that individuals with very large incomes did not really need these deductions, so Congress adopted a phase-out of these deductions based upon the amount of the individual's income.[82] A ten-step formula, which includes subcategories of calculations, was still used in 2009 to phase out a portion of the itemized deductions for individuals whose incomes exceeded defined amounts.[83]

As another example, under current law, retired individuals who receive only Social Security benefits as their income generally do not pay individual income taxes on those benefits payments. However, Congress decided more than two decades ago that individuals who have other income that is greater than certain amounts should begin to pay income taxes on the Social Security benefits that they receive. Again, complex formulas exist that phase in taxes on a portion of these Social Security benefits under these circumstances.[84]

Providing Elective Tax Subsidies in Multiple Ways

For this purpose, an "elective tax subsidy" is defined as a tax provision that allows an individual to pay reduced income taxes based on a choice of spending for personal benefit. The existence of elective tax subsidies does not necessarily have to lead to undue complexity. Current subsidies of this type, however, take so many different forms that their comparative impacts on an individual's taxes or on federal tax receipts as a whole are difficult to discern.

Again, some examples will illustrate this problem.

Some tax subsidies are in the form of reductions or partial reductions from income before the tax rates are applied to the income. Examples are the itemized deductions for home mortgage interest paid during the tax year (an initial 100 percent deduction) and unreimbursed moving expenses for changing job locations (also an initial 100 percent deduction, but only to the extent that the sum of those expenses and other described expenses exceeds 2 percent of adjusted gross income).[85] Some of these elective tax subsidies can also be affected by the phase-out of itemized deductions for individuals with larger incomes.

Using income reductions, the amount of the tax subsidy in terms of taxes avoided depends upon the marginal tax rate that applies to the taxpayer's income. Under the current graduated–tax rate approach, individuals with larger incomes receive a greater tax subsidy because their marginal rates are higher. This feature also affects tax fairness, not only by providing greater subsidies for individuals with larger incomes, but also by magnifying differences between the taxes owed by individuals with larger incomes who have or do not have the allowed income reduction.

Other elective tax subsidies are in the form of credits against taxes owed, either wholly or partially. Examples are the education and adoption credits.[86] Subsidies via tax credits are the simplest to compare against each other and also to analyze in terms of their impacts on total tax receipts, especially if they are calculated from simple formulas.

Applying an Alternative Minimum Tax

Sometime in the 1970s, information became public that some individuals with very large incomes were paying small amounts of individual income taxes because they had been able to take advantage of Internal Revenue Code provisions that greatly reduced the amount of their incomes that would be subject to tax. During this decade, Congress addressed the inequities caused by these kinds of maneuvers by enacting the "Alternative Minimum Tax" in 1978.[87]

This new tax was conceptually designed to prevent excessive tax avoidance notwithstanding the public policy purposes that allowed selected reductions in the amount of income subject to tax. The **alternative minimum tax** is a taxing scheme that exists alongside the regular individual income tax, with a different set of rates and a smaller set of allowed tax subsidies. The calculations used to determine the alternative minimum tax were complicated to begin with but have gotten worse in recent years as more special tax rates have been adopted for different kinds of incomes, especially capital gains and qualified dividends.

Complicating Features of the Corporation Income Tax

The current federal corporation income tax is a tax on corporation *net profit* and should properly be called the "corporation net profit tax."[88] Like the individual income tax, the corporation income tax rates are graduated, although the rates and their applicability are very different than the rates for individuals.[89]

What makes the corporation income tax complicated is not the determination of the tax, but the determination of taxable net profit. Net profit, of course, is the difference between revenue and expenses.

Many rules exist on what kinds of payments are properly considered to be corporate business expenses that can be used to reduce revenue in the calculation of taxable net profit. These rules exist in addition to rules regarding expenses under general accounting principles. Some rules, like those allowing accelerated depreciation for some assets, can significantly affect the amount of taxable income.

In addition, tucked within the expenses allowed in some industries are some expenses that can properly be considered tax subsidies because they reflect an arbitrary calculation of an expense that can be greater than the actual expense.

Classic examples are the depletion allowances in the oil and gas and mineral extraction industries.[90] These substitute for what otherwise would be expenses spread out over time as depreciation of an asset, such as oil in the ground (the value being calculated by the cost of finding the deposit and setting up an extraction facility). Depletion allowances are actually simpler than alternative ways to calculate depreciation, but they are perpetual. As a result, the total allowable expenses over time can greatly exceed the amount of money invested in the property.

These and other tax subsidies via corporate expense determinations may be appropriate, but their total cost in terms of lost tax receipts is difficult to calculate. They flunk my accountability criterion.

Complicating Features of the Tax on Deceased's Estates

When the value of a deceased's estate exceeds a certain amount, a set of graduated tax rates has historically applied to its value above that amount. At least two features complicate the federal estate tax.

One complication is the morass of rules that determine what estate assets are subject to the tax and when. Estate planning seeks to avoid excessive tax payments like double tax payments on the same assets in a short time, thereby preserving more assets for the deceased's heirs and future heirs as well.

A second complication with the federal estate tax is its interrelationship with the federal gift tax. The federal gift tax exists so that individuals cannot avoid the estate tax simply by giving their assets away to family members, friends, or other individuals. Although the gift tax uses the same set of graduated rates as the estate tax,[91] gifts can occur over a long period of time, so record keeping alone can make proper accounting for all gifts a nightmare.

As an example of the special tax provisions applicable only to tax year 2010, the estate tax was rescinded for that year.[92] Special rules applied only during that year, which complicated even this apparently simple change.

Addressing These Complicating Features

Armed now with knowledge about complicating features of the current individual income tax, corporation income tax, and estate and gift taxes, we are ready to look at ways to simplify those taxes while also preserving the goals of fairness and accountability.

The preview of the FAST Plan in the next chapter will highlight how this can be done.

Chapter 8

———◆•◆•◆———

The FAST Plan's Bottom Line

The current federal tax thicket did not just suddenly appear out of nowhere. Congress has created this thicket over many years as it has sought ways to raise money to provide for government operations, programs, and services. Current federal taxes reflect practical and philosophical considerations as well as political compromises. The statutory provisions represent the best judgment of those who enacted them. Many provisions made good sense at the time they were adopted and still do, at least in their intent.

Any attempt to overhaul federal taxes will be doomed if current tax provisions are ignored. Despite an overwhelming American frustration with federal taxes, many provisions have been around for a long time and are familiar to taxpayers. As noted in the Introduction, familiarity alone breeds a certain comfort level that will be difficult to dislodge. Yet tinkering with the details of only a few tax provisions will not achieve our overall fairness, accountability, and simplicity goals. The next series of chapters takes on this broader task by examining the FAST Plan proposals in the context of many well-known federal tax provisions. For consistency, I have used 2009 tax law as the benchmark for what is "current" because 2010 and later year tax laws featured important temporary provisions.

Context is more than a recitation of what the current tax law *is*. Sometimes *why* Congress adopted a particular tax feature provides the best guidance on what changes can be made. That is why many of the following chapters describe the underlying reasons for the feature covered by the chapter. Proposed changes can then address those reasons. Equally important is an understanding about how various tax provisions work together. The following attempts to reform federal taxes also address whether and how the reasons for many provisions can be advanced in ways that are less interdependent.

Obvious to any individual taxpayer is the fact that total federal taxes, not just one particular tax, is what determines how much money a person has left over for other purposes. It does not matter whether the tax is labeled "income," "Social Security," or "Medicare." The money paid to the United States is simply gone from a person's budget. Ignoring this fact will prevent full and meaningful solutions to the current federal tax thicket. That is why all of these individual taxes are considered in the following chapters. What may be surprising is how current corporation income tax and estate tax features also can affect an individual's federal income tax, mostly through special individual income tax provisions that are derived largely from those features. The chapters that discuss these taxes are thus relevant to all taxpayers and not just corporate executives and people with large estates.

An attempt to critique every current tax provision is unnecessary to the task of proposing new ideas to make federal taxes more fair, accountable, and simple. Such an attempt would be far beyond my knowledge and impossible anyway in a relatively short book.[93]

The next sections of this chapter summarize my FAST Plan without discussing the reasons for its proposals. Be prepared for a few jolts. Some of my proposals are radical in the sense that they reject longstanding approaches to federal taxes.

The FAST Plan Overview

Five groups of taxes that create the current federal tax thicket will be addressed in this book. These are (1) the individual income tax, (2) the Social Security tax on individuals and employers, (3) the Medicare tax on individuals and employers, (4) the corporation income tax, and (5) the complementary estate and gift taxes. Collectively, these five tax groups accounted for 92 percent of all federal receipts in fiscal year 2008.[94]

The mere existence of five different tax groups is not what creates the federal tax thicket. Instead, that thicket arises from complexity within each tax group and current interrelationships among the five groups. Indeed, I propose eliminating only the estate and gift taxes and only after changing related individual income tax rules. The chapters that follow describe why certain current tax features should be retained, changed, replaced, or eliminated. Specific proposals on how to accomplish these results are found at the end of many chapters.

How, then, do we reform federal taxes to achieve fairness, accountability, and simplicity?

The FAST Plan for individuals will have an individual income tax that uses a single standard tax rate. Taxable income will be determined by allowing only a few selected reductions from income, such as a standard deduction. All tax subsidies will be allowed only in the form of tax credits. The income tax will coordinate with Social Security and Medicare taxes so that no individual's *total* federal tax rate will exceed the standard rate.

For corporations, the FAST Plan will replace the corporation income tax on net profit with a much lower standard-rate income tax on revenue.

And for estates and gifts, the FAST Plan will have no estate or gift tax in return for treating an estate for tax purposes as if the decedent were still alive.

Three summary versions of the FAST Plan are found in this book:

- A version that is designed to introduce politicians and economists to the core new ideas of the FAST Plan (This version is found in chapter 31. It assumes considerable knowledge about current federal tax law, which you will have achieved by that point in this book.)
- A version of the FAST Plan that contains all of the specific proposals found at the end of chapters in this book (This version is found in appendix 1A. This version collects in one place all of the changes needed to create the full FAST Plan. It can serve as a checklist for preparing legislation to accomplish the FAST Plan.)
- A version that is designed to introduce the new ideas of the FAST Plan in an integrated way and to guide you to the chapter(s) that provide the reasoning and facts behind these ideas (This version of the FAST Plan is what follows in the remainder of this chapter.)

The FAST Plan for Individual Income, Social Security, and Medicare Taxes

- Retain a tax on individual income with income being defined the same as under current law, but replace all graduated–tax rate structures with a standard-rate income tax that applies to all filing categories and that is determined initially neither to increase nor decrease federal individual income tax receipts (chapters 10 and 27).
- Retain the current 12.4 percent Social Security and 2.9 percent Medicare tax rates and their application to earned income, the current cutoff for Social Security tax application, and the current payment obligations by employers, employees, and self-employed individuals (chapter 11).
- Allow all Social Security and Medicare tax payments by an individual as nonrefundable credits against the individual's income tax, but only after making the credits for Social Security and Medicare tax payments equivalent between employees and self-employed individuals (chapters 10 and 11).
- Apply the standard-rate income tax to all kinds of individual income:
  - Wages (chapter 13)
  - Capital gains (chapter 14)
  - Dividends (chapter 15)
    - For dividends, make the standard rate applicable in conjunction with the proposed change in the tax base for the corporation income tax (chapters 15 and 29).

- Interest (chapter 13)
- Personal business income (chapter 13)
- Partnership and S corporation income (chapter 13)
- A portion of Social Security benefits depending upon other income (chapter 16)
  - For Social Security benefits, simplify the current methods for calculating the portion of the benefits that is taxable if Social Security benefits are to be taxable at all (chapter 16).
- Pension payments and retirement-plan distributions based on deferred income or untaxed contributions (chapter 17)
- All miscellaneous income (chapter 13)
- Retain most current statutory exclusions from gross income, but revisit some current exclusions from gross income to determine if the tax subsidy represented by the exclusion should be accomplished instead with a nonrefundable tax credit (e.g., interest on state and local bonds) (chapter 18).
- In determining taxable income, retain as reductions from income payments that postpone tax liability, such as contributions to qualified retirement plans, or that are taxable to another person, such as alimony and maintenance (chapter 20).
- In determining taxable income, allow as reductions from income all payments necessary for a healthy life, including the current standard deduction, current exemptions, *and* payments for qualified medical expenses that exceed 1 percent of an individual's adjusted gross income (chapter 21).
  - Eliminate permanently all phase-out rules for itemized deductions and exemptions (chapter 19).
- Allow nonrefundable income tax credits instead of reductions from income or special tax rates as the only way to provide tax subsidies to individuals (chapter 24).
  - To the extent these tax subsidies are retained, recast as tax credits all current reductions from income for elective payments that benefit oneself (e.g., mortgage interest) or that benefit others as gifts to charity (chapter 22).
  - Allow no reductions from income or tax credits for payments of state and local taxes (chapter 23).
  - To the extent these tax subsidies are retained, recast as tax credits all current itemized deductions for uncompensated losses (chapter 23).
  - Allow no reductions from income for Social Security and Medicare taxes paid by self-employed individuals (part of the changes needed to make these taxes equivalent as paid by employees and self-employed individuals in connection

with allowing these payments as nonrefundable credits to an individual's income tax) (chapters 11 and 23).

- Except for a taxpayer's money held by the United States, label every individual refundable tax credit as a direct subsidy (chapter 24).
- Retain current individual nonrefundable and refundable tax credits so long as the tax and direct subsidies represented by those credits remain appropriate (chapter 25).
  - Recast the Earned Income Credit in more simple ways that separate its two subsidies (chapter 25).
  - Reexamine every individual tax credit that derives from current law that would be changed by the proposals of the FAST Plan (chapter 25).
- Provide a temporary tax subsidy to eligible retirees to allow time for retirement planning to take into account a standard-rate income tax (chapter 26).
- Eliminate the alternative minimum tax, but only if all tax subsidies are recast as nonrefundable tax credits (chapter 28).

The FAST Plan for Corporation Income Tax

- Replace the current corporation earnings (net profit) tax with a corporation standard-rate revenue tax on revenues from operations in the United States (chapter 29).
  - Use an initial standard rate determined from five-year historic data on corporate revenues (rate estimated at 1.5 percent) (chapter 29).
  - Treat all entities with corporation-like attributes as corporations subject to any corporation revenue tax that is adopted in place of the corporation earnings (net profit) tax (chapter 29).
- Impose no tax on corporation revenue or earnings from operations outside the United States and concurrently eliminate all corporation foreign tax credits (chapter 29).

The FAST Plan for Estate and Gift Taxes

- Repeal all estate and gift taxes, but only upon eliminating the automatic stepped-up basis rule for all property in an estate, without exception, and preferably along with adopting a standard-rate income tax for all income, including all capital gains (chapter 30).

Using the FAST Plan's Bottom Line

With the FAST Plan's bottom line now revealed, we are ready to launch into the details of and reasoning behind all parts of the FAST Plan. The fairness, accountability, and simplicity criteria described in chapter 4 will continue to drive my assessment of current law and potential alternatives.

The next chapters contain not only descriptions of current law and potential alternatives, but also many facts presented in new ways that shed light on whether and how current law should be reformed. If you have particular interest in some topics or new ideas of the FAST Plan, the references in this chapter can help direct you to those topics or new ideas.

Part II:

Reforming Taxes on Individual Income

Chapter 9

———◆·◆·◆———

How Individual Income Is Taxed Today

The words of the Sixteenth Amendment to the US Constitution are clear:

> The Congress shall have power to lay and collect taxes on incomes, from whatever source derived, without apportionment among the several States, and without regard to any census or enumeration.

Congress has exercised this power many times since the states ratified the Sixteenth Amendment in 1913.[95]

In exercising this power, Congress has adopted broad definitions of income and has categorized income differently for different tax purposes. This chapter presents an overview of the three current taxes on individual income that account for a huge portion of all federal tax receipts—the Social Security tax, Medicare tax, and individual income tax. This overview will allow us to critique current features of those taxes and to propose reforms that will meet our fairness, accountability, and simplicity criteria.

Social Security and Medicare Taxes

Social Security and **Medicare** taxes comprised about 34 percent of all federal receipts in fiscal year 2008 (excluding deficit borrowings).[96] As emphasized in chapter 3, combined outlays for Social Security and Medicare hospital benefits were less than those amounts.[97]

The Social Security and Medicare taxes use standard rates that are levied only against **earned income**. Earned income consists of wages of employees and net earnings from self-employment by self-employed individuals. Both taxes apply to earned income above a very small amount without any reductions, but the Social Security tax ends once an individual's earned income exceeds a certain amount ($106,800 in 2009). The Medicare tax, on the other hand, applies to all earned income no matter how large.

Individual Income Tax

The federal individual income tax is the primary source of tax receipts used for US government operations and services other than Social Security and Medicare hospital benefits. Receipts from this tax comprised 45 percent of total federal receipts in fiscal year 2008 (excluding deficit borrowings). These receipts comprised 69 percent of total receipts other than receipts from Social Security and Medicare taxes (also excluding deficit borrowings).[98]

Although many Americans are familiar with the general way that the individual income tax is determined, a brief overview is in order as a reminder and for those who may not have had experience with this tax.

At this point, three concepts can set the framework for understanding the federal individual income tax. These concepts are taxable income, income tax, and tax credits. The chapters that follow address these concepts and propose changes in the way that the individual income tax is determined.

Taxable Income

The calculation of an individual's **taxable income** starts with a broad definition of **gross income** that initially sweeps in almost every conceivable form of income.[99] The Internal Revenue Code first whittles away at this definition by specifically excluding some forms of actual or arguable income from being treated as gross income.[100] Then the code allows a host of reductions from gross income to determine taxable income. These reductions are grouped in ways that include some seemingly odd features like an "adjusted gross income" as an interim step. Many of these reductions are tax subsidies.

Income Tax

Once taxable income is calculated, tax rates are applied to that amount to determine an individual's income tax.

For many decades, the income tax rates have been graduated. As described previously, under graduated tax rates, different tax rates apply to different segments of an individual's taxable income. These segments are known as tax brackets.

Under 2009 law, the graduated tax rates on an individual's ordinary taxable income ranged from 10 percent to 35 percent.[101] Starting in 2013, the 2012 fiscal cliff tax compromise raised the maximum rate to 39.6 percent for individuals whose income exceeds a threshold amount (e.g., $400,000 for a single individual).[102]

Different sets of graduated tax rates exist for different filing categories, such as "married filing jointly," although the ultimate maximum rate is the same for all filing categories. Special sets of lower graduated tax rates also exist for capital gains income and dividends income, with the lowest rates applying to long-term capital gains and qualified dividends.[103]

Tax Credits

Finally, a number of tax credits are potentially available that may be applied against the income tax to arrive at the tax due (or sometimes money to be refunded). Some of these credits are just ways to account for money that has already been paid to the United States by or on behalf of the taxpayer. Other tax credits are tax subsidies or direct subsidies.

What Is Coming Up

Part 2 of this book focuses primarily on the individual income tax. We need to consider Social Security and Medicare taxes only in how they relate to the individual income tax.

Armed with our overview of the individual income tax, the many remaining chapters in part 2 critique all major features of that tax. These chapters form five topical groups:

- Fundamental structure of the individual income tax (chapters 10–11)
- What individual income to tax (chapters 12–18)
- Reductions from income to determine taxable income (chapters 19–23)
- Individual income tax credits (chapters 24–25)
- Important special cases (chapters 26–28)

Most chapters end with FAST Plan proposals to change or often to retain the feature considered.

Meeting the Most Difficult Reform Challenge

Does the fundamental structure of the current individual income tax need to change to accomplish fairness, accountability, and simplicity?

The next two chapters answer this overriding question.

Chapter 10

<hr />

Should We Retain Graduated Income Tax Rates?

The use of graduated income tax rates has an apparent logic that people who have larger incomes are better able to pay a greater portion of their incomes as taxes because smaller portions of those incomes are needed for essential living expenses. This logic has been challenged on and off for many years. Whether or not this logic has merit, the goals of simplicity and fairness require us to reevaluate the use of graduated income tax rates.

Historic Effects of Graduated Income Tax Rates

By themselves, graduated tax rates are not overly complex. The Internal Revenue Service has created tax tables and straightforward formulas to allow individuals to calculate easily the income tax due on a specified amount of taxable income. Graduated income tax rates, however, have spawned other complicated tax provisions that try to address some odd effects caused by graduated rates.

Filing Categories

One group of those provisions consists of different sets of income tax rates for different **filing categories**. Current law recognizes four categories. The IRS labels these as "single," "married filing jointly" (or "qualified widow(er)"), "married filing separately," and "head of household."[104] The different sets of rates that apply to these filing categories try to address the effects of graduated tax rates on total tax when total income can or cannot be split equally between two people.

Odd results like the "marriage penalty" (or "marriage bonus") occur from the combination of graduated tax rates and different sets of tax rates for different filing categories. A **marriage penalty** occurs when a married couple's income tax owed per individual is more than the income tax owed by a similarly situated single individual with the same taxable income per individual. A **marriage bonus** occurs when a married couple's income tax owed per individual is less than the income tax owed by a similarly situated single individual with the same taxable income per individual. (See chapter 27 for an in-depth look at the marriage penalty and bonus.)

Capital Gains

Another group of tax provisions spawned in part by graduated income tax rates is the historic use of lower tax rates for capital gains. Among other purposes, these lower rates try to decrease the effects of graduated tax rates on total tax when all capital gains occurring over more than one year or even many years are bunched in just one tax year. (See chapter 14.)

Tax Discrimination

A more subtle effect of graduated income tax rates should also be noted. Graduated tax rates have created an atmosphere in which taxpayers who have larger incomes and find themselves in higher tax-rate brackets have resented their tax rates as compared to others. They have successfully lobbied for tax deductions, tax credits, or special rates on certain kinds of income that will effectively reduce their overall tax rates.

Often the stated rationales for these total tax reductions are couched in other terms. But if one looks behind some tax deductions, credits, and special rates, we see that few people other than taxpayers with larger incomes can take advantage of them or that people with larger incomes can take much greater advantage of them than people with smaller incomes. All of these provisions add complexity and discrimination to the federal taxes system. Reducing the pressures that lead to these provisions can more easily allow them to be changed. Changes can then be directed toward creating greater simplicity and fairness in the federal tax system overall.

Marginal Total Federal Tax Rate

At least during the last ten years, the federal graduated income tax rate system did not follow its original logic when an individual's total federal tax obligation is considered (adding income, Social Security, and Medicare taxes). We can best represent that total obligation by an individual's **marginal total federal tax rate**, which is the effective rate that results from applying income, Social Security, and Medicare taxes on the last dollar earned by the individual.

When all three of these taxes are added, you might be surprised to learn that the highest marginal total federal tax rate from 2003 to 2012 did not occur for individuals with exceptionally large earned incomes who could best afford to pay higher tax rates. Instead, it occurred for self-employed individuals having earned incomes as small as roughly $78,000 up to roughly

$115,000 depending upon filing category. The actual numbers for this "middle group" tell a sobering story.

We will use tax year 2009 as an example for the 2003–2012 time period.

In 2009, individuals in the middle group of self-employed individuals faced marginal total federal tax rates of 40.15 percent (in very rare cases, the rate could be even higher for a small slice of income). The next highest marginal total federal tax rate was 37.21 percent for self-employed individuals having earned incomes exceeding roughly $385,000.[105]

Among wage earners, the highest marginal total federal tax rate in 2009 occurred for individuals having wages exceeding roughly $385,000 (36.45 percent), closely followed by individuals having wages as low as roughly $80,000 up to roughly $107,000 (35.65 percent).[106]

All of these rates decreased by two percentage points in 2011 and 2012 because of the temporary decrease in Social Security tax rates for those years.

The 2012 fiscal cliff tax compromise changed this picture somewhat. The compromise increased the income tax rates for large incomes above designated threshold amounts, while retaining the 2003 to 2012 income tax rates for all other incomes.

With these increases, the highest marginal total federal tax rate in 2013 became 41.75 percent for self-employed individuals having taxable earned incomes exceeding the threshold amount (e.g., $400,000 for a single individual).[107] The marginal total federal tax rate for the middle group of self-employed individuals in 2013 remained at 40.15 percent.

Among wage earners, the highest marginal total federal tax rate in 2013 became 41.05 percent for individuals having taxable wages exceeding the threshold amount.[108] The marginal total federal tax rate for the middle group of wage earners remained at 35.65 percent.

Common proposals to modify current graduated income tax rates but still retain a graduated-rate approach noticeably omit disclosure of an individual's total federal tax obligation under the proposal. For example, a 28 percent maximum income tax rate on earned income will impose a very different highest marginal total federal tax rate if it is effective before rather than after the amount of income reaches the Social Security tax cutoff. Beware of any federal tax-reform proposal that does not candidly reveal its effect on marginal total federal tax rates.[109]

Say Good-Bye to Graduated Tax Rates

The only way to remove the historic effects of graduated tax rates is not to use them at all. In this regard, I respectfully disagree with the recommendation in the Fiscal Commission's 2010 report to maintain or increase the progressivity of the federal tax code.[110]

To replace graduated income tax rates, I propose one standard income tax rate for *all* kinds of income, including all capital gains. A standard rate will eliminate the perceived need for separate tax rates for different filing categories and will eliminate one rationale historically used to justify special low rates for long-term capital gains. (See respectively chapters 27 and 14.) Using one standard tax rate for all individual income also makes tax receipts more predictable than the current multirate approach. This predictability clarifies decisions needed to avoid annual deficit spending and national debt increases.

Of course, the idea of a single standard-rate income tax is not new. Challengers to the logic behind graduated tax rates have long proposed a **flat tax,** with one rate being applied to all ordinary income. Their arguments typically rely on a simple rhetorical question: What could be more fair than everyone having to pay the same percentage of their taxable incomes as taxes? With this appeal to fairness, why have these proposals consistently failed to generate much popular support?

Flaws in Flat-Tax Proposals

Many historic flat-tax proposals share two flaws, at least in terms of their ability to gain that elusive popular support. The first flaw is their failure to take into account an individual's total federal tax obligation, including payment of Social Security and Medicare taxes.[111] The second flaw is their proposed zero tax on capital gains and often also other forms of capital-based income, such as interest and dividends.

With respect to Social Security and Medicare taxes, if a flat tax is applied to earned income without addressing Social Security and Medicare taxes on that income, individuals with smaller earned incomes will pay a higher marginal total federal tax rate on taxable income than will individuals with much larger earned incomes. This will occur because the Social Security tax will be an add-on, but it ends at the Social Security tax cutoff. With this result, it is no wonder than many people have not embraced historic flat-tax proposals.

With respect to zero tax on capital gains and other capital-based income, many people first ask a simple question: Who would mostly benefit from this exclusion?

Those same people will likely answer "mostly the wealthy." Logic supports this answer because wealthy people have more money than less-wealthy people, and a larger portion of their money is available to buy land, stock, bonds, and other assets that have the potential for capital gains or that can provide dividend or interest income. Facts also support this answer, as demonstrated by the following data:

> IRS data from tax year 2007, the last tax year before the Great Recession, illustrate who does and does not have substantial capital-based income. In 2007, for the group of 125 million tax returns that reported less than $100,000 adjusted gross income, only 5 percent of that income was capital-based income ($220 billion of a $4,047 billion total). In contrast, for the group of 18 million tax returns that reported $100,000 or more adjusted gross income, that percentage was 25 percent ($1,181 billion of a $4,641 billion total). The further up the income scale you go, the larger that percentage becomes. For the select group of less than 20,000 tax returns that reported $10 million or more adjusted gross income, 69 percent of that income was capital-based income ($387 billion of a $562 billion total). This 69 percent figure is calculated by adding the percentages of total income reported respectively for net capital gains (56 percent), dividends (7 percent), and taxable interest (6 percent).[112] Of course, within each income group, and more prevalent in the groups with larger incomes, all or nearly all of the income of some individuals will be in the form of capital-based income.

Many Americans intuitively recognize these disparities and so will not embrace a flat tax or standard-rate income tax that excludes from the tax capital gains, dividends, and interest or even only capital gains.

The Standard-Rate Tax of the FAST Plan

The standard-rate tax of the FAST Plan is not a flat tax because it removes both flaws found in historic flat-tax proposals. Here is how it removes those flaws.

The FAST Plan takes into account the effects of Social Security and Medicare taxes by allowing their payment as a credit against income tax determined from a standard rate. This approach not only solves the problem of people with small incomes having higher marginal total federal tax rates, but also recognizes the interconnection that Social Security tax receipts have had with income tax receipts under endemic deficit spending.

Remember from chapter 3 on borrowings from federal trust funds that for many years, the money received from the Social Security taxes has exceeded the payments for benefits each year, and not by small amounts. That money has been spent for other government services and programs. As a result, receipts from Social Security taxes have been an integral part of the total federal budget and federal expenditures for things other than Social Security. Although the United States has created IOUs to the Social Security trust funds for that money, those IOUs may not be paid back. So I reject the notion that Social Security taxes must always be considered separate from income tax policy. That notion rests on the false assumptions that funds from the Social Security taxes will only be used for Social Security benefits and that only other federal taxes pay for general federal expenditures. The next chapter shows how income tax credits for payment of Social Security and Medicare taxes can be applied comparably for wage earners and self-employed individuals.

The FAST Plan proposals address the rationales used to support low or zero income tax rates for capital gains (chapter 14) and other kinds of capital-based income, especially dividends (chapter 15). Although I conclude that fairness and simplicity require capital-based income to be subject to the same standard tax rate as other income, I also propose other changes along with a standard rate in order to address rationales that are used to support low or zero rates for some kinds of capital-based income.

The Amount of the Standard Rate

What should be the amount of the standard rate?

Ultimately, a standard rate is best determined from calculations that show how much tax revenue will be raised by alternative standard rates, tempered by politically determined absolute maxima. As compared to using multiple tax rates in a graduated tax scheme or for different kinds of income, using a standard rate allows the United States more easily to frame a budget of expenses that matches tax receipts, or to frame tax receipts to match a budget of expenses. This feature will help to minimize deficit spending, except for emergencies.

As an example of how to calculate a standard tax rate on individual income, an initial standard rate can be calculated from tax year 2007 data, the last normal tax year before the Great Recession. The goal of this rate would be to achieve the same amount of individual income tax receipts that actually occurred from the tax year 2007. In that way, the initial rate determination will not be used as an excuse to increase or decrease federal income taxes generally. Using this goal, I estimate the standard income tax rate at 29 percent.[113]

Surprised at this high a percentage? In evaluating this rate, remember that Social Security and Medicare taxes paid by individuals will be credits against the income tax. As calculated in the next chapter, that credit will be about 14.2 percent of all earned income up to the Social Security tax cutoff, so the pure "income tax" portion of the tax rate paid under the standard rate would be 14.8 percent for earned income up to the cutoff.

These two numbers—14.8 percent for a net marginal income tax rate up to the Social Security tax cutoff and 29 percent for a standard tax rate—are eerily close to the nominal graduated income tax rates passed by Congress and approved by President Reagan in the Tax

Reform Act of 1986. The two rates in that act were 15 percent for initial amounts of taxable income and 28 percent for all taxable income above those amounts, including capital gains (the initial amounts of income varied according to filing category).[114] Although that act eliminated a host of discriminatory tax provisions, it still left in place many income reductions, complicating tax provisions, and tax-obligation disparities that are reassessed in this book. Tax receipts after the effective date of that act in 1988 continued to be inadequate to cover federal outlays.[115]

The estimated standard rate of 29 percent necessarily has some built-in assumptions that derive from the FAST Plan proposals in this book. These are identified as part of appendix 10A, which has the calculations for a standard rate. In general, the 29 percent rate assumes that the current standard deduction and personal exemptions would remain, that the only other reductions from income to determine taxable income would be payment of medical expenses, and that all payments of Social Security and Medicare taxes would be used as income tax credits. In addition, the 29 percent rate assumes *no* individual tax subsidies or direct subsidies, whether taken as income reductions or as tax credits, that would decrease individual income tax receipts. Every tax or direct subsidy that is added to the income tax system will increase the calculated standard rate needed to achieve the same tax receipts target.

If you have read about flat-tax proposals that use lower tax rates than 29 percent, especially proposals that use zero rates for some kinds of income, ask yourself whether the proponents of those rates have demonstrated how those rates will raise the same amount of individual income tax receipts that the United States has obtained in recent ordinary tax years like 2007.

What Should Be the Target for Tax Receipts?

A standard rate of 29 percent is strictly a calculated rate using the individual income tax receipts from tax year 2007 as the target amount. As forewarned in chapter 2, sound fiscal policy will require at least a balanced budget in future years, and probably also surpluses that would be used to diminish the national debt. With the goal of a balanced budget, are the individual income tax receipts from 2007 the best target amount to be used in determining an initial standard rate?

The individual income tax receipts that were allocated to each of the US fiscal years 2008 and 2007 are close to the amount of those tax receipts for the 2007 tax year. What happened budget-wise in those two fiscal years?

Sadly, the total federal deficits in those fiscal years were substantial, and the on-budget deficits were even larger. So if receipts from taxes other than the individual income tax were to remain the same (such as the corporation income tax), the receipts obtained from a 29 percent standard-rate tax on individual income would have been inadequate to pay for US expenditures in either fiscal year 2008 or 2007. As the next paragraph demonstrates, the actual numbers are daunting.

The federal deficit in fiscal year 2008 was $459 billion and in fiscal year 2007 was $161 billion.[116] As discussed in chapters 2 and 3, payments of Social Security benefits did not contribute to either deficit because receipts from Social Security taxes in both fiscal years exceeded benefits payments. Excluding the use of Social Security trust funds for general expenditures, the "on-budget" deficits for fiscal years 2008 and 2007 were respectively $642 billion and $342 billion.[117]

This disconnect between tax receipts and expenditures shows that calculating an initial standard rate by targeting the individual income tax receipts from tax year 2007 may be unwise. That target may create a false sense that a 29 percent rate is enough by itself to create future balanced budgets. The truth is more sobering.

A 29 percent standard rate could not have achieved a balanced budget in fiscal years 2008 or 2007 without taking other steps. Looking at fiscal year 2007 as a less-daunting example than 2008, at least three options existed to achieve a balanced budget under similar fiscal circumstances. These options assume that only the individual income tax would have been available to use in achieving a balanced budget.

(1) We could have diminished federal expenditures in a total amount that was at least as large as the total federal deficit (or the larger on-budget deficit if all Social Security trust fund tax receipts and interest income had remained in the Social Security trust funds).[118]

(2) We could have adopted a standard rate that was sufficiently higher than 29 percent to obtain increased individual income tax receipts in an amount at least as large as the total federal deficit (or the on-budget deficit). For example, a standard rate of 34.4 percent would have been required to obtain increased individual income tax receipts equal to the on-budget deficit of $342 billion.[119]

(3) We could have combined diminishing federal expenditures and adopting a higher standard rate so that the combination would have achieved a balanced budget.

Having a standard rate for individual income taxes and using simple methods to calculate that rate help to frame decisions about how to achieve a balanced budget. Simple methods remove the mystery and at least some uncertainty in figuring out how much to reduce federal expenditures or to increase a standard rate to achieve that goal. These methods can also be used to determine the effect on a standard rate caused by combinations of direct and tax subsidies that are not counterbalanced by decreases in federal expenditures.

Testing an Alternative Approach with Facts

An alternative school of thought about determining a standard or flat-tax rate, or even income tax rates generally, should also be addressed. That school of thought asserts that lower federal individual tax rates will increase economic activity so much that total receipts from that tax will actually increase.[120]

Since 1980, significant changes in individual income tax rates have occurred six times, with five of those times being important tax decreases.[121] Appendixes 10C and 10D look at the most obvious data—individual income tax receipts and US GDP (economic activity) from 1981 to 2012—to see whether they support this school of thought. In my opinion, they do not, without forced interpretations of the data using many qualifiers about other factors that also can influence tax receipts and economic activity. The following example supports this opinion with data.

As one example from appendix 10C, fiscal year 2000 was the high mark for annual tax receipts from the federal individual income tax ($1,145 billion in constant dollars). After the tax decreases adopted in 2001 and 2003, tax receipts at first declined from 2001 through fiscal year 2004. The mild recession that began in 2001 probably partially caused the initial part of this decline,[122] as most of these tax decreases did not become fully effective until 2003. Beginning in fiscal year 2005, tax receipts rebounded some and reached a peak in fiscal year 2007 before the Great Recession ($1,093 billion in constant dollars). Tax receipts per person show a similar but greater decline and a similar but less-great rebound.

These data show that after seven years, tax receipts did not return to the amount obtained in fiscal year 2000. Compared to fiscal year 2000, diminished tax receipts during the seven-year period from 2001 to 2007 comprise one factor that contributed to an increase of $3,322 billion in the national debt during that same time period.[123] Of course, even the tax receipts increases that occurred between 2005 and 2007 were squelched by the Great Recession, which caused individual income tax receipts to decline to levels even below those of fiscal year 2004.[124]

Applying the Standard-Rate Tax

As noted earlier in this chapter, a standard-rate tax is simple but carries a potential flaw. If adopted alone, it will cause individuals with smaller incomes to have higher marginal total tax rates than individuals with larger incomes because Social Security taxes will be add-ons. The

FAST Plan prevents this result by allowing the payment of Social Security taxes (and Medicare taxes) as credits against the income tax. The next chapter shows how to implement this critical idea.

Chapter 10 Proposal
Should We Retain Graduated Income Tax Rates?

Reform

- Replace all current graduated individual income tax rate schedules with a single standard income tax rate.
- Determine an initial standard rate from an analysis that keeps total federal individual income tax receipts constant in a non-recession economy.
- Allow all Social Security tax and Medicare tax payments by an individual as nonrefundable credits against income taxes owed, but only after making the Social Security and Medicare tax payments equivalent between employees and self-employed individuals (as shown in chapter 11).
- Apply the standard-rate income tax to all kinds of income.

Chapter 11

---·◆·◆·◆---

Solving the Social Security and Medicare Taxes Dilemma

Why are Social Security and Medicare taxes a dilemma when using a standard-rate income tax?

The answer is twofold: they are add-on taxes to the income tax, and they apply differently to employees (wage earners) and self-employed individuals.

Solving the Add-On Dilemma

As identified in the previous chapter, the add-on feature of Social Security and Medicare taxes means that using a standard-rate income tax with no other changes will fail the fairness criterion. This is so because individuals with smaller incomes will pay higher marginal total federal tax rates than individuals with larger incomes (adding together income, Social Security, and Medicare taxes).

Also as identified in the previous chapter, the FAST Plan solves this add-on dilemma by allowing the payments of Social Security and Medicare taxes as nonrefundable credits against an individual's income tax. With this approach, an individual's marginal total federal tax rate will never exceed the standard rate.

Solving the Different Applications Dilemma

Because Social Security and Medicare taxes apply differently to employees and self-employed individuals, credits for payment of these taxes will also be different for those two groups if current law remains unchanged. These differences will lead many people to perceive that the credits are unfairly applied. Fortunately, we can make relatively simple changes that will allow employees and self-employed individuals to have comparable income tax credits for their payment of Social Security and Medicare taxes.

Showing how this can be done is a multistep process that requires considerable detail and some mathematics. I will first describe in general terms current Social Security and Medicare taxes as applied to employees and self-employed individuals. These descriptions lead us to briefly examine the history and future of Social Security and Medicare taxes. I will then illustrate how these taxes work with the individual income tax under current law and would work with a standard-rate income tax superimposed on current law with no other changes. Finally, I will show the changes in current law that will allow employees and self-employed individuals to have comparable income tax credits for their payments of Social Security and Medicare taxes. That showing will include proof that the changes will indeed work to achieve fairness.

This is by far the most technical chapter in the main text of this book. Accordingly, here is a preview of its remaining contents as shown by its subheadings.

- Important Features of Social Security and Medicare Taxes
  Social Security and Medicare Taxes on Employees
  Social Security and Medicare Taxes on Self-Employed Individuals
      The self-employment-tax multiplier
      Self-employment tax payment as a reduction from income
- Social Security and Medicare Taxes in Context
- Marginal Total Federal Tax Rates
  Under Current Law
  Under a Standard-Rate Tax within Current Law
- The Parity Challenge: Employees and Self-Employed Individuals
- Equalizing Credits for Employees and Self-Employed Individuals
  Adjustments for Employees
  Adjustments for Self-Employed Individuals
- The Dilemma Recap

Important Features of Social Security and Medicare Taxes

Social Security and Medicare taxes are charged against an individual's earned income. As noted previously, in general, **earned income** is money received as wages by an employee or as net earnings from self-employment by self-employed individuals. It does not include income from investments or bank accounts or a number of other specified forms of income.[125]

For many years, Social Security and Medicare taxes have been charged against an individual's earned income that exceeds only a small minimum amount, such as $400 or $1,000, no matter what financial circumstances exist for that individual.[126] The trade-offs, of course, are (1) that Social Security benefits will be available to those same people when they are no longer able to work because of disability or have qualified to stop working through retirement and (2) that Medicare hospital benefits will be available to those same people after they qualify for Medicare.

To achieve comparable income tax credits for Social Security and Medicare tax payments by employees and individuals, we also have to keep in mind how these taxes apply to earned income.

Since 1990, the full rate for the Social Security tax has been 12.4 percent. The Social Security tax ends when an individual's income exceeds a certain amount, which I will call the "Social Security tax cutoff" ($106,800 in 2009).[127]

Since 1986, the full rate for the Medicare tax has been 2.9 percent.[128] Unlike the Social Security tax, which has a maximum income cutoff, the Medicare tax is charged against all of an individual's earned income, no matter how large.[129]

I say "full rate" because the way in which these taxes are paid differs between employees and self-employed individuals.

Social Security and Medicare Taxes on Employees

Employees do not directly pay their Social Security and Medicare taxes.

Instead, the employer is required to pay one-half of the employee's full Social Security tax and also to collect the other half from the employee and submit it to the United States.[130] Thus, an employee is directly charged and sees only one-half the Social Security tax. For the employer, the other one-half is an additional cost beyond the employee's wages, although this cost is a business expense along with other business expenses that are subtracted from revenue to determine net profit. This additional cost has caused some employers to figure out ways to classify people as self-employed "independent contractors" rather than as employees, thereby avoiding the employer's portion of the Social Security tax payment.

Like the Social Security tax, the employer is required to pay one-half of the employee's Medicare tax and also to collect the other half from the employee and submit it to the United States.[131] Thus, an employee is directly charged and sees only one-half the Medicare tax.

Social Security and Medicare tax rates paid by employees and employers are shown in table 11.1.

Table 11.1. Comparing 2009 Social Security and Medicare tax rates paid by employees and employers

	Rate employee pays	Rate employer pays	Total rate
Social Security tax	6.2%	6.2%	12.4%
Medicare tax	1.45%	1.45%	2.9%
Total rate	7.65%	7.65%	15.3%

A nuance for the Social Security tax on employees occurred for 2011 and 2012. The December 2010 tax compromise temporarily reduced an employee's Social Security tax payment in 2011 from 6.2 percent to 4.2 percent of earned income (the employer's payment remained unchanged). The Social Security tax receipts that were lost because of these reductions were to be reimbursed by transfers from the general federal fund.[132] Thus, the rate reduction for the Social Security tax in 2011 was just a *mechanism* used to provide more money to many individuals from the general federal fund to try to stimulate economic activity. Congress extended these lower 2011 rates through 2012, with a similar reimbursement of lost Social Security tax receipts.[133]

Using this mechanism unfortunately has prompted some people to claim incorrectly that Social Security is already far in the red and an important contributor to the national debt. They cite the large shortfall between Social Security tax receipts and benefits paid in 2011 and 2012. Had this mechanism for stimulus money not been used, however, Social Security tax receipts would have been much closer to the benefits paid.[134] The 2012 fiscal cliff tax compromise ended the temporary lower Social Security tax rate by not extending it.[135]

Social Security and Medicare Taxes on Self-Employed Individuals
Self-employed individuals are required to pay both Social Security and Medicare taxes under the **self-employment tax**. Under that tax, the full Social Security tax rate is 12.4 percent, and the full Medicare tax rate is 2.9 percent.[136]

A nuance for the Social Security tax on self-employed individuals also occurred in 2011 and 2012. The December 2010 tax compromise temporarily reduced a self-employed individual's full Social Security tax rate in 2011 from 12.4 percent to 10.4 percent of earned income. Like the reduced Social Security tax rate for employees, Social Security tax revenues that were lost because of the reduced tax rate on self-employed individuals were to be reimbursed by transfers from the general federal fund.[137] Congress also extended these reductions through 2012.[138] Just as for employees, the 2012 fiscal cliff tax compromise ended the lower Social Security tax rate for self-employed individuals by not extending it.[139]

Two features of federal law applicable to the self-employment tax modify the full rates that self-employed individuals pay for Social Security and Medicare taxes:

- A multiplier used to determine the earned income amount against which the self-employment tax applies
- A reduction from income allowed for part of the payment of the self-employment tax when calculating the amount of income that is subject to the individual income tax

The self-employment-tax multiplier

To calculate a self-employed individual's Social Security and Medicare taxes under the self-employment tax, the rates are applied against business net profit times 0.9235.

Why 0.9235?

This is the mathematical result of allowing a self-employed individual to subtract from business net profit one-half the combined Social Security and Medicare tax rates applied to that net profit when determining that individual's "earned income," which is subject to the full Social Security and Medicare tax rates.[140]

Conceptually, this subtraction treats a self-employed individual as his or her own employee. This is one way to try to equalize tax treatment between employees and self-employed individuals. The numbers show how it works.

As an employee, wages subject to Social Security and Medicare taxes would not include Social Security and Medicare tax payments made by the employer on the employee's behalf. For wages up to the Social Security tax cutoff, those payments by the employer would be one-half of 15.3 percent, namely 7.65 percent, applied to the employee's wages, where 15.3 percent is the sum of the Social Security tax rate of 12.4 percent and the Medicare tax rate of 2.9 percent.

The 0.9235 factor achieves a similar result for a self-employed individual mathematically in this way. Just like for employees, the sum of the Social Security and Medicare tax rates for self-employed individuals is 15.3 percent. One-half the combined rate is 7.65 percent. Subtracting this factor from one equals 0.9235. For application of Social Security and Medicare taxes, the 0.9235 factor applied against net profit is thus a simplified way to make a self-employed individual's earned income like an employee's wages, which do not include the employer's one-half payment of Social Security and Medicare taxes on those wages.

Self-employment tax payment as a reduction from income

When calculating income subject to the income tax, current law allows a self-employed individual to reduce gross income by one-half the self-employment tax paid by the individual.[141] This reduction is the second prong of conceptually treating a self-employed individual as his or her own employee. As described above, an employer is required to pay one-half the total Social Security and Medicare taxes on his or her employee's wages, but also is allowed to recognize that payment as a business expense, thereby reducing net profit potentially subject to an income tax. The reduction for this same amount from a self-employed individual's gross income accomplishes an equivalent business-expense result for that individual, even though this amount is not technically classified as a business expense.

Social Security and Medicare Taxes in Context

Before suggesting changes to the way that Social Security and Medicare taxes interact with the individual income tax, we should consider whether those taxes should or are likely to change significantly in the future.

The full rate of 12.4 percent for the Social Security tax and the Social Security tax cutoff have historically produced more than adequate money each fiscal year for Social Security benefits paid in that year. As previously noted in chapter 3, that history ended in fiscal year 2010. In that fiscal year, receipts from Social Security taxes did not cover all Social Security benefits paid out.[142] The Great Recession is blamed for this circumstance because its larger unemployment has both reduced the amount of Social Security tax receipts and forced more people to retire early to get benefits due to their inability to find employment.[143] I view this circumstance as temporary and reversible when the Great Recession wanes. Thus, in the context of reforming federal taxes, I do not propose to change the 12.4 percent Social Security tax rate, the presence of a Social Security tax cutoff, or the application of this tax rate to earned income that exceeds only very small minimal amounts.

The full rate of 2.9 percent for the Medicare tax, together with other income owed to the Medicare hospital insurance trust fund, has historically produced adequate money each fiscal year for the Medicare hospital benefits paid in that year until 2009.[144] In the context of reforming federal taxes, I also do not propose to change this rate or its application to all earned income.

The original 2010 health insurance reform legislation, commonly known as Obamacare, included a Medicare hospital insurance surcharge tax of 0.5 percentage points on large earned incomes.[145]

The apparent rationale behind the surcharge was that individuals with large earned incomes could easily afford the surcharge. Payment of this surcharge should *not* be allowed as a credit against an individual's income tax because then it would no longer be a surcharge. This treatment under the FAST Plan would not be unfair to these individuals in light of the FAST Plan's standard-rate income tax, which would be lower than the current marginal income tax rate applicable to those individuals. Similar reasoning would apply to other surcharges that Congress may adopt in the future.

Although existing Social Security and Medicare tax rates and applications will likely work to provide current benefits once the Great Recession wanes, these structures cannot be self-sustaining in the longer future. The "baby-boomer" demographic bulge of people who will soon be retiring and other factors will cause the trust funds for Social Security and Medicare hospital insurance to run out of money if no changes are made. Projections vary on when this will occur for each fund. As expressed in chapter 3 on borrowings from federal trust funds, the first crisis with these funds will occur when their respective tax receipts are regularly less than the benefits paid out. This first crisis is earlier than the projections that assume that the United States will be able to pay back the money borrowed from these funds, with interest, before the "runs out" crisis occurs. Hopefully, Congress will soon address these upcoming problems in ways that will be fiscally sound and generally accepted by the American people.

Marginal Total Federal Tax Rates

Armed with basic facts about current Social Security and Medicare taxes, let's now examine how these taxes can affect marginal total federal tax rates for different individuals under current law and under any standard-rate income tax with no other changes in current law. Seeing the scope of these effects will illustrate why these two taxes cannot be ignored in any attempt to simplify individual income taxes. This illustration requires moving beyond generalities and into numeric examples.

Under Current Law

Let's first consider marginal total federal tax rates under current law (2009 tax law).

For an employee, the Social Security and Medicare taxes that the employee has paid are direct add-ons to the employee's income tax.

For a self-employed individual, the Social Security and Medicare taxes (self-employment tax) that the individual is required to pay are also direct add-ons to the individual's income tax, but the income tax is affected by the amount of these two taxes. This occurs because of the rule that allows one-half the self-employment tax paid as a reduction from income in determining taxable income.[146]

When combined with current law, which features graduated income tax rates, some odd disparities between the marginal total federal tax rates of similarly situated individuals occur because of three factors:

(1) The treatment of Social Security and Medicare taxes as add-ons
(2) The reduction from income allowed for half of these taxes paid by self-employed individuals
(3) The fact that graduated individual income tax rates do not key off the amount of the Social Security tax cutoff

The third factor means that in some cases, an individual whose earned income is below but near the Social Security tax cutoff will have the same marginal income tax rate but a higher marginal total federal tax rate (adding income, Social Security, and Medicare taxes) than an individual whose earned income is above the Social Security tax cutoff.

The disparities caused by all three factors are best illustrated by numeric examples using individuals whose only income is earned income. These disparities for all earned income levels also are shown visually in figures 10F.1 and 10F.4 of appendix 10F using a single individual as an example.

First, let's consider employees. Under current law, an employee U ("Unlucky"), whose wages are just below the Social Security tax cutoff, will pay a marginal total federal tax rate that is 6.20 percentage points higher than another employee L ("Lucky"), whose wages are just above that cutoff. The comparative rates are 35.65 percent for U and 29.45 percent for L when these employees are filing as a single person. This 6.20 percentage point disparity, of course, is exactly the amount of the Social Security tax that U pays on an additional dollar of wages but that L does not pay because L's earned income is above the Social Security tax cutoff. This specific 6.2 percentage point disparity occurs because both U and L pay the same marginal income tax rate of 28 percent on their wages.[147]

Next, let's consider self-employed individuals. Under current law, an individual SU ("Self-Employed Unlucky"), whose self-employed income is just below the Social Security tax cutoff, will pay a marginal total federal tax rate that is 9.85 percentage points higher than another individual SL ("Self-Employed Lucky"), whose self-employed income is just above that cutoff. The comparative rates are 40.15 percent for SU and 30.30 percent for SL when these individuals are filing as a single person. As highlighted in chapter 10, the 40.15 percent rate was the highest marginal total federal tax rate that any individual paid under the law effective from 2003 to 2012. This specific 9.85 percentage point disparity results from the interplay of Social Security, Medicare, and income tax provisions that apply to self-employed individuals.[148]

These examples illustrate the maximum disparities in marginal total federal tax rates that occur under current law between individuals with similar earned incomes. The picture is more complicated when other income tax brackets are considered. Using the employee example, those employees whose taxable income is small enough to be in a lower marginal tax bracket than U will have a lower marginal total federal tax rate than U. Conversely, those employees whose taxable income is large enough to be in a higher marginal income tax bracket than L will have a higher marginal total federal tax rate than L (but not as high as employee U except in the highest income tax bracket). Similar comparisons also apply in the example of self-employed individuals.

These maximum disparities in the examples matter even more when considering an approach that uses a standard-rate income tax and no other changes to current law.

Under a Standard-Rate Tax within Current Law

Now let's consider marginal total federal tax rates under a standard-rate income tax within current law.

If a standard rate were to replace the current graduated rates, with no other changes in the tax laws, the total tax-rate disparities shown in the examples used to describe current law would extend up and down the earned income amounts from the Social Security tax cutoff. That is, for those individuals who had some taxable income, *all* such individuals whose total earned income was below the Social Security tax cutoff, would face a marginal total federal tax rate on their earned incomes that is higher than the marginal total federal tax rate faced by *all* individuals whose total earned incomes exceeded the Social Security tax cutoff (even those who had earned incomes in the millions of dollars). Again, here are example numbers to illustrate the extent of these disparities.

Comparing employees, that universal disparity would be 6.2 percentage points (e.g., 32.65 percent compared to 26.45 percent if 25 percent were the standard rate).[149] Comparing self-employed individuals, that universal disparity would depend upon the standard rate. If 25 percent were the standard rate, the disparity would be 10.02 percentage points (e.g., 37.36 percent compared to 27.34 percent).[150] These are not trivial disparities, especially considering that individuals with small incomes would be paying *higher* marginal total federal tax rates than individuals with large incomes. These disparities for all earned income levels are shown visually in figures 10F.3 and 10F.6 of appendix 10F, using a single individual as an example under a 25 percent flat-tax approach.

The Parity Challenge: Employees and Self-Employed Individuals

The FAST Plan prevents the disparities described above by allowing the payments of Social Security and Medicare taxes as nonrefundable credits against the income tax calculated from a standard rate. The FAST Plan approach assures that the maximum total federal tax rate for every individual will not exceed the standard income tax rate. This approach also promotes simplicity by avoiding multistep calculations to determine the credit.

At present, the effective Social Security and Medicare tax rates for self-employed individuals are nearly twice the rates for employees.[151] The rates for self-employed individuals will thus generate much larger income tax credits than the rates for employees. Despite these differences in credits, the marginal *total* federal tax rates for employees and self-employed individuals will both be the standard income tax rate. However, many employees will object to the credits for self-employed individuals because employees will perceive that they are paying higher net income tax rates than self-employed individuals. To avoid these objections and a rebellion against a standard-rate income tax, the credits for employees and self-employed individuals should be the same or nearly the same for the same amounts of earned income.

How can parity between these two groups be achieved?

One possible way to create parity would be (1) to apply directly to employees the full Social Security tax of 12.4 percent and full Medicare tax of 2.9 percent on wages and (2) to eliminate the current 0.9235 factor against business net profit used to determine the amount of a self-employed individual's earned income that is subject to Social Security and Medicare taxes. In that way, the combined Social Security and Medicare tax credits would be at the rate of 15.3 percent of earned income for both employees and self-employed individuals.

Even if mathematically sound in terms of the amount of the credit, this approach is not feasible at this stage in history. Decades of reliance on a system where half the full Social Security and Medicare taxes on wages are paid by employers has created employee/employer agreements and net wages expectations that cannot be swept aside by mere fiat.

Does this reliance end the possibility of treating the payment of Social Security and Medicare taxes as a credit to income taxes?

Fortunately, the answer is no.

Equalizing Credits for Employees and Self-Employed Individuals

The challenge is to figure out how to create nearly the same effective income tax credits for Social Security and Medicare tax payments on the earned incomes of employees and self-employed individuals while maintaining the current system where employers pay one-half of these taxes on the wages of their employees.

This challenge can be met by a method with two parts. The first part deals with the way that Social Security and Medicare taxes on wages are treated for income tax purposes. The second part deals with the two previously summarized unique features of federal tax law that are applicable to the self-employment tax. The next discussion identifies each part of the method and then shows why that part works.

Adjustments for Employees

Let's start with the wages part of this method. Luckily, two accounting adjustments can create a close equivalent of applying the full Social Security and Medicare taxes on employees' wages without disrupting any established net wages.

First, designate Social Security and Medicare tax payments by the employer as income to the employee. These payments can be designated as income because the payments are on behalf of and directly benefit the employee.

Second, for tax credit purposes, also treat Social Security and Medicare tax payments by the employer as Social Security and Medicare tax payments by the employee. This credit is appropriate because it exactly matches the increased income designated to the employee. That increased income is not actually received but instead paid to the United States by the employer on behalf of the employee.

These two accounting adjustments should make no difference to the employer, who is already paying out the same total amount of wages, Social Security taxes, and Medicare taxes for each employee and is treating the total amount as a deductible business expense. From the employer's point of view, the money paid out does not even get classified differently.

Now let's put some numbers to these changes for employees so that changes for self-employed individuals will have a target to match.

Using these two accounting adjustments, the employee will have the full Social Security and Medicare taxes paid on the employee's wages potentially available as a credit for payment of Social Security and Medicare taxes. For Social Security taxes, those payments would be 12.4 percent of an employee's wages up to the Social Security tax cutoff, consisting of 6.2 percent paid directly by the employee and 6.2 percent paid by the employer on behalf of the employee. For Medicare taxes, those payments would be 2.9 percent of an employee's wages, consisting of 1.45 percent paid directly by the employee and 1.45 percent paid by the employer on behalf of the employee.

These two accounting adjustments are almost, but not quite, the equivalent of the employer paying the employee additional wages equal to the amount of the employer's Social Security and Medicare tax payments on the employee's original wages. What prevents equivalency is the fact that the full Social Security tax of 12.4 percent and Medicare tax of 2.9 percent are paid on the original wages that precede the two accounting adjustments, not the increased total income from wages. This is so even though the increased total income from wages becomes the employee's employment income for income tax purposes. Considering the increased total income from wages in amounts up to the Social Security tax cutoff, under the two accounting adjustments, the effective combined full Social Security and Medicare tax rate is 14.21 percent as applied against the increased total income from wages. This effective rate is the same as 92.90 percent of the full combined 15.3 percent rate on the increased total income from wages (a factor of 0.9290).[152]

This effective total Social Security and Medicare taxes rate of 14.21 percent (0.9290 times the full 15.3 percent rate) provides a target for the effective total Social Security and Medicare taxes rate to be paid by self-employed individuals.

Another nuance should be considered. For employees, the increased income in the amount of Social Security and Medicare taxes paid by the employer will be subject to my proposed standard-rate income tax. Should some fine adjustment be made for this increase?

The answer is no because allowing credits against income tax for an individual's payment of Social Security and Medicare taxes and using a standard-rate income tax will change the total tax regimen so much that this small increase in income will not affect the fairness of total federal taxes paid by employees.

Adjustments for Self-Employed Individuals

Now let's turn to the Social Security and Medicare taxes paid by a self-employed individual. Remember that a 0.9235 factor is currently used against business net profit to calculate a self-employed individual's earned income that is subject to the self-employment tax (Social Security and Medicare taxes). This factor is very close to the 0.9290 factor just calculated for employees as the effective combined rate of Social Security and Medicare taxes on increased total income from wages up to the Social Security tax cutoff (using the two accounting adjustments applicable to employees).

Which factor should be used to create parity between the Social Security and Medicare tax rates paid by self-employed individuals and employees?

The current 0.9235 factor has some arbitrary built-in features already, so parity between employees and self-employed individuals favors replacing it with the 0.9290 factor. Thus, the

FAST Plan uses the 0.9290 factor. Appendix 11B contains detailed reasoning behind this conclusion.

Of course, this 0.9290 factor could be rolled into the Social Security and Medicare tax (self-employment tax) rates applicable to self-employed business income, thus saving one calculation step (resulting rates are 11.52 percent for Social Security and 2.69 percent for Medicare). However, keeping the rates at 12.4 percent and 2.9 percent but using an earned income factor has the advantage that these rates for employees and self-employed individuals will not only be the same, but will also appear to be the same.

We are not done yet.

Should we keep or eliminate the current reduction from income allowed for one-half the Social Security and Medicare taxes (self-employment tax) paid by a self-employed individual?

This reduction decreases the amount of an individual's income that is taxable. If retained, this decreased amount will increase the effective credit for payment of Social Security and Medicare taxes because that credit will be applied against a smaller income tax. That increase will destroy the parity just achieved between income tax credits allowed to employees and self-employed individuals. Thus, the FAST Plan eliminates this historic reduction from income.

The Dilemma Recap

In this chapter, we examined the dilemma caused by the interrelationship between Social Security and Medicare taxes and the FAST Plan's proposed standard-rate tax on individual income. The FAST Plan achieves fairness in marginal total tax rates by allowing a credit against an individual's income tax for the payment of Social Security and Medicare taxes. The FAST Plan achieves fairness between employees and self-employed individuals by creating comparable credits through four changes in current law. For employees, the FAST Plan designates the employer's payment of Social Security and Medicare taxes as income to the employee and treats the employer's payment as payment by the employee. For self-employed individuals, the FAST Plan replaces the current 0.9235 self-employment-tax multiplier with a 0.9290 multiplier and eliminates the current reduction from income allowed for one-half the payment of self-employment taxes.

With these fundamental changes now in place, we are ready to critique other ways that the current individual income tax works in practice.

Chapter 11 Proposal
Solving the Social Security and Medicare Taxes Dilemma

Retain

- Retain the current 12.4 percent Social Security and 2.9 percent Medicare tax rates, earned income cutoff for Social Security tax application, and payment obligations by employers, employees, and self-employed individuals.

Reform

- If a standard-rate income tax is adopted for all income, allow all Social Security tax and Medicare tax payments by an individual as nonrefundable credits against the individual's income tax, but only after making the credits for Social Security and Medicare tax payments equivalent between employees and self-employed individuals in accordance with the following accounting adjustments:
    (1) For an employee, designate the Social Security and Medicare tax payments by his or her employer on the employee's wages
        (a) as income to the employee and also
        (b) as Social Security and Medicare tax payments to the United States by the employee as well as by the employer.
    (2) For a self-employed individual, use a 0.9290 factor in place of the current 0.9235 factor against business net profit to determine the amount of earned income on which to apply the Social Security and Medicare taxes.
- If Social Security and Medicare tax payments are allowed as nonrefundable credits against an individual's income tax, then also eliminate the current reduction from income allowed for one-half the self-employment tax (Social Security and Medicare taxes) paid by self-employed individuals.

Chapter 12

———◆●◆●◆———

What Income Should Be Taxed?

Although Congress has the power "to lay and collect taxes on income, from whatever source derived,"[153] the scope of the individual income tax in any tax reform depends upon how that power should be exercised. We begin with basics.

What Is Income?

Webster's New Universal Unabridged Dictionary defines "income" as "the monetary payment received for goods or services or from other sources, as rents or investments."[154] The Internal Revenue Code defines "gross income" as "all income from whatever source derived, including (but not limited to) the following items: [followed by a list of fifteen kinds of income]."[155]

Both definitions share the common trait that generally income does not exist unless an event occurs in which a person receives money or other new value.[156] For example, if a person owns a building continually for ten years and the value of that building doubles during that ten years, the increased value is not income because no event has occurred in which the person receives money or other new value. This common trait has the practical advantage that a tax on income is usually payable when the person with income has received money or sometimes other new value that is convertible to money, which is available for paying a tax.

There is no good reason to alter this historic common trait for defining income. Any attempt to do so would greatly complicate a federal income tax. For example, if mere increases in value were considered income, at the least, periodic valuations would have to be done that probably would require a new federal bureaucracy and would involve contentious questions about the methods used to determine value.

The Webster's and code definitions also share the common trait that income occurs only if the money or value received is owned fully by the recipient. Under this trait, borrowings are not income because the amount borrowed is owed to the lender, whether or not the amount borrowed can be used however the borrower desires. I use this example because Edward J. McCaffery, in his excellent book *Fair Not Flat*, has proposed including borrowing as income in his plan to turn the current individual income tax into a true consumption tax. In my opinion, his idea is analytically sound when done in conjunction with other parts of his plan. Nevertheless, this treatment of borrowing is so far outside the way that most people think of income that too much confusion would result if this treatment were to be adopted.[157]

What Is Taxable Income?

Not all income is taxable under the current Internal Revenue Code. The code identifies taxable income in two basic ways.

First, as described in chapter 19, the code allows a huge variety of reductions from gross income to determine the amount of taxable income. These reductions are categorized and discussed in later chapters.

Second, the code defines "gross income" both to include and to *exclude* some specific items that one could reasonably assert are "income" in the normal sense. These definitions identify what kinds of income are subject to tax. Examples of excluded items are "gifts and inheritances" and "qualified scholarships."[158] These particular exclusions lay to rest any uncertainty whether these monetary benefits are taxable income. Other exclusions from the definition of "gross income" are clearly income under any normal understanding of that term. A notable example is interest from qualified state and local bonds,[159] which usually are held as investments.

Excluding any normal kind of income from a definition of taxable income is just another mechanism by which tax subsidies occur. That is, people who receive money or new value designated as tax-exempt receive that money or new value just as surely as people who receive the same amounts that are not designated as tax-exempt. Similarly situated people thus pay very different taxes on the same amounts of real income. Whether excluding certain kinds of income from the definition of income is an appropriate way to achieve any tax subsidy is addressed in chapter 18 on tax-exempt income items.

The Most Important Kinds of Individual Income

Different *kinds* of individual income account for widely different *amounts* of annual individual income. This obvious fact severely limits the potential tax receipts from some kinds of income and also greatly increases the effects that special treatment of some kinds of income will have on total tax receipts.

The chapters that follow consider all of the eight kinds of income that collectively accounted for 99.3 percent of all reported individual income in the 2007 tax year. As categorized in IRS statistical data and summarily identified in the following chapters, these eight kinds of income are shown in table 12.1.[160]

Table 12.1. Major kinds of reported individual income, tax year 2007

__Kind of individual income__	__% of all 2007 reported individual income__
Wages	66.3%
Capital gains income	10.2%
Pensions and retirement-plan distributions	7.3%
Partnership and S corporation income	4.7%
Personal business income	3.2%
Interest income	3.0%
Dividends income	2.7%
Social Security benefits	1.9%
Total	99.3%

To place these eight kinds of income in a broader historical context, appendix 12A contains tables that show the amounts of income reported for these kinds of income in three recent tax years: 2007 (the last tax year before the Great Recession), 2000 (the year preceding broad tax decreases that were adopted in 2001), and 1993 (the first year of broad tax increases adopted in 1993).

In each of those three years, "wages" was by far the largest kind of income reported. However, its percentage of total income has been declining. The figures are 76.9 percent for 1993, 69.4 percent for 2000, and 66.3 percent for 2007 (shown in the table above). Thus, other kinds of income are playing an increasingly important role for potential receipts from an individual income tax.

Analytically, these eight kinds of individual income can also be lumped into four categories:

(1) Wages
(2) Capital-based income (capital gains, dividends, and interest)
(3) Business income (personal business income, and partnership and S corporation income)

(4) Retirement and disability income (Social Security benefits, and pensions and retirement-plan distributions)

These unifying categories are helpful for some purposes, but the historic special treatment of four of these eight kinds of individual income dictate considering those kinds of income in separate chapters (capital gains, dividends, Social Security benefits, and pension payments and retirement-plan distributions). The remaining four kinds of income will be considered in chapter 13 (wages, personal business income, partnership and S corporation income, and interest). Chapter 13 will also consider miscellaneous income because of its importance to some individuals, even though miscellaneous income does not rank in the top eight in terms of potential for income tax revenues.

Chapter 12 Proposal
What Income Should Be Taxed?

Retain
- Retain current definitions of what is included in "gross income."

Reform
- Retain current definitions of what is *excluded* from "gross income," but only to the extent that the subsidy represented by the exclusion remains appropriate after other FAST Plan changes are made to current federal taxes.

Chapter 13

———◆●◆●◆———

Historic Ordinary Income

Five kinds of income are considered in this chapter: wages, personal business income, partnership and S corporation income, interest, and miscellaneous income.

All of these kinds of income have for many years been fully subject to the individual income tax rates in effect each tax year. Income that has been so treated will be referred to as **ordinary income**. Historic treatment, of course, does not guarantee similar treatment in the future. Indeed, recently some politicians have proposed special tax treatment for interest income. Thus, it is useful to examine each of these five kinds of income to see why or whether they should continue to be taxed as ordinary income.

Wages

Wages are the classic and simplest form of gross income.[161] Simply put, an employee performs work for an employer and receives money in return. As noted in the preceding chapter, in tax year 2007, wages accounted for 66.3 percent of the total individual gross income of $8,811 billion reported by all individuals who filed income tax returns.[162] The tax on wages is the bedrock of receipts obtained from the individual income tax. This fact alone requires wages to be taxed as ordinary income.

Tax Withholding on Wages

The United States and many state governments have stepped into the employer-employee relationship by requiring the employer to withhold a portion of the money paid as wages.[163] The employer sends the withheld money to these governments as advance payment for individual income taxes that the employees will owe on their wages. The obvious reason for withholding is to guarantee that the governments will actually receive the taxes owed to them. If withholding did not exist, some employees would not have enough money to pay their taxes when owed because they would already have spent that money. In general, the withholding formulas result in amounts being withheld that are close to the amount of taxes that will be owed on the wages received, at least where employees correctly exercise their limited discretion in adjusting withholding amounts based on their numbers of dependents and exemptions. These basic features of the individual income tax on wages make good sense and should continue.

A Contentious Wages Issue

Despite the outward simplicity of the individual income tax on wages, at least one contentious issue permeates this tax. Namely, what benefits that an employee receives other than money, if any, should be classified as taxable wages?

The simplest answer to this question is "none," so that only money received by an employee is taxable wages. This answer, however, would allow employers to pay employees in a variety of creative ways other than money just so that the employee could avoid paying some or most individual income taxes (and Social Security and Medicare taxes as well). Tax simplicity in this instance runs afoul of tax fairness. This question of what employee benefits should be taxable is just one example of the fact that no matter how simple one tries to make any tax, its practical application inevitably raises complicating issues that will have to be resolved. Resolution of these issues may depend in part upon policy decisions about what should or should not be taxable.

With respect to what employee benefits should be taxable, two questions can help categorize these benefits in ways that will assist making this decision. If the answer to either question is yes, then the employee benefit should be eligible for classification as wages because it is something that the employee and not the employer would normally pay for if the employee wanted it. Whether the benefit should actually be classified as wages may depend upon whether a strong policy reason exists not to classify the benefit as taxable wages (such as health insurance paid by an employer).

Question 1: Did the employer pay someone else a fee or charge on behalf of the employee for a personal benefit that the employee received?

Example A: The employer pays the annual country club dues for a company vice president (currently not a deductible business expense of the employer, and thus likely to be reported by the employer as taxable wages to the employee).[164]

Example B: The employer pays the monthly health insurance premium for an employee and the employee's family (currently not treated as taxable wages).[165]

Question 2:   Did the employer provide the employee with a thing or service for personal use for free or at greatly reduced cost?

            Example A: The employer provides to the executive secretary of the company's president free personal use of a Cadillac sedan owned by the employer (currently treated as taxable wages).[166]

            Example B: The employer provides free meals to all main office employees at a dining room located in the company's main office building (currently not treated as taxable wages to any employee).[167]

Personal Business Income

Many individuals prefer to have their own businesses as their financial livelihoods. Historically, in some professions, the vast majority of individuals have preferred this approach (e.g., lawyers and dentists). Today the information age with electronic communications has opened up many more opportunities for individual businesses because more work can be done effectively without a traditional workplace than previously possible. From an income tax perspective, the different forms of individual businesses are treated similarly, but not identically. This section focuses on the personal business of a self-employed individual.

Any self-employed individual who has filled out Schedule C of Form 1040 may be surprised to learn that "net profit from business" is not a designated taxable income item in the Internal Revenue Code. Instead, net profit from business as taxable income results from the interplay of three code sections. Section 61 defines gross income as including "gross income derived from business,"[168] Section 63 defines taxable income as "gross income minus the deductions allowed by this chapter (other than the standard deduction),"[169] and Section 162, which is within "this chapter," allows "as a deduction all the ordinary and necessary expenses paid or incurred during the taxable year in carrying on any trade or business, including (...) [specific descriptions follow]"[170]

Despite this arrangement in the code, the IRS has sensibly provided Schedule C so that individuals can easily calculate business income that is subject to the federal income tax (described as "Profit or Loss from Business (Sole Proprietorship)").

An individual's business income, whether from full-time or part-time self-employment, is analogous to an employee's wages. Accordingly, personal business income is properly subject to the federal income tax in the same manner as wages.

Partnership and S Corporation Income

Partnerships and S corporations are forms of group business enterprises that tax law treats as collections of personal businesses.

Partnerships

Under current federal tax law, individuals carrying on business as partners are subject to the income tax only in their separate or individual capacities.[171] In effect, each partner's distributive share of the partnership's taxable income (net profit) is treated as if each partner had his or her own business income in that amount. Certain kinds of partnership payments, however, cannot be used as deductions in calculating taxable income. Instead, these must be separately allocated to each partner individually (e.g., charitable contributions).[172] This treatment is consistent with the general treatment of partnership income as self-employed business income.[173] Thus, an individual's partnership income is properly included as ordinary income subject to a standard-rate income tax under the FAST Plan.

S Corporations

An S corporation is a corporation that has a limited number of individual shareholders, all of whom agree that the corporation should be an S corporation.[174] Like partnerships, the S corporation's net profit is attributed directly to the individual shareholders.[175] Indeed, S corporations are so much like partnerships that the IRS treats income from these sources in the same statistical category. Like partnership income, S corporation income is properly included as ordinary income subject to a standard-rate income tax.

The question whether any particular form of partnership or S corporation should also be taxed as an entity is addressed in chapter 29 in its section on when to treat noncorporate business entities as corporations.

Interest

Simply stated, **interest** is money paid by a borrower to a lender for the use of the lender's money. Interest payments to an individual are made in a variety of contexts.

Interest is typically paid on bank or credit union savings accounts, on corporate bonds, on US treasury bills or savings bonds, and on state and local government bonds. Sometimes interest is also paid to an individual on a personal loan to a friend or relative. All interest fits a classic definition of income.[176]

Historically and today, most forms of interest have been taxed as ordinary income, with no special rates.

For most people, interest is a very small portion of their total incomes. For those people, the rates at which interest is taxed does not make a big difference in their overall federal taxes. However, for a few people, interest can be a major or maybe the primary source of income. For them, the income tax rate on and taxability of interest will significantly affect their total federal income taxes. So we have to look carefully at whether we should continue the historic treatment of interest as ordinary income.

Should Interest Have Special Tax Rates?

Some people have proposed that some or all interest be taxed at lower rates or not at all to encourage savings. Others have proposed zero tax on interest, based on an assertion that taxing interest is a double tax on savings, while ignoring the fact that interest is an increase in the amount of that savings.[177] If adopted, these proposals would fail the fairness criterion because they would create a significant tax subsidy to individuals who have large amounts of interest income. Based on tax year 2007 data, wealthier people are far more likely to have interest income than less-wealthy people, although this slant toward wealthier people is not as pronounced as it is for capital gains and dividends (see following chapters).[178] In addition, proposals not to tax some interest based on income levels or other criteria introduce new complexity in the tax code beyond what already exists today. Accordingly, we should continue to treat as ordinary income all currently taxable income. This approach is consistent with long-standing historic precedent that is both simple and fair.

Municipal Bonds Interest

An important exception to the general rule on interest exists for interest from state and local government bonds (collectively often just called "municipal bonds"). Interest from state and local bonds is exempt from the federal individual income tax.[179] This interest is reported on federal tax forms along with other tax-exempt interest, but is not included in the calculation of gross income.[180] From a tax standpoint, this income never occurred, even though recipients of this income have money in hand just the same as people who receive ordinary interest or wages. The tax-exempt status of state and local bond interest is considered further in chapter 18 on tax-exempt income items.

Miscellaneous Income

As might be expected, human ingenuity has created and will continue to create many other forms of income beyond the eight most important kinds of income identified in the preceding chapter. Among these are net rents from real estate (a special form of business income), royalties (such as payments from proceeds of extracted minerals or payments from the sale or use of copies of creative works like a popular song), payments from trust or estate income, and winnings from a lottery.[181] More subtle forms of income are received in the form of a free benefit, such as cancellation of a debt owed by the taxpayer.[182] Miscellaneous forms of income have historically been considered ordinary income that is subject to the normal income tax rates unless specifically made tax-exempt.

Given the variety of forms of miscellaneous income, understandably special rules have been developed to deal with some of these forms of income, although fortunately those rules do not include special tax rates. Perhaps some of these special rules can be simplified in a full reexamination of all federal taxes or may even result from simplifying other aspects of federal taxes as proposed in the FAST Plan.

Congress also appears to have been watchful to exclude from miscellaneous income some benefits like qualified scholarships, which could be considered income but the taxation of which would significantly reduce their effectiveness.[183] My FAST Plan proposals do not affect these kinds of exclusions.

Consistent with the goals of fairness and simplicity, the historic treatment of miscellaneous income as ordinary income should remain.

Historic Ordinary Income Recap

We have seen in this chapter that we should continue to treat as ordinary income wages, personal business income, partnership and S corporation income, interest, and miscellaneous income. The FAST Plan applies a standard-rate income tax to all of these kinds of income.

Our next chapter tackles capital gains, a kind of income that historically has had special treatment in income tax law. Whether its special treatment should continue will be a contentious issue in any serious tax reform. Let's now see how the FAST Plan approaches this issue.

Chapter 13 Proposal
Historic Ordinary Income

Retain
- Treat these five kinds of income as ordinary income:
    - Wages
    - Personal business income
    - Partnership and S corporation income
    - All interest income except as specifically excluded by statute
    - All miscellaneous income not otherwise excluded from the definition of gross income

Reform
- Apply a standard-rate income tax rate to all of this ordinary income.

Chapter 14

———◆•◆•◆———

Capital Gains

Individual capital gains income has had special treatment in the tax law for most of the last fifty years. To critique this treatment, this chapter begins by defining capital gains and describing how capital gains are treated under current law. We then look at four related questions in deciding how to treat capital gains in the FAST Plan reform:

- Who has significant capital gains income?
- How does capital gains income affect tax owed?
- Do rationales for special capital gains tax treatment have merit?
- What other capital gains issues should be considered?

What Is a "Capital Gain"?

To understand the technical term "capital gain," first we need to understand the meaning of "capital asset." The Internal Revenue Code defines a **capital asset** as "property held by the taxpayer (whether or not connected with his trade or business), but does not include—[followed by a list of exceptions, such as business inventory]."[184] "Property" can be as widely different as ranchland, a house, an antique car, or shares of stock in a corporation.

The lingo in federal tax law describes a **capital gain** as the difference between the **amount realized** (received) from the sale or other disposition of a capital asset (property) and its **adjusted basis**.[185] The **basis** of property is its cost, which usually is its purchase price but may also be other value given when the owner obtained the property.[186] Tax rules allow the basis to be increased or decreased by certain actions relating to the property. For example, the cost of a new roof for a building could increase its basis. These allowed changes create the **adjusted basis**.[187] Simple arithmetic shows that there is no capital gain potentially subject to tax unless the amount realized is greater than the adjusted basis of a capital asset. A capital gain tax thus cannot be a double tax on the adjusted basis of the capital asset.

Under current law, a capital gain is not realized (taxable) unless there is a sale.[188] Usually, when a sale occurs, the seller receives money, and that money is then the amount realized. Money is thus available to pay a tax on a capital gain if it is treated as income subject to tax.

Current Tax Treatment of Capital Gains

Current tax law divides capital gains into two categories—short-term and long-term. By definition, a long-term capital gain occurs only if the property that is sold has been held (owned) for more than one year.[189] All other capital gains are short-term. The current graduated ordinary income tax rates apply to short-term capital gains. In contrast, special lower income tax rates apply to long-term capital gains.

During the last ten years and using 2009 tax law as the reference, most long-term capital gains have had a maximum tax rate of 15 percent, no matter how large these total gains may have been for an individual during the tax year.[190] I say "most" because special tax rates higher than 15 percent applied to long-term gains from some kinds of property, like "collectibles" (such as works of art).[191] The 2012 fiscal cliff tax compromise increased the maximum tax rate of 15 percent to 20 percent for individuals whose income is larger than a threshold amount (e.g., $400,000 for a single individual), but the compromise retained the concept of significantly lower tax rates for long-term capital gains.[192]

Taxation of capital gains is further affected by statutory provisions that allow some kinds of income to be classified as long-term capital gain, even though that income does not fit the normal description of a capital gain.[193]

Current Tax-Law Consequences

No doubt, special rates for long-term capital gains add complexity to the calculation of federal income taxes for those people who have this kind of income.[194] This added complexity and the special low rates for these gains have been justified by a variety of rationales. Some people have even proposed that capital gains not be taxed at all, a proposal that would simplify income taxes but also take an important bite out of federal tax receipts while creating a class of income that is even more privileged than currently.

However one views the merits of the rationales used to support special low income tax rates on most long-term capital gains (or no tax at all), decisions based on those rationales have real consequences in terms of who benefits most from those decisions. So that the rationales are not discussed in a cold intellectual vacuum, let's first examine who actually has significant capital gains income and how the current special rates can create very different tax results for people who have comparable cash incomes.

Who Has Significant Capital Gains Income?

Everyone, of course, has an opportunity to buy property like corporate stocks or real estate or to start a business as a new corporation that has stock that can later be sold. However, that opportunity does not mean much unless money is available to exercise that opportunity. Thus, people with the most available money are the most able to buy property or start a new business. Generally these are people who have considerably more money than they need to live what they consider to be a decent life. Initially, that money may come through significant wage or service earnings, a successful new business, inheritance, or good luck (e.g., winning a lottery). Later, that money may also come from long-term capital gains in a ballooning effect made possible in part by paying less tax on that income than would be paid on equal amounts of wages or business income. Additional money may also be available from loans because more personal assets exist as security for the lenders.

These may be nice statements, but are they supported by facts?

Indeed they are, as shown by data compiled by the Internal Revenue Service.[195] These data show that wealthier taxpayers are indeed far more likely than less-wealthy taxpayers to get the benefit of special low tax rates on long-term capital gains. Real numbers provide greater meaning to this general statement.

Data from tax year 2007, the last tax year before the Great Recession, show that the group of taxpayers whose tax returns reported adjusted gross incomes of $100,000 or more accounted for 93 percent of the reported net capital gains. Was that because this group also had 93 percent of total reported income? Not at all. This same group had only 53 percent of all reported adjusted gross income. This means that this group of taxpayers had a disproportionately large amount of net gains (18 percent of their total adjusted gross incomes) compared to the group of taxpayers whose tax returns reported adjusted gross incomes less than $100,000 (2 percent of their total adjusted gross incomes).[196]

This disproportion increases with each larger and larger adjusted gross income category above $100,000 that is reported in the IRS data. That very select group of taxpayers whose tax returns each reported adjusted gross incomes of $10,000,000 or more accounted for 35 percent of all net capital gains reported by all taxpayers. That same group had only 6 percent of all reported adjusted gross income. For this group, net capital gains comprised 56 percent of their total adjusted gross incomes. I call this group "very select" because it had fewer than 20,000 tax returns (less than 0.02 percent of all filed returns). Comparable data exist for the tax year 2000, before the broad tax decreases that Congress adopted in 2001 and the specific capital gains tax decreases that Congress adopted in 2003.[197]

How Does Capital Gains Income Affect Tax Owed?

An individual's sale of property with capital gains makes cash available to use however that individual wants. That cash is no less useful than cash received at the same time from wages or business income. Yet the current low tax rates on long-term capital gains and resulting diminished tax can make the net cash available to an individual who has income from long-term capital gains far greater than the net cash available to an individual who earns the same amount of money as wages or business income. A simple example based on 2009 tax law will illustrate this point.[198]

Example Comparison of Tax Owed

In this example, Surgeon S is self-employed and single, and has taxable income of $300,000 as earned income, all from her personal services. She would pay $77,900 in federal income taxes.

Investor I also is self-employed and single, and has taxable income of $300,000, but his income is all from long-term capital gains that he received by selling stock that he held just over one year. He would pay $38,688 in federal income taxes.

The difference is $39,212, with Surgeon S's income tax being more than double Investor I's income tax.

The disparity in total federal taxes owed between Surgeon S and Investor I is even greater because Surgeon S is required to pay Social Security and Medicare taxes, but Investor I is not. Surgeon S's total federal tax would be $99,177, which is $60,489 greater than and over two and a half times Investor I's total federal tax liability of $38,688. Of course, Investor I would not be building up Social Security credits for Social Security benefits upon retirement, although he would get Medicare benefits provided that he paid Medicare taxes on earned income for a total of at least ten years before reaching the age of sixty-five.[199]

Primary Beneficiaries of Less Tax Owed

The above example is not only possible, but also leads to a larger story about who benefits and how much from the current low tax rates on long-term capital gains. A previous section in this chapter has already shown that wealthier individuals have a disproportionately large amount of capital gains income that enjoys special low tax rates. The IRS has compiled data that reveal how much that disproportion has benefited those wealthier individuals.[200] Like the data on sources of income, these data divide taxpayers into categories based upon their reported adjusted gross incomes. For each category, the IRS has calculated the total income taxes paid as a percentage of reported taxable income and also as a percentage of reported adjusted gross income. In light of the current graduated income tax rates, one would expect that these percentages would increase for each category as the amount of adjusted gross income increases, maybe reaching a plateau as the maximum tax rate applies to a very large portion of income received.

The data do *not* fit this expectation.

Instead, again using tax year 2007 as an example, the total income taxes paid as a percentage of both taxable income and adjusted gross income reach a high plateau in the categories that encompass adjusted gross incomes from $500,000 to $5,000,000 but then decrease. Again, specific data will illustrate this fact.

> For that very select group of taxpayers who reported adjusted gross incomes of $10,000,000 or more, the total income tax as a percent of adjusted gross income was 19.8 percent. That is about the same as the percentage for the group of taxpayers having adjusted gross incomes of $200,000 to $500,000, and considerably less than the high plateau of 24.2 percent for the group of taxpayers having adjusted gross incomes of $1,500,000 to $2,000,000. The total income taxes paid as a percentage of *taxable* income show a similar pattern.[201]

I can discern only one explanation for these percentages: the relatively large proportion of total income within this very select group that consists of net capital gains measurably decreases the income taxes paid by this group.

These data, of course, combine in a group all taxpayers with the specified adjusted gross incomes. Within each group, there can be large tax disparities such as shown by my example of Surgeon S and Investor I. Indeed, within the wealthiest group of taxpayers, there can be individuals such as professional athletes who pay income taxes on almost all of their incomes at the maximum marginal rate of 35 percent (2009 law), and other individuals such as stock speculators who pay income taxes on almost all of their incomes at a maximum capital gains marginal rate of 15 percent (2009 law).

Conclusions from the Data

These IRS data show that the special low tax rates on long-term capital gains fail all three criteria for tax reform set forth in this book. They fail the fairness criterion because they benefit primarily wealthier individuals and those benefits are significant. They fail the accountability criterion because the special low rates are a tax subsidy and the impacts of this subsidy on tax receipts are not easily known. They fail the simplicity criterion because they require unique and complex calculations.

Do Rationales for Lower Capital Gains Taxes Have Merit?

Having shown with data that the special low tax rates on long-term capital gains fail the fairness, accountability, and simplicity criteria, the question now is whether the rationales used to justify those special rates have such great merit that they overcome those failures.

Three common rationales in favor of lower capital gains tax rates will be addressed here. According to these rationales, the purposes of lower capital gains rates are (1) to minimize income "bunching" disadvantages, (2) to encourage investment, and (3) to benefit society. As summarized in the conclusion to this section, these rationales do not overcome the failure of special capital gains tax treatment to meet our tax-reform criteria when considered in the context of FAST Plan reforms.

To Minimize Income "Bunching" Disadvantages

Income "bunching" for capital gains can occur because a long-term capital gain reflects an increase in value over time, sometimes many years. The model often portrayed in this context is a person who puts life savings into a business, works hard for twenty years, expands the business, and finally sells the business for a large sum. All of the capital gains over time in this model are bunched in one tax year. Remember that current ordinary income tax rates are graduated so that larger incomes get taxed at higher rates. If treated as ordinary income, bunching the long-term capital gains income of our model businessman in one year would result in higher marginal tax rates being applied to that income than the marginal tax rates that would have been applied if the same capital gain had occurred in smaller equal amounts each year the business had been owned. Applying special lower income tax rates to long-term capital gains is thus one rough way to accomplish spreading the gain over more than one year.

The maximum rate of 15 percent is the equivalent of assuming that the gain is spread over so many years that no more than the second lowest rate in the 2009 graduated income tax schedules applies to all of that income, no matter how large.[202] Somewhat surprisingly, for our model businessman, the federal tax law is even more complex and potentially more favorable than using the special low tax rates on long-term capital gains. He may qualify for a different approach that allows decreased tax on his capital gains if the sale of his business occurs through the sale of "small business stock."[203]

If all kinds of individual income were to be taxed at a single standard rate, as proposed in the FAST Plan, the "bunching" rationale disappears. Under a standard tax rate for all income, the tax rate on the total long-term capital gain in the year of sale would be the same as the tax rate calculated as if the same capital gain had occurred equally each year that the property had been owned.[204]

To Encourage Investment

People who support special low tax rates for capital gains income most often claim "encouraging investment" as their justification. In this respect, the term "investment" has a very broad meaning. This is so because the current low tax rates on long-term capital gains apply to almost every kind of property except collectibles.

We can agree that the low tax rates encourage people to buy more property that has the potential for capital gains, such as corporate stocks or real estate, than would be the case with higher tax rates.

A more important question is whether this encouragement gives the desirable results claimed by the proponents of special capital gains tax treatment. Let's now examine the claims of those proponents, the counter-assertions by critics, and facts relevant to those claims and assertions.

Proponents' claims

Proponents of special capital gains tax treatment say that the low tax rates are also designed to encourage the formation of new businesses and the expansion of existing businesses, especially businesses conducted as corporations. The low tax rates on long-term capital gains provide incentive for these activities because a larger portion of the increased value of the business, as represented by increased stock value, will actually be received upon sale than if higher tax rates applied to that increase. According to one school of thought, these encouragements will increase investments that are needed for the American economy to "increase output, productivity, and employment," thus improving the standard of living for all Americans.[205]

In a somewhat different vein, proponents of low tax rates on capital gains also claim that low tax rates increase investments and risk taking by those who have capital, which in turn creates jobs, expands the American economy, and ultimately even increases total federal tax receipts.[206] According to these claims, increased tax receipts will occur because those expanded investments will create overall larger wages and taxable business income. Even though wage earners and individuals with business income will be paying more federal taxes, they will be better off because they will also have additional income available for other purposes.

Critics' assertions

Critics of special low tax rates on capital gains respond to these claims by asserting that projected profit from perceived demand for goods, services, and facilities is what stimulates investment and risk taking, not lower tax rates on capital gains. According to these critics, if projected profit or perceived demand are lacking, investments and risk taking will also be lacking, no matter how low the capital gains tax rates. Furthermore, if actual demand for goods and services is lacking, the overall economy suffers, and so do jobs and federal tax receipts.

Tax subsidy effect

True to my admonition in the discussion of tax subsidies, anytime you hear or see words like "encourage" or "incentive" related to tax features, think "tax subsidy." Stripped down, an argument that low tax rates on capital gains are needed to encourage investment and thereby obtain enough investment money "for the economy" is really an argument that all taxpayers must subsidize "investment" activity, in this case, the activity of buying and owning nearly all kinds of property that have the potential to increase in value. The current special low rates on long-term capital gains and resulting diminished tax receipts mean that everyone else has to pay more taxes to cover all federal expenditures than if the investment activity were taxed the same as personal services activity.

Available facts

In the time period between 1987 and 2009, Congress has twice specifically decreased the tax rates on long-term capital gains. What do available data from this time period show that prove or disprove the claims by proponents or assertions by critics of low tax rates on capital gains?

Appendix 14D looks at changes in the number of American jobs and appendix 10D looks at changes in the US GDP during that time period. These data are inconclusive. They do not prove the proponents' assertions because the decreased capital gains tax rates adopted in 1997 and 2003 did not demonstrably increase the number of American jobs or the US GDP as compared to time periods preceding those tax decreases. These data do not necessarily prove the critics' assertions either, because the effects of decreased capital gains tax rates may be more subtle than the data can show.

As for increased tax receipts, the data on individual income tax receipts, including lower rates for capital gains, have *not* resulted in greater federal tax receipts (see appendix 10C).

To Benefit Society

According to the proponents of no tax on capital gains, *any* tax tends to "lock in" an owner's assets, which might better be sold to someone else who could use the assets more efficiently. The owner in turn could also invest the proceeds in more efficient ways. Society or the economy as a whole would benefit from more efficient use of its capital assets.[207] Under this philosophy, supported by some economists, low capital gains rates are better than regular income tax rates, but no tax at all on all capital gains would give the best societal benefit.[208]

Whether or not society as a whole would benefit through the efficiency asserted in this philosophy, the cost of achieving this efficiency is the same as the cost of achieving the encouragement for investment described in the previous section. Indeed, as compared to current low tax rates for long-term capital gains, a "no-tax" approach to capital gains would create an even greater tax subsidy and a more-select group of people with wealth who pay far less tax on their cash incomes than people who obtain the same or even less cash income through wages or business income. A no-tax approach also has the potential for capital gains income not being reported at all on federal income tax forms, thus hiding the very data that are needed to demonstrate the amount and uneven distribution of this form of income among individuals.

The societal benefits argument thus raises the question whether equity among taxpayers should trump potential capital asset efficiency.

In a democracy such as the United States, I believe that it should.

This belief stems not only from an idea of equity among taxpayers, but also from a broader view of societal benefits than expressed by those who decry the lock-in potential for capital caused by a capital gains tax. Capital assets do not exist in a world separate from people. In a free society, the demand by people for those assets is what gives them monetary value. Similarly, the monetary value of human capital in the form of human services is determined by the demand by people for those services. Choices by people on how to use their time, intelligence, and physical abilities, whether to develop expertise in the use of capital (their own or someone else's) or expertise in the use of personal skills and other tools potentially available to them, should be uninfluenced by different tax consequences from those choices. Only then can a true free market exist for services and capital assets, where demand by people primarily determines how society's human and physical resources are allocated.

The Rationales Fail Their Burden of Proof

This section has shown that the claimed investment and ancillary benefits from special low tax rates on capital gains income are not supported by strong evidence. Without this strong evidence, the broad capital gains tax subsidy must be challenged because of its two unusually strong discriminatory effects.

As shown in the first part of this chapter, the existing low maximum tax rate for long-term capital gains clearly (1) benefits primarily a select group of people with wealth who have substantial capital gains cash income and (2) allows individuals with long-term capital gains income to pay far less tax on their cash incomes than people who obtain the same or even less cash income through wages or self-employed personal services. These unfair discriminatory effects far outweigh whatever alleged potential benefits are generated by this blanket tax subsidy. Indeed, dogged insistence on special low tax rates for capital gains has created an "entitlement" for individuals with substantial capital gains income that negatively affects the federal budget in much the same way that expenditures for "entitlements" negatively affect that budget. The FAST Plan rejects this tax subsidy by applying the standard-rate tax to all capital gains.

Beyond its unfair discriminatory effect, treating capital gains as unique for tax purposes also reinforces a flawed vision of capital assets as being apart from the people who own them. Capital assets are just one tool among many tools that people use to generate income, so their use should not be treated differently than those other tools. For example, the tools of a truck driver who gets paid for his services include not only a truck, but also good eyes, good reflexes, driving experience, and other personal and physical assets that provide value to what the truck driver does. Similarly, the tools of a surgeon who gets paid for her services include not only an operating facility, but also a steady hand, a medical education, surgical experience, surgical instruments, and an organized team of assistants to achieve value for what the surgeon does. An investor such as a real estate developer brings more than money or land to a development. He or she brings other tools like real estate market understanding, relationships with contractors, personal time devoted to the project, and a vision for the development. Ultimately, the combination of good decisions and the money, land, and other assets invested is what produces value for what this investor does. Accordingly, the reflection of this value in the form of money received from capital gains should be treated no differently than the reflection of value received as money in the form of wages or business income. A standard-rate income tax for all income, including all capital gains, would provide this equal treatment.

What Other Capital Gains Issues Should We Consider?

The law on capital gains is extensive and complex. This book is not designed to cover all aspects of every federal tax. Undoubtedly many capital gains–related rules will have to remain so long as capital gains are taxed as income. Examples are the rules on carryover basis, how the adjusted basis of property is determined, and what combinations of capital gains and losses can be used to determine taxable capital gains income.[209]

To the extent that complexity and unfairness derive from what qualifies as a capital gain as compared to ordinary income, this complexity and unfairness should be reduced if my proposed standard-rate income tax is applied to all capital gains as well as historic ordinary income. With a standard rate, classifying income as ordinary income or capital gains will make no difference in the tax. This fact will produce at least two favorable effects:

- Complex schemes to create capital gains–style income instead of ordinary income will no longer have any purpose. Choices for compensation between receiving money as wages or property such as stock options will be based on actual value rather than tax advantages or disadvantages.
- Because classifying capital gains as short-term or long-term will make no difference in the tax owed, property will be bought or sold entirely because of the inherent advantage of doing so at the time, rather than being influenced by different tax consequences if a sale is delayed or accelerated.

Two unique issues regarding income tax on capital gains do merit some discussion. The first concerns the effects of inflation on capital gains. The second is capital gains from sale of a principal residence.

Dealing with Inflation

Should capital asset values be indexed to general inflation?

Throughout most of the last thirty years, the United States has had a modest inflationary economy, with the Great Recession being an important exception. As everyone knows, in an inflationary economy, most property values rise.

If a person buys property at the beginning of a time period in which the property's value increases exactly the amount of general inflation over that time period, that person is no better off at the end of the time period than at its beginning. In relative terms, the property has not increased in value. If the property is sold at the end of the time period, there is no real gain in value because the money received is worth no more in relative terms than the money that was used to buy the property. Yet a taxable capital gain would still exist, as represented by the difference between the property's sale price and its original purchase price.

Some people cite this example as effectively a confiscation of property and even go beyond this example to assert that all capital gains are really just illusory income because they all result from inflation. Therefore, according to these people, capital gains should not be taxed at all or, at worst, should be taxed at special low rates such as the maximum 15 percent rate that was effective from 2003 to 2012 for long-term capital gains.

The FAST Plan rejects these contentions because the bludgeon of a special low tax rate on capital gains (or no tax at all) gives unfair discriminatory favorable treatment to capital gains income that far exceeds gains caused only by inflation.

But what about that portion of capital gains that *is* the result of inflation? Should inflation's effect on capital gains be neutralized by indexing capital asset values to general inflation over time? After all, the applications of many tax rates are already indexed to one measure or another of general inflation. An example is the annual increase in the Social Security tax cutoff.[210] The starting point for indexing a capital asset would be its original basis.[211]

When examined in practice, the indexing approach for capital gains fails the goals of tax simplicity and probably also tax fairness. This approach would work against tax simplicity in at least three different ways.

First, and most fundamentally, an indexing approach for capital gains reintroduces a need to designate clearly what income is capital gains so that special indexing rules can apply to that income. Unique treatment of capital gains will also reintroduce the pressures that historically have led to special rules under current law that give the benefit of capital gains tax rates to some kinds of income that do not fit the classic description of capital gains. If Congress again succumbs to those pressures, tax fairness will again suffer.

Second, especially for real property, each change in the adjusted basis of the capital asset would have to carry its own amount and date for indexing. Just keeping track of the basis and adjusted basis of capital assets is a challenge for some individuals. Indexing would greatly compound that challenge. This very challenge would also contribute to tax unfairness. Individuals who could afford to hire experts to do the accounting and indexing for them would have an advantage over individuals who could not afford that expertise. That advantage would translate into some individuals having less *taxable* capital gains than other individuals having the same capital gains just because of differences in the documented indexing of their capital assets.

Third, an indexing approach raises multiple questions about how an index should be applied, the answers to which can affect tax liability and tax fairness. After first solving the problem of what index to use for capital assets in the first place, how often should the index be updated? Many capital assets are bought and sold throughout the year, so a typical annual index would not be able to reflect short-term inflationary changes, particularly in a strongly inflationary economy. Maybe this question could be resolved by stringent rules that use annual indices only, but maybe not. In addition, should the index approach also apply in determining capital losses that are used to reduce capital gains in a year? Indexing when capital losses occur presumably would increase losses because the adjusted basis would be increased by an inflationary index, thus further decreasing the net capital gains that are taxable.

As for tax fairness, in addition to the fairness issues already raised, indexing values in determining capital gains introduces a tax-free return in the amount of the indexed value for individuals who have capital gains. Wage earners, whose inflation-adjusted wages are fully taxable, can question whether a tax-free safe haven is an appropriate guarantee for all property when the value of property is determined by many factors other than inflation.

Remember also who would benefit from an indexing approach. The vast majority of capital gains are enjoyed by individuals who have much larger total incomes than most Americans. Historically, taxable capital gains have not been reduced by inflation indexing. If any extra tax payment results solely from inflation's effect on capital gains, the tax payment will be borne by those who can most afford to pay it.

Capital Gain on the Sale of a Principal Residence

An individual's principal residence is an asset that might actually increase so much in value over time that a significant capital gain can exist when the residence is sold.[212] For many people, their principal residence is the largest single asset that they own, whether it is a modest trailer home in a trailer park or a 5,000-square-foot suburban Tudor-style house. A principal residence, however, is much more than an investment asset. It is home.

Congress has recognized this fact by providing special rules for the sale of a principal residence.[213] Under qualified circumstances relating to the time period a principal residence is owned and used, these rules exclude from any income tax a certain amount of capital gain from its sale. The exclusion can be exercised no more than once every two years. The exclusion amount varies depending upon ownership and tax filing status. So long as the capital gain is within the exclusion amount, these rules allow the full proceeds from sale of a principal residence to be used to buy another residence (or to be saved or used to buy anything else).[214] This obviously is a tax subsidy, but simply applied.

These rules are appropriate for a principal residence under current tax law. This tax subsidy and its lack of accountability with limited reporting requirements could be subject to reevaluation along with all other tax subsidies if federal taxes are revamped as proposed in the FAST Plan.

Capital Gains Recap

This chapter has covered a lot of ground. Beginning with a definition of capital gain, we have examined who has significant capital gains income, how the current special treatment of capital gains affects taxes owed, and whether rationales used to support that special treatment have merit. This examination has concluded that the special low tax rates on long-term capital gains should be rejected in overall tax reform. The FAST Plan reflects this conclusion by applying its standard income tax rate to all capital gains as well as ordinary income. We are now ready to examine another kind of income that recently has had special tax treatment just like capital gains: dividends.

Chapter 14 Proposal
Capital Gains

Reform
- Treat all capital gains as ordinary income.
- Apply a standard-rate income tax to all capital gains.
- For a principal residence that is sold, keep the current methods to exempt a portion of any capital gain from the individual income tax, but only if reporting is required and this tax subsidy remains appropriate as other FAST Plan changes are made to current federal taxes.

Chapter 15

———◆·◆·◆———

Dividends

For many years, **dividends** from corporate stocks were considered to be ordinary income subject to ordinary income tax rates. In 2003, Congress changed this treatment by adopting special lower tax rates for "qualified dividend" income.[215] Those rates are the same as the rates applied to long-term capital gains.

In the FAST Plan, dividends income is subject to the standard income tax rate, but to understand why this makes sense despite their current treatment, I will first summarize the conflicting arguments about whether or not to tax dividends income, and if so, to what extent. My proposed reform of the current corporation income tax will also play an important role here.

Arguments for Special Treatment of Dividends Income

Some proponents of the special low tax rates on dividends income actually argue that *any* tax on dividends income is unfair. They base that argument primarily on a double taxation claim that has two variations: the corporation's perspective and the shareholder's perspective. Some proponents raise other arguments as well.

The Corporation's Perspective

Proponents of low or no tax on dividends assert that this tax represents double taxation of corporation income (meaning net profit or "earnings," the term used in the Internal Revenue Code and in the remainder of this chapter). According to this argument, dividends are distributions of a corporation's earnings, and these earnings have already been taxed. This concern was even noted back in 1954 when Congress adopted what is still largely the framework of the Internal Revenue Code.[216] This argument is consistent with the notions expressed by many economists that all business income should be treated the same tax-wise and that corporations are just economic business entities that take a particular legal form.[217] Other business income, such as that from a personal business, does not have this extra layer of taxation.

The Shareholder's Perspective

Proponents of low or no tax on dividends assert that a corporation's shareholder is an owner of the corporation, and as an owner, the shareholder has already paid taxes on the corporation's earnings. As a corollary to the ownership idea, some proponents of low or no tax on dividends assert that dividends are an "after-tax" gift to the corporation's owners (shareholders).

Other Proponents' Arguments

Expanding beyond the corporation itself, some proponents of a low or no tax on dividends also assert that a regular tax on dividends adversely affects retirees who depend upon dividends income for their livelihood.

Yet other proponents assert that no tax or a low tax on dividends, much like a low tax on capital gains, encourages investment in corporations, thus assisting the American economy overall.

Arguments for Treating Dividends as Ordinary Income

Opponents of special low tax rates or no tax on dividends income respond to their proponents in a variety of ways.

Opponents first assert that a corporation is a separate legal entity, with a separate obligation to pay taxes as an entity. How much tax the corporation pays as an entity, even from earnings, is irrelevant to the taxability of dividends income paid to shareholders, who get the benefit of the income received just like an employee gets the benefit of wages paid by the corporation.

Opponents also assert that the amounts of any dividends are determined solely by the corporation, are not directly tied to earnings, and are therefore not really distributions of previously taxed earnings. For example, the directors could choose to use some earnings to repurchase outstanding stock.[218] Indeed, the total amounts designated for dividends could be less or even more than a corporation's taxable earnings in a particular year. Opponents point out that a variety of maneuvers can affect *taxable* earnings in a year when actual earnings exist and significant dividends are paid to shareholders. These include the use of carryover (or carryback) losses and a variety of accounting maneuvers that can reduce or eliminate taxable earnings.[219]

As for the ownership rationale, opponents of low tax rates for dividends assert that this idea is just a trumped-up argument for special treatment of dividends. They say that a shareholder does not have normal rights of ownership, like the ability to use or sell corporate assets. At most, a shareholder has the right to vote for directors and sometimes bylaws changes (in proportion to the number of shares owned). Except for majority shareholders who are also directors, shareholders cannot participate in many decisions that determine the amount of a corporation's earnings that potentially is available to pay dividends that would benefit them.

In response to the alleged plight of retirees who depend upon dividends income, opponents note that the benefits of a low tax rate on dividends extend far beyond retirees, and even among retirees, include many people who have incomes that are much larger than average. Indeed, taking tax year 2007 as an example, taxpayers having adjusted gross incomes of $100,000 or more had 77 percent of all ordinary dividends income reported that year.[220]

Finally, opponents to special low tax rates for dividends say in response to the "encourages investment" argument that this language alone shows that a low or no tax on dividends is a tax subsidy. They further assert that the alleged benefits of this tax subsidy are not observable in any pertinent data if they exist at all.

A somewhat unique argument also exists that favors taxing dividends like all other income. This approach compares different payments by corporations to people and how income tax law treats those payments. Corporations pay wages to employees for their services in providing time and expertise to benefit the corporation. Those wages are taxable as ordinary income. Corporations also pay individuals who are independent contractors for their services in providing time and expertise to benefit the corporation. The business net profits of those independent contractors, which are derived from the corporation's payments, also are taxable to those individuals as ordinary income. Similar to these payments to employees and independent contractors, dividends represent payments to shareholders for their service of providing capital (money) to benefit the corporation. Therefore, dividends to shareholders should also be taxable as ordinary income.

Changing the Tax Framework for Dividends Income

The ebb and flow of majority congressional views about the conflicting philosophies reflected in the arguments just described (and maybe others) has determined whether dividends are taxed as ordinary income under the normal income tax rates, under special lower rates, or not at all.[221]

Many arguments for a low or no tax on dividends income hinge greatly on the taxation of corporations being based on earnings and on the corporate practice that dividends are often closely related to earnings (albeit many times not). If we eliminate the corporation net profit (earnings) tax, the support for these arguments disappears. Then dividends become just like any other income and properly subject to a standard income tax rate. This is what I propose in chapter 29 on corporation taxes, although I do not suggest that corporations be free from all federal taxes (chapter 29 proposes a small corporation revenue tax).

Even if we do not adopt a corporation revenue tax, the lack of direct connection between dividends and taxed earnings, combined with the discriminatory nature of who has substantial dividends income, favors return of dividends to their historic treatment as ordinary income.

Retirees who rely on modest dividends for their retirement income have special circumstances that may merit a temporary tax subsidy when we apply a standard-rate income tax to dividends. Retirees who rely on modest incomes from pensions or retirement-plan distributions have similar circumstances. In chapter 26 we will examine the special case of these retirees under a newly adopted standard-rate income tax.

Having now raised the question of income to retirees, the next two chapters take a close look at the most common forms of income that retirees rely upon: Social Security benefits, pension payments, and retirement-plan distributions.

Chapter 15 Proposal
Dividends

Reform
- Treat all dividends as ordinary income.
- Apply a standard-rate income tax to all dividends.
- Preferably adopt this reform in conjunction with replacing the corporation income tax with a corporation revenue tax.

Chapter 16

————◆•◆•◆————

Social Security Benefits

Among those Americans who lost almost everything during the Great Depression in the 1930s, the elderly were particularly hard-hit because they were not in a position to recoup their losses over time. The Social Security system is an outgrowth of this feature of the Great Depression. It was and is a way to ensure that most Americans have minimal funds for life's essential needs when they retire or become disabled.

Statutory headings name the Social Security legislation "old age, survivors, and disability insurance."[222] Social Security is thus a form of *insurance* designed to provide funds for those who need them. Those who reach old age, survive a spouse's death, or become disabled are conclusively presumed to need Social Security funds.[223] In Social Security lingo, the funds received from Social Security are called *benefits*.

Competing Taxation Philosophies

Whether to treat all or some portion of **Social Security benefits** as taxable income pits two competing philosophies against each other.[224]

Some people assert that Social Security benefits should not be taxable at all because they represent paybacks to individuals who have paid Social Security taxes over a long time to support others. The amounts of those paybacks are properly related to the amounts of Social Security taxes paid by each individual each year over time. Thus, these paybacks should not be diminished by treating Social Security benefits as taxable income.

Other people assert that, true to Social Security's formal name, Social Security benefits represent solely insurance against financial deprivation. If an individual who qualifies for Social Security benefits has substantial other income, that individual does not need all of this insurance to have a comfortable financial life. Treating part or all of that individual's Social

Security benefits as taxable income allows some Social Security money to be returned for eventual distribution to those who truly need Social Security benefits.

How has Congress dealt with these competing philosophies and other ideas in determining whether or how to treat Social Security benefits as taxable income? More important, how should Social Security benefits be treated in the future, especially under the proposals advanced in the FAST Plan?

Historic and Current Taxation of Social Security Benefits

For many years, Social Security benefits were not considered to be taxable income. As part of its overhaul of Social Security legislation in 1983, Congress decided otherwise for tax years beginning in 1984.[225] According to the Senate report that described the reasons for the change, the new statute would "improve tax equity by treating more nearly equally all forms of retirement and other income that are designed to replace lost wages," would assure that individuals with smaller incomes would not be taxed on their Social Security benefits, and would assure that "only those taxpayers who have substantial taxable income from other sources will be taxed on a portion of the benefits they receive."[226] In other words, Congress partially aligned itself with the "insurance" philosophy regarding the taxation of Social Security benefits.

The basic idea of the new statute was to include in an individual's gross income a portion of the individual's Social Security benefits if the individual's total income exceeded a threshold amount. The new statute created formulas that would determine what income amounts must be compared to the threshold and the portion of the Social Security benefits that would be included in gross income.[227] This new statute also featured the restriction that no more than one-half of an individual's Social Security benefits could be included in his or her gross income. The legislation required that the income taxes that were collected on taxable Social Security benefits were to be transferred to the Social Security trust funds.[228]

In 1993, Congress reexamined the taxation of Social Security benefits as part of a massive set of tax changes designed to reduce federal deficits.[229] At that time, Congress decided that up to 85 percent of an individual's Social Security benefits could be taxable income, again when the individual's total income exceeds threshold amounts. To accomplish this increase, Congress inserted yet another formula in the 1983 statute that used 85 percent in place of one-half in the practical application of the formula. Congress also inserted a second threshold concept.[230] The reasoning stated in 1993 for this second threshold was "to more closely conform the income tax treatment of Social Security benefits and private pension benefits by increasing the maximum amount of Social Security benefits included in gross income for certain higher-income beneficiaries."[231] This legislation also required the added income taxes collected on taxable Social Security benefits resulting from these changes to go to the Medicare hospital insurance trust fund, not to the Social Security trust funds.[232]

The provisions of the 1983 and 1993 legislation are now embodied in Section 86 of the Internal Revenue Code. Section 86 is multilayered, complicated, and arguably overreaching in the way that it taxes Social Security benefits.

Flaws in Section 86

Even if one accepts the philosophy that the Social Security benefits of people with substantial other income should be at least partially taxable, Section 86 has two readily apparent flaws in the way that it now applies that philosophy.

Excess Complexity

From a simplicity point of view, Section 86 is a monster. It has quirks that defy cogent explanation or easy calculation. Because of Section 86, an eighteen-step worksheet is required to figure out the amount of an individual's annual Social Security benefit that is taxable. The rationales for many line items in that worksheet are wholly obscure. And that worksheet is only a basic worksheet that does not apply to all situations.[233]

Section 86 and its basic worksheet greatly complicate any attempt to estimate income taxes when an individual who receives Social Security benefits has to decide how much money to withdraw from a retirement account, to obtain by selling investments, or to seek from working. Retirees are justifiably frustrated by this difficulty. Some retirees are surely surprised and angered at the amounts of their Social Security benefits that are taxable when they prepare tax returns at the end of the year after having made those decisions.

Inadequate Thresholds

In determining those individuals who have significant other income that will trigger the taxation of their Social Security benefits, the threshold amounts for "significant" in Section 86 have not kept up with inflation. Many individuals whom Congress would not have considered in 1983 or even 1993 to have significant other income now have to contend with Section 86.

For example, the threshold "base amount" for individuals filing a joint return in 1984 was $32,000, and remained $32,000 in 2009. An equivalent dollar amount in 2009 would be $62,420 using one common inflation adjustment.[234] Even the $44,000 for the "adjusted base amount" that Congress inserted for 1994 remained the same in 2009 (equivalent to $62,610 in 2009).[235] Partly for this reason, the amount of taxable Social Security benefits as a portion of all gross income reported to the IRS by all individuals has risen from 0.7 percent in 1993 to 1.4 percent in 2000 and 1.9 percent in 2007.[236]

FAST Plan Treatment of Social Security Benefits

I support the philosophy that Social Security benefits represent insurance against financial deprivation, not a guaranteed payback for all people. Actual reliance on that insurance, however, extends much further than allowed by the current treatment of Social Security benefits as taxable income.

- One form of reliance is for basic life necessities, as represented by some estimated amount that covers those needs. This form of reliance appears to underlie the complex formula approach used in current tax law to determine a threshold amount beyond which Social Security benefits become taxable, even though the threshold amount has become a less and less adequate reflection of the cost of necessities.
- A second and equally important form of reliance is based on expectations for retirement income resulting from different levels of Social Security tax payments over time. Those expectations affect planning for other retirement income that is largely locked-in once retirement occurs. Of course, the larger this other retirement income becomes, the less important are untaxed Social Security benefits as a component of expectations for total retirement income.

Proposal 16A.1 in appendix 16A is an attempt to recast Section 86 in a much simpler and less onerous way to apply the "insurance" philosophy while respecting both forms of reliance on Social Security benefits. This recast version has three simple features:

(1) For every dollar of other income that exceeds a threshold amount, a fixed percentage of a dollar of the individual's Social Security benefits will be included in gross income (and therefore taxable).
(2) The maximum amount of an individual's Social Security benefits that can be added to other gross income is calculated by applying the same fixed percentage in (1) to the individual's total Social Security benefits in the tax year.
(3) The threshold amount is large enough not only to provide income needed for basic necessities, but also to respect expectations for Social Security retirement income resulting from different levels of Social Security tax payments over time.

Calculations under this recast version would be possible with nine line entries, each having easily understood components (see figure 16A.1 in appendix 16A).

For the recast version of Section 86, I use 50 percent for the fixed percentage and a threshold amount for other income equal to ten times the standard deduction applicable to the individual. Using the standard deduction as the base automatically tailors thresholds to an individual's filing category and also incorporates cost-of-living increases over time. Of course, a different percentage could be used as politically determined, and the threshold could be a fixed amount for each filing category provided that this amount is subject to automatic cost-of-living adjustments.

The final question regarding taxation of Social Security benefits is whether the tax receipts from this taxation should be designated to specific purposes. As noted in the historic summary above, Congress has required all of these receipts to go to trust funds. Some receipts go to the Social Security trust funds, and some receipts go to the Medicare hospital insurance trust fund. In the FAST Plan, all of the receipts from taxation of Social Security benefits would go to the Social Security trust funds. This approach keeps Social Security unified. In that way, decisions about needs for Social Security and Medicare can be made uninfluenced by subsidies from one to the other or to general government programs.

Social Security Benefits Recap

In this chapter, we have examined how Congress has historically chosen to tax Social Security benefits, the complexity of the way that current law determines taxable Social Security benefits, and the FAST Plan's simplified method to determine taxable Social Security benefits. Our next chapter considers the other major sources of retirement income for most individuals: pension payments and retirement-plan distributions.

Chapter 16 Proposal
Social Security Benefits

Reform
- Treat a portion of Social Security benefits as ordinary income based on the excess of other income over a threshold amount that
    (1) provides sufficient funds for basic necessities and
    (2) respects expectations for Social Security retirement income resulting from different levels of Social Security tax payments over time.
- Apply a standard-rate income tax to the calculated ordinary income.
- Transfer all income taxes paid on taxable Social Security benefits to the Social Security trust funds.

Chapter 17

Pension Payments and Retirement-Plan Distributions

Pension payments and selected retirement-plan distributions have long been regarded as deferred income that is taxable as ordinary income. This deferred income usually falls into one of two categories.

One category is delayed payment for services, such as a pension paid by an employer to its retired former employee. Had the employer paid the employee more wages instead of promising a pension, the extra wages would have been taxable income.

A second category of pensions is money paid from funds in a retirement plan where the source of the funds is money that was not taxed when contributed to the plan. A common example is payment from an individual retirement account that was funded by untaxed money contributed by an employee or self-employed individual. Had the money that was contributed into a retirement plan been received by the employee or self-employed individual and otherwise used, the extra money would also have been taxable income.

Under these circumstances, both pension income and retirement-plan distributions derived from untaxed contributions to the plan are properly taxed as ordinary income.

Unfortunately, the story on retirement-plan distributions cannot end there.

A Non-Taxation Advantage

Current law regarding non-taxation of money paid into qualified retirement plans gives an odd non-taxation advantage to those employees whose employers have a retirement plan over both self-employed individuals and those employees whose employers do not have a retirement plan. This advantage fails our fairness criterion. It arises from the non-application or application of Social Security and Medicare taxes to money that ends up in a retirement plan.

As noted previously, Social Security and Medicare taxes are paid on earned income in the form of wages and self-employment business income.[237]

For an employee, the "wages" subject to these taxes specifically exclude payments made by the employer or employee to a qualified retirement plan established by the employer.[238] Pensions paid from this type of retirement plan also are not "wages" subject to Social Security and Medicare taxes.[239] Thus, Social Security and Medicare taxes are never paid on money that is contributed to an employer-established retirement plan.

In contrast, for a self-employed individual, the calculation of self-employment income that is subject to Social Security and Medicare taxes does not subtract payments to a qualified retirement plan as a deductible trade or business expense.[240] This means that a self-employed individual will have paid Social Security and Medicare taxes on any money that he or she contributes to a retirement plan from self-employed income. These taxes are add-ons to any income tax owed by a self-employed individual.

A similar result occurs for an employee whose employer does not have a retirement plan. In the absence of an employer-established retirement plan, this employee will also have paid Social Security and Medicare taxes on any wages money that the employee contributes to an otherwise qualified retirement plan, such as an individual retirement account. Just as with a self-employed individual, these taxes are add-ons to any income tax owed by this employee.

Removing the Non-Taxation Advantage

A reconfiguration of federal taxes should address these disparities.

The FAST Plan proposal to allow payments by an individual for Social Security and Medicare taxes as credits to the individual income tax will largely remove the consequences of these disparities. Under this treatment, Social Security and Medicare taxes that are paid on money contributed to a qualified retirement plan will not be added to the individual income tax as they are now. Thus, an individual who makes a contribution to a qualified retirement plan that is not an employer-established plan will end up paying no more total federal taxes (adding income, Social Security, and Medicare taxes) at the time of the contribution than an individual with the same taxable income who makes or whose employer makes a contribution to an employer-established retirement plan.

This chapter concludes our consideration of the major kinds of currently taxable individual income. We now turn to those kinds of individual income that Congress has deemed to be tax-exempt.

Chapter 17 Proposal
Pension Payments and Retirement-Plan Distributions

Retain

- Treat pension payments and retirement-plan distributions as ordinary income to the extent that they represent deferred income or are derived from untaxed money contributed to a retirement plan.

Reform

- Apply a standard-rate income tax to this form of ordinary income.

Chapter 18

------ ◆•◆•◆ ------

Tax-Exempt Income

The Internal Revenue Code lists a host of items that are excluded from its definition of gross income, thereby excluding those items from taxable income and making them tax-exempt.[241] We will first categorize these tax-exempt items to help us determine whether this approach meets our three criteria of fairness, accountability, and simplicity for these items. We will then critique the long-standing policy tradition of excluding state and local bond interest from the definition of gross income.

Categorizing Exclusions from Gross Income

Current exclusions from gross income can be divided into four general categories:

(1) Personal benefits
(2) Healthy life necessities
(3) Miscellaneous exclusions
(4) Tax subsidies

Personal Benefits

Some of the gross income exclusions apparently are designed to remove any doubt about whether a described personal benefit should be considered income at all. Examples of this kind of exclusion are "gifts and inheritances,"[242] "improvements by lessee on lessor's property,"[243] and "qualified scholarships."[244] Using exclusions from gross income appears to be a proper way to create clarity for the taxability or nontaxability of these personal benefits. This clarity fits all three of our criteria.

Healthy Life Necessities

Some of the gross income exclusions are in the nature of money necessary for a healthy life, which I describe in the context of reductions from income as money that should be excluded from taxation as a matter of basic human rights (chapter 21). Examples of this kind of exclusion from taxable income are "amounts received under accident and health plans,"[245] "contributions by an employer to accident and health plans,"[246] and "dependent care assistance programs."[247] These kinds of exclusions from gross income should remain if you agree with me that money necessary for a healthy life should not be taxed. Exclusions are the simplest way to accomplish that purpose for these kinds of income.

Miscellaneous Exclusions

Some gross income exclusions can best be described as miscellaneous exclusions because they are tucked away in other parts of the Internal Revenue Code and do not fit a general category. A notable example is the effective exclusion from income of payments by an employer or employee to a qualified retirement account that has been established by the employer. These payments are excluded from reportable wages as deferred compensation (payments to a "deferred arrangement").[248] They are also excluded from the definition of wages subject to Social Security and Medicare taxes.[249] Of course, distributions from these plans *are* income subject to the federal income tax in the year received, so ultimately these initial exclusions are effectively rescinded, at least for federal income taxes (see chapter 17). Because of their variety, miscellaneous exclusions from gross income would have to be judged individually on whether they meet our three criteria.

Tax Subsidies

The final general category of items excluded from gross income consists of items that are truly ordinary income items but for their statutory exclusion. These exclusions create tax subsidies to the people who receive these forms of income. Examples are "interest on any State or local bond,"[250] "exclusion of gain from sale of principal residence" (a partial exclusion),[251] and "certain foster care payments."[252] The issue here is not whether the tax subsidies are appropriate, but whether the way in which the tax subsidies occur is appropriate. To be sure, excluding these items from taxable income is simple. That simplicity, however, comes at the cost of accountability.

The Tax Subsidy Exclusion of State and Local Bond Interest

The exclusion of state and local bond interest from the definition of gross income will be used as an example of problems that are inherent in using exclusions to provide a tax subsidy.

This exclusion has been around a very long time. Whether this exclusion is viewed as an extension of the reserved rights of the states under the Tenth Amendment to the US Constitution[253] or as a political concession to the states, this exclusion encourages people to buy state and local bonds because their interest is tax-exempt. This tax-exempt treatment allows the issuing governmental entities to offer comparatively low interest rates that are nevertheless acceptable to investors. Clearly this approach aids local governments and the people who pay local taxes within their jurisdictions. Unfortunately, the tax-exempt treatment of state and local bond interest also provides a significant tax subsidy to the recipients of that interest.

Fairness Issues

Making interest on state and local bonds tax-exempt raises fairness concerns. Should any individual be able to manage his or her investments to obtain a very large income and yet pay little or no income taxes as compared to an individual with comparable or even much less income like wages? Are the benefits to local governments and their citizens so great as to override this discrimination, which is far more likely to benefit individuals with large enough wealth to be able to afford significant investments in state and local bonds? Can this discrimination be minimized while retaining most of the benefits to local governments from the current tax-exempt status of state and local bonds interest?

Ultimately, answering these questions are political decisions on balancing costs and benefits. I do not take a position in this book on these questions other than to note the discriminatory effect of the current tax-exempt status of state and local bond interest. The Fiscal Commission's 2010 report is not so circumspect. That report recommends that the interest on newly issued state and local bonds be taxable the same as other interest.[254]

Accountability Issues

Under current law, the cost of treating state and local bond interest as tax-exempt in terms of lost federal tax receipts can only be estimated. To be sure, for many years, Form 1040 has included a space in which to report tax-exempt interest. The IRS has compiled statistics from that information that show how much total tax-exempt interest was reported and also how that tax-exempt interest was distributed among various taxpayers classified by their adjusted gross incomes.[255] That information, however, does not reveal how much tax revenue the United States did not receive because state and local bond interest was not taxed. The tax receipts lost from each individual who has reported tax-exempt interest depend upon the unique income tax bracket of that individual. In addition, the current tax-exempt interest category includes tax-exempt interest other than state and local bond interest. The real fiscal impact caused by the tax-exempt status of state and local bond interest is not clearly known.

Accountability Using the FAST Plan

A somewhat more complex, but far more accountable, way exists to provide the tax subsidies that now occur through treating state and local bond interest as tax-exempt. First, include the income in the definition of gross income, but then provide a tax credit based on the amount of that specific income.

For example, the total amount of this interest would be included in an individual's gross income, but a nonrefundable tax credit would be allowed in the amount of the standard income tax rate times the total amount of this interest. This approach would clearly reveal the impact of this tax subsidy on total federal individual income tax receipts. This approach also would permit the use of simple mechanisms for limiting the amount of this tax subsidy allowed to each individual if that becomes a policy decision by Congress (see chapter 24 on using only tax credits for subsidies).

On to Taxable Income

We have come to the end of our journey covering potential reforms affecting the most important kinds of income that are now subject to the individual income tax, as well as current tax-exempt items. We now turn to potential reforms relating to the determination of taxable individual income.

Chapter 18 Proposal
Tax-Exempt Income

Retain

- Retain most current statutory exclusions from gross income.

Reform

- Revisit some current exclusions from gross income, such as interest from state and local bonds, primarily to determine whether the tax subsidy created by the exclusion should remain, and if so, recast the subsidy as a nonrefundable tax credit.

Chapter 19

———◆·◆·◆———

Evaluating Current Reductions from Income

Armed with knowledge about the kinds of income that are (or should be) subject to the individual income tax, we are now ready to critique how taxable income is determined through the use of multiple reductions from income.

In this chapter, we first take a broad view of the ways that current tax law uses reductions to determine taxable income. We then will identify structural problems with those ways as compared to our fairness, accountability, and simplicity criteria. We also will examine one way that Congress has attempted to increase fairness for some reductions. Finally, we will categorize current reductions from income as a logical guide to the more detailed reevaluations of current reductions that occur in the following four chapters.

Determining Taxable Income

As initially described in chapter 9, once an individual's total income is determined by adding all categories of reportable income (the total being called "gross income"), current tax law allows many potential subtractions from that total to calculate taxable income. Tax law and tax forms group these **reductions from income** in different ways that impact differently the calculation of taxable income.

The first group of reductions from income is positioned **above the line** and is used to reduce an individual's gross income to what is called the **adjusted gross income**.[256] The IRS calls these reductions **statutory adjustments**.[257] All other reductions from income are positioned **below the line**. This term simply means that the entries on the individual tax forms for these reductions all occur below the line where the adjusted gross income figure appears.

A second group of reductions from income is labeled "deductions." Within this group, individuals have a choice between using a **standard deduction** or **itemized deductions**. The standard deduction is a specific dollar amount for the tax year that applies to each individual filing category, with a few possible adjustments for special circumstances. In contrast, itemized deductions are unique to each individual taxpayer. Many different kinds of deductions are allowed within the itemized deductions category. Current law allows itemized deductions in place of but not in addition to the standard deduction. Tax law in 2009 required the total dollar amount of itemized deductions to be diminished for individuals with large incomes. Because this specific group of reductions is labeled "deductions," I will not use that term here except when referring to that specific group.

A third group of reductions from income is labeled **exemptions**. These reductions are specific dollar amounts for each individual filing a tax return and for children and others who are dependent upon those individuals. Tax law in 2009 also required the total dollar amount of exemptions to be diminished for individuals with large incomes.

Subtracting all of these allowed reductions from income gives the taxable income against which to apply the current graduated individual income tax rates.

Structural Problems with Current Reductions from Income

Congress has used reductions from income extensively to promote a large variety of politically determined policies. Congress appears to have arbitrarily positioned some of these reductions above or below the line for adjusted gross income. As we shall see, that positioning can affect the amount of tax owed. In addition, expanding the use of reductions from income to promote policies can have negative ripple effects on state governments.

Problems Inherent with Many Current Reductions

Because Congress has used reductions from income so extensively, many reductions are available only to select groups of people. This selectivity fails the fairness criterion. In addition, by trying to be precise in the way that some reductions are allowed, Congress has used complex formulas to calculate those reductions. These formulas fail the simplicity criterion. The next four chapters provide specific examples of these failures.

The biggest problem inherent with most reductions from income, however, arises from a mathematical feature common to all reductions under current law. Because income tax rates are graduated, the same dollar amount of a specific type of reduction can affect the total tax liability of different taxpayers differently. That is, an individual whose marginal taxable income is in a higher bracket (e.g., 28 percent) will have income taxes reduced *more* by a given dollar amount of an allowed reduction than an individual whose taxable income is in a lower bracket (e.g., 15 percent). The tax revenue lost because of that specific reduction thus depends upon circumstances that are unique to each taxpayer. This fact greatly complicates any effort to figure out how much each existing or proposed type of reduction from income collectively diminishes or will diminish total federal tax receipts. Accountability suffers. The FAST Plan's standard-rate income tax would alleviate this mathematical problem, but if adopted without other changes, would still require calculations to determine the effects on tax receipts of each type of reduction from income.

Problems Inherent with Above-the-Line Reductions

Unfortunately, some current reductions from income share a second mathematical problem in terms of tax accountability. This problem arises from the positioning of different reductions in the determination of taxable income.

The adjusted gross income figure is not just a handy midpoint among all of the allowed reductions from income. Instead, this figure is used in a variety of calculations that have real impacts on the ultimate amount of an individual's taxable income. Thus, where an income reduction is designated to occur in the determination of taxable income makes a practical difference for an individual's tax liability and ultimately to total tax receipts.

In one type of calculation, adjusted gross income is used to trigger thresholds for allowing some itemized deductions. An example is medical expenses. Under 2009 law, only those medical expenses that were greater than 7.5 percent of adjusted gross income were allowed as an itemized deduction from income (see chapter 21).

In another type of calculation, adjusted gross income is used both to trigger and to determine adjustments to otherwise allowed reductions from income. An example is the way that exemptions have been adjusted for individuals with large incomes. As stated earlier in this chapter, under 2009 law, the dollar amount of each allowed exemption was adjusted downward according to a formula based on adjusted gross income when an individual's adjusted gross income exceeded a certain amount.

Because of these calculations, any reduction from income that is allowed above the line to determine adjusted gross income can have a multiplying effect on other reductions used to determine taxable income. Discerning the effects on tax receipts caused by each of these reductions is thus hopelessly complex. Although a consistent policy rationale may originally have dictated when a reduction should occur "above the line" in determining adjusted gross income, the current group of reductions above the line fits no consistent rationale and needs to be reexamined and changed.

Ripple Effects of Reductions on Many State Governments

Many states use an income tax as one way to raise money for their governmental services. Among these states, some states use federal taxable income as the base on which the state income tax is applied, with only a few adjustments (e.g., Colorado). This approach greatly simplifies state income tax forms and the task of paying state income taxes.

This simplification, however, comes at a price. The price is greater uncertainty in the amount of revenue that can be raised by the state income tax each year because changes in allowed federal reductions from income will directly affect that revenue.

Historically, federal income reductions in the form of the standard deduction and exemption have been predictable because these have changed only to reflect inflation adjustments. Other reductions, however, have been less predictable, and in recent years have expanded. For example, under the broad tax decreases adopted by Congress in 2001, the previous ratcheting-down of itemized deductions for wealthy taxpayers ended for 2010.[258] This change increased the total amount of itemized deductions, which in turn diminished overall federal taxable income. This change caused an automatic reduction in state income tax receipts in states that base their income tax on federal taxable income. For these states, all federal tax subsidies that are adopted in the form of reductions from income rather than tax credits will reduce federal taxable income and thus state income tax receipts.

Congress's Attempts at Reductions Fairness

More than two decades ago, Congress formally addressed one aspect of unfairness caused by its extensive use of reductions from income to promote a variety of policies. Congress decided that individuals with large incomes in higher tax brackets really did not need some reductions, especially when those reductions reduced their taxes much more than the same reductions reduced the taxes of individuals with smaller incomes. Here is how Congress implemented that decision.

In 1990, Congress decided to limit the availability of itemized deductions to taxpayers who have large incomes. Congress adopted a formula that diminished otherwise allowable itemized deductions by a percentage of the taxpayer's adjusted gross income that is greater than a specified amount. The end result, however, could not be less than 20 percent of the otherwise allowable deductions.[259]

In the same year, Congress used a similar approach to limit the allowable dependents' exemptions for taxpayers who have large incomes. This formula also diminished the amounts of these exemptions by a percentage of the taxpayer's adjusted gross income that is greater than a specified amount. Unlike the 20 percent floor to which itemized deductions could be diminished, allowed exemptions could reach zero if the taxpayer's adjusted gross income was large enough.[260]

Both of these limitations were backhanded ways to increase the federal taxes on taxpayers with large incomes without increasing the tax rates applicable to those incomes. Both of these limitations also added complexity to the calculation of federal taxes, not only for people with large incomes, but also for people with smaller incomes just to see whether or not they would be subject to the limitations.

In the 2001 Tax Act, Congress decided that the overall limitations on itemized deductions and exemptions should be phased out and then ended for tax years that began after December 31, 2009.[261] This decision simplified the calculation of federal taxes beginning in 2010. This change in the law would have expired automatically beginning in 2011, but Congress extended this change through 2012 as part of the December 2010 tax compromise.[262] The 2012 fiscal cliff tax compromise reintroduced phased-in limitations on the amounts of itemized deductions or exemptions available to taxpayers with large incomes.[263]

The ebb and flow of Congressional attitudes about limiting or not limiting overall reductions from income shows that the idea of limits has to be dealt with in any major federal tax reform.

Should Itemized Deductions as a Whole Be Limited?

An early thesis suggested in chapter 10 was that the historic use of graduated tax rates has led to many current reductions from income that are used to determine taxable income. That is, people in higher rate brackets chafe at the perceived unfairness of higher *rates*, and thus lobby for and sometimes get reductions from income that decrease the effective total tax rates on their incomes. Many of these reductions are in the form of itemized deductions. Many of these itemized deductions are tax subsidies that in practice are more available to people with large incomes than small incomes.

Under the FAST Plan's proposed standard-rate income tax on all kinds of income, these reductions will have to be reassessed because their retention would give many individuals with larger incomes effective tax rates that are *lower* than the rates of individuals with smaller incomes. Greatly limiting reductions from income overall will avoid this unfairness. Through this approach, no tack-on limits on reductions from income will be necessary because the few remaining reductions from income will not be tax subsidies that should be limited.

Should Exemptions Be Limited?

Any phase-out rule for exemptions also complicates the calculation of taxable income. Simplicity alone favors eliminating any phase-out approach. The policy importance of exemptions for all individuals is discussed in chapter 21, which addresses reductions from income for payments necessary for a healthy life.

Categorizing Reductions from Income

Three important questions should be answered regarding each current reduction from income:

(1) Should we retain the incentive, subsidy, or other policy that supports the current reduction?

(2) If retained, should the current reduction remain as a reduction, or should we convert it to a tax credit?

(3) If remaining as a reduction, should the reduction occur above the line in the determination of adjusted gross income?

Current reductions from income can be assigned to six broad categories that will help in answering those three questions:

(1) *Business reductions used to determine individual business income*

These reductions are the familiar trade and business expenses that are subtracted from business gross income to determine personal business income (see chapter 13) and from other individual business activities that are taxable.

(2) *Reductions for business-related activities*

Reductions for business-related activities do not have to be part of a personal business. These reductions are nearly always tax subsidies.

(3) *Income transfers that ultimately will be taxable*

These are money transfers that only postpone income tax liability (e.g., payments to a qualified retirement plan) and transfers that are taxable to another person (e.g., alimony payments).

(4) *Payments necessary for a healthy life*

This category represents a broad policy that encompasses some long-standing current reductions (e.g., the personal exemption).

(5) *Elective payments*

This category includes both payments that benefit oneself (e.g., interest on a home mortgage) and payments that benefit others (e.g., cash donation to a charity).

(6) *Nonelective payments*

This category includes well-known reductions for payments of taxes (e.g., state income tax) and presumed payments for uncompensated losses (e.g., replacing an uninsured home destroyed by a tornado).

These categories and subcategories do not correspond directly to the way in which current tax-reporting forms are organized. Indeed, some categories include well-known line items that currently occur both above and below the line used in determining adjusted gross income.

The next four chapters establish principles that lead to answers to the three questions posed above for each currently allowed reduction from income. Those principles are somewhat different for each of the six categories numbered above. Under current law, reductions in categories (1), (2), and (3) mostly occur above the line in determining adjusted gross income. They will be examined in the next chapter, which will establish principles for when a reduction should be placed above the line. Reductions in categories (4), (5), and (6) are sufficiently unique to require separate chapters.

The detailed examinations that follow conclude that only a few reductions should be allowed when a standard-rate income tax is adopted. If the policies behind other current reductions remain viable, those policies can be promoted more accountably and simply through tax credits rather than reductions from income.

Chapter 19 Proposal
Evaluating Current Reductions from Income

Reform
- If a standard-rate income tax is adopted, eliminate permanently all rules that diminish the availability of itemized deductions or exemptions based on the amount of an individual's income.

Chapter 20

————————— ◆•◆•◆ —————————

Appropriate Reductions Above the Line

As described in the previous chapter, current reductions from income are positioned either "above the line" in determining adjusted gross income or "below the line" when calculating taxable income. An interim step such as "adjusted gross income" can have value so long as sensible principles govern which reductions lie above the line. Here we will describe those principles and then use them to identify reductions from income that should occur above the line.

Limiting the Types of Reductions Placed Above the Line

So that the effects of tax subsidies are not multiplied, two principles should govern which reductions are placed above the line to determine adjusted gross income.

The first principle is that the reduction is a means of defining the income from a business activity that is subject to tax. This is a concession to the odd way that the Internal Revenue Code makes the net profit of an individual's business activity the taxable income from that activity.

The second principle is that the reduction is for an income transfer where the transferred income ultimately will be subject to the federal individual income tax, whether by the taxpayer or someone else. This is money that is not available to the taxpayer in the year that the transfer is made.

A reduction that fits either principle should be placed above the line when calculating adjusted gross income. Other reductions should be moved below the line, or the reduction should be changed to a tax credit, assuming that the tax subsidy represented by the reduction is retained at all in a general revision of federal taxes.

Using these principles, let's examine three categories of reductions from income that are currently placed above the line in determining adjusted gross income.

Business Reductions for Determining Individual Business Income

Business reductions used to determine individual business income match the first principle for placing reductions above the line.

As described in chapter 13 on personal business income, the interplay of three sections of the Internal Revenue Code makes the net profit from a business activity the taxable income of a self-employed individual (reported on Schedule C of Form 1040).[264] The same code approach is used to make net income from rental real estate the taxable income from that business (reported on Schedule E of Form 1040). One of the three code sections used in determining net profit allows ordinary and necessary trade and business expenses as a reduction to gross income in the determination of net profit. Because business net profit and net income are reported as income on Form 1040 above the line, ordinary and necessary business expenses are effectively used as a reduction from income to determine adjusted gross income.

Perhaps the code should be rearranged to fit the ways that Schedules C and E determine net profit from all individual business activities. Whether or not this is done, these kinds of business reductions for individuals should remain in determining individual business income that is reported as income subject to the federal income tax.

A unique type of personal business-related expense that is currently allowed as a reduction from income above the line is one-half the payment of Social Security and Medicare taxes by a self-employed individual. Under the FAST Plan, this reduction will be eliminated for the reasons expressed in chapter 11 on solving the Social Security and Medicare taxes dilemma.

Reductions for Business-Related Activities

Other business-related activities also are currently available as reductions from individual income above the line. I use the term "activities" because these other reductions encompass both payments by the taxpayer and other subsidies tied to particular kinds of income. Reductions for these activities are tax subsidies that are available to any person, not just self-employed individuals. Examples will highlight the broad variety of these reductions.

Examples of business-related payments that can be reductions are certain educator expenses,[265] certain business expenses of select groups of people such as performing artists,[266] and job-related moving expenses.[267] These particular reductions also occur above the line in determining adjusted gross income. This placement of these tax subsidies can magnify their effect on taxable income.

An allowed reduction from income that is a subsidy for an activity rather than a payment by the taxpayer is the reduction for domestic production activities.[268] This reduction is calculated as a percentage of the taxpayer's income from qualified domestic production activities. This tax subsidy also now occurs above the line in determining adjusted gross income.

Again, the question here is not whether these tax subsidies are appropriate, but whether the way in which they are allowed is appropriate. My answer is no. They fit neither principle for placement above the line.

All tax subsidies for business-related activities should be recast as tax credits so that their effects on tax receipts can clearly be known. The current subsidies for business-related activities that occur as reductions from income above the line are particularly problematic because they can have magnified income tax consequences.

Income Transfers That Ultimately Will Be Taxable

Income transfers where the transferred income ultimately will be taxable fit precisely the second principle presented above for reductions above the line.

Current tax law recognizes two varieties of these kinds of transfers: (1) money transfers that only postpone income tax liability and (2) money transfers that are taxable to another person.

Money Transfers That Only Postpone Income Tax Liability

Money transfers that only postpone income tax liability are nearly always transfers to some form of retirement plan.

Current tax law allows reductions from an individual's income for payments to a variety of personal retirement plans.[269] Individual retirement accounts (IRAs) may be the most familiar retirement plans because they are available to any individual who has earned income.[270] Some other retirement plans are available specifically to self-employed individuals, which includes partners in a business.[271] Current law limits the amount of payments to these kinds of plans that can be used as reductions from income. These limits are based on the amount of an individual's income. All of these payments are thus transfers of a portion of an individual's gross income received during the tax year to an account where the money is not generally available to the individual until some later year.

Many employees also exclude from their income payments to their retirement plans that are not IRAs, but the mechanism is not a reduction from the employee's income. Instead, payments by an employee or employer to a qualified retirement plan established by the employer are classified as deferred compensation and are excluded from the definition of wages.[272] Thus, the money used for these payments is not considered to be income in the first place.

Qualified retirement plans have several common features. Transactions within the plan, such as selling shares of stock for a gain, are not taxable events when they occur.[273] Money withdrawn from a retirement plan is ordinary income subject to normal taxation in the year of withdrawal[274] in the proportion that original payments into the plan were taken as reductions from taxable income or were deferred compensation.[275] Stringent rules exist that discourage an individual from prematurely withdrawing funds from a retirement plan, such as severe tax penalties on those withdrawn funds. Conversely, stringent rules also exist that require funds in a retirement plan to be withdrawn over time after an individual reaches a certain age.[276]

So long as personal retirement plans remain public policy, treating payments to those plans as reductions from income or as deferred income makes good sense because the money ultimately will be subject to the federal income tax. Where allowed as reductions from income, these ultimately taxable payments logically should be subtracted from gross income in the determination of adjusted gross income.

Money Transfers That Are Taxable to Another Person

Upon divorce, a potential legal outcome is for one ex-spouse to be required to pay alimony or maintenance to the other ex-spouse. In effect, this is legally required sharing of one ex-spouse's income much like what would have occurred if the two people had remained married. One or the other ex-spouse should be required to pay taxes on that income, but not both or the similarity to married people breaks down. Current tax law reflects that logic.

Historically, alimony and maintenance have been treated as taxable income to their recipients.[277] Congress probably adopted this approach because the recipient of alimony typically has little other taxable income and so might be in a lower tax bracket than the paying ex-spouse. Thus, more after-tax money would be available for the living expenses that alimony is designed to cover.

Alimony and maintenance payments historically also have been reductions from the income of the paying ex-spouse.[278] This approach makes sense because this money is no longer available to the paying ex-spouse.

Alimony and maintenance are the prime and maybe only example of reductions from income that are money transfers that are taxable to another person. Like payments to a retirement plan, alimony payments ultimately are subject to the federal income tax. Thus, these reductions logically should be subtracted from gross income in the determination of adjusted gross income.

Above-the-Line Recap

Using our two principles for allowing reductions above the line, we find that only two kinds of current reductions fit those principles: business reductions for determining individual business income, and income transfers that ultimately will be taxable. We find also that current reductions above the line for other business-related activities do not fit those principles. We will now consider the myriad of other current reductions from income that do not fit those principles.

Chapter 20 Proposal
Appropriate Reductions Above the Line

Retain

- Treat payments of ordinary and necessary trade and business expenses for individual businesses (such as a self-employed business or rentals from property) as reductions from income used to determine business income that is subject to the individual income tax.
- Treat money transfers that only postpone income tax liability (such as payments to qualified retirement plans up to defined limits) as reductions from gross income to determine adjusted gross income.
- Treat money transfers that are taxable to another person (such as alimony and maintenance payments) as reductions from gross income to determine adjusted gross income.

Reform

- Recast all other business-related reductions from income as nonrefundable tax credits so long as the tax subsidies represented by those reductions remain appropriate.
- Allow no other reductions from gross income to determine adjusted gross income.

Chapter 21

Reductions for Payments Necessary for a Healthy Life

As a matter of human dignity, the United States should not tax that portion of a person's income that is necessary for a healthy life. The most basic human survival needs are water, food, clothing, and shelter. In our modern era, medical care has become a fifth basic human survival need, and certainly a fifth need for a healthy life. Reductions from income are potentially the simplest way not to tax income that is necessary for a healthy life.

Two current reductions from income support this purpose. These are exemptions and the standard deduction. In contrast, current federal tax law regarding payments for medical care creates greatly different results for people having similar medical expenses and similar incomes. Let's take a closer look at each of these three types of reductions from income. Then we will figure out changes that meet our fairness, accountability, and simplicity criteria.

Exemptions

As introduced in chapter 9, **exemptions** are specific dollar amounts allowed as reductions from income for an individual and the individual's spouse, children, and others who are dependent upon the individual.

Under 2009 tax law, the basic exemption for each person was $3,650.[279] This is an inflation-adjusted amount calculated from a base amount of $2,000 established more than two decades ago.[280]

The concept of a basic monetary exemption from taxation for each person is sound when viewed as a minimal amount of money necessary for a person's survival needs of water, food, clothing, and shelter.

In 2009, exemptions were phased out as reductions from income for individuals whose incomes exceed designated amounts.[281] For those individuals, Congress decided that part or all of the exemption was not needed because those individuals had incomes that were more than adequate to pay for the survival requirements represented by the exemption. As noted previously, phase-outs are just a backhanded way to increase taxes on individuals with larger incomes. They also complicate the calculation of taxable income. Phase-out rules are also illogical in the sense that everyone has the basic survival requirements represented by the exemption. Thus, exemptions should remain as reductions even if an individual otherwise has a large income. All phase-outs of exemptions should be eliminated under my simplicity goal.

Standard Deduction

The standard deduction is a specific dollar amount allowed as a reduction from income for each individual filing category.

Under 2009 tax law, the basic standard deduction was $5,700 per taxpayer ($8,350 for a head of household).[282] Some add-ons also existed for certain situations. People over the age of sixty-five, for example, were entitled to an increased standard deduction,[283] perhaps in recognition that the elderly are more likely to have larger medical expenses, such as long-term prescription drugs. As with exemptions, the 2009 basic standard deduction of $5,700 is an inflation-adjusted amount calculated from a base amount established more than two decades ago. Whatever the amount, the standard deduction is a simple way not to tax some income that can be used for a variety of payments that are part of normal living in the United States.

The standard deduction can be viewed as augmenting the exemption in order to provide additional money for water, food, clothing, and shelter. However, the current availability of itemized deductions in place of the standard deduction shows that the standard deduction has broader purposes by permitting relatively small reductions in income that parallel the variety of itemized deductions now available. These itemized deductions include not only reductions for a portion of medical payments, but also some state and local taxes, interest on home mortgages, gifts to charitable and religious organizations, and unreimbursed losses from casualty and theft.

Tax Treatment of Medical Expenses

The availability and cost of medical care have become major issues for many Americans. In 2010, new medical insurance legislation arose out of the debate that began in 2009 on what to do about both issues.[284] Whether this legislation is retained, modified, or rescinded, many people or their employers will still have to pay for medical insurance, medical procedures, dental work, prescription medicine, and many other medically related services or products if they can afford to do so. Many provisions of the 2010 legislation are not effective until the year 2014, so an appropriate benchmark for examining the tax-law treatment of medical expenses is the year 2009. "Current law" in the following discussion is the 2009 tax law.

Current Law

Current federal income tax law relating to medical expenses can create very different tax consequences for people whose medical expenses are exactly the same in a year. As such, current law flunks the fairness test. Current law also flunks the simplicity test because complex interrelations among medically related special tax provisions defy short, cogent explanation. Bear with me as I try to illustrate the current mess with a group of six examples:

(1) Employees of an employer that provides full medical insurance or medical services to its employees as a benefit of employment receive that benefit tax-free even though the benefit is provided in lieu of larger wages, which would be subject to income, Social Security, and Medicare taxes.[285]

(2) Employees of an employer that provides no medical insurance or medical services to its employees have to pay for medical insurance and medical care with after-tax money except to the extent that (a) the payments qualify for itemized deductions from income[286] or (b) the employee is qualified to and does adopt an allowed medical savings account and the payments for medical services are made from that account (Health Savings Account or pre-existing Archer Medical Savings Account).[287]

(3) Self-employed individuals have to pay for medical insurance and medical care with after-tax money except to the extent that (a) the payments qualify for reductions from income allowed for medical insurance established under a business, (b) the payments qualify for itemized deductions from income,[288] or (c) the individual is qualified to and does adopt an allowed medical savings account and the payments are made from that account (Health Savings Account or pre-existing Archer Medical Savings Account).[289]

(4) Payments for medical care, including medical insurance, can qualify as itemized deductions from income, but this is not allowed unless the standard deduction is forfeited.[290] Only payments that exceed 7.5 percent of adjusted gross income can be deducted. The deducted amount is immunized from the federal income tax, but not the Social Security or Medicare tax.

(5) If an individual is qualified to and does establish a Health Savings Account, then limited amounts of money can be deposited annually in the account and used to reduce taxable income (but not Social Security and Medicare taxable earned income).[291] That money will not be taxed so long as it is used to pay qualified medical expenses.

An individual with a Health Savings Account must also have and pay for a qualified "High Deductible Health Plan" (meaning a designated form of health insurance).[292] Payments for that health insurance plan cannot be made from the Health Savings Account and so can reduce taxable income only if otherwise allowed as an itemized medical expense.[293]

(6) Self-employed individuals who have enough profit can reduce their taxable income by their payments for medical insurance if the medical insurance plan is "established under your business."[294]

Confused? So am I. And the descriptions in these examples skirt around the many special rules applicable to most of the examples.

A Better Way

If you agree with my propositions that medical care is needed for a healthy life and that income necessary for a healthy life should not be taxed, we can unravel the fabric of special tax laws and rules regarding medical expenses. A simple goal will guide this unraveling: money paid out for medical care should not be taxed.

The model for this goal is example (1) above, where an employer provides full medical insurance or medical services to its employees as a benefit of employment, and the benefit is not income subject to tax.

How can we reform current law to similarly protect money needed for medical expenses by uninsured employees and self-employed individuals?

The answer is surprisingly simple. Allow payments for medical care to be reductions from income *in addition to* the standard deduction. This is not as favorable as having someone else pay for one's medical care, but at least income used to pay for medical care will not be taxed. Two tweaks on this approach probably would be advisable, both of which tend to avoid reductions for minor, optional medical expenses.

- First, continue the idea of a threshold for allowed income reductions, but reduce the current threshold of 7.5 percent of adjusted gross income (that's $2,250 for a modest adjusted gross income of $30,000). A percentage more like 1 percent is less discriminatory and fits better with the idea that a small portion of the standard deduction is already intended to cover some medical expenses.
- Second, maybe reexamine and tighten the definition of medical expenses that qualify for the income reduction. In terms of need for a healthy life, there is indeed a difference between chemotherapy to cure aggressive cancer and hair implants to cover natural balding (cosmetic surgery is already excluded from qualifying medical expenses).[295]

If we allow payments for medical care as reductions from income in addition to the standard deduction, what should be the future of Health Savings Accounts and Archer Medical Savings Accounts? These are trust accounts dedicated solely to the payment of qualified medical expenses into which an individual can make limited payments that are allowed as reductions from income.[296] Payments from these trusts are not taxed when made for qualified medical expenses.

Reductions from income are all that these accounts accomplish tax-wise now, so the current need for these accounts diminishes or even disappears when we allow payments for medical care as reductions in addition to the standard deduction. To be sure, these accounts do allow an individual to accumulate some tax-free money for the "rainy day" medical expense. But under the FAST Plan approach, an individual can also accumulate money for the rainy day medical expense secure in the knowledge that if the money has to be paid out, an equal amount of income in that year will be tax-free. If the FAST Plan proposals are adopted, rather than deciding the fate of these accounts at that juncture, both Health Savings Accounts and Archer Medical Savings Accounts can be continued for a while to see whether their usage wanes over time.

The Only Below-the-Line Reductions

We began this chapter with a strong policy statement: the United States should not tax that portion of a person's income that is necessary for a healthy life. The reductions from income described in this chapter fit that policy.

No similar broad policy applies to the other reductions from income allowed in current law. Many of those reductions are classic tax subsidies. If the subsidy survives tax reform, then we should implement it with a nonrefundable tax credit, not a reduction from income. The next two chapters show why this is so for both elective and nonelective payments by an individual.

Chapter 21 Proposal
Reductions for Payments Necessary for a Healthy Life

Retain
- Regardless of the amount of an individual's income, allow the full standard deduction to cover some basic survival needs and also minimal payments that are part of normal living in the United States.

Reform
- Regardless of the amount of an individual's income, allow full exemptions as reductions from income to cover basic survival needs (a reform, but like 2010–2012 and some previous tax law).
- Allow reductions from income in addition to the standard deduction for payments for qualified medical expenses that exceed 1 percent of an individual's adjusted gross income.
- Allow no other reductions from income after adjusted gross income has been determined.

Chapter 22

---◆·◆·◆---

Reductions for Elective Payments

Current federal tax law provides a variety of reductions from income for elective payments by an individual. For this purpose, payments are elective when they are not required by law, by survival or health needs, or by events beyond an individual's control. Two very different kinds of elective payments historically have been recognized as reductions from income. These are payments that benefit oneself and payments that benefit others (gifts to charity).

Payments That Benefit Oneself

Many commonly recognized reductions from income are payments for services or things that are for personal benefit. All of these reductions are tax subsidies to the individual claiming the reduction. Some of these currently allowed reductions occur above the line in calculating adjusted gross income, whereas other allowed reductions occur below the line and are available only if itemized deductions are chosen in place of the standard deduction.

As noted previously, I do not object to the concept of tax subsidies or to the policies behind some current tax subsidies, but I do object to the disparate ways in which they occur in the federal tax laws. This disparate treatment fails our accountability criterion (some specific reductions also fail the fairness and simplicity criteria). This disparate treatment is illustrated by the following examples, which show the arbitrary way that current law assigns as above or below the line many reductions from income for elective payments that benefit oneself. These examples are found in Form 1040 and its Schedule A for 2009 (the number is the line in the form).

Reductions from income allowed "above the line" (line item from 2009 Form 1040)
30—Penalty on early withdrawal of savings (initiated by elective early withdrawal)

33—Student loan interest deduction
34—Tuition and fees deduction

Reductions from income allowed as itemized deductions (line item from 2009 Schedule A)
10–12—Home mortgage interest and points
13—Qualified mortgage insurance premiums
14—Investment interest
21—Unreimbursed employee expenses
22—Tax preparation fees
23—Other expenses (investment, safe deposit box, etc.)

As described more fully in chapter 24, tax subsidies will be simpler and far more accountable if all tax subsidies occur as nonrefundable tax credits, not as reductions from income. Thus, all of the reductions listed above should be recast as nonrefundable tax credits if the tax subsidy continues to have merit when federal taxes are reformed as proposed in the FAST Plan. Even if retained, some of these tax subsidies should have monetary limits when judged in conjunction with a standard-rate income tax for all income. Examples showing how some existing reductions can be recast as tax credits are found in chapter 24.

Payments That Benefit Others (Gifts to Charity)

Federal tax law has long encouraged American generosity by allowing charitable contributions to be reductions from gross income in the form of an itemized deduction.[297] Like all itemized deductions, charitable contributions can be reductions from income only if the standard deduction is forfeited.

"Gifts to charity," as the IRS dubs this reduction in 2009 Schedule A, are elective payments or donations that monetarily benefit someone other than the individual taxpayer. That is, the recipient gains and the donor individual gives up all rights to and use of the donated money or goods. Although gifts to charity are a form of tax subsidy to the individual because they reduce an individual's income tax, they also are subsidies to the recipient organizations because the reductions encourage gifts at the expense of diminishing tax receipts.

Current federal tax law already provides many limits on the total amount of gifts to charity that an individual can take as an itemized deduction to income.[298] These limits vary depending upon both the type of charity and the nature of the gift (money, property, or capital gain property). These limits are expressed as different percentages of the "contribution base," which for most people is their adjusted gross income. Predictably, there are special exceptions within the general rules.

Recall also that 2009 tax law required the total dollar amount of itemized deductions to be diminished for individuals with large incomes. Gifts to charity were among those diminished deductions.[299] Under the 2001 Tax Act, these overall limitations on itemized deductions, such as gifts to charity, were eliminated for 2010.[300]

When combined with the current graduated income tax rates, the multiple existing limitations on gifts to charity make almost impossible the task of calculating the impact that the "gifts to charity" tax subsidy has on federal tax receipts. As with other tax subsidies, transforming the itemized deduction for gifts to charity to a tax credit would greatly increase its accountability and also would simplify an individual's calculation of a gift's effect on income taxes owed. Also, with the reasonable assumption that the standard deduction already includes a small portion of money for gifts to charity, fairness and simplicity will be enhanced if the tax credit applies only to gifts that exceed a modest amount, such as $200.

Chapter 22 Proposal
Reductions for Elective Payments

Reform

- Recast as nonrefundable tax credits all current reductions from income for elective payments that benefit oneself and then revisit each tax subsidy to determine if it remains appropriate.
- Recast as a nonrefundable tax credit the itemized deduction for gifts to charity, with these two additional features:
    (1) Allow the tax credit only for total gifts that exceed a modest amount, such as $200.
    (2) Recast in the form of limitations on allowed tax credits all current limitations on the amount of allowed reductions from income for gifts to charity.

Chapter 23

———◆•◆•◆———

Reductions for Nonelective Payments

In addition to elective payments and payments necessary for a healthy life, nearly all individuals make a variety of payments that are required by law or by circumstances beyond their control. Congress has regularly considered proposals concerning whether and how these kinds of payments should be allowed as reductions from income used to determine taxable income. The recent lineup of these proposals that Congress has approved includes allowing reductions for payment of some state and local taxes, for a portion of the payment of federal self-employment taxes (Social Security and Medicare taxes), and for presumed payments for uncompensated losses. All of these reductions fit our description of tax subsidies. We will consider them in sequence.

Reductions for Payment of State and Local Taxes

Taxes are a form of nonelective payment where the person who makes the payment has no direct control over its amount. Payments for state and local taxes have been eligible reductions from income in varying ways over the years, although they have been consistently classified as itemized deductions and so can be claimed only if the standard deduction is forfeited.

Which States and Local Taxes Are Favored as Reductions?

State and local taxes come in many forms. Different states use different kinds of taxes to support their governmental services. Many states use all three of the most common forms of state taxation to raise most of their revenues, namely income, property, and sales taxes (e.g., New York).[301] Some states, however, have no state income taxes, but instead rely on property, sales, and other taxes to fund their governmental services (e.g., Washington). Some states rely extensively on severance taxes on natural resources located within the state (e.g., Alaska and Wyoming).

Congress has viewed this variety of state and local taxes in different ways over the years in terms of which kinds of taxes should qualify for reductions from income.

For example, sales taxes at one time were fully deductible when supported by receipts submitted with a tax form (a paper mess), then were not deductible at all, and in 2009 were deductible if supported by receipts or according to a formula, but not if state or local income taxes were claimed as a deduction.[302] Payments for state real property taxes are now and have consistently been allowed as itemized deductions to income. On the other hand, payment of some common state taxes, such as those on gasoline, have not been allowed as deductions.[303]

The payment of *all* state and local taxes is nonelective and reduces the amount of an individual's income that is available for other purposes. So why has Congress treated different state and local taxes in such disparate ways?

An answer to this question lies in the different relative amounts that states have chosen to spend on governmental operations and services and in the different ways that states have chosen or been able to raise revenues to pay for those operations and services.

Competing Schools of Thought

Three different schools of thought can illustrate core issues that create divided opinions on what state and local tax payments, if any, should be allowed as itemized deductions from an individual's income.

The "no deductions" school

One school of thought asserts that *no* state and local tax payments should be deductions because the deductions are unfair to citizens of states that choose to have relatively small state and local governments and therefore lower state and local taxes.

The unfairness argument goes this way. Relative to their incomes, the citizens of states with low state and local taxes will have smaller federal itemized deductions for their payment of these taxes than will citizens of states that have higher state and local taxes. This might not appear to matter because these citizens will also have more money in hand relative to their incomes. However, they will also have to pay a portion of that extra money as federal income taxes. They will end up paying more federal income taxes on the same amount of gross income than will citizens of states with higher state and local taxes.

One counterargument to this "unfairness" argument rests on the ability of Americans to move from state to state freely. People in states that have relatively higher state and local taxes claim that they provide correspondingly more services, especially to the needy. They then argue that they have extra governmental expenses in part because people migrate to their state from states that have fewer governmental services. So they not only provide more services per person, but they also have an increasing number of people to serve because of this migration. In short, these states claim their higher state taxes are covering the unwillingness of those other states to provide needed services. Lower federal income taxes resulting from deducting payments of state taxes helps them perform those needed services. This whole argument is complicated further by some federally mandated (but not fully funded) benefits to those migrants, such as Medicaid.

The "unfair choices" school

A second school of thought about the deductibility of state and local tax payments criticizes Congress's choices about which categories of state and local taxes are eligible as itemized deductions. This school of thought claims that those choices are unfair to citizens of states whose citizens pay fewer or none of those particular categories of taxes. Unfairness occurs because citizens of these states will have smaller deductions for state and local taxes relative to their incomes than will citizens of states that have the types of state and local taxes that are eligible as itemized deductions.

One counterargument to this unfairness claim derives from the different ways that states are able to fund these governmental services. For example, some states have small or no deductible state income taxes because they are lucky to have abundant natural resources like coal, oil, natural gas, and minerals, from which they receive significant revenues via state severance taxes or shared federal lease receipts. These alternative revenues can allow a state to have these low taxes while still providing a relatively large level of governmental services. For those states, one can argue that these natural resources are *national* assets that these states happen to be able to tap for revenues. These states cannot therefore legitimately complain that their citizens are disadvantaged by having relatively small state and local taxes that qualify for income deductions in the calculation of federal taxable income.

The "all qualify" school

A third school of thought about the deductibility of state and local tax payments asserts that *all* state and local taxes paid by an individual should qualify as deductions no matter what kind of tax it is. This school adopts the simple approach that the payment of all state and local taxes is nonelective and reduces the amount of an individual's income that is available for other purposes. Therefore, the United States should not tax that money.

The FAST Plan Solution

These three different schools of thought probably account for much of the ebb and flow in Congress about what categories of state and local taxes should qualify for income deductions in determining federal taxable income. This ebb and flow has occurred for many years and likely will continue if our current income tax structure remains.

As a consequence of this ebb and flow, many state and local taxes are not currently allowed as deductions, so denying the eligibility of some taxes while recognizing the eligibility of other taxes has built-in disparities that fail our fairness criterion. In addition, many disparities are hard to rationalize and hard for the public to understand and accept. Citizens can legitimately ask why state taxes on gasoline or telephone services are not eligible as deductions when real estate taxes are. Similarly, why are state income taxes not eligible as deductions if an individual chooses to deduct state sales taxes even though the individual pays both in his or her state? Simply saying that these quirks are the result of compromise or power politics provides little comfort to the average citizen and can lead to disrespect for the whole tax-determination process.

The simplest approach, of course, is not to allow *any* state and local tax payments as income deductions. In support of this approach, state and local taxes can be viewed simply as an ordinary cost of living in a state and enjoying the advantages of its governmental services. The standard deduction against income already allows an income reduction for some ordinary living expenses, which include payment of state and local taxes. Amounts beyond that level are tax subsidies that historically have been available primarily to individuals with larger incomes who also were paying higher marginal federal income tax rates.

Under the FAST Plan's standard-rate income tax, the justification for this tax subsidy declines. Indeed, allowing deductions or tax credits for payment of state and local taxes would end up providing a greater tax subsidy to those individuals with larger incomes, who need it less. For these reasons, no income deductions or tax credits should be allowed for the payment of state and local taxes beyond those already inherent in the standard deduction.

Reductions for Payment of Federal Self-Employment Taxes

As noted in chapter 11 on solving the Social Security and Medicare taxes dilemma, current law allows a reduction from income for one-half the federal self-employment taxes paid by self-employed individuals (Social Security and Medicare taxes).[304] This reduction occurs above the line in the calculation of adjusted gross income. For the reasons described in chapter 11, this reduction should be eliminated provided that payments of Social Security and Medicare taxes are allowed as credits against an income tax determined from a standard rate.

Reductions for Uncompensated Losses

Current tax law allows income reductions in the form of itemized deductions for certain uncompensated losses incurred by an individual taxpayer. Although the 2009 version of Schedule A of Form 1040 (Itemized Deductions) refers to eligible losses as "Casualty and Theft Losses," the statute that allows these deductions sweeps in a variety of other losses as eligible income deductions.[305] For example, the statute allows income deductions for losses incurred in a trade or business, as well as nonbusiness losses incurred in any transaction entered into for profit.[306] Special rules exist for losses from the sale or exchange of capital assets.[307] The statute also identifies a unique category of eligible losses in the form of lost deposits in a qualified financial institution that becomes bankrupt or insolvent.[308]

Uniqueness of the Uncompensated Losses Deduction

A deduction for losses is a unique tax subsidy in at least two respects.

First, other tax subsidies reimburse all or part of a payment made by an individual for some kind of expense. To be sure, losses are not voluntary, and losses in the form of lost bank deposits are cash diminutions analogous to the payment of an expense. But a casualty or theft loss of an item is not analogous to payment of an expense unless an individual chooses to replace the destroyed or stolen item. In this respect, this tax subsidy either assumes that an individual will always want to replace the lost item or that everyone is entitled to some recompense for a lost item, even if the individual chooses not to replace the item.

Second, the tax subsidy for losses favors those who did not carry insurance that would have covered the loss (whether caused by choice, lack of funds, or unavailability of insurance). Note that losses are eligible to be income reductions only if they are "not compensated for by insurance or otherwise."[309] Those people who did have insurance that covered their losses receive no analogous tax subsidy because premiums for casualty insurance are not recognized income reductions. In this respect, application of the tax subsidy for losses can sometimes be unfair.

The Uncompensated Losses Deduction in Practice

Like some other income reductions, the itemized deduction for casualty and theft losses (but not for some of the other eligible losses) is available only if the losses are not trivial. The general approach used here is to allow deductions only where the loss arising from each casualty or theft exceeds $100 and where the aggregate amount of net losses in the year exceeds 10 percent of the taxpayer's adjusted gross income.[310] Exceptions to the 10 percent rule apply to casualty and theft losses occurring in federally designated disaster areas.

The FAST Plan Approach

As with some other income reductions, I do not challenge here the desirability of some tax subsidy relating to losses sustained by an individual. However, the present itemized deduction from income should be recast in the form of a tax credit to enhance accountability of the subsidy. Limits similar to those now existing can be incorporated in this recasting.

The recasting process should also open up a discussion about possible changes in the variety of items now eligible for this tax subsidy so that unfair and overly complex subsidies are changed or removed.

Nonelective Payments Recap

In this chapter, we have examined three kinds of nonelective payments that current tax law allows as reductions from income—payment of state and local taxes, payment of self-employment taxes, and presumed payment for uncompensated losses. Only the reduction for uncompensated losses survives as a tax subsidy for inclusion in the FAST Plan, and even then only if it is recast as a tax credit. As introduced at the end of chapter 19 and proposed in the preceding several chapters, tax credits are better vehicles than reductions from income for providing many subsidies. It's time now to develop that idea as a firm part of the FAST Plan.

Chapter 23 Proposal
Reductions for Nonelective Payments

Reform

- Allow no reductions from income and allow no tax credits for payments of state and local taxes.
- If Social Security and Medicare tax payments are allowed as nonrefundable credits against an individual's income tax, then also eliminate the current reduction from income allowed for one-half the self-employment tax (Social Security and Medicare taxes) paid by self-employed individuals.
- Recast as a nonrefundable tax credit the current itemized deduction for uncompensated losses and then revisit this tax subsidy to determine if it remains appropriate.

Chapter 24

———— •◆•◆• ————

Expanded Role of Tax Credits for Subsidies

The US government provides subsidies to individuals for many purposes. These range from helping people in dire financial straits to encouraging people to spend their money in particular ways to achieve goals that the political process has deemed worthy. Providing subsidies through the individual income tax system is probably far more efficient than would be a system of grants that requires applications, approvals, and deliveries of money through multiple agencies. Whether or not this is correct, Congress has regularly used and probably will continue to use the individual income tax system to provide subsidies.

The question before us now is how to provide subsidies in the individual income tax system that will nevertheless meet our fairness, accountability, and simplicity criteria. When those criteria are met, we can easily discern whether each subsidy remains viable over time.

Problems with Current Tax and Direct Subsidies

Let's begin an answer to this question by recapping what we have covered already about subsidies in the current individual income tax system.

Chapter 6 describes what constitutes a tax or direct subsidy. That chapter also gives examples of current tax and direct subsidies that illustrate the fact that current subsidies occur in so many different ways that fairness, accountability, and simplicity are lost for many subsidies.

Chapter 19 describes a structural lack of accountability with all tax subsidies in the form of reductions because reductions have a different effect on federal tax receipts depending upon the individual's marginal income tax rate (because of current graduated tax rates). The succeeding chapters on specific reductions from income show that many reductions are tax subsidies. Those chapters already propose that we recast as tax credits all tax subsidies that are now in the form of reductions from income that remain viable when we reform the individual income tax.

156

The FAST Plan Solution

In the FAST Plan reform, we will use only tax credits for all subsidies that Congress provides through the individual income tax system.

Our accountability criterion will be met because this approach allows both individuals and the United States to see exactly how much money is saved (individuals) or lost (United States) as the result of any particular subsidy. Our simplicity and fairness criteria will be met because the tax credit approach allows simple limits to be placed on subsides so that they are neither complex to determine nor discriminatorily generous.

Showing how our three criteria will be met requires us to look first at the way that tax credits work today in the individual income tax system and then at the practical merits of using only tax credits for subsidies.

The Way Tax Credits Work Today

Current federal law provides two basic types of individual income tax credits:

- The first type of credit is strictly a credit against income tax that otherwise would be due. If the credit is greater than the income tax, no income tax would be owed, but the excess credit does not generate a payment from the United States to the taxpayer. The Internal Revenue Code labels this type of credit a **nonrefundable credit**.[311] Examples are the credits allowed for adoption expenses and for elderly or disabled individuals who have small incomes.[312]
- The second type of credit is essentially a payment from the United States to the individual in the amount of the credit. With this type of tax credit, the "payment" first applies to any income tax that is due. If the payment is greater than the income tax, the United States owes the excess to the individual. The Internal Revenue Code labels this type of credit a **refundable credit**.[313]

Form 1040 has long recognized the distinction between these two types of credits by organizing nonrefundable credits in the section for "Tax and Credits" and by organizing refundable credits in the section for "Payments."

The "payments" (refundable credits) type of credits can also be divided into two groups:

- One group can best be described as an accounting credit for a taxpayer's money held by the United States. Examples are money held by the United States from taxes withheld on wages, overpayments of tax, and payments of estimated tax.[314] These credits really do represent taxpayer payments.

- A very different group of "payments" (refundable credits) consists of direct subsidies to an individual. A well-known example is the "Earned Income Credit," through which the individual receives from the United States any excess of the EIC over income taxes owed if the income taxes are less than the EIC.[315] Other examples are the recent temporary "First Time Homebuyer Credit" and the credit for 65 percent of the health insurance costs for a select group of eligible individuals.[316] All of the "payments" or "refundable credits" in this latter group should be renamed as "direct subsidies," because that is what they are.

Practical Merits of Using Only Tax Credits for All Subsidies

As described in chapter 6, a tax subsidy is a tax provision that reduces taxes owed as compared to a standard taxpayer. A direct subsidy, on the other hand, can require the United States to pay an individual money that is not otherwise held by the United States on behalf of the individual. This division should be reflected in tax-reporting forms when we use only tax credits for all subsidies. We will thus consider tax and direct subsidies separately.

Tax Credits for Tax Subsidies

At present, when a tax subsidy is provided through a tax credit, it is a nonrefundable credit. Tax subsidies that now occur in other ways, for example, reductions from income or special low tax rates, should be recast as nonrefundable tax credits because they already are nonrefundable subsidies.

Adopting a strict rule that all tax subsidies be in the form of nonrefundable credits provides at least these benefits:

- Simple and understandable limits can be placed on each tax subsidy and on the totality of tax subsidies for an individual if the political process so dictates.
- For those tax subsidies that now occur in the form of special low tax rates for some kinds of income, using tax credits instead of special tax rates allows the tax subsidy to be reduced more easily without a bogus claim of "tax increase" for what is really a decrease in a discriminatory tax advantage.
- Using only tax credits for all tax subsidies exposes these subsidies to everyone. This knowledge will permit periodic reevaluation of those subsidies by Congress and the public based on the cost of obtaining the goals that the subsidies are supposed to promote. That cost is measured by lost tax receipts.

Figure 24.1 is an example that shows how tax subsidies can be exposed and simply limited if they take the form of nonrefundable tax credits. In this example, the standard income tax rate is 29 percent, and the tax credits achieve tax subsidies for some goals that are similar to those in current tax law.

Figure 24.1. Example form for income tax credits with limits (29 percent standard rate)

Income tax credits

1.a. Qualified moving expenses . . . . _____

1.b.   Multiply line 1.a by 0.29 (29%) . . . . _____

1.c. Enter the lesser of $1,000 or the amount in line 1.b . . . . _____

2.a. Home mortgage interest on primary residence . . . . _____

2.b.   Multiply line 2.b by 0.29 (29%) . . . . _____

2.c. Enter the lesser of $3,000 or the amount in line 2.b . . . . _____

3.a. Qualified child and dependent care expenses from
        form 2441 . . . . _____

4.a. Total income tax credits (add lines 1.c , 2.c, and 3.a) . . . . _____

45. Subtract line 4.a from tax in line 44 . . . . _____

This short example uses tax subsidies that are currently available in three different ways:

(1) An individual's payment of moving expenses is currently allowed as an income reduction above the line.
(2) An individual's payment of interest on a home mortgage for a primary residence is currently allowed as an itemized deduction from income.
(3) An individual's payment of qualified child and dependent care expenses is currently allowed as a nonrefundable income tax credit.[317]

The example in figure 24.1 also illustrates different ways that these three tax subsidies can be calculated and limited.

If a political decision were made to limit the total amount of all tax subsidies to any one individual, we could easily determine the allocation of amounts to each tax subsidy. Simply multiply each line item subsidy by a calculated ratio for that taxpayer. An example ratio would be the allowed limit divided by the total amount of all tax subsidies claimed as credits.

Similarly, if a political decision were made to have a tax subsidy with a sliding scale based on income levels (adjusted gross income or otherwise), the amount could be calculated using a separate form like the current Form 2441 referenced in figure 24.1 for child and dependent care expenses. The result of this calculation would still show the impact of the subsidy on taxes owed or tax receipts lost. Of course, sliding-scale tax subsidies introduce complexity into the tax system and should be discouraged because they are inconsistent with the goal of simplicity for all federal taxes.

If Congress adopts my FAST Plan proposal that a standard-rate income tax applies to all individual income, however derived, the groups that lose special tax-rate status will try to get a tax subsidy for their particular situations. Even if Congress obliges one or more of those groups, so long as their subsidies are all recast as nonrefundable tax credits, the cost of those subsidies will be known.

Tax Credits for Direct Subsidies

A direct subsidy provided through the income tax system already normally takes the form of a credit in federal income tax returns. As noted previously, direct subsidy credits are currently labeled as "refundable" credits in the Internal Revenue Code and as "payments" on Form 1040.

For accountability, credits for direct subsidies should be separate from both nonrefundable credits for tax subsidies and refundable credits for money held by the United States on behalf of the individual (these latter credits are truly payments). The most honest way to create that separation is to label every direct subsidy as a "direct subsidy," even though for some taxpayers all of the direct-subsidy credit will be used to offset income tax otherwise owed.

Tax Credits Recap

As shown in this chapter, using nonrefundable tax credits for all tax subsidies and refundable tax credits for all direct subsidies, especially when renamed as "direct subsidies," has two practical benefits: (1) the subsidies can be simply limited, and (2) accurate, clear, and simple data on the cost of each subsidy will be available so that periodic reevaluation of each subsidy will be more likely to occur than under current law.

What, then, should be the fate of current tax credits? We address this question in the next chapter.

Chapter 24 Proposal
Expanded Role of Tax Credits for Subsidies

Reform

- Use nonrefundable income tax credits, and not reductions from income or special tax rates, as the only way to provide tax subsidies to individuals.
- Use refundable credits on individual income tax returns as the only way to provide direct subsidies to individuals in the individual income tax system, and label each such refundable credit as a direct subsidy.

Chapter 25

———————◆·◆·◆———————

Current Individual Income Tax Credits

Any federal tax reform in the near future will occur in a political atmosphere of an expanding national debt. This atmosphere probably will and should create strict scrutiny of all tax and direct subsidies because these affect the amount of money available to cut annual deficits in the federal budget.

This chapter will look at two popular kinds of subsidies that tax law currently provides in the form of tax credits. These are the Earned Income Credit and certain business-related income tax credits. These examples will illustrate the challenges that exist in reforming existing tax credits to accomplish our fairness, accountability, and simplicity goals.

The Earned Income Credit

The current Earned Income Credit (EIC) is a refundable tax credit. It is a direct subsidy designed to provide extra money to eligible individuals with small incomes whose income is almost exclusively earned income. The way that the current EIC accomplishes this purpose, however, fails our fairness and simplicity criteria by being both oddly discriminatory and extraordinarily complicated.

As one example of odd discrimination, married individuals who file jointly may claim the EIC whereas married individuals who prefer to file separately are barred from claiming the EIC, even if their total earned incomes are exactly the same small amount.[318]

Even for those individuals eligible to claim the EIC, the current EIC is so complicated that one set of the Form 1040 Instructions used in 2009 devoted twenty-three pages to this one item. The IRS offers—maybe pleads—to calculate the EIC for you.[319] This complexity alone supports a wholesale reexamination of the EIC to try to achieve better simplicity.

The EIC's Mixture of Two Ideas

A reexamination of the current EIC should start by recognizing that it is a mixture of two very different ideas about providing extra money to individuals with small incomes.

One idea is to refund some or all Social Security and Medicare taxes paid to the United States by an eligible individual with a small income. The EIC uses a 7.65 percent multiplier against earned income as the credit for eligible individuals with no qualifying children. This percentage matches the combined rate of 7.65 percent for Social Security and Medicare taxes that is applied against wages to determine an employee's Social Security and Medicare tax payment.[320]

The second idea in the current EIC is to provide extra money based on the number of "qualifying" children who are dependent upon the eligible individual. This extra money is calculated by using add-on percentages to the 7.65 percent multiplier against earned income and also by using larger eligible amounts of earned income against which those higher percentages can be applied.[321] These add-on portions of the EIC are not refunds of money paid by the individual to the United States. Instead, they are direct cash subsidies from the United States. To improve accountability, these add-on portions should be separated from the EIC and called the "qualifying child" direct subsidy.

This separation would highlight another anomaly in the Internal Revenue Code. An independent nonrefundable "Child Tax Credit" of $1,000 also existed in 2009 for "each qualifying child."[322] Like the Earned Income Credit, the amount of the Child Tax Credit decreases for individuals with large enough incomes (e.g., decreases begin for adjusted gross incomes exceeding $110,000 in the case of a joint return). But the rules for how and when these decreases occur are very different from the formula approach used with the Earned Income Credit.

The Earned Income Credit and Child Tax Credit both support a policy to provide extra money to people with children. Unfortunately, they are examples of how the piecemeal tack-on approach to federal tax law has created mind-boggling complexity for individual taxpayers and hidden costs in terms of lost tax receipts because of that policy.

Future Fate of the EIC

Focusing again on the Earned Income Credit, Congress will likely continue to favor a general policy to provide extra money to individuals with small incomes and to provide that money via the federal tax code. Many individuals rely on this extra financial help. Also, the proponents of this policy strongly believe that it causes many people to seek work who might otherwise not do so. Data show that the EIC has real impacts.

In tax year 2007, more than 24 million tax returns claimed the EIC, for a total of $48 billion in credits. Of that $48 billion, refundable credits (payments by the United States to individuals) were $42 billion.[323]

Improving the EIC

How can the EIC be improved?

If this general policy continues, separating its two core ideas—the idea of giving a refund of Social Security and Medicare tax payments, and the idea of giving money for a qualifying child—is an important first step to addressing each idea in more simple, nondiscriminatory, and understandable ways than found in the current EIC. That separation will also allow the "qualifying child" direct subsidy to be consolidated with the Child Tax Credit tax subsidy.

I do not have magic methods to simplify the EIC's two ideas for subsidies to individuals with small incomes, but I encourage others to try to create them.

In light of the FAST Plan's proposal to allow an individual's payment of Social Security and Medicare taxes as a nonrefundable tax credit, someone might suggest making this tax credit refundable as a way to give automatic refunds of those taxes to individuals with small incomes. The goal of this maneuver, of course, would be to create essentially the same result as the current EIC for that portion of the EIC that refunds Social Security and Medicare taxes paid by an eligible low-income individual.

This maneuver, however, will *not* achieve that goal. Showing why is complex, and thus relegated to appendix 25A.

Business-Related Income Tax Credits

Current federal tax law allows a large number of "business-related" income tax credits. These are all nonrefundable tax credits. Thankfully, these credits are summarized under one section of the Internal Revenue Code that refers to other code sections that describe the qualifications for the credits.[324] The sum of these credits is generally limited in scope, although not in total amount, if the taxpayer's taxable income is large enough.[325]

The tax subsidies represented by business-related income tax credits are available to self-employed individuals and also to corporations and other business entities. These tax subsidies promote a great variety of policies.

The practical availability of these tax subsidies to self-employed individuals is equally varied. Some of the business-related credits are targeted at small businesses that often are conducted by self-employed individuals. An example is the credit for expenditures to provide access to disabled individuals as required by federal law, which are particularly applicable to restaurants and retail stores.[326] Other business-related credits are primarily available to the kinds of business that most likely would be conducted by a corporation, such as clinical testing expenses for certain drugs for rare diseases or conditions.[327] Still other business-related credits by their very nature are available only to very large business enterprises that almost always would be conducted by corporations. For example, only a very large business enterprise has any chance to qualify for the credit for electricity production from an advanced nuclear power plant.[328]

Whatever the policy merits of these business-related tax credits, accountability dictates using tax credits as the best way to provide the subsidy. For individuals, many current tax credits would not have to be revised if my FAST Plan proposals are adopted. For corporations, however, the limits on these tax subsidies would have to be revised if my FAST Plan proposal for a tax on corporations, as outlined in chapter 29, is adopted.

Upcoming Issues

At this point in our journey on individual income taxes, we have examined and proposed reforms regarding the basic structure of the individual income tax, the kinds of income that should be taxed, reductions from income to determine taxable income, and tax credits. We need three more chapters to complete this part of our journey. Chapter 26 will address new issues created by the FAST Plan's standard-rate income tax. Chapters 27 and 28 will then show how the FAST Plan resolves two contentious features of the current individual income tax: the marriage penalty (and marriage bonus) and the Alternative Minimum Tax.

Chapter 25 Proposal
Current Individual Income Tax Credits

Retain

- Retain current individual nonrefundable tax credits so long as the tax subsidies represented by those credits remain appropriate.
- Retain current individual direct subsidies provided as refundable tax credits so long as the subsidies represented by those credits remain appropriate.

Reform

- Except for the credits for a taxpayer's money held by the United States, label all refundable individual tax credits as direct subsidies.
- Reexamine every individual tax credit that derives from any feature of current tax law that would be changed by the proposals of the FAST Plan.
- Recast the Earned Income Credit in simpler ways that separate the direct subsidy for qualifying children from the refund of Social Security and Medicare tax payments.

Chapter 26

———◆·◆·◆———

Two Special Cases: Investors and Retirees

As described in detail in chapter 11 on solving the Social Security and Medicare taxes dilemma, any income tax approach that relies on a standard tax rate instead of graduated rates has a potential flaw that affects fairness. It can create a marginal total federal tax rate on individuals with smaller earned incomes that is higher than the marginal total federal tax rate on similarly situated individuals with larger earned incomes. The FAST Plan prevents this result by allowing the payment of Social Security and Medicare taxes as a nonrefundable credit against the income tax, using simple accounting adjustments to the current treatment of those taxes (as shown in chapter 11).

The credit method works well for employees and self-employed individuals whose primary incomes are earned income subject to Social Security and Medicare taxes. However, two groups of people have circumstances that deserve separate consideration under our fairness criterion. Both groups consist of people whose primary income is from sources that are specifically excluded from being classified as earned income subject to Social Security and Medicare taxes.[329]

One group consists of people who are not retired but whose primary income is capital-based income. We will call this group the "Investors."

Another group consists of people who are retired. Their incomes can be from a variety of non-earned income sources, such as Social Security, pensions, retirement plans, or invested capital. We will call this group the "Retirees."

Investors

Under the FAST Plan's standard-rate income tax for all kinds of income, on an equal amount of income, Investors would pay the same total federal tax as would employees and self-employed individuals with the same amount of earned income. However, part of an employee's and self-employed individual's total federal tax would be for Social Security and Medicare taxes.

The Potential Inequity

Unlike an employee or self-employed individual, none of an Investor's total tax payment would be classified as Social Security or Medicare taxes. The Investor would not be building up Social Security credits that could increase the Social Security benefits that the Investor would receive upon retirement. The Investor also would not be building up annual Medicare credits needed to become eligible for Medicare benefits.

Addressing the Potential Inequity

One way to address this potential inequity is to give Investors the option to designate as Social Security and Medicare taxes a portion of the income tax on their income that is specifically excluded from earned income. In general, those kinds of income are rents from property, dividends, interest, and capital gains.[330] These will be referred to as "investment income." Although to present this concept I have described the "Investors" group as those people whose *primary* incomes are from sources other than earned income, this concept can also apply to investment income received by individuals whose primary income is earned income. The following practical rules for exercising this option would advance both simplicity and fairness through consistency with the application of Social Security and Medicare taxes to earned income.

- The option would be available only to an individual whose investment income exceeds a specific amount, such as $1,000 (to avoid trivial bookkeeping).
- The Investor can choose or not choose the option independently for each tax year.
- The option is "all in" or "all out" in the sense that all of the tax year's investment income must be included in the option.
- The option requires that the designation be for both Social Security and Medicare taxes.
- The income tax designation for Social Security and Medicare taxes is calculated as if the investment income is self-employed earned income.
- Payments of Social Security taxes on any wages and self-employed business income of the Investor (as calculated when determining the allowed income tax credit for these payments) come first when calculating the maximum payment designated for the Social Security tax based on the Social Security tax cutoff.

These rules are designed to keep the option consistent with the normal application of Social Security and Medicare taxes to earned income, rather than having the option available only for Social Security taxes. By exercising this option, an Investor would build up credits for future Social Security benefits and eligibility for future Medicare benefits.

Will this option be attractive to the Investors group?

I do not know.

To the extent that it is attractive, the extra money that will come into the Social Security and Medicare hospital insurance trust funds can help deal with the baby boomers' demographic bulge of retirees expected during the next two decades. This possibility alone makes trying the option worthwhile.

Retirees

An increasingly large group of people has or soon will have their primary income from Social Security, pensions, qualified retirement plans, or investments set aside for retirement. Decades of retirement planning have occurred in a dual context of future Social Security benefits that are largely untaxed for individuals with small incomes and future pension payments, retirement-plan distributions, and investment income that are subject to graduated or even special low income tax rates. Analytically, reliance on Social Security benefits, pension payments, and retirement-plan distributions differs somewhat from reliance on investment income, so these forms of reliance will be considered separately.

Reliance on Social Security, Pensions, and Retirement Plans

Pensions and retirement-plan distributions are not considered to be earned income that is subject to the Social Security and Medicare taxes.[331] Similarly, the portion of Social Security benefits that currently is taxable when an individual's other income is large enough is not considered to be earned income. Thus, the total federal tax on these kinds of income has historically only been the graduated income tax, which featured low rates on relatively small amounts of income. This feature of low tax rates has influenced decisions about how much money to try to set aside for retirement. A standard-rate income tax on all income will upset the expectations of individuals with smaller incomes for spendable money from their Social Security credits, pensions, and retirement plans until they have had an opportunity to adjust their retirement planning.

This circumstance calls for a temporary focused tax subsidy for Retirees with these kinds of income. I propose a temporary tax credit that will have the effect of bringing the actual income tax paid more in line with what would have occurred under historic graduated rates. One way to calculate this credit would be to give a credit as if the Retiree's taxable Social Security benefits, pension payments, and retirement-plan distributions were self-employed earned income and the Retiree had paid Social Security and Medicare taxes on that income up to the Social Security tax cutoff. The income tax credit would be the amount of the simulated Social Security and Medicare taxes. This method would be consistent with the general income tax credit for Social Security and Medicare taxes under the FAST Plan, as well as the option available to the Investor group to designate some of their income taxes as Social Security and Medicare taxes. It would also limit the credit to the income that would have been subject to historic graduated income tax rates that are lower than the new standard rate.

Who should qualify for this credit?

The most obvious and readily identifiable group of eligible Retirees consists of those people above the age of fifty-nine-and-a-half who have taxable pensions or qualified retirement-plan distributions. That is the age when distributions from an IRA retirement plan are no longer penalized for being early.[332] The credit would be calculated on that taxable income.

Reliance on Investment Income

Another group of Retirees consists of people who depend upon steady income from investments that are not part of a qualified retirement plan (what I will call the "Investor Retirees"). Although one could argue that if a person's income is not from a pension or qualified retirement plan, retirement planning was not involved, this argument views the process of retirement planning too narrowly.

Dividends income is a common example of income relied upon by Investor Retirees instead of income from pensions or qualified retirement plans. Especially with respect to dividends, a temporary tax subsidy would be warranted more because of the long history of graduated income tax rates with low rates for initial amounts of income than the more recent low tax rates on dividends since 2003.

I propose a temporary focused tax subsidy for the Investor Retirees that is the same as the tax subsidy described above for Retirees with taxable Social Security benefits, pension payments, and retirement-plan distributions.

One possible and simple way to identify the Investor Retirees is by age. Using age fifty-nine-and-a-half and older would be consistent with the Retirees having IRA retirement plans. The temporary income tax credit for Investor Retirees would be calculated on all taxable investment income that is subject to the standard-rate income tax, such as rents, interest, dividends, and capital gains.

As is apparent from the name, the group of Investor Retirees is a subclass of the Investors group described in the previous section. As such, an Investor Retiree could have a choice to be treated as an Investor, with the option to have part of his or her income taxes treated as Social

Security and Medicare taxes, or as an Investor Retiree entitled to the temporary tax credit described in this chapter. Although options generally work against the goal of simplicity, the fairness goal trumps simplicity in this instance.

How Long Is "Temporary"?

How long should "temporary" be for this tax subsidy?

A good answer to this question may require research on how much time is reasonably needed for people to adjust their retirement planning to take into account a standard-rate income tax on all income. Whether and how Social Security benefits are taxed in the future as compared to currently should also be considered in answering this question. A number like ten years is appealing for people not yet in retirement, but that time period may be unreasonably short or unnecessarily long. The difficulty of choosing a temporary time period should not, however, be an excuse to make this tax subsidy a permanent feature of federal tax law.

Chapter 26 Proposal
Two Special Cases: Investors and Retirees

Reform

- If a standard-rate income tax is adopted for all income and if all Social Security and Medicare tax payments by an individual are allowed as nonrefundable credits against the individual's income taxes, then also:
  - Allow individuals who have taxable income in excess of $1,000 that is specifically excluded from the individual's earned income and thus is not subject to Social Security and Medicare taxes, the option each year to designate as Social Security and Medicare taxes an amount of their income taxes determined as if all of that taxable income had been self-employed earned income.
- To allow retirement planning adjustment to a standard-rate income tax, provide a temporary tax subsidy to eligible retirees in the form of a nonrefundable income tax credit determined as if they had paid Social Security and Medicare taxes on their taxable Social Security benefits, pension payments, qualified retirement-plan distributions, and investment income up to the Social Security tax cutoff.
  - Define eligible retirees as those individuals age fifty-nine-and-a-half and older.

Chapter 27

———◆•◆•◆———

The "Marriage Penalty" (and "Marriage Bonus")

A "marriage penalty" sounds terrible. Upon hearing about a "marriage penalty," some people automatically conclude that Congress has strangely disfavored marriage in the tax law and that all married people somehow pay more taxes per person than single people who have the same income.

This conclusion is wrong.

Under current law, married taxpayers and single individual taxpayers do have different sets of tax rates. Heads of household have a unique set of tax rates, and surviving spouses are treated like a married couple for some purposes.[333] Applying these different sets of tax rates can give a different income tax figure for the same amount of taxable income depending upon filing category. As introduced in chapter 10, when we examined those sets of tax rates, there is indeed a "marriage penalty" for some married taxpayers as compared to single individual taxpayers, but there is also a "marriage bonus" for other married taxpayers.

The description of the marriage penalty and marriage bonus in chapter 10 bears repeating. A **marriage penalty** occurs when a married couple's income tax owed per individual is more than the income tax owed by a similarly situated single individual with the same taxable income per individual. A **marriage bonus** occurs when a married couple's income tax owed per individual is less than the income tax owed by a similarly situated single individual with the same taxable income per individual. Both circumstances can and do occur under current graduated income tax rates. Those tax differences can be significant. Recognizing the marriage-penalty anomaly, Congress has adopted a special provision that eliminates the "marriage penalty" for married taxpayers in the 15 percent tax bracket.[334] A person's filing status thus has a real impact on the amount of tax that will be owed.

How did these different sets of tax rates occur?

More important, what can be done to remove their inequities?

The answer to what can be done about these inequities can best be understood by describing how these different sets of tax rates occurred in the first place and then briefly explaining why different sets of tax rates create some tax inequities depending upon filing status. This chapter concludes with the FAST Plan's proposal to remove those inequities.

Origin of Different Sets of Tax Rates

Federal Income Taxation by Klein and associates succinctly describes the history behind the different sets of tax rates for different filing categories that are now present in the Internal Revenue Code.[335] The problems addressed by these sets of rates are caused by the interplay of two features in historic and current federal income tax law. The first is graduated tax rates with higher rates applying to larger incomes. The second is the ability of married people to combine their incomes and then split that total equally, with each spouse then being treated as one taxpayer who has just one-half the total taxable income.

As described in the Klein treatise, this latter feature came about over sixty years ago as a response by Congress to state community property law, which dictated the same result. By allowing the joint tax return for married couples, Congress equalized the income tax treatment of all married people, whether or not they lived in a state that used community property law, at least if they filed a joint tax return rather than filing separate tax returns.

The Bonus Effect of the Joint Return

The interplay of the graduated income tax rates and the joint return works like this. Treating each spouse as having one-half the total taxable income of the married couple has the effect of allowing the lowest tax rates to apply to each half of the income. Where one spouse earns all of the income, doubling the tax computed this way will normally be less than if the graduated rates apply once to the full taxable income. This is so because that full taxable income may reach higher marginal tax rates than one-half the income reaches and because the lowest rates will only be applied once on that full income. The federal tax rates for married couples filing jointly reflect the double application of the lowest rates inherent in the equal split of total income between spouses.

At the time Congress adopted the split-income approach for married couples filing a joint return, the vast majority of married couples had one primary breadwinner (back then, usually the husband). This meant that a married couple who relied on that primary income paid less income tax than a single person who had the same income.

Perceived Unfairness of the Joint Return

Single people declared foul. They asserted a double disadvantage. Not only was a single person paying more income tax than a married couple on the same amount of income, but the cost of living per person for a single person was higher than for a married couple.

Congress responded by creating a new and reduced set of income tax rates for "unmarried individuals" only. Under this new set of rates, a single individual who had the same income as a married couple with one breadwinner could still pay more income taxes than the married couple if the married couple filed a joint return, but that difference would be less than existed before Congress adopted the new rates. Even after this change, the married couple with one breadwinner still enjoyed a "marriage bonus" as compared to a single individual because of the couple's ability to split equally one primary income in computing their income tax obligation.

Later, Congress complicated this picture further by creating yet another set of graduated income tax rates for heads of household.[336]

Structural Flaws in the Different Sets of Tax Rates

By using the different sets of tax rates applicable respectively to married couples and to single individuals, structural flaws existed from the very beginning that could create two forms of a "marriage penalty" as well as a "marriage bonus." These became more obvious as time passed and more and more spouses joined the workplace in jobs that generated comparable incomes. These are the "separate returns" penalty and the "equal incomes" penalty.

The Separate Returns Penalty

One form of marriage penalty occurs when, for whatever reason, spouses want to file separate tax returns. In that case, each spouse is treated as a married person subject to the married person set of tax rates, not as a single person who is subject to the reduced set of single individual rates.[337] Each spouse would, therefore, pay more income tax on his or her income than a single person with that same taxable income. For married couples whose spouses have very different incomes, a simple way to avoid this result is to file a joint tax return, even if they prefer not to do so. For other married couples, however, this maneuver will not significantly reduce their taxes because of the second and more subtle form of marriage penalty.

The Equal Incomes Penalty

This second form of marriage penalty occurs most clearly when spouses have nearly equal incomes. When filing a joint return, these spouses are subject to the married person set of tax rates. But combining and splitting nearly equal incomes will not shift some of the taxable income from a higher tax-rate bracket to a lower tax-rate bracket such as occurs when spousal incomes are very different. Applying the married person set of tax rates on these equal taxable incomes will give a greater total income tax per spouse than applying the single individual tax rates on that same taxable income would give for a single person.

How to Remove the Tax Inequities

One reasonable way to address the "marriage penalty" issue is to apply the single individual tax rates to spouses who file separate returns. Formulas could be developed that would allow married couples to choose rationally whether to file a joint return or separate returns based on the amount of tax that would be owed under each method. This approach, however, further complicates a situation that is already complicated with multiple sets of tax rates that depend upon filing status. It also does not address the "marriage bonus" issue that contributed to the development of these multiple sets of tax rates in the first place. As that issue illustrates, having different sets of tax rates that depend upon one's filing status leads to resentment as one filing status group or another believes that its position is unfair compared to some other group's position.

Graduated income tax rates are the core cause of the discrepancies that created impetus for different sets of tax rates. The FAST Plan's standard income tax rate for all individuals eliminates this core cause. Under a standard rate, filing status will not matter. Splitting income between spouses who file jointly will create no different total income tax per person than if each spouse filed a separate return or if each spouse had been single.

Of course, the amount of a standard deduction may differ depending upon filing status, and that has an effect on the amount of income tax. This difference does and should reflect a balanced decision on needs, rather than a mathematical result from the interplay of disparate sets of tax rates. The special needs of single heads of household, for example, can be and currently are dealt with via adjusted standard deductions.[338]

You may question whether the FAST Plan's proposed nonrefundable tax credit for payment of Social Security and Medicare taxes will reintroduce some form of marriage penalty or bonus. It will not because these taxes are already treated individually.

That is, the amount of Social Security and Medicare taxes owed is calculated from each individual's earned income, not some allocation of income between spouses. Under the FAST Plan, the payment of Social Security and Medicare taxes will be treated the same for employees and self-employed individuals. Allowing subtraction of these payments from an income tax determined by a standard rate will give consistent and equal results for each individual who pays those taxes, no matter what the individual's filing status.

Chapter 27 Proposal
The "Marriage Penalty" (and "Marriage Bonus")

Reform

- Use a standard-rate income tax for all individual taxpayers regardless of their filing status.

Chapter 28

The Alternative Minimum Tax on Individuals

In 1978, Congress adopted the Alternative Minimum Tax as a way to keep individuals from adroitly taking advantage of numerous tax subsidies in the form of tax "preferences" to greatly minimize their income taxes.[339]

Any real tax reform has to address the Alternative Minimum Tax (AMT) because over time, the number of people who have been swept into the AMT has increased significantly. From 2002 to 2007, the number of returns filed with the IRS that included the AMT more than doubled, and this doubling does not record the number of individuals who had to do preliminary calculations just to find out whether they were subject to the AMT.[340]

As stated in chapter 7, the Alternative Minimum Tax is a taxing scheme that exists alongside the regular individual income tax, with a different set of rates and a smaller set of allowed tax subsidies.[341] As stated in the Klein treatise, "The alternative minimum tax (AMT) imposes a tax at a reduced rate on a broader base."[342] In general terms, this broader base is determined by targeting some tax subsidies as being potentially abused, adding part or all of those tax subsidies back into taxable income, and imposing alternative minimum tax rates on part of this result. The tax owed is the greater of this AMT or the regular tax.

If that process seems complicated, well, it is!

Part of the frustration individuals have with the AMT is the effort required to figure out whether or not it applies to that individual, even if ultimately it does not. The AMT resoundingly fails our simplicity criterion.

Can the goals of the AMT be achieved in different and simpler ways?

Developing an answer to this question first requires brief summaries of how the AMT works in practice and what tax subsidies the current AMT does or does not target.

How the AMT Works in Practice

The AMT on individuals is designed to apply minimum tax rates on "alternative minimum taxable income" that exceeds certain amounts.[343] These amounts are triggers for applying the AMT calculation, which may or may not result in a greater total income tax than the regular income tax.

The amount of taxable income that triggers a calculation of the AMT is relatively small. These amounts are called "exemption amounts." In 2009, the exemption amount was $70,950 for taxpayers filing a joint return. No wonder so many people have had to fuss with the AMT. To add to this calculation nightmare, even the exemption amount is phased out for taxpayers whose alternative minimum taxable income exceeds certain amounts (e.g., $150,000 for taxpayers filing a joint return).[344]

When the AMT is triggered for an individual, the first step is to recalculate the amount of taxable income, which then becomes the "alternative minimum taxable income."

At the outset of this first step, the current Internal Revenue Code applies special rules to net capital gains. These rules generally allow the special tax rates for long-term capital gains to be unaffected by the AMT, including the maximum 15 percent tax rate for most such gains (15 percent under 2009 law; increased to 20 percent beginning in 2013).[345]

Targeted Tax Subsidies

With capital gains income being excluded from any AMT adjustment, what are the targeted tax subsidies that do affect an individual's alternative minimum taxable income?

The code deals with these tax subsidies in two categories, but the effect of each category is to add back to regular taxable income all or a portion of the tax subsidy. One category is called "adjustments," and the second category is called "items of tax preference."[346]

The adjustments category of targeted tax subsidies includes a number of itemized deductions. Examples are the itemized deductions for state and local taxes (real property, personal property, and income or alternative sales taxes), the group of miscellaneous allowed deductions, and a portion of allowed medical expenses.[347] Left intact as tax subsidies are such itemized deductions as interest payments on home mortgages.[348] In calculating the alternative minimum taxable income, no standard deduction or personal exemption is allowed either.[349]

Other targeted tax subsidies for individuals are more in the nature of business-related tax subsidies, which can be categorized as tax preferences. A handy list of these subsidies is found at Lines 9 through 28 of Form 6251 used in 2009.[350] A common, although not universal, approach to these tax subsidies is to require recalculation of the tax subsidy when computing alternative minimum taxable income. Examples of these targeted business-related tax subsidies are reductions in income for investment interest expense, depletion allowances, and research and experimental costs.

The rules, exceptions, and recalculations that permeate the AMT are mind-boggling. Its goal is laudable—to keep individual taxpayers from abusing tax subsidies and thereby avoid paying taxes—but the method used to accomplish this goal stinks.

Ending the Alternative Minimum Tax

What is an alternative to the AMT?

The answer is to recast all tax subsidies as nonrefundable tax credits.

As described in chapter 24, when provided as a tax credit, each tax subsidy can easily be limited in amount. The totality of tax subsidies also can be limited, either in amount or percentage of adjusted gross income, giving a de facto minimum tax rate for everyone when a standard-rate income tax is used as proposed in the FAST Plan. This combined approach makes an Alternative Minimum Tax unnecessary.

Moving On

These last two chapters illustrate the power of the FAST Plan in reforming the individual income tax. Its proposals automatically eliminate two of the most contentious features of current tax law: the marriage penalty and the Alternative Minimum Tax. With that conclusion, we are now leaving the individual income tax to focus on two related federal taxes: the corporation income tax and the estate (and gift) tax.

Chapter 28 Proposal
The Alternative Minimum Tax on Individuals

Reform

- Eliminate the Alternative Minimum Tax for individuals, but only if all tax subsidies are recast as nonrefundable tax credits.

Part III:

Reforming
Related Taxes

Chapter 29

————•◆•————

Reforming the Corporation Income Tax

On first thought, the current corporation income tax would appear to be independent from the individual income tax.

However, we have already seen one way that the corporation income tax relates to the individual income tax when we considered whether and how to tax dividends income in chapter 15. That relationship alone requires us to take a hard look at the way the current corporation income tax operates in practice. As we will soon see, there are many more reasons to reevaluate the corporation income tax when considering tax reform.

Beyond its relationship to dividends, the current corporation income tax is politically and fiscally important. It is often criticized by a wide range of people with different viewpoints because of the perceived excessive subsidies to some corporations or industries and not others tucked within its provisions. Taxes on corporations are the second most important revenue source for general US government outlays.[351] As such, they deserve especially careful attention to assure that they comply with our fairness, accountability, and simplicity criteria.

In this chapter, we will first summarize the Internal Revenue Code's current approach to taxing corporations, suggest and critique a historic underpinning for that approach, and identify the flaws in that approach. We will then reveal and examine the FAST Plan's new proposal for taxation of corporations, how that proposal affects some corporation tax history, and what tax rate(s) would be appropriate under that proposal. Finally, we will consider what other entities should be treated as corporations subject to the same tax proposal.

The Code's Approach to Taxing Corporations

If you look in the Internal Revenue Code, you will find a section that imposes a tax on the taxable income of every corporation, but you will not find a separate group of sections that describes what a corporation's taxable income is.[352] Instead, corporations are lumped together with individuals in the sections that define gross income, taxable income, and allowable reductions from gross income that may be used to determine taxable income.

In sifting through these code sections, what emerges is a "corporation income tax" that is a tax on a corporation's net profit. That is, a corporation's taxable income is calculated as its gross income minus a variety of reductions allowed by statute,[353] by far the most significant of which are trade or business expenses (such as employee salaries).[354] This net profit tax base is termed **earnings** or **earnings and profits** throughout the code.[355] The term "earnings" is also commonly used in annual reports of publicly traded corporations. In deference to that usage, I will use "earnings" rather than "net profit" in this chapter on the corporation income tax.

Like the individual income tax rates, the current corporation tax rates are graduated. Again using 2009 tax law as the reference, the rate starts at 15 percent, but jumps to 25 percent for earnings above $50,000, then to 34 percent for earnings above $75,000. The rate increases slightly to 35 percent for earnings above $10,000,000.[356]

Challenging the Code's Historic Underpinning

Why are corporations and individuals lumped together in the code sections that determine taxable income?

This approach may have its genesis in a philosophical attempt to treat all business income the same way.[357] After all, one effect of this approach is that the taxable earnings of a corporation are calculated similarly to the taxable business income of a self-employed individual. Despite this nominal similarity, the code provides a number of reductions to determine taxable income that are unique to individuals (e.g., medical expenses),[358] are unique to corporations (e.g., organizational expenditures),[359] or in practice are potentially available to corporations but hardly ever to individuals (e.g., elections to expense certain refineries).[360]

Whatever the initial philosophical motivation, the corporation and self-employed forms of business are not synonymous and need not be treated similarly. Significant differences exist between the two kinds of businesses that are directly relevant to whether they should be taxed on the same basis.

Personal Business Features

Self-employed individuals have very strong incentive to maximize their net profits from a personal business. Only that money is available for personal expenses and investments because the trade or business expenses that are allowed to determine net profit are confined to the individual's business operations. These allowed expenses at most provide only indirect personal benefits. Also, many self-employed businesses are not readily salable, so spending business revenues to increase the assets of the individual business is not nearly as attractive as creating net profit for personal use. Collectively, these features mean that taxing the net profit of a self-employed business is very much like taxing the wages of an employee.

Corporate Business Features

The picture regarding corporation earnings is more complex. To be sure, corporate officers and directors also have incentive to maximize the corporation's earnings, but that incentive competes with other goals.

One other goal is to maximize the value of the corporation's stock. Annual earnings are a factor in creating that value, but so also are the accumulation of business assets and development of new products that involve expenses that reduce earnings.

An attitudinal goal with some corporate executives and directors is to minimize corporation income taxes or not pay any taxes at all. This goal can be achieved by giving priority to certain kinds of business expenses over providing earnings available for dividends.

Conflicting personal goals of decision makers, especially executives, can also affect earnings. One such goal could be to increase their own salaries, which are deductible business expenses for a corporation that reduce its earnings. Another such goal could be to spend more corporate money on new assets, which would reduce earnings but increase stock value to the benefit of those executives whose compensation includes stock options.

Corporations also have other features that make their business enterprises very different from the business of a self-employed individual.

Perhaps most important, corporations can raise money by selling stock of the corporation. Indeed, the goal of many founders of start-up corporations is to build up the business so that it can "go public" through an initial public offering of the corporation's stock. In that way, the corporation can raise more money for expanded operations, and the founders can get cash for their business by selling some of their stock if they choose to do so. Corporations also have enhanced ability to acquire or combine with other corporations via stock trades or issuances as part of the purchase price.

In addition, the classic initial reason to do business as a corporation is to limit the personal liability of owners for damages caused by business operations, such as a truck accident caused by an employee delivering products. Potential personal liability resulting from business operations in practice limits the scope of a self-employed individual's business as compared to the scope of a corporation's business.

Conclusion from Comparative Business Features

These comparisons between personal and corporate business features illustrate that business by corporations is fundamentally different from business by self-employed individuals. Now is the time to recognize that corporations should be treated as unique entities and not just another business operation in how they are taxed or not taxed by the United States.

Flaws in the Earnings Tax Base

The current use of a corporation's earnings as its taxable income base has at least three flaws.

The most important flaw is that some enormous corporate business enterprises pay zero or minuscule federal income taxes. Indeed, some of those corporate enterprises have paid zero or minuscule federal income taxes for multiple years.[361] Yet some of these same corporations receive direct benefits from programs and services provided by the US government, and all of them receive the general benefit of the security for their business operations in the United States provided by federal institutions and national security mechanisms. A free ride for these corporations can hardly be considered fair to individual taxpayers or to other corporations that do have earnings on which they pay the corporation earnings tax.

A second flaw is that earnings have little relationship to the costs that the United States incurs both in providing services that the corporate business enterprise uses and in regulating some activities that the corporation conducts so that people in the United States are protected from harmful consequences of those activities. These costs are more closely related to the size of the corporate business enterprise than to its earnings. Fairness dictates that corporate tax obligations have some relationship to those costs.

A third flaw relates to the taxability of dividends, as discussed in chapter 15 on dividends income. Taxing a corporation's earnings has encouraged arguments to reduce or eliminate federal individual income taxes on dividends because of alleged double taxation of the same income (earnings). If a corporation income tax were not based on earnings, the asserted basis for these arguments would disappear. Special tax rates for dividends income would be less likely, thus increasing simplicity in federal income taxes overall.

Proposals for corporation tax reform that focus solely on changing some accounting maneuvers or deductions from revenues that reduce taxable earnings may partially remove the first flaw, but not the second and third flaws. Fortunately, a very different but more bold approach to a corporation income tax is available that has none of these three flaws.

A New Taxable Income Base for Corporations

At present, a natural person's gross income for federal tax purposes includes such moneys received as wages, interest, dividends, self-employed business income, capital gains, and distributions from partnerships and trusts.[362] Setting aside the variety of specific tax subsidies allowed to particular individuals, a natural person's taxable income is that person's gross income minus only two small reductions: the personal exemptions and the standard deduction. As shown in chapter 21 on income reductions for payments necessary for a healthy life, both of these reductions are designed in part to exempt basic survival expenses from taxation.[363] Except at the poverty end of the spectrum, the basic taxable income of a natural person is a large percentage of that person's gross income.

A corporation is a "person" for most legal purposes. A corporation can own, buy, and sell property; it can make, spend, and raise money; and it can sue and be sued in courts. Compared to a natural person, about the only thing a corporation cannot legally do is vote. As a legal "person," a corporation can properly be compared to a natural person in determining an appropriate federal taxable income base for the corporation.

As noted in the first section of this chapter, at present, a corporation's gross income is defined by the same code section that defines the gross income of a natural person, even though corporations do not receive wages.[364] If wages were excluded from that definition, a corporation's "gross income" becomes essentially its revenue as commonly reported today under generally accepted accounting principles applicable to corporations. Setting aside specific tax subsidies allowed to corporations, a corporation's revenue rather than its earnings is the closest analogy to the gross income of a natural person, most of which is the individual's taxable income.

I propose that the federal tax on corporations use a corporation's revenue from operations in the United States as the tax base, not a corporation's earnings. I also propose that a single standard corporation tax rate be used. Of course, the tax rate cannot be anywhere close to the current tax rates that apply to a corporation's earnings or to an individual's taxable income. Because this new corporation tax would not apply to revenues or earnings from corporate operations outside the United States, it would reflect the territorial tax approach commonly used by other nations.[365]

What then are the advantages of using revenue from operations in the United States instead of earnings as the tax base? Equally important, what would be a proper standard tax rate to apply to corporation revenue?

Advantages of Using Corporation Revenue as the Tax Base

There are at least nine advantages to using a corporation's revenue from operations in the United States as its tax base instead of a corporation's earnings:

(1) *A tax on revenue aligns with the "bigger is better" philosophy of most of the corporate world.* Just about every corporation has a goal to grow in size, and that means to increase revenue. Increased size means expanded product lines and more assets for production. This goal will normally override any reluctance to pay taxes, so tax avoidance will be more difficult to achieve by taxing revenue instead of earnings.

(2) *A tax on revenue rather than earnings removes reducing taxes from the set of conflicting goals that now influence decisions that affect the amount of earnings reported by a corporation.* Removing a tax on earnings should allow executives, directors, and shareholders to see more clearly the effects of decisions that balance the conflicting goals that affect earnings, such as whether to pay out more dividends or to invest in more research and development. This removal could also reduce what some regard as the gamesmanship used by some corporate executives in determining their corporation's earnings in a particular year. Recent reported examples include the use of deferred tax expenses and accelerated depreciation to reduce corporate earnings and even create refundable tax benefits (direct subsidies).[366]

(3) *The size of a corporate business enterprise in the United States as reflected by revenue rather than earnings is a better measure of the total direct and indirect benefits the corporation receives from the US government, as well as the cost of the corporate enterprise to the US government.* As an example of direct benefits, all publicly traded corporations receive direct benefits from the Securities and Exchange Commission, without which investors would be less likely to buy corporate stocks because information about corporate performance would be less certain. As an example of direct costs, in the industrial sector, a large chemical corporation owning twenty processing plants in fifteen states is probably more likely to have a toxic chemical spill that requires federal directed or actual cleanup than a similar corporation owning one plant.

(4) *Using a corporation's revenue rather than earnings as the tax base allows sensible taxation of the US operations of foreign corporations, including those that are now "foreign" strictly for tax purposes.* Foreign corporate operations in the United States have the general benefit of the security provided by federal institutions and national security mechanisms just as much as do the

operations of domestic corporations. A tax on revenues will reflect that benefit better than a tax on earnings from those operations. In addition, revenues from a corporation's sales and other operations in the United States should be more readily apparent, measurable, and less subject to manipulation than earnings from those sales and operations.

(5) *Using revenue rather than earnings as the tax base will make it much more difficult to create transactions whose major goal is to hide real income from taxation.*

A simple tax on revenue will also encourage transactions to be measured on their business merit, not their tax advantages because there will be none.

(6) *Using revenue rather than earnings as the tax base allows the federal tax to be considered just another cost of doing business.*

For example, a corporation pays for utilities in proportion to its size and gets the benefit of reliable electricity for lights and computers used in its operations. Similarly, under a federal tax on revenue, a corporation will pay in proportion to its size for the direct benefits of many federal governmental services, such as federal courts in which to enforce its contracts, and the indirect benefits of a secure nation in which to do business.

(7) *Corporation revenues vary less than earnings from year to year.*

Some of the variation in earnings has little relationship to actual profits. For example, sometimes the use of carryover (and carryback) losses reduces taxable earnings when real profits nevertheless exist. This particular maneuver also can involve an extraordinarily complex set of rules.[367] A tax on corporation revenue is not only simpler but also provides a more predictable stream of tax receipts for the United States than a tax on corporation earnings.

(8) *Using corporation revenues rather than earnings with their accompanying carryover and carryback rules will eliminate the odd practice of losses being considered purchasable assets.*

Historically, some corporations could and did buy other corporations primarily to use the losses of those other corporations to shield their own earnings from the corporation earnings tax. That practice fortunately has been minimized by the current version of federal law and its regulations dealing with this subject.[368] These regulations would not be needed under a corporation revenue tax.

(9) *Using revenue rather than earnings as the tax base removes the underpinning of the argument asserted by some people that a tax on dividends is a double tax on the same income, namely corporate earnings.*

Using revenue rather than earnings as the corporation tax base should remove much of the impetus to treat dividends differently than other kinds of income received by individuals, thus removing from federal individual income taxes the complexity and discriminatory treatment arising from a set of special low tax rates.

Dealing with Corporation Tax History

The Internal Revenue Code has a long history of taxing only the earnings of a corporation, and in many circumstances those earnings have included earnings from operations outside the United States.[369] How will this history be disrupted by a tax on corporation revenue only from operations in the United States?

Corporations with Small Earnings

Replacing earnings with revenue as the corporation tax base will have a significant effect on those corporations that rarely have reported earnings (whether by design, because of an unsuccessful business model, because of poor management, or because of a historically low-margin type of business[370]). Those corporations will have to pay federal taxes for the first time, in some cases even substantial taxes because of their large size. My primary answer to their complaints is, "Your free ride is over; the time has come for you to pay for your fair share of benefits received." In short, historic reliance on a flawed method used to tax corporations should not be a good reason to continue that method.

International Treaties

Another long history that potentially could be disrupted by a corporation revenue tax, at least temporarily, is represented by the treaties or international conventions that the United States has signed over time. To the extent that treaties assume that the taxable "income" of a business enterprise is earnings, these treaties may not automatically fit with a tax that uses corporation revenue as the base.

In this international context, however, taxation of revenue as income has an important advantage over taxation of earnings as income: using revenue as income should be easier and less amenable to manipulation than earnings when identifying what income of a corporation is foreign-based or United States–based. These identifications matter because international treaties typically try to avoid double taxation of the same income, and identifying where that income occurred is one criterion used to establish rules on income taxability by different nations.

Foreign Tax Credits

The Fiscal Commission's 2010 report recommends that the United States adopt a territorial tax system to make US corporations more competitive on the international scene. Under a territorial system, the United States would not tax foreign operations of US corporations, nor would foreign nations tax the US operations of their domestic corporations.[371] The FAST Plan achieves this result by restricting its corporation revenue tax to revenue from operations in the United States.

Because the FAST Plan's corporation revenue tax does not apply to revenue or earnings from corporate operations based outside the United States, corporation foreign tax credits also have to be eliminated under the FAST Plan. Those credits are designed solely to reduce double taxation on foreign income that can occur under the current corporation income tax, a circumstance that does not exist under the FAST Plan.

Taxable Business Income Symmetry

Of course, using revenue rather than earnings as the taxable income of a corporation also removes a historic symmetry between a corporation's taxable business income and a self-employed individual's taxable business income. As described above, however, that symmetry ignores many important differences between these two types of business enterprises. Continued use of a flawed symmetry of treatment in the code will not diminish those differences.

Tax-Exempt Nonprofit Corporations

The FAST Plan does not attempt to change the tax-exempt status of existing nonprofit corporations or organizations. Although we might consider reassessing the current categories of tax-exempt corporations and other organizations as part of tax reform, this reassessment is not essential to achieving the FAST Plan's most important fairness, accountability, and simplicity features.

S Corporations

Finally, we need to address the unique corporation tax history of the "S corporations."[372] These are "small business corporations" that have a limited number of individual shareholders, all of whom agree that the corporation should be an S corporation. S corporations are not subject to the current corporation earnings (net profit) tax.[373] Instead, the S corporation's specially determined net profit is attributed directly to the individual shareholders.[374]

In this regard, S corporations are more like partnerships than corporations. With the restricted nature of their ownership, S corporations do not have other attributes of regular corporations that support our replacing the corporation earnings tax with a corporation revenue tax. Thus, S corporations should not be subject to the FAST Plan's proposed corporation revenue tax, even though keeping the S corporation classification does retain some federal tax complexity.

Appropriate New Tax Rate on Corporation Revenue

Tax rates are often primarily a function of political wrangling. In this situation, however, a logical and simple way exists to set an initial standard tax rate that would apply to the revenue of every corporation. We can use a "status quo" method that relies upon an average annual tax receipts target derived from a recent five-year history of tax receipts from the current corporation income tax. Using this method for the five-year period from 2003 through 2007, the tax rate would be 1.5 percent.[375] Adjustments in the rate could be made after the first few years the rate is used if tax receipts prove to be much less or more than calculated.

A Potential Tweak to Taxable Revenue

An additional tweak to the corporation revenue tax could include a "corporation standard deduction" that is designed to insulate very small corporations with very small revenues from the tax in much the same way that the standard deduction operates for individuals. Extreme caution must be exercised in creating such a tweak so that it does not become a loophole through which a corporation could minimize its revenue tax by creating hundreds or thousands of small subsidiary corporations.

Adjustments in Tax Credits Available to Corporations

The current Internal Revenue Code contains a large variety of "business-related" income tax credits that apply to both individuals and corporations.[376] In the code, the total amount of many of these credits for corporations is limited based on the amount of a corporation's calculated earnings tax for the year.[377] This limitation and other limitations on subsidies available to corporations will have to be reexamined and made consistent with the FAST Plan's proposed corporation revenue tax. This task can be minimized by reexamination and elimination of many of these subsidies, as recommended generally by the Fiscal Commission's 2010 report.[378] If *any* corporation subsidies survive this reexamination, they should be allowed only as separate nonrefundable or refundable tax credits. Then they will meet our accountability criterion. Just like subsidies for individuals, corporate subsidies can then easily be limited in amount and their costs exposed so that periodic reevaluation of each subsidy will be more likely to occur than under current law.

As noted above, federal law on foreign tax credits will also have to be changed to eliminate foreign tax credits because the FAST Plan's corporation revenue tax would not apply to revenue or earnings from corporate operations based outside the United States.

When to Treat Noncorporate Business Entities as Corporations

If a federal income tax on corporation revenue is adopted to replace the current income tax on earnings, how should other business entities or organizations be treated?

The variety of legally recognized entities other than corporations has expanded over time. Some of these entities are designed specifically to take advantage of certain tax benefits. Others exist to limit the personal liability of owners for acts of the enterprise encompassed by the entity. Still others exist simply as alternative ways for people to work together in a common business enterprise. Today a list of business entities other than corporations would include at least these commonly used forms:

- General partnership
- Limited partnership
- Union
- Limited liability company
- Limited liability partnership
- Mutual insurance company
- Business trust (such as a real estate investment trust)

Whether any of these entities should be treated as a corporation subject to a federal corporation revenue tax logically should depend on the extent to which the entity has attributes like those of a corporation. Most important are those attributes that can assist the entity to become a very large business enterprise that takes advantage of significant governmental resources and affects many people beyond the entity itself. After all, those attributes of a corporation provide one important justification for replacing the current corporation earnings tax with a revenue tax.

Corporation-Like Attributes

The two most obvious such attributes are the ability of the entity to sell ownership interests or bonds to the public. The next two paragraphs provide more detail about those two attributes.

The most important corporation-like attribute is the ability of the entity to sell ownership interests to the public without the holders of those interests having to take on any responsibility within the entity. This attribute is analogous to the stock ownership feature of a corporation. As noted previously, the stock feature assists a corporation in creating a very large enterprise in at least two different ways. One way is to raise significant money by selling its stock, such as through an initial public offering. Another way is to issue stock as payment for all or part of an acquisition, typically another corporation. Among the entities listed above, limited partnerships, business trusts, and maybe mutual insurance companies have the ability to sell ownership interests to the public in order to raise money for the enterprise. Other listed entities may have this ability as well, although most general partnerships and unions would not have this ability.

The second corporation-like attribute is the ability of the entity to issue bonds that can be purchased by the public. This attribute is exactly the same as a corporation's ability to sell bonds to fund expansion of its operations, again to assist the entity or corporation in becoming a large enterprise. I do not know which, if any, of the entities listed above have this ability. Even if none of these entities has this ability now, the rule should be clear that the ability to sell bonds alone is enough to cause the entity to be treated as a corporation subject to the corporation revenue tax. Otherwise, the investment community will establish entities having this singular ability instead of an ability to sell an ownership interest just to avoid the federal corporation revenue tax.

Closing a Potential Loophole

Partnerships between corporations, often called "joint ventures," represent a potential loophole that corporations could use to minimize their revenues subject to a corporation revenue tax. Historically, net profits of partnerships, but not revenues, have been assigned to partners in accordance with their ownership interests in the partnership. Rules will have to be developed that assign partnership revenues to partners that are corporations so this potential loophole is closed.

Fairness for All Noncorporate Business Entities

By applying the concepts in this section as an initial step in the FAST Plan, existing business entities other than corporations will be paying their fair share of federal taxes along with corporations.

The variety of business entities other than corporations will probably continue to evolve, some being in response to any existing or new federal tax structure. New forms of entities can be dealt with as they arise.

Chapter 29 Proposal
Reforming the Corporation Income Tax

Reform

- Replace the current corporation earnings (net profit) tax with a standard-rate corporation revenue tax on revenues from operations in the United States.
- Determine an initial standard rate from five-year historic data on corporation revenues and corporation income taxes paid in a non-recession economy (estimated at 1.5 percent from a method designed solely to obtain historic levels of corporation tax receipts).

- Impose no tax on corporation revenue or earnings from operations outside the United States and concurrently eliminate all corporation foreign tax credits.
- Create phase-out and phase-in rules that will allow corporations a reasonable time in which to adjust to the new tax base and standard rate.
- Treat entities with corporation-like attributes as corporations subject to any corporation revenue tax that is adopted in place of the corporation earnings (net profit) tax.

Chapter 30

---●◆●---

New Rules for Estates and Gifts

What is an **estate**?

It is all property, including money, that a deceased person owned at the time of death.

What is an **inheritance**?

It is the property, including money, that a person receives from an estate (excluding earnings from the estate).

These terms matter because historically federal taxes have been levied on estates, but not on inheritances.[379] Although inheritances could have been treated as income, long-standing federal law specifically excludes inheritances from gross income that is potentially subject to the federal income tax.[380]

No genius is required to see that an easy way to avoid a tax on an estate would be to give money and property to the intended heirs before dying. That is why a gift tax also exists that complements the estate tax. The gift tax is designed to collect the taxes that would have been paid on the estate of a person who makes the gift. That is the gist of the gift tax, even though specific rules, such as money that is exempt from the gift tax, complicate this complement. Gifts, like inheritances, are specifically excluded from federal gross income.

Our examination of federal taxes relating to estates and gifts will focus on estates, while sometimes recognizing related features of the gift tax. We will begin with a summary of the estate tax, including its recent variations. We will then critique the important historic connection between estates and individual income taxes. Finally, we will look at the proper fate of estate and gift taxes in comprehensive federal tax reform.

The Current Estate Tax

Federal taxes on estates and gifts have historically been separate from federal individual income taxes, probably so that they could be subject to different rules and use different rates.

Comparison to the Individual Income Tax

Two examples from the estate taxes that were applicable in 2009 will illustrate the differences between the estate tax and individual income tax.

First, the estate tax in 2009 applied against the "amount of the taxable estate" (with some adjustments taking into account taxable gifts).[381] That amount was determined by deducting from the "gross estate" a variety of expenses, payments, and transfers as allowed by statute, including transfers for public, charitable, and religious uses.[382] The gross estate included the value at the time of the decedent's death of all property in the estate.[383] Thus, property valuations were needed to determine the base on which to apply the estate tax, unlike the income tax, where money transactions usually provide the base on which to apply the tax.

Second, the estate tax in 2009 used fourteen graduated rates applicable to different amounts of a taxable estate, with a maximum rate of 45 percent.[384] In contrast, the income tax in 2009 used only five graduated rates applicable to different amounts of taxable income in each filing category, with a maximum rate of 35 percent.[385]

Recent Estate Tax History

I use the year 2009 as an example because the 2001 Tax Act included repeal of the estate tax for the year 2010 (but not repeal of the gift tax).[386] The estate tax that existed before 2001 would have reappeared automatically in 2011 without further congressional action.[387] Congress reinstated a version of the estate tax for 2011 and 2012 in the December 2010 tax compromise. In this two-year version, the maximum estate tax rate was reduced to 35 percent (among other changes).[388] Congress again modified the estate tax in its 2012 fiscal cliff tax compromise. This time, Congress increased the maximum estate tax rate to 40 percent (among other changes).[389] Particularly in light of their contentious history, estate taxes cannot be ignored when trying to make all federal taxes more fair, accountable, and simple.

Despite the separation between estate taxes and income taxes, a very important connection also has existed historically between them. It is called the "stepped-up basis."

The "Stepped-Up Basis" Rule of Federal Income Tax Law

The "stepped-up basis rule" in federal income tax law effectively reduces income taxes that would have been owed but for the unhappy circumstance of a person's death. It works this way.

Recall that a capital gain is the difference between the selling price of a capital asset (property) and the adjusted basis of that capital asset (property) (e.g., its original purchase price). Before 2010, all property in an estate other than cash automatically received an increase in its basis to the fair market value of the property at the time the decedent died, assuming, of course, that the property had increased in value.[390] This **stepped-up basis** has the effect of excluding from the federal income tax all of the gains in the property's value that preceded the decedent's death whenever the heirs eventually sell that property. I will call these gains the "**embedded capital gains.**" Had the same property been sold by the decedent just a day before he or she died, those embedded capital gains would have been subject to the federal individual income tax on capital gains. The heirs are thus better off, income tax–wise, than the property's owner would have been, and the US Treasury is less well-off.

Congress's Short-Term Reform

In the 2001 Tax Act, Congress changed the "stepped-up basis" rule effective for 2010.[391] This change made the basis of property in an estate the lesser of the property's adjusted basis or the fair market value at the time of the decedent's death. This is the same basis rule that historically has applied and still applies to the basis of property received by gift.[392] For a later sale and calculation of capital gains, this basis rule generally treated the property the same as if the decedent were selling the property.

This new basis rule, however, applied in practice only to large estates. This is so because the change for 2010 also carved out significant exceptions by allowing the basis of estate property to be increased by selected maximum amounts depending upon the identity of the heirs. As the specific numbers show, these exceptions effectively continued the stepped-up basis rule for all but the largest estates.

Under those exceptions, embedded capital gains up to $3,000,000 for a spouse and $1,300,000 for other heirs still escaped income taxation just because the owner died before selling the property.[393] For example, even under the approach used for 2010, if Wily investor had paid $2,000,000 for a corporation's stock in 2006 that had a value of $5,000,000 at the time of his death in 2010, Wily's widow could sell the stock for $5,000,000 a few weeks later and pay no income tax on the $3,000,000 gain. This is a good deal for Wily's widow, but a bad deal for the US Treasury (and indirectly other taxpayers), and a huge difference from Wily or anyone else who sold stock with the same gains while living. Within the million-dollar limits of 2010, just as under the historic rule allowing a stepped-up basis for *all* estate property, the heirs are better off, income tax–wise, than the property's owner would have been, and the US Treasury is less well-off.

In the December 2010 tax compromise, Congress reinstated the stepped-up basis rule when it reinstated a version of the estate tax for 2011 and 2012.[394] The 2012 fiscal cliff tax compromise effectively continued the stepped-up basis rule for all future estates.[395]

Future Fate of the Stepped-Up Basis Rule

For a federal tax system that is fair, accountable, and simple, what should be the rules regarding the basis of property in an estate?

Using a rule that allows an automatic stepped-up basis, or even keeping a rule that allows no stepped-up basis as applied in 2010 with large exceptions, would be a huge discriminatory mistake. These rules should properly be called "tax escape" rules because they give a large income tax subsidy to heirs of an estate by excluding significant embedded capital gains from taxation. Both rules fail our fairness criterion that individuals with the same amount of income pay comparable amounts of federal income tax. Both rules also tend to lock in capital assets because they encourage the elderly owners of capital assets to hold onto those assets rather than sell them so that the owner's heirs can receive and then sell those assets without being taxed on the assets' embedded capital gains.

So, should a rule with no stepped-up basis apply to all estate property without exceptions, or should some exceptions exist such as provided in 2010 but with much smaller amounts?

The rule should be universal without exceptions. Remember that this is just a rule regarding the basis of inherited property. No individual income taxes will be owed unless or until the property is sold by the estate or heirs of the property. By having no exceptions, heirs will be treated the same as the decedent would have been treated if he or she had sold the estate property before dying.

Having no exceptions also avoids a sticky problem for executors of estates. If exceptions exist that allow increases in the basis of estate property up to a maximum amount, whenever the total embedded capital gains for all estate property exceed that amount, an executor has to decide whose inherited property gets the benefit of an increased basis. Maybe the heirs will agree on an allocation of the increased basis, but maybe not. Potential controversy is built into this method of providing exceptions.

Answering Critics of a No Stepped-Up Basis Rule

Critics of a rule that does not allow a stepped-up basis for estate property will point out that heirs may not be able to establish the decedent's adjusted basis that will be carried over with some inherited property. Unlike the decedent, the heirs may not know when the decedent bought some property, how much the decedent paid for the property, and where to find existing documentation of the purchase. According to these critics, this lack of knowledge will cause some heirs to be saddled with larger capital gains income than they actually receive when selling inherited property. They will thus also be saddled with unfair income tax payments on their capital gains from that sale.

There are at least two responses to these critics' concerns.

First, some decedents may also have had this difficulty if they had sold the property before dying, especially for property that had been owned a long time. That difficulty would not and should not have excused the decedent from paying income taxes on the gains received from that sale. Heirs of that property should not be given a better income tax position than the decedent would have had.

Second, any potential difficulty for heirs in establishing the adjusted basis of property in an estate can be minimized through estate planning. Very simply, without a stepped-up basis rule, a new element of estate planning will be to include organized documentation of assets that shows and confirms the adjusted basis of all major property owned by the person doing the planning. If there is no estate tax, this could become the primary element of estate planning rather than trusts, disclaimers, and other legal mechanisms now employed to minimize estate tax possibilities. As for continuing records for property passed from generation to generation, state estate law already requires an inventory of all estate property with its fair market value, so new forms of inventory could also include the adjusted basis. Indeed, to deal with this issue, the IRS in 2010 was creating a form to be filed with the decedent's last income tax return that would list the decedent's properties and their adjusted bases.[396]

Of course, heirs can choose to postpone paying income taxes on embedded capital gains merely by continuing to own the inherited property. That is a big difference from the historic estate tax, where the tax is owed promptly on the value of all taxable estate property even if no heir wants to sell any of that property.

An Option for Heirs

Despite their ability to postpone income taxes on embedded capital gains, some heirs may want to increase the basis of inherited property to its fair market value because of their own tax situations. A simple rule can accommodate this desire. Give the heirs an option to pay income tax on the property's embedded capital gains and thereby achieve a stepped-up basis for that property equivalent to its fair market value at the time of the decedent's death.

Even executors of estates could be given this option on behalf of heirs and could use assets of the estate to pay the income tax if agreed by all heirs. Whether an heir chooses to continue to own inherited property and then sell it at some later date or to pay income taxes on embedded capital gains, the United States will ultimately achieve the same income tax receipts from the embedded capital gains as if the decedent had sold the property just before dying.

Having dealt with the basis of property inherited from an estate, what about the estate itself? Should there be a federal estate tax and a complementary gift tax?

To Have or Not to Have Federal Estate and Gift Taxes

Whether or not to have federal estate and gift taxes has been a contentious issue for many years. Focusing on the estate tax, what are some of the arguments against and for having any estate tax at all?

Arguments Against an Estate Tax

Those who oppose, and even abhor, the federal estate tax call it the "death tax." They assert that this tax steals a person's hard-earned assets. Cutting through their rhetoric, these are their logical arguments:

(1) The decedent has already paid taxes, and so the estate tax is double taxation on the assets (true for many assets, but as seen above, not true for embedded capital gains).[397]
(2) The estate tax rates are absurdly high.
(3) An estate tax on the value of all property in an estate, including cash, is a partial confiscation of that property.
(4) Certain kinds of business assets, like the "family farm," have to be sold to pay estate taxes rather than the heirs being able to continue the business uninterrupted.

Arguments For an Estate Tax

Those who favor the estate tax point out that it is levied only on the extremely wealthy. They could easily call the estate tax the "anti-dynasty tax." Cutting through their rhetoric, their logical arguments include:

(1) The tax moderates the existence of a perpetual aristocracy of wealth that is not based, at least in part, on the personal accomplishments of the heirs of the estate.

(2) The tax is a fair payment to society at large for providing the stability and legal framework that allowed the person to accumulate the estate assets in the first place.

(3) Estate taxes encourage significant donations to public, charitable, and religious organizations (these donations being deductible at their fair market value from the total value of the estate[398]).

(4) Few estates are actually of the business "family farm" type that will be broken apart by having to pay estate taxes. Proponents further contend that special rules could be developed to accommodate those few estates that fit the family-farm type that deserves to remain intact.[399]

In this book, I will not weigh in on these largely philosophical arguments about the desirability or lack of desirability of an estate tax and complementary gift tax.

The FAST Plan Approach

Philosophical arguments aside, no doubt the presence of estate and gift taxes complicates overall federal taxes and also complicates and even drives much estate planning. People understandably want to minimize the application of these taxes to their estates and the potential future estates of their heirs. The nuances and complexity of estate and gift taxation and related planning are far beyond my understanding or the purpose of this book. How to deal with legalities related to estates and gifts like generation-skipping transfers, marital trusts, disclaimers of rights, and unified credits is strictly for the experts. That fact alone is one of the problems with the historic estate and gift tax structure. It may be that the very nature of estate taxes will prevent them and their complementary gift taxes from ever being simple. Absent a clear path to simplicity for these taxes, our simplicity goal for all federal taxes favors their demise.

As with any tax reduction or elimination, if we eliminate current federal estate and gift taxes, the tax receipts lost will have to be accounted for. Either the receipts lost will have to be made unnecessary by comparable decreases in federal expenditures, or other taxes will have to raise replacement receipts.

Elimination of the stepped-up basis rule for all estate property without exception is a change that can provide revenues to replace some or maybe even all revenues lost if estate and gift taxes are repealed altogether. This change has the advantage that it builds upon the concepts and financial data already existing with federal individual income taxes and their application. Revenue replacement will be more likely if the proposed standard-rate income tax of the FAST Plan applies to all income, including all capital gains.

To put in context these receipts from historic estate and gift taxes, in fiscal year 2008, estate and gift taxes accounted for $29 billion of the $1,623 billion in federal receipts, excluding social insurance and retirement receipts (mostly receipts from Social Security and Medicare taxes).[400] Others will have to judge whether losing this $29 billion by not having any federal estate or gift taxes is deemed a significant or insignificant amount of lost tax receipts, especially when weighed against (1) increased tax receipts that will result from eliminating the automatic stepped-up basis rule and (2) general savings for many individuals that will result from greatly simplified estate planning.

Chapter 30 Proposal
New Rules for Estates and Gifts

Reform

- Eliminate the automatic stepped-up basis rule for all property in an estate, without exception.
- Repeal all estate and gift taxes, but only upon eliminating the automatic stepped-up basis rule for all property in an estate, without exception, and preferably along with adopting a standard-rate income tax for all income, including all capital gains.
- Give heirs the option to pay income taxes on embedded capital gains of selected property in an estate based on its fair market value at the time of the decedent's death, thereby establishing a new basis for that property.
- Subject to approval by all of the estate's heirs, give the executor of an estate two options:
    (1) To pay income tax on embedded capital gains of selected property in the estate based on its fair market value at the time of the decedent's death, thereby establishing a new basis for that property
    (2) To pay the income tax from estate assets

Part IV:

Making Change Happen

Chapter 31

———◆•◈•◆———

The First Step

The FAST Plan for Tax Reform is not an academic exercise.

As stated in the introduction, we need action *now* to achieve comprehensive federal tax reform. The FAST Plan provides a blueprint for that reform.

So that we can achieve the reforms of the FAST Plan, many people will have to become familiar with its proposed changes and their merits. Only then can we create impetus for its reforms.

This chapter provides a FAST Plan summary to serve as a quick reference guide to its basic elements. As such, the summary is a launching pad for further discussion, especially in the political arena, where change has to originate. Because the FAST Plan summary contains little explanation about why the FAST Plan's elements have merit, anyone who uses the summary to promote the FAST Plan should also have read *The FAST Plan for Tax Reform* or have had prior experience with federal tax law that can be used to understand all parts of the FAST Plan.

The FAST Plan summary in this chapter has been formatted to allow it to be photocopied on three sheets of paper. Feel free to do so if you want to get involved in promoting the FAST Plan.

To provide further impetus to adopting the FAST Plan, the next two chapters deal with practical transition to the FAST Plan and its tax payment impacts. The final chapter steps back with a challenge to us all on how to achieve real federal tax reform.

The FAST Plan for Tax Reform

The **F**air, **A**ccountable, and **S**imple **T**ax Plan

Complaints about federal taxes abound, but workable proposals for fixing them are rare. Three criteria—fairness, accountability, and simplicity—provide sensible goals for all federal taxes. These goals can be met without having to overhaul the tax collection system. Here are workable proposals that do this.

FAST Plan Summary

Individual Income Tax

Retain the individual income tax as the primary revenue source for general federal expenditures.

- Use one standard tax rate for *all* kinds of income and all individuals.
- Allow an individual's payment of Social Security and Medicare taxes as a nonrefundable income tax credit.
- To determine taxable income, allow reductions from income only for expenses necessary for a healthy life.
- Permit tax subsidies only as nonrefundable income tax credits.
- Identify as a direct subsidy any subsidy payment that is provided through the income tax system as a refundable credit.

Social Security and Medicare Taxes

Retain the current rates and payment responsibilities for Social Security and Medicare taxes, but adjust their application and income tax treatment so that income tax credits for their payments are comparable for all individuals.

Corporation Income Tax

Replace the current corporation earnings (net profit) tax with a small corporation revenue tax that uses one standard rate applied against revenues from US operations only.

Estate and Gift Taxes

Eliminate federal estate and gift taxes, but allow no automatic stepped-up basis for property in an estate or received as a gift.

More detailed descriptions show how these proposals create a Fair, Accountable, and Simple Tax Plan. For a full presentation of the FAST Plan, consult www.fastplanfortaxreform.com for information on the book *The FAST Plan for Tax Reform*.

FAST Plan Highlights

1. The Three Criteria for Federal Taxes

"Fairness" requires that each comparable individual or entity with the same income pay nearly the same total federal taxes. "Accountability" is the ability to know the impact on tax receipts of every tax provision, especially tax subsidies. "Simplicity" means that the tax is both easy to calculate and easy to understand.

2. One Standard Individual Income Tax Rate

Using one standard tax rate for all individual income treats all income as equal, eliminates rate distinctions between filing categories, and makes tax receipts more predictable than the current multirate approach. This predictability clarifies decisions needed to avoid annual deficit spending and national debt increases.

One method to calculate a standard rate in the absence of tax and direct subsidies gives a 29 percent rate when the target for revenue is the individual income tax receipts for tax year 2007. That target may be inadequate because the total deficits in federal fiscal years 2007 and 2008 were, respectively, $161 billion and $459 billion, and on-budget deficits were $342 billion and $642 billion (on-budget excludes using any surplus Social Security trust funds for general expenditures).

3. Social Security and Medicare Tax Payments as Allowed Credits

By allowing nonrefundable credits for payment of Social Security and Medicare taxes, an individual's marginal *total* federal tax rate (adding income, Social Security, and Medicare taxes) will not exceed the standard rate.

Four changes will make these credits the same for employees and self-employed individuals (two each for employees and self-employed individuals).

- For employees, treat the payment by the employer as income to the individual and as a payment also by the individual.
- For self-employed individuals, use 0.9290 as the earned income multiplier and eliminate the current reduction from income for one-half the payment of Social Security and Medicare taxes through the self-employment tax.

These four changes give a universal credit of 14.2 percent of earned income up to the Social Security tax cutoff.

4. Reductions from Income Only for Expenses Necessary for a Healthy Life

Retain standard deductions and exemptions as representing a policy not to tax expenses that are necessary for survival (food, water, clothing, and shelter) and for some other minimal living expenses.

Allow an additional reduction for the payment of all unreimbursed medical expenses above 1 percent of adjusted gross income as essential to maintain a healthy life and to more nearly equalize tax treatment between individuals who have employer-paid health insurance and those who do not.

To determine adjusted gross income, allow only reductions for payments that will ultimately be taxable (e.g., alimony taxable to someone else).

Allow no other reductions from income.

5. Tax Subsidies Only as Nonrefundable Income Tax Credits

The term "tax subsidy" is used here for all current itemized deductions other than medical expenses, all other reductions from income except the standard deduction and exemptions, and all nonrefundable tax credits.

Permitting tax subsidies only as nonrefundable tax credits allows simple limits to be placed on them individually and collectively and the fiscal impact of each tax subsidy to be known accurately. This approach eliminates any need for an alternative minimum tax.

Reevaluate every tax subsidy in light of a standard-rate income tax. For example, do not allow a tax subsidy for payment of state and local taxes.

6. Corporation Income Tax Replacement

Replace the corporation earnings (net profit) tax with a small corporation revenue tax that uses one standard rate applied against revenues from US operations only. This makes the corporation income tax a simply determined and predictable business expense that aligns more closely with the benefits the corporation receives from conducting business in the United States.

One method to calculate a corporation revenue tax gives a standard rate of 1.5 percent when using as a target recent average historic receipts from the corporation earnings (net profit) tax.

7. New Estate and Gift Tax Rules

The estate and complementary gift tax breed complex estate plans and odd tax trade-offs. Eliminating these taxes but allowing no automatic stepped-up basis for property in an estate treats the heirs the same tax-wise as the decedent before death.

Chapter 32

---◆•◆•◆---

Transition

Change is difficult.

Change can generate fear.

Some of my FAST Plan proposals change long-standing approaches to federal taxation. One way to alleviate fear of change is to develop clear pathways on how to get from one set of policies to another. The task in this chapter is to demonstrate some pathways that can allow transition from current federal tax law to the different approaches proposed in the FAST Plan.

Many of my FAST Plan proposals are interrelated and will not work well to achieve fairness, accountability, and simplicity unless adopted together. Some proposals may require transitional years for taxpayers to adjust to them. A few proposals can be adopted in the context of current law and can be made effective immediately. Reasonable transition will thus differ depending upon which proposal is considered. We will consider ideas for transition in this sequence:

(1) Standard-rate individual income tax generally
(2) Standard-rate income tax on all capital gains
(3) Standard-rate income tax on all dividends
(4) Corporation revenue tax

Transition to a Standard-Rate Individual Income Tax

The FAST Plan's standard-rate tax for all individual income sweeps in more proposed changes than any other single proposal. A critical allied change to a standard rate is the nonrefundable credit against an individual's income tax for the individual's payment of Social Security and Medicare taxes. As emphasized throughout this book, without that credit, individuals with small earned incomes would pay significantly higher marginal total federal tax rates (adding their income, Social Security, and Medicare taxes) than individuals with large incomes. Many Americans would find this result to be unacceptable and even cruel because individuals with large incomes have less relative need for their additional dollars.

We need four additional features in transition to assure that the standard-rate income tax fully meets our fairness, accountability, and simplicity criteria:

- Social Security and Medicare tax credits equality
- A fairly determined standard tax rate
- Using only tax credits for subsidies
- Standard-rate universal application

Social Security and Medicare Tax Credits Equality

As discussed in chapter 11 on solving the Social Security and Medicare taxes dilemma, the nonrefundable credits allowed in the FAST Plan for payment of Social Security and Medicare taxes would be applied unequally for employees and self-employed individuals without changes in current tax law. The accounting changes proposed in that chapter make those credits comparable. Allowing a nonrefundable credit for payment of Social Security and Medicare taxes and the FAST Plan's proposed accounting changes all have to be made at the same time.

A Fairly Determined Standard Tax Rate

A standard income tax rate should not be arbitrary. Instead, it should be determined by analyses that show what rate is needed to maintain the federal tax receipts that exist under current law or to provide more or less total tax receipts to cover federal expenditures as determined from the political process. The first standard rate should not be an excuse to increase or decrease total federal taxes. Once a standard rate is determined, both the standard rate and its allied tax credits and accounting changes for Social Security and Medicare taxes can be applied without a transition period other than sufficient time for employers to adjust their payroll systems. Those adjustments could be underway while the initial standard rate is being determined.

Using Only Tax Credits for Subsidies

Also related to a standard-rate tax on individual income are the many reductions from income that current law allows in determining taxable income. Except for standard deductions, exemptions, and reductions for payments for medical expenses, all of these reductions should first be recast as nonrefundable tax credits and then reexamined in light of the standard rate. This reexamination will likely show that a standard rate will dictate the elimination of or strict limitations on the tax subsidies inherent in some or maybe even all long-standing income reductions. These include the itemized deductions for state and local taxes, which I propose be eliminated, and for all elective payments that benefit oneself, such as mortgage interest payments. All of these changes preferably should occur at the same time as the general transition to a standard-rate income tax, but that transition should not be held back by wrangling over details about these tax subsidies.

Standard-Rate Universal Application

A final part of adopting a standard-rate tax on individual income is applying the standard rate to all individual income, including the long-term capital gains and qualified dividends that now enjoy special low rates. These two kinds of income may require transition periods longer than required for a general transition to a standard rate for other individual income. Capital gains and dividends will thus be considered next.

Transition to a Standard-Rate Income Tax on All Capital Gains

The reasons for applying a standard-rate income tax to all capital gains are addressed in chapter 14 on capital gains. The sole question here is how best to transition to a standard rate applicable to capital gains.

The current special low capital gains rates apply primarily to what can loosely be called long-term investment capital gains. As such, people who made those long-term investments did so in part because of their tax advantages as a tax subsidy. "Long-term" qualification for this purpose is only one year. If a standard-rate income tax looms ahead, how much time should investors have to sell their long-term capital assets if they choose to do so before their tax subsidy disappears?

The purpose of a waiting period is solely to allow reasonable time for desired sales to develop for those capital assets that individuals prefer to sell before an increased tax on capital gains occurs. Thus, an appropriate waiting period might be different for different kinds of assets. Shares of a publicly traded corporation, for example, would ordinarily be easier to sell than unimproved land. Also factoring into an ability to sell capital assets is the fact that for many investors, a new standard income tax rate applied to short-term capital gains will be lower than their marginal tax rate applied to those same gains under the current graduated rate structure. These investors will have greater short-term investment flexibility that could increase the general demand for capital assets.

On balance, a two- or three-year waiting period—but not longer—may be appropriate in which to make the standard-rate income tax applicable to long-term capital gains. So many factors other than tax rates affect the salability of capital assets that a transition period exceeding two or three years assigns too much importance to the tax aspects of those sales. For example, a general recession, a change in consumers' desires, and stock market fluctuations caused by global events can have far greater impacts on the salability of a capital asset than the tax rate for capital gains.

An approach that phases in the standard rate on long-term capital gains is undesirable because it not only would add complexity, but also could provide pressure for prompt sales of some long-term capital assets that are not suited to prompt sale.

Transition to a Standard-Rate Income Tax on Dividends

The special low income tax rate on qualified dividends that exists in current tax law represents, at least in part, a compromise in the debate over double taxation fueled by the current tax on corporation earnings. Despite this relationship, applying the standard-rate income tax to dividends does not have to await a full transition to a corporation revenue tax.

The dividends tax transition can occur in the same time frame as the change in rates on capital gains because the low rates on qualified dividends are the same as the low rates on long-term capital gains. Besides, these special low rates have only been around since 2003.[401] At least this method would have some consistency among related investments.

An alternative but more complicated approach would be to make the standard rate applicable to dividends in the same time chosen for the transition to a corporation revenue tax. If a phase-in method is used like the method outlined below for the corporation revenue tax, the phase-in period would be five years.

Transition to a Corporation Revenue Tax

Perhaps the boldest proposal in the FAST Plan is my rejection of the corporation earnings (net profit) tax in favor of a corporation revenue tax.

Although I strongly urge that earnings be replaced as the income tax base for corporations, I recognize that an immediate transition to a revenue-based tax could create serious dislocations for some corporations. Corporations that historically have had healthy earnings would probably want to make an immediate change because their tax bills will decrease. Corporations that historically have had small or no earnings, however, may balk and complain that they will go bankrupt if they suddenly have to pay more or any income taxes to the United States. A transition period, therefore, makes good sense.

For corporations, I suggest that a fair transition over a number of corporate fiscal years could occur by calculating two taxes, one using the old tax on earnings with its rates (the "historic tax") and another using the new tax on revenue with its much-reduced standard rate (the "new tax"). As an example, if the full change were to be made complete after five years, for each fiscal year after the new tax is adopted, the total tax could be as shown in table 32.1.

Table 32.1. Potential staged transition to a new corporation revenue tax

First fiscal year	80% historic tax + 20% new tax	= total tax
Second fiscal year	60% historic tax + 40% new tax	= total tax
Third fiscal year	40% historic tax + 60% new tax	= total tax
Fourth fiscal year	20% historic tax + 80% new tax	= total tax
Fifth fiscal year	100% new tax	= total tax

Is this enough time for such a major change?

I do not know.

This example is just a starting point for a dialogue on an appropriate time frame and phase-in method. Of course, any phase-in method will increase rather than decrease corporate tax complexity. Temporary increased complexity may be necessary to establish a taxation method for corporations that ultimately is far more simple and nondiscriminatory than the current method.

Three Potential Changes within Current Law

We can adopt three of my FAST Plan proposals as changes in the context of current law without having to adopt other FAST Plan proposals.

The most far-reaching such proposal is to recast all subsidies as tax credits. Mostly this would involve changing current tax subsidies to nonrefundable tax credits. Credits can be based on a variety of methods, including a flat percentage of payments made or a small percentage of adjusted gross income. All subsidies can easily be limited in amount using the tax credits method. Credits can be devised that reflect existing subsidy policies in a reasonable way, so the credits methodology can be applied immediately. Then these subsidies can be revisited when their true cost in terms of lost tax receipts becomes evident.

Two of the FAST Plan proposals that we can adopt in the context of current law relate to estates and gifts and should be adopted together, as discussed in chapter 30. These are my proposals to eliminate the automatic "stepped-up basis" rule for deceased's estates, with no exceptions, and to eliminate the federal estate tax and its complementary gift tax. These proposals can also be applied immediately because their effects are triggered only by the unplanned event of a person's death. The gift tax exists because of the estate tax, and so should end when the estate tax ends.

Transition Reality

Having now shown how we can transition to the FAST Plan, the next chapter takes a look at the tax payment impacts of the FAST Plan on different groups of individuals and entities when that transition has occurred.

Chapter 33

---◆•◆•◆---

Tax Payment Impacts of the FAST Plan

If the FAST Plan achieves fairness, accountability, and simplicity, then arguably it really will not matter whether any particular individual or entity will end up paying less or more federal taxes. Those who end up paying more federal taxes are not really disadvantaged because they were underpaying under the previous system. Conversely, those who end up paying less federal taxes are not really beneficiaries of change because they were overpaying under the previous system.

This argument avoids the legitimate question of who is likely to pay more federal taxes and who is likely to pay less federal taxes under the FAST Plan. Here is an attempt to answer this question. Recognize, however, that even though the FAST Plan is designed to eliminate or at least greatly reduce many tax subsidies, specific defined tax subsidies with clear accountability probably will and should remain. Those tax subsidies can significantly affect the amount of federal taxes any particular individual will pay.

Decreased Compliance Costs for Everyone

In one respect, everyone will gain from the FAST Plan because its proposals are designed to increase taxpaying simplicity. Greater simplicity creates both direct and indirect cost savings.

The most obvious direct cost saving for both individuals and entities will be less money spent for tax advice and on the preparation of federal tax returns. Especially for individuals, greater simplicity also means freeing up time for other endeavors. Of course, the industry that provides tax advice and tax return preparation will diminish, so some people in that industry will have to retool for other work.

Greater simplicity can also create indirect cost savings for most individuals and entities. How this will occur has already been summarized in chapter 4 but bears repeating here.

Greater simplicity will save the US government money and will also increase federal tax receipts generally. Either effect will provide indirect cost savings for most individuals and entities because each effect can potentially allow overall tax decreases or prevent otherwise-needed tax increases. These benefits can occur in at least two different ways.

(1) Greater simplicity will diminish tax-reporting errors and will require less federal resources to process, check, and audit tax returns, thus reducing federal expenditures for these purposes.

(2) Greater simplicity will make tax cheating more difficult, whether the cheating is attempted by outright false reporting or by complex tax-avoidance schemes. Odd information will be more visible and easier to detect under simplified reporting and calculations. Less successful cheating should increase federal tax receipts from the same amount of economic activity.

Individuals Who Will Likely Pay More Federal Taxes

Individuals whose primary income is from long-term capital gains will pay more income taxes under the FAST Plan's proposed standard-rate income tax than under the current preferentially low maximum rates (15 percent in 2009 law; 20 percent in 2013 law). My initial estimated standard income tax rate is 29 percent, using 2007 tax receipts as the target amount (even though this rate would not have achieved a balanced budget that year).

A 29 percent rate is not a complete departure from historic precedent and thus will not cast the American economy into uncharted waters. This rate is close to the 28 percent maximum income tax rate on long-term capital gains that was part of the Tax Reform Act of 1986 approved by President Reagan. The Reagan 28 percent rate existed up to 1997, when Congress reduced that maximum rate to 20 percent. The 15 percent maximum rate is relatively new, with Congress having adopted that rate in 2003. Of course, Congress reinstated the 20 percent rate for very large incomes beginning in 2013. (See rate discussions in chapters 10 and 14 and in appendix 10B.)

In addition, individuals who are heirs of estates that have embedded capital gains will no longer be able to avoid paying income taxes on all or a portion of those gains when they ultimately sell these assets. These heirs will end up paying more federal taxes as compared to 2009 tax law if the estate would not have been subject to the federal estate tax (albeit in the form of income taxes and only if and when they sell these assets). On the other hand, if the estate had been subject to the federal estate tax, these heirs may end up paying less federal taxes as compared to 2009 tax law because the FAST Plan eliminates estate taxes in return for later taxing embedded capital gains.

Individuals Who Will Likely Pay Less Federal Taxes

Formulas can be developed to compare an individual's total federal taxes under the FAST Plan to total federal taxes under current law. Appendixes 33A and 33B illustrate how this can be done by using the filing category "married filing jointly" as an example and a standard income tax rate estimated at 29 percent. In making these comparisons, "total federal taxes" means the sum of income, Social Security, and Medicare taxes paid by an individual. These comparisons use only the standard deduction and regular exemptions as income reductions. Also, the calculations of the income tax under current law use no tax credits (subsidies) that might be applicable under current law.

Excluding the effects of specific tax subsidies, the vast majority of individuals who are employees or have self-employed businesses will pay total federal taxes under the FAST Plan that are less than or about the same as total federal taxes under current law. This favorable result occurs mostly because Social Security and Medicare taxes will no longer add to the income taxes of employees and self-employed individuals.

Another group that will likely pay less federal taxes under the FAST Plan than currently consists of individuals who have relatively large incomes that are primarily earned income and who have no or few currently allowed reductions from income (such as mortgage interest payments). For these individuals, the 2009 maximum marginal income tax rate of 35 percent would be reduced to the assumed standard rate of 29 percent used in the examples.

Individuals with significant out-of-pocket medical expenses, including medical insurance costs, will pay less income tax under the FAST Plan because payments for medical expenses will be reductions from income *in addition to* a standard deduction. This approach will make these individuals more equal tax-wise to those individuals whose employers provide them significant medical insurance or medical care.

Individuals with Significant Dividends Income

The FAST Plan will apply a standard income tax rate against all dividends income instead of the current preferentially low tax rates on qualified dividends. Although an individual's income tax on dividends will therefore increase, an individual's net amount of after-tax money from dividends will not necessarily decrease. This is so because the FAST Plan also includes replacing the current corporation earnings (net profit) tax by a much-lower-rate tax on corporation revenue. This new tax method will affect dividends in different ways for different corporations.

The dividends of highly profitable corporations should increase substantially. This is so because the revenue tax in the FAST Plan will affect the amount of earnings available for dividends from these corporations far less than the current 35 percent corporation net profit tax affects those earnings. The increase in dividends can more than offset the increased tax from a standard tax rate on an individual's dividends. Individuals who receive those dividends will have more after-tax money than under current law.

There will be a threshold point where dividends from less-profitable or marginally profitable corporations may not increase at all or may not increase enough to offset the increased tax on dividends resulting from a standard income tax rate. Individuals who receive those dividends will have less after-tax money than under current law.

Thus, the increase or decrease of an individual's after-tax net income from dividends will be specific to each corporation that pays dividends.[402]

The Corporate World

Among corporations, those that will pay more federal taxes are corporations that currently have very small or no earnings, whatever the reason for that result. This is so because the much lower standard-rate corporation tax will be applied to revenue, not earnings. The free ride for some corporations of paying no or very little federal income taxes will disappear.

Those corporations that will likely pay less federal income taxes will be corporations with large earnings. As noted above, however, a significant part of these large earnings may be paid out as dividends. Those dividends will be taxable at a standard rate to the individuals who receive them.

Whether the sum of the federal tax payments by a corporation and the income tax payments by its shareholders on their dividends from the corporation will be more or less than currently will be difficult to assess. That sum will be different for different corporations. If that sum is less under the FAST Plan than current law, maybe that is a proper reward for profitability, rather than the current deterrent for reporting large earnings because of the relatively high marginal tax rates on the earnings of very profitable corporations.

Reform Reality

Notwithstanding the FAST Plan's many new tax ideas, can we really accomplish comprehensive tax reform today? The next and final chapter tackles this difficult question.

Chapter 34

---•◆•◆•◆•---

Are We Ready?

It's easy to complain that federal taxes are too complicated or unfair. Many people, whether politicians, pundits, or ordinary folk, have done so. Translating complaints into ideas for improvement and then taking action are altogether different exercises.

I have tried in this book to provide new ideas on how to reform federal taxes by setting forth understandable goals, defining those goals, and showing how my FAST Plan can achieve those goals. Whether or not you agree that fairness, accountability, and simplicity are proper goals as I have defined them, at least they provide a basis for evaluating current and proposed federal tax law and approaches. Similarly, whether or not you agree with some or all of the FAST Plan proposals, at least they have been made with candor about any policies or philosophies that underlie them and how they relate to and affect existing federal tax approaches and each other.

If we really want to chop away the current federal tax thicket, comprehensive changes have to be made in federal tax laws and approaches. My proposals in the FAST Plan represent one way that comprehensive changes can be made. Even if the FAST Plan or some other set of proposals is seriously considered in Congress, comprehensive changes will likely not occur without the support of most American citizens.

With what criteria will each citizen judge any set of comprehensive changes?

An initial and appropriate criterion will undoubtedly be whether an individual or entity will pay less total federal taxes (yay!) or more (boo!) if a set of comprehensive changes is adopted. If that is the sole criterion, however, we will never chop away the current federal tax thicket.

Unless it is somehow possible to reduce federal expenditures so much that everyone can have less federal taxes that are fairly applied, any set of comprehensive changes will have some who will pay more and some who will pay less after the changes. Beware of people who decide to oppose any set of changes solely because they currently have large discriminatory tax advantages that might be diminished. Those same people may try to block changes by raising a fuss that has little relationship to the actual proposed changes.

Another criterion that citizens—and more likely politicians—may use to judge changes is preconceived views about how income taxes affect citizens' lives. In this respect, current income tax law reflects an uneasy truce between two very different views by incorporating both views in the income tax structure. Graduated tax rates reflect the view that people with larger incomes can afford to and should pay a greater portion of their incomes as taxes because they need a smaller portion of those larger incomes for normal living expenses. Low tax rates for long-term capital gains (and now also ordinary dividends) reflect the view that capital-based income, especially capital gains, should have exceptionally low tax rates in order to encourage investments that create economic benefits for everyone.

My FAST Plan rejects both views for many different reasons, as expressed in previous chapters. If those who hold these views insist that their view be incorporated in federal income tax law, then real tax reform will be impossible. The grand compromise that we need is for *neither* view to be incorporated.

Compromise is a disfavored concept in much of today's political wrangling. Despite this political atmosphere and the possibility that those with large current tax advantages will strive mightily to retain them, hope nevertheless exists that real change can occur.

Americans have in the past supported significant changes in other areas by looking at the big picture beyond their personal situations and preconceived notions. Examples are the Nineteenth Amendment to the US Constitution (women's right to vote) and legislation establishing Social Security (widespread taxes to provide benefits for the elderly and disabled to avoid their abject poverty).

The current federal tax thicket can be chopped away if most American citizens are willing to look at a big picture regarding federal taxes while also giving value to goals like fairness, accountability, and simplicity that would be achieved by comprehensive changes.

Are we ready?

Appendixes

APPENDICES

Introduction

————◆•◆•◆————

Why have appendixes? Three reasons:

First, they provide proof that the data and other facts stated in the main text of this book are correct and that discussions of data fairly represent what the data show.

Second, they provide information that can be used to test or modify some proposals in this book based upon adopting alternative philosophies. An example would be calculating different standard rates for the individual income tax based on whether or how Social Security benefits are taxed.

Third, they present historic information about current federal taxes and spending in accurate and new ways that can help citizens and decision makers better understand the federal tax and budget issues facing the United States today.

Most of the appendixes provide statistical data that are summarized from official US government reports or that are calculated from data in those reports. Particularly valuable as sources are the Statistics of Income (SOI) tables compiled by the Internal Revenue Service and the Historical Tables in the budgets of the US government compiled by the Office of Management and Budget.

The statistical data in these appendixes are presented mostly in tables but also in some figures. Most data cover federal fiscal years 1981 to 2012. Fiscal year 1981 was chosen as the starting point because that is the last fiscal year before the major tax-law changes that occurred during the Reagan presidency and later, which had important effects on federal deficits and national debt increases.

Other appendixes show how example numbers cited in the main text were calculated. Still other appendixes provide detail to augment statements in the main text.

Except for appendix 1A, the appendixes are numbered according to the primary chapter that uses information found in that appendix. Each appendix has a brief statement about its purpose and a comments section that summarizes its content. Data sources are cited in the appendixes.

List of Appendixes

Appendix 1A   Collection of specific FAST Plan proposals. 237

Appendix 1B   Federal spending, total outlays and receipts (with tables 1B.1 and 1B.2 and figures 1B.1 and 1B.2). 247

Appendix 1C   Federal spending, on-budget outlays and receipts (with tables 1C.1 and 1C.2 and figures 1C.1 and 1C.2). 253

Appendix 2A   Federal deficit spending, total deficit with its on-budget and off-budget components (with table 2A.1) 259

Appendix 2B   Federal deficit spending, total deficit with its federal funds and trust funds components (with table 2B.1) 262

Appendix 2C   Federal deficit spending, deficits compared to outlays, total receipts, and total receipts without social insurance and retirement receipts (with tables 2C.1, 2C.2, 2C.3, 2C.4, and 2C.5) 265

Appendix 2D   Federal national debt with its public debt and government accounts debt components (with tables 2D.1 and 2D.2 and figure 2D.1) 272

Appendix 2E   Federal national debt, US interest obligations by lender category compared to total outlays, total receipts, and total receipts without social insurance and retirement receipts (with tables 2E.1, 2E.2, and 2E.3) 277

Appendix 2F   Federal national debt, approximate average annual net interest rates on the national debt (with table 2F.1). 282

Appendix 3A   Federal national debt, the debt to Social Security trust funds (with table 3A.1) 284

Appendix 5A   Individual total tax, example calculation of the total federal taxes paid by a top income group 286

Appendix 9A   Federal receipts by major source (with tables 9A.1, 9A.2, 9A.3, and 9A.4) 290

Appendix 9B   Individual income tax, the duty to file individual income tax returns 295

Appendix 10A   Individual income tax, calculation of a standard rate under the FAST Plan using tax year 2007 data (with tables 10A.1 and 10A.2) 298

Appendix 10B   Individual income tax, summary of significant individual income tax rate changes, 1980–2012 305

Appendix 10C   Individual income tax, comparing tax-rate changes to annual receipts from the individual income tax (with table 10C.1 and figures 10C.1 and 10C.2) 309

Appendix 10D   Individual income tax, comparing tax-rate changes to GDP (with table 10D.1 and figures 10D.1, 10D.2, 10D.3, and 10D.4) 314

Appendix 10E   Individual income tax, comparing marginal total federal tax rates under 2010 tax law (with tables 10E.1, 10E.2, 10E.3, 10E.4, 10E.5, 10E.6, 10E.7, and 10E.8) 321

Appendix 10F   Individual income tax, comparing marginal total federal tax rates under alternative tax-rate approaches (with figures 10F.1, 10F.2, 10F.3, 10F.4, 10F.5, and 10F.6). 335

Appendix 11A   Individual income tax, example marginal total tax-rate comparisons under one standard rate and no other 2009 tax-law changes (with tables 11A.1 and 11A.2) 344

Appendix 11B   Social Security and Medicare taxes, determining the self-employment-tax multiplier 347

Appendix 12A   Individual income and tax data, identifying kinds of individual income and reductions to reach taxable income using sample years (with tables 12A.1, 12A.2, and 12A.3) 350

Appendix 14A   Individual income and tax data, identifying which individual income groups have what kinds of income using sample years (with tables 14A.1, 14A.2, 14A.3, 14A.4, 14A.5, 14A.6, 14A.7, and 14A.8). . .354

Appendix 14B   Individual income and tax data, comparing effective tax rates on all income paid by individuals in different income categories using sample years (with tables 14B.1 and 14B.2). 364

Appendix 14C   Individual income tax, capital gains, example showing tax-payment effect of special capital gains tax rates under 2009 tax law (with tables 14C.1 and 14C.2). 368

Appendix 14D   Individual income tax, capital gains, comparing capital gains tax-rate changes to jobs (with table 14D.1 and figures 14D.1 and 14D.2) . . .372

Appendix 14E   Individual income tax, capital gains, comparing capital gains tax-rate changes to reported net capital gains (with table 14E.1 and figures 14E.1 and 14E.2) 377

Appendix 14F   Individual income tax, capital gains, evaluating Congress's "Reasons for Change" for decreasing capital gains tax rates in 1997 (with table 14F.1). 382

Appendix 16A   Individual income tax, new approach to taxation of Social Security benefits (with figures 16A.1 and 16A.2) 386

Appendix 25A   Individual income tax, can refundable tax credits for payments of Social Security and Medicare taxes achieve the goals of the Earned Income Credit?. 390

Appendix 28A   Individual income tax, identifying tax subsidies targeted by the Alternative Minimum Tax in 2009 tax law (with figure 28A.1) 392

Appendix 29A   Corporation income tax, calculation of a standard rate for a corporation revenue tax (with table 29A.1) 394

Appendix 33A   Individual income tax, examples comparing tax payments under 2009 tax law to tax payments under the FAST Plan standard-rate approach: married wage earners filing jointly .397

Appendix 33B   Individual income tax, examples comparing tax payments under 2009 tax law to tax payments under the FAST Plan standard-rate approach: married self-employed individuals filing jointly 402

Tables and Figures in the Appendixes

Table 1B.1   Federal spending, total outlays and receipts in current and constant (FY 2005) dollars, 1981–2012 249

Table 1B.2   Federal spending, total outlays and receipts per resident person in constant (FY 2005) dollars, 1981–2012 250

Figure 1B.1   Federal spending, total outlays and receipts in constant (FY 2005) dollars, 1981–2012 251

Figure 1B.2   Federal spending, total outlays and receipts per resident person in constant (FY 2005) dollars, 1981–2012 252

Table 1C.1   Federal spending, on-budget outlays and receipts in current and constant (FY 2005) dollars, 1981–2012 255

Table 1C.2   Federal spending, on-budget outlays and receipts per resident person in constant (FY 2005) dollars, 1981–2012. 256

Figure 1C.1   Federal spending, on-budget outlays and receipts in constant (FY 2005) dollars, 1981–2012. 257

Figure 1C.2   Federal spending, on-budget outlays and receipts per resident person in constant (FY 2005) dollars, 1981–2012. 258

Table 2A.1   Federal deficit spending, total deficit with on-budget and off-budget components in current dollars, 1981–2012 261

Table 2B.1   Federal deficit spending, total deficit with federal funds and trust funds components in current dollars, 1981–2012 264

Table 2C.1   Federal deficit spending, three alternative federal deficit versions in current dollars, 1981–2012. 267

Table 2C.2   Federal deficit spending, three alternative federal amounts in current dollars against which to compare deficits, 1981–2012. 268

Table 2C.3   Federal deficit spending, total deficit as % of total outlays, total receipts, and total receipts without social insurance and retirement receipts, 1981–2012 269

Table 2C.4   Federal deficit spending, on-budget deficit as % of total outlays, total receipts, and total receipts without social insurance and retirement receipts, 1981–2012 270

Table 2C.5   Federal deficit spending, federal funds deficit as % of total outlays, total receipts, and total receipts without social insurance and retirement receipts, 1981–2012 271

Table 2D.1   Federal national debt with its public debt and government accounts debt components in current dollars, 1981–2012 274

Table 2D.2   Federal national debt, annual changes in the public debt and government accounts debt components in current dollars, 1981–2012 . .275

Figure 2D.1   Annual national debt increases in current dollars compared to presidents, 1981–2012 276

Table 2E.1   Federal national debt, US interest obligations on the national debt by lender category in current dollars, 1981–2012 279

Table 2E.2   Federal national debt, net interest payment as % of total outlays, total receipts, and total receipts without social insurance and retirement receipts, 1981–2012 280

Table 2E.3   Federal national debt, gross interest payment as % of total outlays, total receipts, and total receipts without social insurance and retirement receipts, 1981–2012 281

Table 2F.1   Federal national debt, approximate average annual net interest rates on the national debt, 1981–2012 283

Table 3A.1   Federal national debt, the debt to government accounts and to Social Security trust funds in current dollars, 1981–2012 285

Table 9A.1   Federal receipts by major source in current dollars, fiscal year 2008 291

Table 9A.2   Federal receipts by major source as a percentage of total receipts
                  (continuation of table 9A.1), fiscal year 2008 292

Table 9A.3   Federal receipts by major source in current dollars, fiscal year 2001 293

Table 9A.4   Federal receipts by major source as a percentage of total receipts
                  (continuation of table 9A.3), fiscal year 2001 .294

Table 10A.1   Individual income tax, calculation of a standard rate using tax year
                  2007 data in current dollars 300

Table 10A.2   Explanations for line items in table 10A.1 (calculation of an
                  individual income tax standard rate). 302

Table 10C.1   Individual income tax, receipts from the individual income tax in
                  current and constant (FY 2005) dollars, 1981–2012 311

Figure 10C.1   Comparing broad tax-rate changes to receipts from the individual
                  income tax in constant (FY 2005) dollars, 1981–2012 312

Figure 10C.2   Comparing broad tax-rate changes to receipts from the individual
                  income tax per resident person in constant (FY 2005) dollars, 1981–
                  2012. 313

Table 10D.1   Individual income tax, base data for comparing tax-rate changes to
                  GDP, 1981–2012 316

Figure 10D.1   Comparing broad individual income tax rate changes to GDP in
                  constant (FY 2005) dollars, 1981–2012 317

Figure 10D.2   Comparing broad individual income tax rate changes to GDP per
                  resident person in constant (FY 2005) dollars, 1981–2012 318

Figure 10D.3   Comparing long-term capital gains tax-rate changes to GDP in
                  constant (FY 2005) dollars, 1981–2012 319

Figure 10D.4   Comparing long-term capital gains tax-rate changes to GDP per
                  resident person in constant (FY 2005) dollars, 1981–2012 320

Table 10E.1.   Marginal total federal tax rates, single individual, wages income
                  only, 2010 tax law. 323

Table 10E.2.   Marginal total federal tax rates, single individual, self-employment income only, 2010 tax law 324

Table 10E.3.   Marginal total federal tax rates, married couple filing jointly, wages income only, 2010 tax law 326

Table 10E.4.   Marginal total federal tax rates, married couple filing jointly, self-employment income only, 2010 tax law 327

Table 10E.5.   Marginal total federal tax rates, married couple filing separately, wages income only, 2010 tax law 329

Table 10E.6.   Marginal total federal tax rates, married couple filing separately, self-employment income only, 2010 tax law 330

Table 10E.7.   Marginal total federal tax rates, head of household, wages income only, 2010 tax law. 332

Table 10E.8.   Marginal total federal tax rates, head of household, self-employment income only, 2010 tax law 333

Figure 10F.1   Marginal total federal tax rates, 2009 tax law, single individual employee with wages income only or with long-term capital gains and qualified dividends income only 338

Figure 10F.2   Marginal total federal tax rates, FAST Plan (at 29%), single individual employee with wages income only or with long-term capital gains and qualified dividends income only 339

Figure 10F.3   Marginal total federal tax rates, flat-tax proposal (at 25%), single individual employee with wages income only or with long-term capital gains and qualified dividends income only 340

Figure 10F.4   Marginal total federal tax rates, 2009 tax law, single individual with self-employment income only or with long-term capital gains and qualified dividends income only. 341

Figure 10F.5   Marginal total federal tax rates, FAST Plan (at 29%), single individual with self-employment income only or with long-term capital gains and qualified dividends income only 342

Figure 10F.6   Marginal total federal tax rates, flat-tax proposal (at 25%), single individual with self-employment income only or with long-term capital gains and qualified dividends income only 343

Table 11A.1   Marginal total federal tax rates, single individual, wages income only, standard rate (at 25%) within 2009 tax law 345

Table 11A.2   Marginal total federal tax rates, single individual, self-employment income only, standard rate (at 25%) within 2009 tax law 346

Table 12A.1   Individual income and tax data, all returns, kinds of individual income and reductions types in current dollars, tax year 2007 351

Table 12A.2   Individual income and tax data, all returns, kinds of individual income and reductions types in current dollars, tax year 2000 352

Table 12A.3   Individual income and tax data, all returns, kinds of individual income and reductions types in current dollars, tax year 1993 353

Table 14A.1   Kinds of income by individual income category in current dollars, tax year 2007 356

Table 14A.2   Kinds of income by individual income group in current dollars, tax year 2007 357

Table 14A.3   Kinds of income by individual income group shown as % of all income for that kind, tax year 2007 358

Table 14A.4   Kinds of income by individual income group shown as % of all income for the group, tax year 2007 359

Table 14A.5   Kinds of income by individual income category in current dollars, tax year 2000 360

Table 14A.6   Kinds of income by individual income group in current dollars, tax year 2000 361

Table 14A.7   Kinds of income by individual income group shown as % of all income for that kind, tax year 2000 362

Table 14A.8   Kinds of income by individual income group shown as % of all income for the group, tax year 2000 363

Table 14B.1   Income tax by individual income category in current dollars, tax year 2007 366

Table 14B.2   Income tax by individual income category in current dollars, tax year 2000 367

Table 14C.1   Calculation of federal taxes owed by Surgeon S under 2009 tax law 369

Table 14C.2   Calculation of federal taxes owed by Investor I under 2009 tax law 370

Table 14D.1   Individual income tax, capital gains, data used to compare nonfarm employee jobs (private sector) to capital gains tax-rate changes, 1981–2012 374

Figure 14D.1   Comparing nonfarm employee jobs (private sector) to changes in long-term capital gains tax rates, 1981–2012 .375

Figure 14D.2   Comparing nonfarm employee jobs (private sector) per US resident population to changes in long-term capital gains tax rates, 1981–2012 . .376

Table 14E.1   Individual income tax, capital gains, reported net capital gains in current and constant (FY 2005) dollars, 1993–2008 379

Figure 14E.1   Comparing changes in long-term capital gains tax rates to reported net capital gains in constant (FY 2005) dollars, 1993–2008 380

Figure 14E.2   Comparing changes in long-term capital gains tax rates to reported net capital gains as a percentage of total adjusted gross income, 1993–2008 381

Table 14F.1   Comparing median incomes in 1998 to median incomes in 2007 in constant (FY 2010) dollars 384

Figure 16A.1   New approach to taxation of Social Security benefits: simplified Social Security benefits worksheet to determine taxable benefits (using 2009 Form 1040 as reference) 388

Figure 16A.2   2009 Form 1040 Social Security benefits worksheet to determine
               taxable benefits. 389

Figure 28A.1   First page of 2009 Form 6251 showing tax preferences targeted by
               the Alternative Minimum Tax 393

Table 29A.1   Calculation of a standard rate for a corporation revenue tax 396

Table 33A.1   Example Set 1A taxes comparison between 2009 law and 29%
               standard rate 398

Table 33A.2   Example Set 2A taxes comparison between 2009 law and 29%
               standard rate 398

Table 33B.1   Example Set 1B taxes comparison between 2009 law and 29%
               standard rate 404

Table 33B.2   Example Set 2B taxes comparison between 2009 law and 29%
               standard rate 404

Appendix 1A

---◆·◆·◆---

Collection of specific FAST Plan proposals

Purpose: To collect in one place all of the specific proposals at the end of chapters in the main text so that these proposals can be examined as a compact whole and form the basis for tax-reform legislation.

Comments

Many chapters in *The FAST Plan for Tax Reform* end with specific proposals. These are collected here verbatim and in chapter sequence to show the overall framework for the FAST Plan that has more detail than the descriptions found in chapter 8 ("The FAST Plan's Bottom Line"). Some FAST Plan proposals are interdependent in the sense that adopting one proposal without the other would not achieve the goals of fairness, accountability, and simplicity. These proposals may not separately even be good ideas if adopted without other FAST Plan changes in current federal tax law.

This appendix can also serve as a checklist for the preparation of specific legislation that is designed to adopt all or part of the FAST Plan.

Prelude

Chapter 5 identifies taxes on individual income, corporation income (potentially redefined), and estates and gifts as the subjects for reform with the FAST Plan.

Part II: Reforming Taxes on Individual Income

Chapter 10 Proposal
Should We Retain Graduated Income Tax Rates?

Reform

- Replace all current graduated individual income tax rate schedules with a single standard income tax rate.
- Determine an initial standard rate from an analysis that keeps total federal individual income tax receipts constant in a non-recession economy.
- Allow all Social Security tax and Medicare tax payments by an individual as nonrefundable credits against income taxes owed, but only after making the Social Security and Medicare tax payments equivalent between employees and self-employed individuals (as shown in chapter 11).
- Apply the standard-rate income tax to all kinds of income.

Chapter 11 Proposal
Solving the Social Security and Medicare Taxes Dilemma

Retain

Retain the current 12.4 percent Social Security and 2.9 percent Medicare tax rates, earned income cutoff for Social Security tax application, and payment obligations by employers, employees, and self-employed individuals.

Reform

- If a standard-rate income tax is adopted for all income, allow all Social Security tax and Medicare tax payments by an individual as nonrefundable credits against the individual's income tax, but only after making the credits for Social Security and Medicare tax payments equivalent between employees and self-employed individuals in accordance with the following accounting adjustments:
  (1) For an employee, designate the Social Security and Medicare tax payments by his or her employer on the employee's wages
      (a) as income to the employee and also
      (b) as Social Security and Medicare tax payments to the United States by the employee as well as by the employer.

(2) For a self-employed individual, use a 0.9290 factor in place of the current 0.9235 factor against business net profit to determine the amount of earned income on which to apply the Social Security and Medicare taxes.

- If Social Security and Medicare tax payments are allowed as nonrefundable credits against an individual's income tax, then also eliminate the current reduction from income allowed for one-half the self-employment tax (Social Security and Medicare taxes) paid by self-employed individuals.

Chapter 12 Proposal
What Income Should Be Taxed?

Retain

- Retain current definitions of what is included in "gross income."

Reform

- Retain current definitions of what is *excluded* from "gross income," but only to the extent that the subsidy represented by the exclusion remains appropriate after other FAST Plan changes are made to current federal taxes.

Chapter 13 Proposal
Historic Ordinary Income

Retain

- Treat these five kinds of income as ordinary income:
  - Wages
  - Personal business income
  - Partnership and S corporation income
  - All interest income except as specifically excluded by statute
  - All miscellaneous income not otherwise excluded from the definition of gross income

Reform

- Apply a standard-rate income tax rate to all of this ordinary income.

Chapter 14 Proposal
Capital Gains

Reform

- Treat all capital gains as ordinary income.
- Apply a standard-rate income tax to all capital gains.
- For a principal residence that is sold, keep the current methods to exempt a portion of any capital gain from the individual income tax , but only if reporting is required and this tax subsidy remains appropriate as other FAST Plan changes are made to current federal taxes.

Chapter 15 Proposal
Dividends

Reform

- Treat all dividends as ordinary income.
- Apply a standard-rate income tax to all dividends.
- Preferably adopt this reform in conjunction with replacing the corporation income tax with a corporation revenue tax.

Chapter 16 Proposal
Social Security Benefits

Reform

- Treat a portion of Social Security benefits as ordinary income based on the excess of other income over a threshold amount that
    - (1) provides sufficient funds for basic necessities and
    - (2) respects expectations for Social Security retirement income resulting from different levels of Social Security tax payments over time.
- Apply a standard-rate income tax to the calculated ordinary income.
- Transfer all income taxes paid on taxable Social Security benefits to the Social Security trust funds.

Chapter 17 Proposal
Pension Payments and Retirement-Plan Distributions

Retain

- Treat pension payments and retirement-plan distributions as ordinary income to the extent that they represent deferred income or are derived from untaxed money contributed to a retirement plan.

Reform

- Apply a standard-rate income tax to this form of ordinary income.

Chapter 18 Proposal
Tax-Exempt Income

Retain

- Retain most current statutory exclusions from gross income.

Reform

- Revisit some current exclusions from gross income, such as interest from state and local bonds, primarily to determine whether the tax subsidy created by the exclusion should remain, and if so, recast the subsidy as a nonrefundable tax credit.

Chapter 19 Proposal
Evaluating Current Reductions from Income

Reform

- If a standard-rate income tax is adopted, eliminate permanently all rules that diminish the availability of itemized deductions or exemptions based on the amount of an individual's income.

Chapter 20 Proposal
Appropriate Reductions Above the Line

Retain

- Treat payments of ordinary and necessary trade and business expenses for individual businesses (such as a self-employed business or rentals from property) as reductions from income used to determine business income that is subject to the individual income tax.
- Treat money transfers that only postpone income tax liability (such as payments to qualified retirement plans up to defined limits) as reductions from gross income to determine adjusted gross income.
- Treat money transfers that are taxable to another person (such as alimony and maintenance payments) as reductions from gross income to determine adjusted gross income.

Reform

- Recast all other business-related reductions from income as nonrefundable tax credits so long as the tax subsidies represented by those reductions remain appropriate.
- Allow no other reductions from gross income to determine adjusted gross income.

Chapter 21 Proposal
Reductions for Payments Necessary for a Healthy Life

Retain

- Regardless of the amount of an individual's income, allow the full standard deduction to cover some basic survival needs and also minimal payments that are part of normal living in the United States.

Reform

- Regardless of the amount of an individual's income, allow full exemptions as reductions from income to cover basic survival needs (a reform, but like 2010–2012 and some previous tax law).
- Allow reductions from income in addition to the standard deduction for payments for qualified medical expenses that exceed 1 percent of an individual's adjusted gross income.
- Allow no other reductions from income after adjusted gross income has been determined.

Chapter 22 Proposal
Reductions for Elective Payments

Reform

- Recast as nonrefundable tax credits all current reductions from income for elective payments that benefit oneself and then revisit each tax subsidy to determine if it remains appropriate.
- Recast as a nonrefundable tax credit the itemized deduction for gifts to charity, with these two additional features:
    (1) Allow the tax credit only for total gifts that exceed a modest amount, such as $200.
    (2) Recast in the form of limitations on allowed tax credits all current limitations on the amount of allowed reductions from income for gifts to charity.

Chapter 23 Proposal
Reductions for Nonelective Payments

Reform

- Allow no reductions from income and allow no tax credits for payments of state and local taxes.
- If Social Security and Medicare tax payments are allowed as nonrefundable credits against an individual's income tax, then also eliminate the current reduction from income allowed for one-half the self-employment tax (Social Security and Medicare taxes) paid by self-employed individuals.
- Recast as a nonrefundable tax credit the current itemized deduction for uncompensated losses and then revisit this tax subsidy to determine if it remains appropriate.

Chapter 24 Proposal
Expanded Role of Tax Credits for Subsidies

Reform

- Use nonrefundable income tax credits, and not reductions from income or special tax rates, as the only way to provide tax subsidies to individuals.
- Use refundable credits on individual income tax returns as the only way to provide direct subsidies to individuals in the individual income tax system, and label each such refundable credit as a direct subsidy.

Chapter 25 Proposal
Current Individual Income Tax Credits

Retain
- Retain current individual nonrefundable tax credits so long as the tax subsidies represented by those credits remain appropriate.
- Retain current individual direct subsidies provided as refundable tax credits so long as the subsidies represented by those credits remain appropriate.

Reform
- Except for the credits for a taxpayer's money held by the United States, label all refundable individual tax credits as direct subsidies.
- Reexamine every individual tax credit that derives from any feature of current tax law that would be changed by the proposals of the FAST Plan.
- Recast the Earned Income Credit in simpler ways that separate the direct subsidy for qualifying children from the refund of Social Security and Medicare tax payments.

Chapter 26 Proposal
Two Special Cases: Investors and Retirees

Reform
- If a standard-rate income tax is adopted for all income and if all Social Security and Medicare tax payments by an individual are allowed as nonrefundable credits against the individual's income taxes, then also:
  - Allow individuals who have taxable income in excess of $1,000 that is specifically excluded from the individual's earned income and thus is not subject to Social Security and Medicare taxes, the option each year to designate as Social Security and Medicare taxes an amount of their income taxes determined as if all of that taxable income had been self-employed earned income.
- To allow retirement planning adjustment to a standard-rate income tax, provide a temporary tax subsidy to eligible retirees in the form of a nonrefundable income tax credit determined as if they had paid Social Security and Medicare taxes on their taxable Social Security benefits, pension payments, qualified retirement plan-distributions, and investment income up to the Social Security tax cutoff.
  - Define eligible retirees as those individuals age fifty-nine-and-a-half and older.

Chapter 27 Proposal
The "Marriage Penalty" (and "Marriage Bonus")

Reform

- Use a standard-rate income tax for all individual taxpayers regardless of their filing status.

Chapter 28 Proposal
The Alternative Minimum Tax on Individuals

Reform

- Eliminate the Alternative Minimum Tax for individuals, but only if all tax subsidies are recast as nonrefundable tax credits.

Part III: Reforming Related Taxes

Chapter 29 Proposal
Reforming the Corporation Income Tax

Reform

- Replace the current corporation earnings (net profit) tax with a standard-rate corporation revenue tax on revenues from operations in the United States.
- Determine an initial standard rate from five-year historic data on corporation revenues and corporation income taxes paid in a non-recession economy (estimated at 1.5 percent from a method designed solely to obtain historic levels of corporation tax receipts).
- Impose no tax on corporation revenue or earnings from operations outside the United States and concurrently eliminate all corporation foreign tax credits.
- Create phase-out and phase-in rules that will allow corporations a reasonable time in which to adjust to the new tax base and standard rate.
- Treat entities with corporation-like attributes as corporations subject to any corporation revenue tax that is adopted in place of the corporation earnings (net profit) tax.

Chapter 30 Proposal
New Rules for Estates and Gifts

Reform
- Eliminate the automatic stepped-up basis rule for all property in an estate, without exception.
- Repeal all estate and gift taxes, but only upon eliminating the automatic stepped-up basis rule for all property in an estate, without exception, and preferably along with adopting a standard-rate income tax for all income, including all capital gains.
- Give heirs the option to pay income taxes on embedded capital gains of selected property in an estate based on its fair market value at the time of the decedent's death, thereby establishing a new basis for that property.
- Subject to approval by all of the estate's heirs, give the executor of an estate two options:
    (1) To pay income tax on embedded capital gains of selected property in the estate based on its fair market value at the time of the decedent's death, thereby establishing a new basis for that property
    (2) To pay the income tax from estate assets

Appendix 1B

———◆•◆•◆———

Federal spending, total outlays and receipts

Purpose: To show how the target amount for all federal tax receipts has changed since 1981 as represented by total federal outlays (expenditures).

Comments

This appendix has two tables and two figures.

Table 1B.1 shows for each fiscal year from 1981 to 2012 the total federal outlays and total federal receipts. These data are presented both in current dollars (columns 2 and 3) and in constant dollars (columns 5 and 6) as a way to remove the effects of inflation on the outlay and receipt figures.

Table 1B.2 shows these outlays and receipts in constant dollars per person in the United States as a way to remove the effects of population increases on increased economic activity and, therefore, outlays and receipts caused solely by an expanded population.

Figure 1B.1 depicts how both total outlays and total receipts in constant dollars have changed from 1981 to 2012. The changing outlays and receipts in this figure include increases that are caused solely by an expanded population.

Figure 1B.2 has the same format as figure 1B.1, but shows total outlays and receipts in constant dollars per resident person in the United States.

With respect to outlays, as shown in figure 1B.2, total outlays per person remained essentially constant from 1989 to 2001. These outlays then steadily increased (from 2002 to 2006), even before the extra outlays that began in 2008 as a response to what became the Great Recession. The Office of Management and Budget has data that categorize these total outlays (e.g., data in the Historical Tables in the US budgets). These data can provide a first step in understanding where the increases in outlays occurred after 2001, but an adequate understanding of these increases would also require an examination behind the numbers into the reasons for changes in the different categories.

With respect to receipts, both figures 1B.1 and 1B.2 show the significant decline in total receipts that has occurred during the Great Recession. As numeric examples, the data in table 1B.1 reveal these figures:

- Total receipts in current dollars declined $463 billion from fiscal year 2007 to fiscal year 2009 (18 percent).
- Total receipts in constant dollars declined $512 billion from fiscal year 2007 to fiscal year 2009 (21 percent).

As will be shown in appendix 1C, most of this decline was caused by declines in receipts from taxes other than the Social Security tax.

Data source:

Budget of the U.S. Government, Fiscal Year 2014, Historical Tables, Tables 1.1, 1.3;
Population Estimates, National (US Census Bureau, 2013).

Table 1B.1. Federal spending, total outlays and receipts in current and constant (FY 2005) dollars, 1981–2012

Federal fiscal year (1)	Total outlays in current dollars (billions) (2)	Total receipts in current dollars (billions) (3)	Composite deflator for constant (FY 2005) dollars (4)	Total outlays in constant (FY 2005) dollars (billions) (5)	Total receipts in constant (FY 2005) dollars (billions) (6)
1981	678	599	0.4790	1,415	1,251
1982	746	618	0.5137	1,452	1,203
1983	808	601	0.5394	1,498	1,114
1984	852	666	0.5677	1,501	1,173
1985	946	734	0.5870	1,612	1,250
1986	990	769	0.6022	1,644	1,277
1987	1,004	854	0.6213	1,616	1,375
1988	1,064	909	0.6400	1,663	1,420
1989	1,144	991	0.6637	1,724	1,493
1990	1,253	1,032	0.6842	1,831	1,508
1991	1,324	1,055	0.7165	1,848	1,472
1992	1,382	1,091	0.7439	1,858	1,467
1993	1,409	1,154	0.7640	1,844	1,510
1994	1,462	1,259	0.7782	1,879	1,618
1995	1,516	1,352	0.7995	1,896	1,691
1996	1,560	1,453	0.8187	1,905	1,775
1997	1,601	1,579	0.8360	1,915	1,889
1998	1,652	1,722	0.8439	1,958	2,041
1999	1,702	1,827	0.8558	1,989	2,135
2000	1,789	2,025	0.8770	2,040	2,309
2001	1,863	1,991	0.8992	2,072	2,214
2002	2,011	1,853	0.9138	2,201	2,028
2003	2,160	1,782	0.9378	2,303	1,900
2004	2,293	1,880	0.9645	2,377	1,949
2005	2,472	2,154	1.0000	2,472	2,154
2006	2,655	2,407	1.0354	2,564	2,325
2007	2,729	2,568	1.0642	2,564	2,413
2008	2,983	2,524	1.1031	2,704	2,288
2009	3,518	2,105	1.1073	3,177	1,901
2010	3,457	2,163	1.1211	3,084	1,929
2011	3,603	2,303	1.1439	3,150	2,013
2012	3,537	2,450	1.1704	3,022	2,093

Table 1B.2. Federal spending, total outlays and receipts per resident person in constant (FY 2005) dollars, 1981–2012

Federal fiscal year (1)	United States resident population at July 1 (millions) (7)	Total outlays in constant (FY 2005) dollars per resident person (8)	Total receipts in constant (FY 2005) dollars per resident person (9)	Federal fiscal year (1)	United States resident population at July 1 (millions) (7)	Total outlays in constant (FY 2005) dollars per resident person (8)	Total receipts in constant (FY 2005) dollars per resident person (9)
1981	229	6,181	5,461	1997	273	7,015	6,919
1982	232	6,260	5,186	1998	276	7,093	7,393
1983	234	6,402	4,762	1999	279	7,128	7,652
1984	236	6,359	4,971	2000	282	7,234	8,188
1985	238	6,771	5,254	2001	285	7,270	7,769
1986	240	6,850	5,321	2002	288	7,641	7,041
1987	242	6,678	5,680	2003	290	7,942	6,555
1988	244	6,814	5,821	2004	293	8,114	6,653
1989	247	6,978	6,045	2005	296	8,351	7,277
1990	250	7,325	6,033	2006	299	8,576	7,775
1991	253	7,304	5,820	2007	302	8,491	7,990
1992	257	7,229	5,707	2008	304	8,895	7,527
1993	260	7,093	5,810	2009	307	10,349	6,192
1994	263	7,143	6,151	2010	309	9,979	6,244
1995	266	7,129	6,357	2011	312	10,095	6,455
1996	269	7,086	6,598	2012	314	9,624	6,667

Figure 1B.1. Federal spending, total outlays and receipts in constant (FY 2005) dollars, 1981–2012

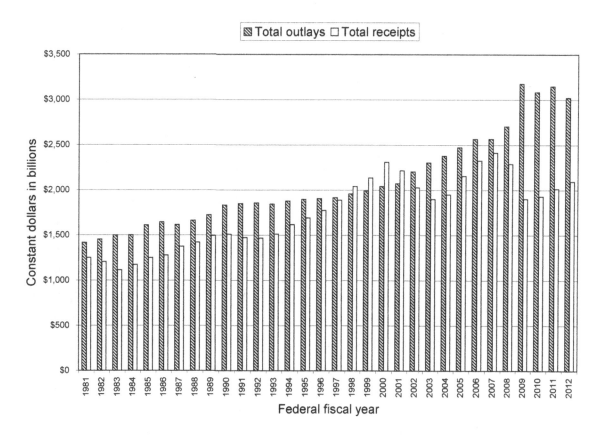

Figure 1B.2. Federal spending, total outlays and receipts per resident person in constant (FY 2005) dollars, 1981–2001

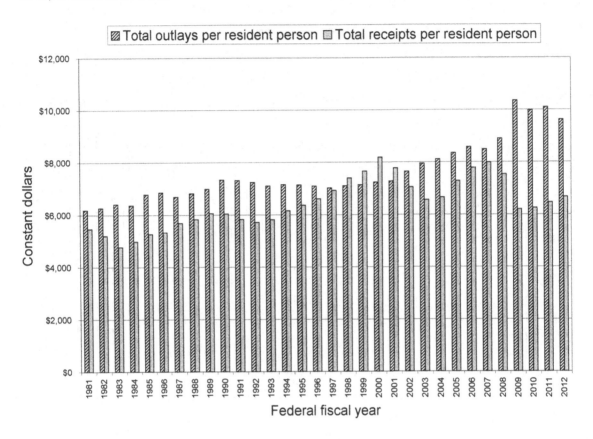

Appendix 1C

———◆•◆•◆———

Federal spending, on-budget outlays and receipts

Purpose: To show how the target amount for federal tax receipts other than Social Security taxes has changed since 1981 as represented by on-budget federal outlays (expenditures).

Comments

The two tables and two figures in this appendix parallel the tables and figures in appendix 1B, but show on-budget outlays and receipts rather than total outlays and receipts.

As described in more detail in appendix 2A, total federal outlays can be divided into on-budget and off-budget components. The **off-budget** component for **outlays** is almost entirely the payment of Social Security benefits. The **off-budget** component for **receipts** is almost entirely the receipts from the Social Security tax. All other outlays and receipts are on-budget.

Annual receipts from the Social Security tax have been more than adequate to pay all annual Social Security benefits in the 1990–2009 time period, and even in 2010 were close to the amount needed to pay those benefits. Thus, the Social Security off-budget outlays and receipts did not contribute to federal deficits during that time period. This fact makes on-budget outlays an appropriate target amount to achieve via the receipts from all federal taxes other than the Social Security tax.

Table 1C.1 shows for each fiscal year from 1981 to 2012 the on-budget federal outlays and on-budget federal receipts. These data are presented both in current dollars (columns 2 and 3) and in constant dollars (columns 5 and 6) as a way to remove the effects of inflation on the outlay and receipt figures.

Table 1C.2 shows these receipts and outlays in constant dollars per person in the United States as a way to remove the effects of population increases on increased economic activity and, therefore, outlays and receipts caused solely by an expanded population.

Figure 1C.1 depicts how both on-budget outlays and on-budget receipts in constant dollars have changed from 1981 to 2012. The changing outlays and receipts in this figure include increases that are caused solely by an expanded population.

Figure 1C.2 has the same format as figure 1C.1, but shows on-budget outlays and receipts in constant dollars per resident person in the United States.

As shown in figure 1C.2, just like total outlays, on-budget outlays per person remained essentially constant from 1989 to 2001. These outlays then steadily increased (from 2002 to 2006), even before the extra outlays that began in 2008 as a response to the Great Recession.

As shown in both figures 1C.1 and 1C.2, on-budget receipts declined precipitously during the Great Recession. They accounted for nearly all of the decline in total receipts during that time period (compare figure 1B.1 in appendix 1B to figure 1C.1; also compare figure 1B.2 in appendix 1B to figure 1C.2). As numeric examples, table 1C.1 reveals these figures:

- On-budget receipts in current dollars declined $482 billion from fiscal year 2007 to fiscal year 2009 (25 percent).
- On-budget receipts in constant dollars declined $506 billion from fiscal year 2007 to fiscal year 2009 (28 percent).

Proportionally, these declines for on-budget receipts of 25 percent (current dollars) and 28 percent (constant dollars) are considerably larger than the declines for total receipts of 18 percent (current dollars) and 21 percent (constant dollars) from fiscal year 2007 to fiscal year 2009. These differences reflect the fact that Social Security tax receipts remained relatively stable in the first part of the Great Recession and so contributed very little to the decline in total receipts.

Data source:
Budget of the U.S. Government, Fiscal Year 2014, Historical Tables, Tables 1.1, 1.3;
Population Estimates, National (US Census Bureau, 2013).

Table 1C.1. Federal spending, on-budget outlays and receipts in current and constant (FY 2005) dollars, 1981–2012

Federal fiscal year (1)	On-budget outlays in current dollars (billions) (2)	On-budget receipts in current dollars (billions) (3)	Composite deflator for constant (FY 2005) dollars (4)	On-budget outlays in constant (FY 2005) dollars (billions) (5)	On-budget receipts in constant (FY 2005) dollars (billions) (6)
1981	543	469	0.4790	1,134	979
1982	595	474	0.5137	1,158	923
1983	661	453	0.5394	1,225	840
1984	686	500	0.5677	1,208	881
1985	769	548	0.5870	1,310	934
1986	807	569	0.6022	1,340	945
1987	809	641	0.6213	1,302	1,032
1988	860	668	0.6400	1,344	1,044
1989	932	727	0.6637	1,404	1,095
1990	1,028	750	0.6842	1,502	1,096
1991	1,083	761	0.7165	1,512	1,062
1992	1,129	789	0.7439	1,518	1,061
1993	1,143	842	0.7640	1,496	1,102
1994	1,182	924	0.7782	1,519	1,187
1995	1,227	1,001	0.7995	1,535	1,252
1996	1,260	1,086	0.8187	1,539	1,326
1997	1,290	1,187	0.8360	1,543	1,420
1998	1,336	1,306	0.8439	1,583	1,548
1999	1,381	1,383	0.8558	1,614	1,616
2000	1,458	1,545	0.8770	1,662	1,762
2001	1,516	1,484	0.8992	1,686	1,650
2002	1,655	1,338	0.9138	1,811	1,464
2003	1,797	1,258	0.9378	1,916	1,341
2004	1,913	1,345	0.9645	1,983	1,395
2005	2,070	1,576	1.0000	2,070	1,576
2006	2,233	1,798	1.0354	2,157	1,737
2007	2,275	1,933	1.0642	2,138	1,816
2008	2,508	1,866	1.1031	2,274	1,692
2009	3,001	1,451	1.1073	2,710	1,310
2010	2,902	1,531	1.1211	2,589	1,366
2011	3,104	1,738	1.1439	2,714	1,519
2012	3,030	1,881	1.1704	2,589	1,607

Table 1C.2. Federal spending, on-budget outlays and receipts per resident person in constant (FY 2005) dollars, 1981–2012

Federal fiscal year (1)	United States resident population at July 1 (millions) (7)	On-budget outlays in constant (FY 2005) dollars per resident person (8)	On-budget receipts in constant (FY 2005) dollars per resident person (9)	Federal fiscal year (1)	United States resident population at July 1 (millions) (7)	On-budget outlays in constant (FY 2005) dollars per resident person (8)	On-budget receipts in constant (FY 2005) dollars per resident person (9)
1981	229	4,950	4,276	1997	273	5,652	5,201
1982	232	4,993	3,977	1998	276	5,736	5,607
1983	234	5,237	3,589	1999	279	5,784	5,792
1984	236	5,120	3,732	2000	282	5,895	6,247
1985	238	5,504	3,923	2001	285	5,916	5,791
1986	240	5,584	3,937	2002	288	6,289	5,084
1987	242	5,381	4,263	2003	290	6,608	4,626
1988	244	5,507	4,278	2004	293	6,769	4,759
1989	247	5,865	4,435	2005	296	6,993	5,324
1990	250	6,010	4,385	2006	299	7,213	5,808
1991	253	5,974	4,198	2007	302	7,079	6,015
1992	257	5,905	4,127	2008	304	7,479	5,564
1993	260	5,754	4,239	2009	307	8,828	4,268
1994	263	5,775	4,515	2010	309	8,377	4,419
1995	266	5,770	4,707	2011	312	8,697	4,870
1996	269	5,721	4,931	2012	314	8,245	5,118

Figure 1C.1. Federal spending, on-budget outlays and receipts in constant (FY 2005) dollars, 1981–2012

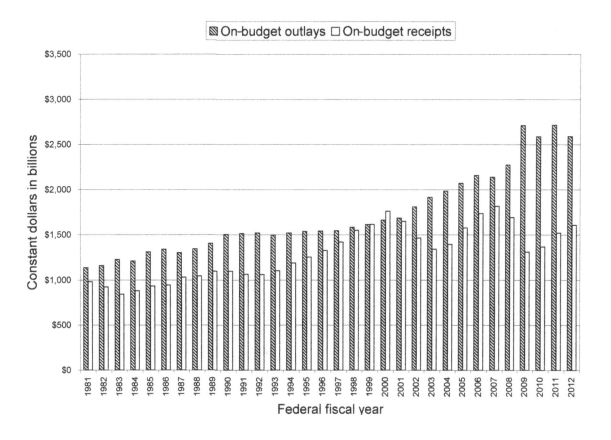

Figure 1C.2. Federal spending, on-budget outlays and receipts per resident person in constant (FY 2005) dollars, 1981–2012

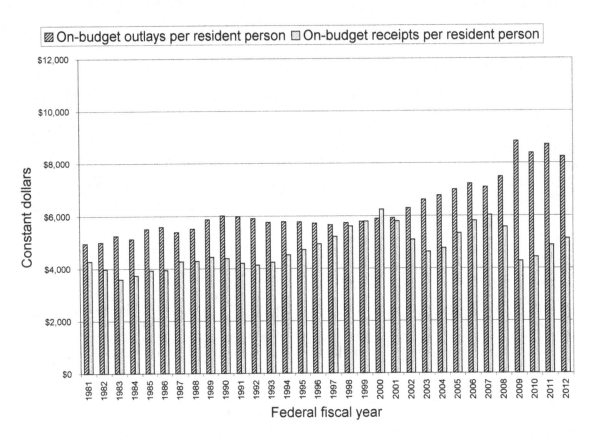

Appendix 2A

———◆•◆•◆———

Federal deficit spending, total deficit with its on-budget and off-budget components

Purpose: To show the approximate monetary contribution to general federal expenditures from Social Security trust funds.

Comments

The total federal deficit or surplus in a fiscal year compares *all* federal receipts to *all* federal outlays. This number is commonly reported as the "federal deficit" or "federal surplus" in a fiscal year. One way to get behind the total federal deficit number is to look at the Office of Management and Budget's division of all federal receipts and all federal outlays into the "on-budget" and "off-budget" categories. Table 2A.1 shows this division.

The two Social Security trust funds (retirement and disability) comprise nearly all of the off-budget number. The deficit or surplus of the United States Postal Service comprises the relatively tiny remainder of this number. A surplus occurs for the Social Security trust funds if benefits payments from those trust funds are less than the receipts allocated to those trust funds (i.e., from Social Security taxes and from other sources, such as interest on federal borrowings from the trust fund). A deficit occurs if benefits payments are more than those receipts. Because a surplus has occurred in the off-budget number in all but the first five of the thirty-two years represented in table 2A.1, the off-budget surplus number closely approximates the amount of money that the United States borrowed from the Social Security trust funds and used for general federal expenditures in each fiscal year.

The on-budget number represents the difference between all federal receipts and all federal outlays other than those designated as off-budget. Example on-budget receipts are those from the individual income tax, corporation income tax, and the Medicare tax. Example on-budget outlays are those for national defense, Medicare benefits, and transportation.

Data source:

Budget of the U.S. Government, Fiscal Year 2014, Historical Tables, Table 1.1.

Table 2A.1. Federal deficit spending, total deficit with on-budget and off-budget components in current dollars, 1981–2012

Federal fiscal year (1)	Total federal (deficit) or surplus in current dollars (billions) (2)	On-budget (deficit) or surplus in current dollars (billions) (3)	Off-budget (deficit) or surplus in current dollars (billions) (4)	Federal fiscal year (1)	Total federal (deficit) or surplus in current dollars (billions) (2)	On-budget (deficit) or surplus in current dollars (billions) (3)	Off-budget (deficit) or surplus in current dollars (billions) (4)
1981	(79)	(74)	(5)	1997	(22)	(103)	81
1982	(128)	(121)	(7)	1998	69	(30)	99
1983	(208)	(208)	0	1999	126	2	124
1984	(185)	(185)	0	2000	236	86	150
1985	(212)	(222)	9	2001	128	(32)	161
1986	(221)	(238)	17	2002	(158)	(317)	160
1987	(150)	(168)	19	2003	(378)	(538)	161
1988	(155)	(192)	37	2004	(413)	(568)	155
1989	(153)	(205)	53	2005	(318)	(494)	175
1990	(221)	(278)	57	2006	(248)	(434)	186
1991	(269)	(321)	52	2007	(161)	(342)	181
1992	(290)	(340)	50	2008	(459)	(642)	183
1993	(255)	(300)	45	2009	(1,413)	(1,550)	137
1994	(203)	(259)	56	2010	(1,294)	(1,371)	77
1995	(164)	(226)	62	2011	(1,300)	(1,367)	67
1996	(107)	(174)	67	2012	(1,087)	(1,149)	62
Average 2001-2008	(251)	(421)	170				

Appendix 2B

———◆•◆•◆———

Federal deficit spending, total deficit with its federal funds and trust funds components

Purpose: To show the monetary contribution to general federal expenditures from all federal trust funds.

Comments

As noted in appendix 2A, the total federal deficit or surplus in a fiscal year compares *all* federal receipts to *all* federal outlays, and this number is commonly reported as the "federal deficit" or "federal surplus" in a fiscal year. A second way to get behind the total federal deficit number is to look at the Office of Management and Budget's allocation of all federal receipts and all federal outlays into the "trust funds" and "federal funds" categories. Table 2B.1 reflects this allocation and shows the deficit or surplus in each category.

Some federal taxes are dedicated by law to particular uses. Examples are Social Security, Medicare, and gasoline taxes. Money obtained from dedicated taxes is allocated to each dedicated tax's trust fund (in an accounting sense, not actual deposits). For the examples cited, these are the two Social Security trust funds (retirement and disability), the Medicare hospital insurance trust fund, and the highway trust fund. A surplus occurs for a trust fund if the payments from that trust fund are less than the receipts allocated to the trust fund (i.e., from all the taxes dedicated to the trust fund and from other sources, such as interest on federal borrowings from the trust fund). A deficit occurs if those payments are less than those receipts.

The trust funds number in table 2B.1 adds up the surpluses and deficits of all federal trust funds in the fiscal year. Because a surplus has occurred in the trust funds number in each of the thirty-two years represented in table 2B.1, the trust funds surplus number shows the amount of money that the United States borrowed from the federal trust funds and used for general federal expenditures in each fiscal year.

The federal funds deficit or surplus number represents the difference between all federal receipts other than those allocated to trust funds and all federal outlays other than those made from trust funds. This number is also named the "true discretionary deficit" in the main text of this book.

Data source:

Budget of the U.S. Government, Fiscal Year 2014, Historical Tables, Table 1.4.

Table 2B.1. Federal deficit spending, total deficit with federal funds and trust funds components in current dollars, 1981–2012

Federal fiscal year (1)	Total federal (deficit) or surplus in current dollars (billions) (2)	Federal funds (deficit) or surplus in current dollars (billions) (3)	Trust funds (deficit) or surplus in current dollars (billions) (4)	Federal fiscal year (1)	Total federal (deficit) or surplus in current dollars (billions) (2)	Federal funds (deficit) or surplus in current dollars (billions) (3)	Trust funds (deficit) or surplus in current dollars (billions) (4)
1981	(79)	(86)	7	1997	(22)	(148)	126
1982	(128)	(134)	6	1998	69	(92)	161
1983	(208)	(231)	23	1999	126	(87)	213
1984	(185)	(218)	33	2000	236	2	235
1985	(211)	(266)	54	2001	128	(101)	228
1986	(221)	(283)	62	2002	(158)	(360)	202
1987	(150)	(222)	73	2003	(378)	(556)	178
1988	(155)	(253)	98	2004	(413)	(605)	193
1989	(153)	(276)	123	2005	(318)	(555)	237
1990	(221)	(341)	121	2006	(248)	(537)	289
1991	(269)	(381)	112	2007	(161)	(409)	249
1992	(290)	(386)	96	2008	(459)	(725)	266
1993	(255)	(355)	100	2009	(1,413)	(1,540)	127
1994	(203)	(299)	95	2010	(1,294)	(1,418)	123
1995	(164)	(263)	99	2011	(1,300)	(1,397)	97
1996	(107)	(222)	115	2012	(1,087)	(1,177)	90
Average 2001-2008	(251)	(481)	230				

Appendix 2C

------◆·◆·◆------

Federal deficit spending, deficits compared to outlays, total receipts, and total receipts without social insurance and retirement receipts

Purpose: To show how three alternative deficit figures portray different impressions about the impact of annual deficit spending, especially when those deficits are presented as a portion of other federal amounts.

Comments

The five tables in this appendix tell a data-based story about how federal deficit spending can be and has been minimized by the way it is commonly reported.

Table 2C.1 shows three different calculations of the annual federal deficit (or rare surplus). As summarized in appendixes 2A and 2B, the "total" federal deficit or surplus in a fiscal year compares *all* federal receipts to *all* federal outlays. The "on-budget" deficit or surplus excludes from general federal receipts and outlays all of the receipts and outlays that are allocated to the two Social Security trust funds (and a relatively tiny amount based on net profit or loss of the United States Postal Service). The "federal funds" deficit or surplus (also named the "true discretionary deficit" in this book) excludes from general federal receipts and outlays all of the receipts and outlays that are allocated to all of the federal trust funds, not just the two Social Security trust funds.

Table 2C.2 collects in one place three federal amounts against which annual deficits can be compared in order to provide context to the deficit number. "Total federal outlays" encompasses all payments made by the United States in a fiscal year, including payments from all trust funds such as the Social Security and Medicare hospital insurance trust funds. Except for a few years during 1981 to 2012, money for these payments came both from federal receipts

265

and from borrowings that increased the national debt. "Total federal receipts" consists of all money collected by the United States in a fiscal year, excluding borrowings. All but a very small portion of this money came from federal taxes. "Total federal receipts without social insurance and retirement receipts" extracts from total federal receipts the money that is collected from Social Security and Medicare taxes and a few related taxes that collect much less money. This extraction treats these taxes as being firmly dedicated to their statutory purposes and thus not available to pay for general government expenditures.

Tables 2C.3, 2C.4, and 2C.5 show the three alternative deficit figures in table 2C.1 as a proportion of each of the three federal amounts in table 2C.2. These data illustrate how differently deficit spending can be portrayed depending upon what deficit figures are used and what federal numbers those figures are compared to.

A proportion that is commonly reported compares the total federal deficit, which is the smallest number used to represent the federal deficit, to total federal outlays, which is the largest annual amount against which federal deficits can reasonably be compared (see table 2C.3, column 9). This comparison minimizes the significance of deficit spending in any particular fiscal year.

At the other end of the calculation spectrum, the proportion that compares the federal funds deficit to total federal receipts without social insurance and retirement receipts maximizes the significance of deficit spending in any particular year. This calculation reflects a policy that no dedicated taxes may be used to pay for any general government expenditure (see table 2C.5, column 17).

Data source:
Budget of the U.S. Government, Fiscal Year 2014, Historical Tables, Tables 1.1, 1.4, 2.1.

Table 2C.1. Federal deficit spending, three alternative federal deficit versions in current dollars, 1981–2012

Federal fiscal year (1)	Total federal (deficit) or surplus in current dollars (billions) (2)	On-budget (deficit) or surplus in current dollars (billions) (3)	Federal funds (deficit) or surplus in current dollars (billions) (4)	Federal fiscal year (1)	Total federal (deficit) or surplus in current dollars (billions) (2)	On-budget (deficit) or surplus in current dollars (billions) (3)	Federal funds (deficit) or surplus in current dollars (billions) (4)
1981	(79)	(74)	(86)	1997	(22)	(103)	(148)
1982	(128)	(121)	(134)	1998	69	(30)	(92)
1983	(208)	(208)	(231)	1999	126	2	(87)
1984	(185)	(185)	(218)	2000	236	86	2
1985	(212)	(222)	(266)	2001	128	(32)	(101)
1986	(221)	(238)	(283)	2002	(158)	(317)	(360)
1987	(150)	(168)	(222)	2003	(378)	(538)	(556)
1988	(155)	(192)	(253)	2004	(413)	(568)	(605)
1989	(153)	(205)	(276)	2005	(318)	(494)	(555)
1990	(221)	(278)	(341)	2006	(248)	(434)	(537)
1991	(269)	(321)	(381)	2007	(161)	(342)	(409)
1992	(290)	(340)	(386)	2008	(459)	(642)	(725)
1993	(255)	(300)	(355)	2009	(1,413)	(1,550)	(1,540)
1994	(203)	(259)	(299)	2010	(1,294)	(1,371)	(1,418)
1995	(164)	(226)	(263)	2011	(1,300)	(1,367)	(1,397)
1996	(107)	(174)	(222)	2012	(1,087)	(1,149)	(1,177)

Table 2C.2. Federal deficit spending, three alternative federal amounts in current dollars against which to compare deficits, 1981–2012

Federal fiscal year (1)	Total federal outlays in current dollars (billions) (5)	Total federal receipts in current dollars (billions) (6)	*Social insurance and retirement receipts in current dollars (billions)* (7)	Total federal receipts without social insurance and retirement receipts in current dollars (billions) (8)
1981	678	599	*183*	416
1982	746	618	*201*	417
1983	808	601	*209*	392
1984	852	666	*239*	427
1985	946	734	*265*	469
1986	990	769	*284*	485
1987	1,004	854	*303*	551
1988	1,064	909	*334*	575
1989	1,144	991	*359*	632
1990	1,253	1,032	*380*	652
1991	1,324	1,055	*396*	659
1992	1,382	1,091	*414*	677
1993	1,409	1,154	*428*	726
1994	1,462	1,259	*461*	798
1995	1,516	1,352	*484*	868
1996	1,560	1,453	*509*	944
1997	1,601	1,579	*539*	1,040
1998	1,652	1,722	*572*	1,150
1999	1,702	1,827	*612*	1,215
2000	1,789	2,025	*653*	1,372
2001	1,863	1,991	*694*	1,297
2002	2,011	1,853	*701*	1,152
2003	2,160	1,782	*713*	1,069
2004	2,293	1,880	*733*	1,147
2005	2,472	2,154	*794*	1,360
2006	2,655	2,407	*838*	1,569
2007	2,729	2,568	*870*	1,698
2008	2,983	2,524	*900*	1,624
2009	3,518	2,105	*891*	1,214
2010	3,457	2,163	*865*	1,298
2011	3,603	2,303	*819*	1,484
2012	3,537	2,450	*845*	1,605

Table 2C.3. Federal deficit spending, total deficit as % of total outlays, total receipts, and total receipts without social insurance and retirement receipts, 1981–2012

Federal fiscal year (1)	Total deficit (-) or surplus as % of total federal outlays (9)	Total deficit (-) or surplus as % of total federal receipts (10)	Total deficit (-) or surplus as % of total federal receipts without social insurance receipts (11)	Federal fiscal year (1)	Total deficit (-) or surplus as % of total federal outlays (9)	Total deficit (-) or surplus as % of total federal receipts (10)	Total deficit (-) or surplus as % of total federal receipts without social insurance receipts (11)
1981	-11.6%	-13.2%	-19.0%	1997	-1.4%	-1.4%	-2.1%
1982	-17.2%	-20.7%	-30.7%	1998	4.2%	4.0%	6.0%
1983	-25.7%	-34.6%	-53.1%	1999	7.4%	6.9%	10.3%
1984	-21.8%	-27.8%	-43.4%	2000	13.2%	11.7%	17.2%
1985	-22.4%	-28.9%	-45.2%	2001	6.9%	6.4%	9.9%
1986	-22.3%	-28.8%	-45.6%	2002	-7.8%	-8.5%	-13.7%
1987	-14.9%	-17.5%	-27.2%	2003	-17.5%	-21.2%	-35.3%
1988	-14.6%	-17.1%	-27.0%	2004	-18.0%	-22.0%	-36.0%
1989	-13.3%	-15.4%	-24.2%	2005	-12.9%	-14.8%	-23.4%
1990	-17.6%	-21.4%	-33.9%	2006	-9.3%	-10.3%	-15.8%
1991	-20.3%	-25.5%	-40.9%	2007	-5.9%	-6.3%	-9.5%
1992	-21.0%	-26.6%	-42.8%	2008	-15.4%	-18.2%	-28.2%
1993	-18.1%	-22.1%	-35.1%	2009	-40.2%	-67.1%	-116.4%
1994	-13.9%	-16.1%	-25.5%	2010	-37.4%	-59.8%	-99.7%
1995	-10.8%	-12.1%	-18.9%	2011	-36.1%	-56.4%	-87.5%
1996	-6.9%	-7.4%	-11.4%	2012	-30.7%	-44.4%	-67.7%

Table 2C.4. Federal deficit spending, on-budget deficit as % of total outlays, total receipts, and total receipts without social insurance and retirement receipts, 1981–2012

Federal fiscal year (1)	On-budget deficit (-) or surplus as % of total federal outlays (12)	On-budget deficit (-) or surplus as % of total federal receipts (13)	On-budget deficit (-) or surplus as % of total federal receipts without social insurance receipts (14)	Federal fiscal year (1)	On-budget deficit (-) or surplus as % of total federal outlays (12)	On-budget deficit (-) or surplus as % of total federal receipts (13)	On-budget deficit (-) or surplus as % of total federal receipts without social insurance receipts (14)
1981	-10.9%	-12.3%	-17.7%	1997	-6.4%	-6.5%	-9.9%
1982	-16.2%	-19.5%	-29.0%	1998	-1.8%	-1.7%	-2.6%
1983	-25.7%	-34.6%	-53.0%	1999	0.1%	0.1%	0.2%
1984	-21.8%	-27.8%	-43.4%	2000	4.8%	4.3%	6.3%
1985	-23.4%	-30.2%	-47.2%	2001	-1.7%	-1.6%	-2.5%
1986	-24.0%	-30.9%	-49.0%	2002	-15.8%	-17.1%	-27.5%
1987	-16.8%	-19.7%	-30.6%	2003	-24.9%	-30.2%	-50.4%
1988	-18.1%	-21.1%	-33.4%	2004	-24.8%	-30.2%	-49.5%
1989	-18.0%	-20.7%	-32.5%	2005	-20.0%	-22.9%	-36.3%
1990	-22.2%	-26.9%	-42.6%	2006	-16.4%	-18.1%	-27.7%
1991	-24.3%	-30.5%	-48.8%	2007	-12.5%	-13.3%	-20.1%
1992	-24.6%	-31.2%	-50.2%	2008	-21.5%	-25.4%	-39.5%
1993	-21.3%	-26.0%	-41.4%	2009	-44.1%	-73.6%	-127.6%
1994	-17.7%	-20.6%	-32.5%	2010	-39.7%	-63.4%	-105.7%
1995	-14.9%	-16.7%	-26.1%	2011	-37.9%	-59.3%	-92.1%
1996	-11.2%	-12.0%	-18.4%	2012	-32.5%	-46.9%	-71.6%

Table 2C.5. Federal deficit spending, federal funds deficit as % of total outlays, total receipts, and total receipts without social insurance and retirement receipts, 1981–2012

Federal fiscal year (1)	Federal funds deficit (-) or surplus as % of total federal outlays (15)	Federal funds deficit (-) or surplus as % of total federal receipts (16)	Federal funds deficit (-) or surplus as % of total federal receipts w/o social insurance receipts (17)	Federal fiscal year (1)	Federal funds deficit (-) or surplus as % of total federal outlays (15)	Federal funds deficit (-) or surplus as % of total federal receipts (16)	Federal funds deficit (-) or surplus as % of total federal receipts w/o social insurance receipts (17)
1981	-12.6%	-14.3%	-20.6%	1997	-9.2%	-9.4%	-14.2%
1982	-18.0%	-21.7%	-32.2%	1998	-5.6%	-5.3%	-8.0%
1983	-28.6%	-38.4%	-59.0%	1999	-5.1%	-4.8%	-7.2%
1984	-25.6%	-32.8%	-51.1%	2000	0.1%	0.1%	0.1%
1985	-28.2%	-36.3%	-56.8%	2001	-5.4%	-5.0%	-7.7%
1986	-28.6%	-36.8%	-58.3%	2002	-17.9%	-19.4%	-31.3%
1987	-22.1%	-26.0%	-40.4%	2003	-25.7%	-31.2%	-52.0%
1988	-23.8%	-27.8%	-44.0%	2004	-26.4%	-32.2%	-52.8%
1989	-24.1%	-27.9%	-43.7%	2005	-22.5%	-25.8%	-40.8%
1990	-27.2%	-33.1%	-52.3%	2006	-20.2%	-22.3%	-34.2%
1991	-28.8%	-36.1%	-57.8%	2007	-15.0%	-15.9%	-24.1%
1992	-28.0%	-35.4%	-57.0%	2008	-24.3%	-28.7%	-44.6%
1993	-25.2%	-30.8%	-49.0%	2009	-43.8%	-73.2%	-126.8%
1994	-20.4%	-23.7%	-37.4%	2010	-41.0%	-65.6%	-109.2%
1995	-17.4%	-19.5%	-30.3%	2011	-38.8%	-60.6%	-94.1%
1996	-14.2%	-15.3%	-23.5%	2012	-33.3%	-48.0%	-73.3%

Appendix 2D

———◆•◆•◆———

Federal national debt with its public debt and government accounts debt components

Purpose: To show both the cumulative effect of deficit spending as reflected in the two components of the national debt and the years when the largest increases in the national debt have occurred.

Comments

The two tables and one figure in this appendix show the huge size of the national debt, how the national debt has been incurred over time, and why annual increases in the national debt are larger than the commonly reported federal deficit.

Table 2D.1 provides basic background by identifying the two components of the national debt: the public debt and debt to government accounts. All numbers are a snapshot in time at the end of each federal fiscal year. The public debt shows the amount of unpaid borrowings from the public. The government accounts debt shows the amount of unpaid borrowings from all the federal trust funds. Both types of borrowings take the form of unpaid treasury securities that are held, respectively, by members of the public and by federal trust funds. The sum of these unpaid borrowings, of course, is the "gross federal debt" (the national debt). "Gross federal debt" is the term used in the Historical Tables in the *Budget of the U.S. Government, Fiscal Year 2014*.

One way to discern whether excessive borrowings may impede the ability of the United States to sell treasury securities is to compare the public debt to annual economic activity in the United States. That is the function of column 5 in table 2D.1. It compares the public debt to the US GDP, which is one measure of economic strength. Many people think that the larger this percentage becomes, the more reluctant investors will be to buy US treasury securities.

Table 2D.2 shows the annual increase or decrease in the national debt and its two debt components. The increase or decrease in the gross federal debt (national debt) is much closer to the annual deficit represented by the "federal funds" deficit than to the commonly reported "total federal deficit" (or "federal deficit"). Both deficit versions are shown in table 2B.1 of appendix 2B. Until recently, the numbers for the federal funds deficit and increase in the gross federal debt each year were similar, but not identical. They were not identical because historically some federal borrowings have been used for purposes other than covering an annual deficit, a practice that expanded beginning in 2007.[1] That is why the increases in the national debt at the end of fiscal years 2009 and 2010 were considerably larger than the federal funds deficits for those fiscal years.

Figure 2D.1 pictorially compares the increases in the national debt for each fiscal year from 1981 to 2012 (there were no decreases). This figure also correlates those numbers to the president in office at the time. In this correlation, the fiscal year that ends on September 30 in the year that the president leaves office (in January) is correlated to that president because the federal budget for that fiscal year was determined or at least proposed before the president left office. The one exception is fiscal year 2009. That fiscal year is attributed to two presidents—George W. Bush and Barack Obama—because President Obama and Congress expanded the fiscal year 2009 budget in early 2009 with a stimulus spending package intended to stop cascading unemployment. The numbers in figure 2D.1 have not been adjusted for inflation because the principal of earlier treasury securities that represent the borrowings does not increase with inflation.

Data source:

Budget of the U.S. Government, Fiscal Year 2014, Historical Tables, Table 7.1.

---

[1] A summary of these other purposes is found in the *Budget of the U.S. Government, Fiscal Year 2014*, Analytic Perspectives, Economic and Budget Analyses, chapter 5, "Federal Borrowing and Debt," at p. 65. It states:

> Over the long run, it is a good approximation to say that "the deficit is financed by borrowing from the public" or "the surplus is used to repay debt held by the public." However, the Government's need to borrow in any given year has always depended on several other factors besides the unified budget surplus or deficit, such as the change in the Treasury operating cash balance. These other factors—"other transactions affecting borrowing from the public"—can either increase or decrease the Government's need to borrow and can vary considerably in size from year to year. ... The other transactions affecting borrowing from the public are presented in Table 5–2 (an increase in the need to borrow is represented by a positive sign, like the deficit).

Table 2D.1. Federal national debt with its public debt and government accounts debt components in current dollars, 1981–2012

End of federal fiscal year (1)	"Gross federal" (national) debt in current dollars (billions) (2)	Less debt to govt accounts in current dollars (billions) (3)	Equals public debt in current dollars (billions) (4)	Public debt as % of GDP (5)
1981	995	205	789	25.8%
1982	1,137	213	925	28.7%
1983	1,372	234	1,127	33.1%
1984	1,565	257	1,307	34.0%
1985	1,817	310	1,507	36.4%
1986	2,121	379	1,741	39.5%
1987	2,346	456	1,890	40.6%
1988	2,601	549	2,052	41.0%
1989	2,868	677	2,191	40.6%
1990	3,206	795	2,412	42.1%
1991	3,598	909	2,689	45.3%
1992	4,002	1,002	3,000	48.1%
1993	4,351	1,103	3,248	49.3%
1994	4,643	1,210	3,433	49.2%
1995	4,921	1,316	3,604	49.1%
1996	5,181	1,447	3,734	48.4%
1997	5,369	1,597	3,772	45.9%
1998	5,478	1,747	3,721	43.0%
1999	5,606	1,973	3,632	39.4%
2000	5,629	2,219	3,410	34.7%
2001	5,770	2,450	3,320	32.5%
2002	6,198	2,658	3,540	33.6%
2003	6,760	2,847	3,913	35.6%
2004	7,355	3,059	4,296	36.8%
2005	7,905	3,313	4,592	36.9%
2006	8,451	3,622	4,829	36.6%
2007	8,951	3,916	5,035	36.3%
2008	9,986	4,183	5,803	40.5%
2009	11,876	4,331	7,545	54.0%
2010	13,529	4,510	9,019	62.9%
2011	14,764	4,636	10,128	67.8%
2012	16,051	4,770	11,281	72.6%

Table 2D.2. Federal national debt, annual changes in the public debt and government accounts debt components in current dollars, 1981–2012

End of federal fiscal year (1)	"Gross federal" (national) debt increase (decrease) in current dollars (billions) (2)	Government accounts debt increase (decrease) in current dollars (billions) (3)	Public debt increase (decrease) in current dollars (billions) (4)	End of federal fiscal year (1)	"Gross federal" (national) debt increase (decrease) in current dollars (billions) (2)	Government accounts debt increase (decrease) in current dollars (billions) (3)	Public debt increase (decrease) in current dollars (billions) (4)
1981	86	8	77	1997	188	150	38
1982	142	8	136	1998	109	150	(51)
1983	235	21	202	1999	128	226	(89)
1984	193	23	180	2000	23	246	(222)
1985	252	53	200	2001	141	231	(90)
1986	304	69	234	2002	428	208	220
1987	225	77	149	2003	562	189	373
1988	255	93	162	2004	595	212	383
1989	267	128	139	2005	550	254	296
1990	338	118	221	2006	546	309	237
1991	392	114	277	2007	500	294	206
1992	404	93	311	2008	1,035	267	768
1993	349	101	248	2009	1,890	148	1,742
1994	292	107	185	2010	1,653	179	1,474
1995	278	106	171	2011	1,235	126	1,109
1996	260	131	130	2012	1,287	134	1,153

Figure 2D.1. Annual national debt increases in current dollars compared to presidents, 1981–2012

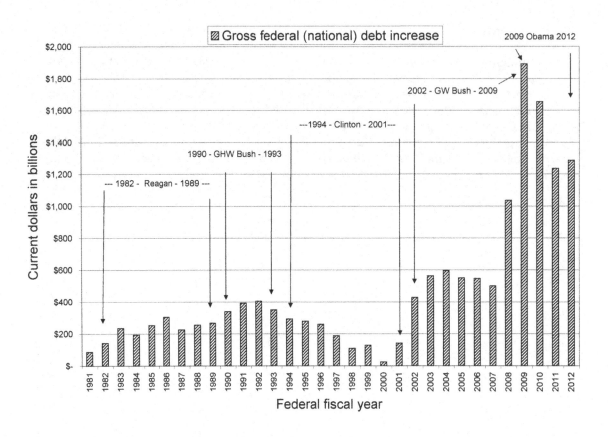

Appendix 2E

◆·◆·◆

Federal national debt, US interest obligations by lender category compared to total outlays, total receipts, and total receipts without social insurance and retirement receipts

Purpose: To show how different categories of US interest obligations caused by the national debt portray different impressions about the demand of the national debt on US government resources (tax receipts), especially when those obligations are compared to other federal amounts.

Comments

The three tables in this appendix tell a data-based story about how interest obligations caused by the national debt can be and have been minimized by the way they are commonly reported.

Table 2E.1 shows the gross annual interest obligations of the United States on its treasury securities and also the four lender categories of interest that comprise the gross annual interest. The "net interest" payment shown in column 6 is money actually paid on the treasury securities that comprise the public debt. This is the number often used when people talk about the interest that the United States is paying on the national debt. The three other categories of interest obligations are collectively called "federal account interest" in this book and in the Historical Tables of the US budgets.

Within the federal account interest are interest obligations of the United States on treasury securities held by two categories of federal trust funds. The "off-budget" trust funds are the two Social Security trust funds. The "on-budget" trust funds are all other federal trust funds. Although these interest obligations to trust funds are noted as "received" in the historical data in the Fiscal Year 2014 Budget, they are "received" only in an accounting sense. If the actual receipts from taxes that are dedicated to a particular trust fund exceed outlays from that trust

277

fund, then the interest owed to that trust fund most likely will just be rolled over into new debt owed to the trust fund in the form of additional treasury securities.

Tables 2E.2 and 2E.3 are analogous to tables 2C.3, 2C.4, and 2C.5 in appendix 2C regarding deficit spending. Tables 2E.2 and 2E.3 provide context to federal interest obligations by showing the net interest payment and gross interest obligation as a proportion of each of the three federal amounts shown in table 2C.2. Like deficit spending, these data illustrate how differently national debt interest payments can be portrayed depending upon what federal outlays those payments are compared to.

A proportion that is commonly reported compares the net interest payment, which is the smallest number used to represent interest obligations on the national debt, to total federal outlays, which is the largest annual amount against which interest obligations can reasonably be compared (table 2E.2, column 7). This comparison minimizes the significance of federal interest obligations in any particular fiscal year.

At the other end of the calculation spectrum, the proportion that compares the gross interest obligation to total federal receipts without social insurance and retirement receipts maximizes the significance of federal interest obligations in any particular year (table 2E.3, column 12). This calculation assumes that all interest obligations will actually be paid and not rolled over into more debt and also that the payments will come from general tax receipts and not dedicated taxes like Social Security and Medicare taxes.

Data source:
Budget of the U.S. Government, Fiscal Year 2014, Historical Tables, Tables 1.1, 2.1, 3.2.

Table 2E.1. Federal national debt, US interest obligations on the national debt by lender category in current dollars, 1981–2012

Federal fiscal year (1)	Gross interest on treasury debt securities in current dollars (billions) (2)	↓ Federal accounts ↓			Public debt
		Interest received by on-budget trust funds in current dollars (billions) (3)	Interest received by off-budget trust funds in current dollars (billions) (4)	Other interest plus investment income in current dollars (billions) (5)	Net interest payment in current dollars (billions) (6)
1981	96	12	2	13	69
1982	117	14	2	16	85
1983	129	15	2	22	90
1984	154	17	3	22	111
1985	179	22	4	23	129
1986	190	27	4	23	136
1987	195	30	5	22	139
1988	214	34	7	20	152
1989	241	40	11	20	169
1990	265	46	16	18	184
1991	285	50	20	20	194
1992	292	54	24	15	199
1993	292	56	27	11	199
1994	296	56	29	8	203
1995	332	60	33	7	232
1996	344	61	37	5	241
1997	356	64	41	7	244
1998	364	67	47	9	241
1999	353	67	52	4	230
2000	362	69	60	10	223
2001	359	75	69	9	206
2002	333	76	77	9	171
2003	318	73	84	8	153
2004	322	68	86	8	160
2005	352	69	92	7	184
2006	406	72	98	9	227
2007	430	72	106	15	237
2008	451	78	114	6	253
2009	383	64	118	14	187
2010	414	67	119	32	196
2011	454	72	116	36	230
2012	359	15	112	12	220

Table 2E.2. Federal national debt, net interest payment as % of total outlays, total receipts, and total receipts without social insurance and retirement receipts, 1981–2012

Federal fiscal year (1)	Net interest payment as % of total federal outlays (7)	Net interest payment as % of total federal receipts (8)	Net interest payment as % of total federal receipts without social insurance receipts (9)	Federal fiscal year (1)	Net interest payment as % of total federal outlays (7)	Net interest payment as % of total federal receipts (8)	Net interest payment as % of total federal receipts without social insurance receipts (9)
1981	10.1%	11.5%	16.5%	1997	15.2%	15.4%	23.5%
1982	11.4%	13.8%	20.4%	1998	14.6%	14.0%	21.0%
1983	11.1%	15.0%	22.9%	1999	13.5%	12.6%	18.9%
1984	13.0%	16.7%	26.0%	2000	12.5%	11.0%	16.2%
1985	13.7%	17.6%	27.6%	2001	11.1%	10.4%	15.9%
1986	13.7%	17.7%	28.0%	2002	8.5%	9.2%	14.8%
1987	13.8%	16.2%	25.2%	2003	7.1%	8.6%	14.3%
1988	14.3%	16.7%	26.4%	2004	7.0%	8.5%	14.0%
1989	14.8%	17.0%	26.8%	2005	7.4%	8.5%	13.5%
1990	14.7%	17.9%	28.3%	2006	8.5%	9.4%	14.4%
1991	14.7%	18.4%	29.5%	2007	8.7%	9.2%	14.0%
1992	14.4%	18.3%	29.4%	2008	8.5%	10.0%	15.6%
1993	14.1%	17.2%	27.4%	2009	5.3%	8.9%	15.4%
1994	13.9%	16.1%	25.5%	2010	5.7%	9.1%	15.1%
1995	15.3%	17.2%	26.8%	2011	6.4%	10.0%	15.5%
1996	15.4%	16.6%	25.5%	2012	6.2%	9.0%	13.7%

Table 2E.3. Federal national debt, gross interest payment as % of total outlays, total receipts, and total receipts without social insurance and retirement receipts, 1981–2012

Federal fiscal year (1)	Gross interest payment as % of total federal outlays (10)	Gross interest payment as % of total federal receipts (11)	Gross interest payment as % of total federal receipts without social insurance receipts (12)	Federal fiscal year (1)	Gross interest payment as % of total federal outlays (10)	Gross interest payment as % of total federal receipts (11)	Gross interest payment as % of total federal receipts without social insurance receipts (12)
1981	14.1%	15.9%	22.9%	1997	22.2%	22.5%	34.2%
1982	15.7%	19.0%	28.2%	1998	22.0%	21.1%	31.6%
1983	15.9%	21.4%	32.9%	1999	20.8%	19.3%	29.1%
1984	18.1%	23.1%	36.0%	2000	20.2%	17.9%	26.4%
1985	18.9%	24.4%	38.1%	2001	19.3%	18.1%	27.7%
1986	19.2%	24.7%	39.2%	2002	16.5%	17.9%	28.9%
1987	19.4%	22.9%	35.4%	2003	14.7%	17.8%	29.8%
1988	20.1%	23.5%	37.2%	2004	14.0%	17.1%	28.1%
1989	21.1%	24.3%	38.1%	2005	14.3%	16.4%	25.9%
1990	21.1%	25.6%	40.6%	2006	15.3%	16.9%	25.9%
1991	21.6%	27.1%	43.3%	2007	15.8%	16.7%	25.3%
1992	21.2%	26.8%	43.1%	2008	15.1%	17.9%	27.8%
1993	20.8%	25.3%	40.3%	2009	10.9%	18.2%	31.6%
1994	20.3%	23.5%	37.2%	2010	12.0%	19.1%	31.9%
1995	21.9%	24.6%	38.3%	2011	12.6%	19.7%	30.6%
1996	22.0%	23.7%	36.4%	2012	10.2%	14.7%	22.4%

Appendix 2F

————◆•◆•◆————

Federal national debt, approximate average annual net interest rates on the national debt

Purpose: To provide data that can be used to illustrate how different interest rates on the national debt can affect the impact of the national debt on resources available to the US government for operations, programs, and services.

Comments

The years from 2002 to 2012, especially 2009 through 2012, witnessed historically low interest rates paid by the United States on treasury securities that represent the public debt portion of the national debt. These low interest rates kept the interest payments on the greatly increasing national debt from increasing commensurately with the national debt increases.

Table 2F.1 shows two simple ways to calculate the approximate average net interest rate paid on the public debt during each fiscal year from 1981 to 2012. Rate B in column 6 requires an extra calculation step and is the more accurate of the two approximate rates.

The methodology in table 2F.1 was tested by comparing rate B to a rate calculated by using Treasury Department data on the "Total Marketable" interest-bearing debt in four fiscal years during 2001 to 2010 (data accessed at www.treasurydirect.gov/govt/rates/pd/avg/avg by searching www.treasurydirect in this sequence: Interest Rate Data > Interest Rates & Prices > Public Debt > Average Interest Rates on U.S. Treasury Securities > Historical Information). For each fiscal year tested, an unadjusted average fiscal year rate was calculated from the twelve end-of-month rates reported in the Treasury Department data. The largest difference between the unadjusted average rate and rate B in table 2F.1 was less than one-tenth the value of the rate, so rate B is a reasonable approximation of the average net interest payment rate for each fiscal year in table 2F.1.

Data source:
  Budget of the U.S. Government, Fiscal Year 2014, Historical Tables, Tables 3.1, 7.1.

Table 2F.1. Federal national debt, approximate average annual net interest rates on the national debt, 1981–2012

Federal fiscal year (1)	Net interest payment (billions) (2)	Public debt at end of fiscal year (billions) (3)	Average public debt using debt at start and end of fiscal year (billions) (4)	Rate A (5)	Rate B (6)
1980		712			
1981	69	789	751	8.7%	9.2%
1982	85	925	857	9.2%	9.9%
1983	90	1,137	1,031	7.9%	8.7%
1984	111	1,307	1,222	8.5%	9.1%
1985	129	1,507	1,407	8.6%	9.2%
1986	136	1,741	1,624	7.8%	8.4%
1987	139	1,890	1,816	7.4%	7.7%
1988	152	2,052	1,971	7.4%	7.7%
1989	169	2,191	2,122	7.7%	8.0%
1990	184	2,412	2,302	7.6%	8.0%
1991	194	2,689	2,551	7.2%	7.6%
1992	199	3,000	2,845	6.6%	7.0%
1993	199	3,248	3,124	6.1%	6.4%
1994	203	3,433	3,341	5.9%	6.1%
1995	232	3,604	3,519	6.4%	6.6%
1996	241	3,734	3,669	6.5%	6.6%
1997	244	3,772	3,753	6.5%	6.5%
1998	241	3,721	3,747	6.5%	6.4%
1999	230	3,623	3,672	6.3%	6.3%
2000	223	3,410	3,517	6.5%	6.3%
2001	206	3,320	3,365	6.2%	6.1%
2002	171	3,540	3,430	4.8%	5.0%
2003	153	3,913	3,727	3.9%	4.1%
2004	160	4,296	4,105	3.7%	3.9%
2005	184	4,592	4,444	4.0%	4.1%
2006	227	4,829	4,711	4.7%	4.8%
2007	237	5,035	4,932	4.7%	4.8%
2008	253	5,803	5,419	4.4%	4.7%
2009	187	7,545	6,674	2.5%	2.8%
2010	196	9,019	8,282	2.2%	2.4%
2011	230	10,128	9,574	2.3%	2.4%
2012	220	11,281	10,705	2.0%	2.1%

Rate A = Net interest payment divided by the public debt at the end of the fiscal year
Rate B = Net interest payment divided by the average of the public debt at the start and at the end of the fiscal year

Appendix 3A

———•◆•———

Federal national debt, the debt to Social Security trust funds

Purpose: To show the full extent of US borrowings from the Social Security trust funds.

Comments

Borrowings from the two Social Security trust funds have made annual deficit spending by the United States appear less significant than it really is. Many people assume that borrowings from these funds will be paid back because Social Security funds must ultimately be used only to pay Social Security benefits (a shaky assumption, as discussed in chapter 3). For this reason and also their predominant size, attention is drawn here to these two federal trust funds.

Table 3A.1 shows the amounts of unpaid debt owed collectively and individually to each of the two Social Security trust funds at the end of each fiscal year from 1981 to 2012. Like the data on the national debt, these figures are a snapshot in time. The two Social Security trust funds are presented separately because the Historical Tables in the Fiscal Year 2014 Budget treat them this way. What is labeled the "retirement trust fund" in table 3A.1 is named the "old age and survivors insurance fund" in the Historical Tables (see Historical Table 13.1). As shown in column 6 of table 3A.1, over time, the debt to the two Social Security trust funds has become an increasing portion of the debt owed to all government accounts.

Data source:
   Budget of the U.S. Government, Fiscal Year 2014, Historical Tables, Tables 7.1, 13.1.

Table 3A.1. Federal national debt, the debt to government accounts and to Social Security trust funds in current dollars, 1981–2012

End of federal fiscal year (1)	Debt to government accounts in current dollars (billions) (2)	Debt to Social Security trust funds total in current dollars (billions) (3)	Debt to Social Security retirement trust fund in current dollars (billions) (4)	Debt to Social Security disability trust fund in current dollars (billions) (5)	Debt to Social Security trust funds total as % debt to government accounts (6)
1981	205	27	24	3	13.2%
1982	213	20	13	7	9.4%
1983	234	32	27	5	13.7%
1984	257	33	28	5	12.8%
1985	310	40	34	6	12.9%
1986	379	46	38	8	12.1%
1987	456	65	58	7	14.3%
1988	549	104	97	7	18.9%
1989	677	156	148	8	23.0%
1990	795	214	203	11	26.9%
1991	909	268	255	13	29.5%
1992	1,002	319	306	13	31.8%
1993	1,103	366	356	10	33.2%
1994	1,210	422	416	6	34.9%
1995	1,316	483	448	35	36.7%
1996	1,447	549	499	50	37.9%
1997	1,597	630	567	63	39.4%
1998	1,747	730	653	77	41.8%
1999	1,973	855	762	93	43.3%
2000	2,219	1,007	893	114	45.4%
2001	2,450	1,170	1,034	136	47.8%
2002	2,658	1,329	1,174	155	50.0%
2003	2,847	1,484	1,313	171	52.1%
2004	3,059	1,635	1,453	182	53.4%
2005	3,313	1,809	1,616	193	54.6%
2006	3,622	1,995	1,793	202	55.1%
2007	3,916	2,181	1,968	213	55.7%
2008	4,183	2,367	2,151	216	56.6%
2009	4,331	2,504	2,296	208	57.8%
2010	4,510	2,586	2,399	187	57.3%
2011	4,636	2,655	2,493	162	57.3%
2012	4,770	2,719	2,587	132	57.0%

Appendix 5A

———◆·◆·◆———

Individual total tax, example calculation of the total federal taxes paid by a top income group

Purpose: To provide a methodology to test by example the hypothesis that the top income groups of individuals pay a disproportionate amount of federal taxes.

Comments

Some people assert that the top income groups of individuals pay a disproportionate amount of federal taxes and, therefore, these individuals unfairly support other individuals.

Typically the figures used to support this assertion compare total income taxes paid by a top income group to total income taxes paid by all individuals. Figures of this type are readily derivable from data found in tables published by the Internal Revenue Service (see figures in appendix 14B).

A broader test of this assertion compares the total federal taxes paid by a top income group to the total federal taxes paid by all individuals (adding income, Social Security, and Medicare taxes). The data needed to make this comparison are *not* readily available in tables published by the Internal Revenue Service. This appendix provides by example a methodology for estimating the total federal taxes paid by a top income group so that these can be compared to the total federal taxes paid by all individuals.

Methodology for Calculating Total Federal Taxes Paid by a Top Income Group of Individuals

The Internal Revenue Service publishes Statistics of Income tables for each *tax year*. For individual income taxes, these tables divide data into income groups based on the adjusted gross income reported on filed returns. These tables include the number of returns filed by each group, the total adjusted gross incomes reported for each group, and the total income taxes paid by each group. These tables provide direct data on the income taxes paid by the top income groups. The data in these tables also allow estimates to be created for the amount of Social Security and Medicare taxes paid by the top income groups. Using tax year 2007 as an example, part A of this appendix shows how to calculate estimates for total federal taxes paid by the income group having adjusted gross incomes of $500,000 and greater in that year.

The Office of Management and Budget publishes historic tables that show the total receipts from individual income taxes, Social Security taxes, and Medicare taxes for a particular *fiscal year*. Fiscal year 2008 is the fiscal year in which most tax receipts from tax year 2007 occurred. These data can be used to estimate a comparison between the total federal taxes paid by a top income group to total federal taxes paid by all individuals in tax year 2007. Part B of this appendix shows how to calculate these estimates for the income group having adjusted gross incomes of $500,000 and greater in tax year 2007.

These calculations show that the total federal taxes paid by the $500,000+ income group was less than 24 percent of the total federal taxes paid by all individuals in tax year 2007. The same group had 21.1 percent of all reported adjusted gross income that year (see appendix 14B, table 14B.1).

Part A: Estimating total federal taxes paid by the $500,000+ income group

(1) Income taxes paid

These data are found in appendix 14B, table 14B.1. Add the numbers in column 8 for all income groups of $500,000 and greater in the adjusted gross income category. The sum is $413 billion.

(2) Social Security taxes paid

Assume that every return was a joint return (two individuals) and that both individuals paid the $12,090 maximum amount of Social Security taxes required in tax year 2007. This assumption overestimates the actual Social Security taxes paid because some returns will not be joint returns and some individuals will have no "earned income" that is subject to the Social Security tax.

Estimate calculation
Total returns: 1,040,662 (added from table 14B.1)
Total individuals: 1,040,662 x 2 = 2,081,324
Total Social Security taxes: $12,090 x 2,081,324 = $25.2 billion

(3) Medicare taxes paid

Assume that all individuals in the group paid Medicare taxes at the self-employment tax rate of 2.9 percent. Also assume that all adjusted gross income reported was earned income subject to the Medicare tax except for capital gains, dividends, and interest. Data in table 14A.4 show that 46 percent of all income of this group was capital gains, dividends, and interest, so the remainder was 54 percent of all income. Both assumptions overestimate the actual Medicare taxes paid.

Estimate calculation

Total adjusted gross income: $1,836 billion (added from table 14B.1)
Total earned income: $1,836 billion x 0.54 = $991 billion
Total Medicare taxes: $991 billion x 0.029 = $28.7 billion

(4) Maximum estimated total federal taxes

Estimate calculation

Total income taxes	$413 billion	
Total Social Security taxes	$ 25 billion	*(estimate)*
Total Medicare taxes	$ 29 billion	*(estimate)*
Total federal taxes	$467 billion	*(estimate)*

Part B: Estimating total federal taxes of the $500,000+ group as a portion of total federal taxes paid in tax year 2007

(5) Total federal taxes paid in tax year 2007

Although fiscal year 2008 data are not exactly the same as tax year 2007 data, the income tax payments (receipts) data are very close in number ($1,116 billion total individual income taxes paid in tax year 2007 according to IRS data; $1,146 billion total individual income taxes paid in fiscal year 2008 according to OMB data). Assume that tax year 2007 data are approximately the same as fiscal year 2008 data for income tax, Social Security tax, and Medicare tax payments.

Calculation (fiscal year 2008 data)

All income tax receipts	$1,146 billion
All Social Security tax receipts	$ 658 billion
All Medicare tax receipts	$ 194 billion
Total individual federal tax payments	$1,998 billion

(6) Estimated total federal taxes for the group as a portion of individual total federal taxes

Estimate calculation
Percentage: $467 billion/$1,998 billion = 23.4%

Data source for (5):
Budget of the U.S. Government, Fiscal Year 2014, Historical Tables, Tables 2.1, 13.1.

Appendix 9A

———•◆•◆•———

Federal receipts by major source

Purpose: To identify potential sources of future federal tax receipts by showing the sources of federal receipts under existing law.

Comments

Proposed changes to federal taxes occur in the context of reliance by the United States on receipts obtained from existing taxes. Knowing which existing taxes and other government activities provide what amounts of receipts can frame discussion about the relative importance of proposed tax changes. For example, a 2 percent decrease in the average rate of the current federal individual income tax will have a far greater effect on tax receipts than a 2 percent decrease in the average rate of the current estate tax.

The four tables in this appendix reflect federal tax and other receipts from tax years 2007 and 2000 that were received in fiscal years 2008 and 2001. These tax and fiscal years serve as examples for many comparisons in this book.

Data source:
   Budget of the U.S. Government, Fiscal Year 2014, Historical Tables, Tables 2.1, 2.4, 2.5.

Note 1: Rounding causes the total receipts for fiscal year 2008 to be $2,523 billion in table 9A.1, rather than $2,524 billion as shown in appendix 1B, table 1.B.1 ($2,524 billion is used consistently in the main text).

290

Table 9A.1. Federal receipts by major source in current dollars, fiscal year 2008

Receipts source fiscal year 2008 (1)	Amount in current dollars (billions) (2)	Amount first subcat in current dollars (billions) (3)	Amount second subcat in current dollars (billions) (4)
Individual income tax	1,146		
Corporation income tax	304		
Social insurance and retirement receipts	900		
Social Security tax (off-budget)		658	
Old-age and survivors insurance			563
Disability insurance			96
Medicare tax for hospital insurance		194	
Railroad retirement pension fund		2	
Railroad Social Security equivalent amount		2	
Unemployment insurance trust funds		40	
Federal employees retirement - employee share		4	
Non-federal employees retirement		<1	
Excise taxes	67		
Other	106		
Estate and gift taxes		29	
Customs duties and fees		28	
Federal reserve deposits		34	
All other		16	
Total receipts	2,523	1,007	659
Social Security tax and Medicare tax receipts		852	
Total receipts less Social Security tax and Medicare tax receipts	1,671		

Table 9A.2. Federal receipts by major source as a percentage of total receipts (continuation of table 9A.1), fiscal year 2008

Receipts source fiscal year 2008 (1)	Amount in Column (2) as % of total receipts (5)	Amount in Column (3) as % of total receipts (6)	Amount in Column (4) as % of total receipts (7)
Individual income tax	45.4%		
Corporation income tax	12.0%		
Social insurance and retirement receipts	35.7%		
Social Security tax (off-budget)		26.1%	
Old-age and survivors insurance			22.3%
Disability insurance			3.8%
Medicare tax for hospital insurance		7.7%	
Railroad retirement pension fund		0.1%	
Railroad Social Security equivalent amount		0.1%	
Unemployment insurance trust funds		1.6%	
Federal employees retirement - employee share		0.2%	
Non-federal employees retirement		0.0%	
Excise taxes	2.7%		
Other	4.2%		
Estate and gift taxes		1.1%	
Customs duties and fees		1.1%	
Federal reserve deposits		1.3%	
All other		0.6%	
Total receipts	100.0%	39.9%	26.1%
Social Security tax and Medicare tax receipts		33.8%	
Total receipts less Social Security tax and Medicare tax receipts	66.2%		

Table 9A.3. Federal receipts by major source in current dollars, fiscal year 2001

Receipts source fiscal year 2001 (1)	Amount in current dollars (billions) (2)	Amount first subcat in current dollars (billions) (3)	Amount second subcat in current dollars (billions) (4)
Individual income tax	994		
Corporation income tax	151		
Social insurance and retirement receipts	694		
Social Security tax (off-budget)		508	
Old-age and survivors insurance			434
Disability insurance			73
Medicare tax for hospital insurance		150	
Railroad retirement pension fund		3	
Railroad Social Security equivalent amount		2	
Unemployment insurance trust funds		28	
Federal employees retirement - employee share		5	
Non-federal employees retirement		< 1	
Excise taxes	66		
Other	85		
Estate and gift taxes		28	
Customs duties and fees		19	
Federal reserve deposits		26	
All other		12	
Total receipts	1,990	781	507
Social Security tax and Medicare tax receipts		658	
Total receipts less Social Security tax and Medicare tax receipts	1,332		

Table 9A.4. Federal receipts by major source as a percentage of total receipts (continuation of table 9A.3), fiscal year 2001

Receipts source fiscal year 2001 (1)	Amount in Column (2) as % of total receipts (5)	Amount in Column (3) as % of total receipts (6)	Amount in Column (4) as % of total receipts (7)
Individual income tax	49.9%		
Corporation income tax	7.6%		
Social insurance and retirement receipts	34.9%		
Social Security tax (off-budget)		25.5%	
Old-age and survivors insurance			21.8%
Disability insurance			3.7%
Medicare tax for hospital insurance		7.5%	
Railroad retirement pension fund		0.2%	
Railroad Social Security equivalent amount		0.1%	
Unemployment insurance trust funds		1.4%	
Federal employees retirement - employee share		0.3%	
Non-federal employees retirement		0.0%	
Excise taxes	3.3%		
Other	4.3%		
Estate and gift taxes		1.4%	
Customs duties and fees		1.0%	
Federal reserve deposits		1.3%	
All other		0.6%	
Total receipts	99.9%	39.2%	25.5%
Social Security tax and Medicare tax receipts		33.1%	
Total receipts less Social Security tax and Medicare tax receipts	66.9%		

Rounding causes numeric discrepancy

Appendix 9B

—————•◆•—————

Individual income tax, the duty to file individual income tax returns

Purpose: To test assertions that filing individual income tax returns (and paying income taxes) is only voluntary.

Comments

Discussion about filing individual income tax returns would not be necessary but for some televised programs that I have seen that complain sarcastically about all federal taxes. These programs have included, with approval, interviews with some people who have not filed federal income tax returns, or paid income taxes, because they assert that filing tax returns is only "voluntary." These people assert boldly that no law requires them to file an income tax return or in some cases even to pay federal income taxes. They further assert that no IRS official or judge who has denied this assertion has shown them, or can show them, any such law.

This assertion can be tested by looking at one of the printed versions of the US Code. Less than an hour is needed to find the full set of provisions that show that this assertion is false. Here they are so that you can see for yourself the falsity of the assertion that filing federal income tax returns is only voluntary.

Documentary Proof that Filing Returns Is Required

Briefly stated, the US Constitution gives Congress the power to tax incomes, Congress has exercised this power in a way that requires individuals to file tax returns as prescribed in regulations adopted by the Secretary of the Treasury, and the Secretary of the Treasury has adopted regulations that require individuals to file income tax returns. The primary provisions that achieve this result are quoted below.

Authority from the people in the US Constitution[2]

The Congress shall have power to lay and collect taxes on incomes, from whatever source derived, without apportionment among the several States, and without regard to any census or enumeration. [US Constitution, Amendment XVI (1913)]

Exercise of that authority by Congress

GENERAL RULE. When required by regulations prescribed by the Secretary any person made liable for any tax imposed by this title, or with respect to the collection thereof, shall make a return or statement according to the forms and regulations prescribed by the Secretary. Every person required to make a return or statement shall include therein the information required by such forms or regulations. [26 U.S.C. § 6011(a) (2009)]

Regulations prescribed by the Secretary

General rule. Every person subject to any tax, or required to collect any tax, under Subtitle A of the Code, shall make such returns or statements as are required by the regulations in this chapter. The return or statement shall include therein the information required by the applicable regulations or forms. [26 C.F.R. § 1.6011-1(a) (2009)]

> *[Note for the General rule: "Subtitle A" is the federal income tax as found in "the Code," meaning the Internal Revenue Code.]*

****

Individuals required to make returns of income

(a) *Individual citizen or resident.*

(1) *In general.* Except as provided in paragraph (2) of this paragraph, an income tax return must be filed by every individual for each taxable year beginning before January 1, 1973, during which he receives $600 or more of gross income, and for each taxable year after December 31, 1972 during which he receives $750 or more of gross income, if such individual is:

(i) A citizen of the United States, whether residing at home or abroad,

(ii) A resident of the United States, even though not a citizen thereof, or

---

[2] Some groups deny that the Sixteenth Amendment to the United States Constitution was ratified properly. With this denial, they then claim that any federal income tax is "unconstitutional." See the 2012 platform of the Constitution Party, especially the section entitled "Taxes," accessed at http://www.constitutionparty.com/OurPrinciples/2012Platform/tabid/127/Default.aspx. The United States Supreme Court held that the Sixteenth Amendment was in accordance with the original Constitution in *Brushaber v. Union Pacific Railroad Co.*, 240 U.S. 1 (1916). See also *United States v. Foster*, 789 F.2d 457, 462–463 (7th Circuit 1986) (rejecting the contention that the Sixteenth Amendment was not ratified properly).

(iii) An alien bona fide resident of Puerto Rico or any section 931 possession, as defined in § 1.931-1-(c)(1), during the entire taxable year. [26 C.F.R. § 1.6012-1(a) (2009)]

[Note for the individual citizen or resident: "paragraph (2)" applies only to individuals who are sixty-five years old or older and simply adjusts the dollar amounts in paragraph (1), not the obligation to file an income tax return.]

Appendix 10A

---❖·◆·❖---

Individual income tax, calculation of a standard rate under the FAST Plan using tax year 2007 data

Purpose: To provide a methodology for calculating a standard individual income tax rate that will be required to produce the same total individual income tax receipts as occurred historically, but using identified FAST Plan proposals; also to show an example that uses this methodology.

Comments

As described in the main text of this book, using a standard-rate tax for all kinds of individual income is a key to achieving fairness, accountability, and simplicity for federal individual income taxes. Other proposals in this book are designed to work with a standard-rate individual income tax to achieve those same three goals. Collectively, these proposals are the FAST Plan.

An initial standard rate under the FAST Plan should be revenue-neutral so that these proposals will not be viewed as excuses to increase or decrease the total amount of money received by the United States from individual income taxes. That is, the standard rate and other proposed changes should produce the same total individual income tax receipts as would have been produced under "current law."

Table 10A.1 presents one methodology that can be used to calculate a standard income tax rate using historic data and identified changes from historic and current tax law. The historic data used in table 10A.1 are from the tax year 2007, which is the last tax year (calendar year) of federal tax payments before the Great Recession. The last part of chapter 10 addresses the question whether the amount of tax receipts from the individual income tax in 2007 is the most appropriate target for an initial standard rate calculation.

For simplicity, table 10A.1 reflects only the proposals in the FAST Plan that have the most impact on total individual income tax receipts. The format of table 10A.1 can be expanded to include other proposals. Changes to current tax law are reflected in the line items of table 10A.1 that have "estimated" numbers. These changes are:

- A standard-rate income tax is applied to all individual income (this calculated rate is shown in line 15).
- All Social Security and Medicare tax payments are used as credits to individual income taxes, including payments made by employers on behalf of employees (lines 13 and 14).
- Social Security and Medicare tax payments made by employers on behalf of employees are income to the employees (line 10).
- Itemized deductions from income are allowed only for medical expenses (lines 6 and 7).
- All medical expenses are allowed as an itemized deduction in addition to the standard deduction (line 7). (The FAST Plan proposals contemplate allowing deductions only for medical expenses in excess of 1 percent of adjusted gross income.)
- Social Security benefits are not taxable income (line 8). (The FAST Plan proposals contemplate taxing some Social Security benefits, but not as much as under current law.)

Note that table 10A.1 starts with adjusted gross income reported on all returns, not total reported income. This approach avoids double counting of some income as taxable. For example, the calculation of adjusted gross income excludes income that is taxable to someone else and that will be reported by that other person as income (e.g., alimony payments). Using adjusted gross income, however, necessarily allows the effects of current tax subsidies that occur "above the line" in calculating adjusted gross income. These are the only tax subsidies included in table 10A.1.

Although table 10A.1 relies upon IRS data for the tax year 2007, estimates have to be made regarding some data that will be different from the data obtained from actual 2007 individual income tax returns. The notes at the end of the table state briefly how the noted estimates were obtained.

Table 10A.2 provides explanations for the data items in table 10A.1, including comments about whether an estimate likely overstates or understates the true number. These extra details are provided because of the overwhelming significance of any proposed rate for a standard-rate individual income tax.

Data source:
Publication 1304, Individual Income Tax Returns, IRS Statistics of Income, Table 1.1, tax year 2007.

Table 10A.1. Individual income tax, calculation of a standard rate using tax year 2007 data in current dollars

Income or reduction description	Number of returns	Amount in current dollars (billions)
(1) Actual adjusted gross income, all returns	142,978,806	$ 8,688
(2) Subtract actual basic standard deductions	90,510,904	$ (636)
(3) Subtract actual additional standard deductions	11,703,100	$ (18)
(4) Subtract actual exemptions	282,613,371	$ (943)
(5) Actual adjusted gross income less actual standard deductions and exemptions		$ 7,091
(6) Subtract estimated basic standard deductions in place of itemized deductions *Note 1*	50,544,470	$ (355)
(7) Subtract estimated medical expenses (all reported itemized medical expenses) *Note 2*		$ (119)
(8) Subtract estimated reduction in gross income from excluding all taxable Social Security benefits *Note 3*	15,011,961	$ (167)
(9) Estimated taxable income without adding employer-paid Social Security and Medicare taxes income to salaries and wages		$ 6,450
(10) Add employer-paid Social Security and Medicare taxes as income to salaries and wages *Note 4*		$ 357
(11) Estimated taxable income after adding employer-paid Social Security and Medicare taxes income to salaries and wages		$ 6,807
(12) Actual individual income tax receipts before credits		$ 1,180
(13) Actual Social Security and Medicare taxes receipts *Note 5*		$ 820
(14) Target for total income tax receipts under standard rate equals actual income tax receipts + Social Security and Medicare taxes receipts *Note 6*		$ 2,000
(15) Standard rate = target for total income tax receipts divided by estimated taxable income after adding employer-paid Social Security and Medicare taxes income to salaries and wages		29%

Note 1: Calculated as average basic standard deduction per return times number of returns using itemized deductions, which is $7,025 x 50,544,470 = $355 billion.

Note 2: Data source is *Publication 1304, Individual Income Tax Returns,* IRS Statistics of Income, Table 2.1, tax year 2007.

Note 3: Assumes no taxable Social Security benefits despite the FAST Plan proposal that some Social Security benefits be taxable.

Note 4: Add 43.5 percent of total Social Security and Medicare taxes paid, as shown in line 13. This is the approximate employer-paid portion of total Social Security and Medicare tax receipts based on salaries and wages being 87 percent of all earned income. As calculated here, earned income consists of salaries and wages ($5,842 billion) plus business or profession net income ($335 billion) plus partnership and S corporation net income ($547 billion). See Note 5 for data source for Social Security and Medicare tax receipts.

Note 5: Data source is *Budget of the U.S. Government, Fiscal Year 2014,* Historical Tables, Table 2.4, fiscal year 2007.

Note 6: Assumes all payments of Social Security and Medicare taxes will be used as income tax credits.

Table 10A.2. Explanations for line items in table 10A.1 (calculation of an individual income tax standard rate)

Income or reduction description	Explanation for amount
(1) Actual adjusted gross income, all returns.	Same as IRS data for tax year 2007.
(2) Subtract actual basic standard deductions.	Same as IRS data for tax year 2007.
(3) Subtract actual additional standard deductions.	Same as IRS data for tax year 2007.
(4) Subtract actual exemptions.	Same as IRS data for tax year 2007. The actual data for 2007 reflect diminished exemptions for individuals with large incomes. A FAST Plan proposal will eliminate those diminutions, so this number slightly understates this reduction if that part of the FAST Plan is adopted (understated by an estimated 1.72 percent of actual exemptions).
(5) Actual adjusted gross income less actual standard deductions and exemptions.	Simple calculation: line 1 minus lines 2, 3, and 4.
(6) Subtract estimated basic standard deductions in place of itemized deductions.	Estimate made by assuming that the basic standard deductions for individuals claiming itemized deductions would have had the same pattern of basic standard deductions as the individuals who used basic standard deductions in tax year 2007. This amount may slightly understate this reduction because it assumes no additional standard deductions for these individuals.
(7) Subtract estimated medical expenses (all reported itemized medical expenses).	Estimate picks up only medical expenses that were reported by individuals who claimed itemized deductions for medical expenses. These are likely the individuals with the largest medical expenses. Nevertheless, this amount understates this reduction when all individuals can claim as reductions medical expenses in addition to their standard deductions. If the true number is twice the estimate in line 7, the standard rate will be calculated as 0.5 percentage points larger than shown in line 15.

(8) Subtract estimated reduction in gross income by excluding all taxable Social Security benefits.	This estimate assumes that no Social Security benefits are taxable, even though the FAST Plan allows for taxing some Social Security benefits received by individuals with large incomes. If the FAST Plan is adopted, this number overstates the reduction in gross income (a counterbalance to other amounts that understate reductions).
(9) Estimated taxable income without adding employer-paid Social Security and Medicare taxes income to salaries and wages.	Simple calculation: Line 5 minus lines 6, 7, and 8.
(10) Add employer-paid Social Security and Medicare taxes as income to salaries and wages (additional gross income from this treatment).	The FAST Plan requires the employer-paid portion of Social Security and Medicare taxes to be treated as income if this same portion is allowed as a nonrefundable credit against income taxes. The note for this line item identifies how this calculation is made. See line 13 for the base data and source.
(11) Estimated taxable income after adding employer-paid Social Security and Medicare taxes income to salaries and wages.	Simple calculation: line 9 plus line 10.
(12) Actual individual income tax receipts.	Same as IRS data for tax year 2007.
(13) Actual Social Security and Medicare taxes receipts.	Same as OMB data for fiscal year 2007. These receipts are the sum of the "old-age and survivors insurance," "disability insurance," and "hospital insurance" line items in table 2.4 of the *Historical Tables, Budget of the U.S. Government, Fiscal Year 2014.*
(14) Total income tax receipts needed to match actual income tax receipts + Social Security and Medicare taxes receipts.	Simple calculation: add lines 12 and 13. This is the target amount of individual income tax receipts for the standard income tax rate to achieve. This target assumes that all Social Security and Medicare tax payments by individuals are used as credits to the income tax. This target overstates the receipts needed because it treats Social Security and Medicare tax payments as refundable credits rather than nonrefundable credits as proposed in the FAST Plan. As nonrefundable credits, any portion of these payments by an individual that exceeds the individual's income tax cannot be used as a credit.

(15) Standard rate = total income tax receipts needed divided by estimated taxable income after adding employer-paid Social Security and Medicare taxes income to salaries and wages.	Simple calculation: line 14 divided by line 11.
No line item	Subsidies will reduce income tax receipts. Each subsidy will require an increase in the standard rate in order to achieve revenue-neutral individual income tax receipts. If each subsidy takes the form of a credit, as provided in the FAST Plan, the impact of each subsidy on the standard rate can be calculated by adding the total amount of the subsidy to the total income tax receipts needed to match the target of revenue-neutral tax receipts shown in line 14.

Appendix 10B

◆•◆•◆

Individual income tax, summary of significant individual income tax rate changes, 1980–2012

Purpose: To identify when individual income tax rates changed in major ways during the time period 1980 to 2012 as a reference from which to compare changes that occurred to a variety of potentially affected economic indicators.

Comments

In the time period from 1980 to 2012, presidents and Congress broadly reassessed the individual income tax four times—in 1981, 1986, 1993, and 2001. Twice they also separately reassessed the taxation of capital gains—in 1997 and 2003. Only one reassessment led to broad tax increases (1993). The other five reassessments led to tax decreases. The years when these tax changes were effective serve as markers against which to compare a variety of economic indicators to see, at least in a general way, whether these tax changes have had any discernible effect on those indicators. Those indicators, in turn, can potentially provide information about the economic effects of the tax changes. The indicators chosen here are tax receipts from the individual income tax (appendix 10C), US GDP (appendix 10D), private-sector jobs (appendix 14D), and net capital gains reported by individuals (appendix 14E).

Summary of Significant Individual Income Tax Rate Changes, 1980–2012

1981 Broad Tax Rate Decreases

As of 1981, no tax was imposed on an individual's taxable income below $3,400 on a joint return and $2,300 on a single return. For income in excess of those amounts, tax rates graduated from a low of 14 percent to a high of 70 percent, with a total of fifteen different rates that were applied to different segments of an individual's income (known as "tax brackets"). A maximum 50 percent rate applied to personal service (earned) income. Capital gains income also had special treatment, with 60 percent of net long-term capital gains being deductible from income. This deduction meant that only 40 percent of net gains were taxed, so the effective maximum tax rate on long-term capital gains was 28 percent (70 percent rate times 40 percent net gains).[3]

The Economic Recovery Act of 1981 decreased all of these tax rates and adopted a maximum rate of 50 percent for all income. The 1981 Act retained the basic 1981 tax structure, with a large number of different tax brackets. The 1981 Act also retained the 1981 tax treatment of long-term capital gains, resulting in a maximum tax rate of 20 percent for long-term capital gains (50 percent rate times 40 percent net gains).

Most of the changes adopted in 1981 began in 1982 and were phased in over three years (1982, 1983, and 1984).[4]

1986 Broad Tax Rate Decreases

The Tax Reform Act of 1986 not only adopted greatly reduced tax rates by creating a 28 percent maximum rate, but also nominally chopped the number of tax brackets from as many as fifteen down to two (15 percent and 28 percent brackets). However, phase-out of the low 15 percent rate for larger taxable income levels effectively created a hybrid structure of tax brackets. These changes became effective in 1988. The 1986 Act adopted an interim five-bracket tax structure for 1987 only, having 38.5 percent as the maximum rate. The 1986 Act also adopted an indexing procedure applicable to all tax brackets so that inflation, by itself, would not create tax increases.[5]

As for capital gains, the 1986 Act rescinded the historic treatment of long-term capital gains income as a partial income deduction. Instead, effective in 1987, the act singled out long-term capital gains as a special kind of income with its own maximum tax rate (28 percent).[6]

Note: In 1990, Congress rescinded the 15 percent rate phase-out and adopted a third tax bracket, with a higher 31 percent rate beginning in 1991.[7]

---

3 S.Rep.No. 97-144, 97th Cong. (1981), 22–27; *Internal Revenue Code, Winter 2009* Ed. (Chicago, CCH, 2008), Vol.1, 75–76 (historic notes on 26 U.S.C. § 1).

4 Economic Recovery Act of 1981, Pub.L.No. 97-34, 95 Stat.172, § 101; S.Rep.No. 97-144, 97th Cong (1981), 27.

5 Tax Reform Act of 1986, Pub.L.No. 99-514, 100 Stat. 2085, § 101; H.R.Rep.No. 99-841, 99th Cong. (1986), II-1 to II-6 (Conf.Rep.).

6 Tax Reform Act of 1986, Pub.L.No. 99-514, 100 Stat. 2085, §§ 301–302.

7 Omnibus Budget Reconciliation Act of 1990, Pub.L.No.101-508, 104 Stat.1388, § 11101(a) and (b).

1993 Broad Tax Rate Increases

Under the Omnibus Budget Reconciliation Act of 1993, Congress adopted a clear five-bracket rate structure for each individual filing category. Except for the lowest 15 percent rate, the 1993 Act increased the rates applicable to each bracket compared to the effective rates under the 1986 Act (as amended in 1990). The new maximum rate was 39.6 percent. These changes were effective starting in 1993.[8]

The maximum rate for net long-term capital gains remained at 28 percent.

1997 Capital Gains Tax Rate Decreases

As part of the Taxpayer Relief Act of 1997, when an individual had long-term capital gains, Congress adopted a multistep formula for calculating that individual's taxes that applied a maximum tax rate of 20 percent on most net long-term capital gains. Selected kinds of capital gains were still subject to maximum tax rates of 28 percent (or 25 percent) rather than 20 percent. These changes applied to taxable years ending after May 6, 1997, so for most individuals, these changes were effective in 1997.[9]

2001 Broad Tax Rate Decreases

Under the Tax Relief Reconciliation Act of 2001, Congress decreased individual tax rates and created a new 10 percent tax-rate bracket for the lowest levels of taxable income, resulting in six tax brackets for each filing category. These decreases occurred in three stages: 2001, 2002, and 2003. For 2003 and later years, the maximum tax-rate bracket was 35 percent.[10] As a unique feature of this act, all of these changes would expire automatically at the end of 2010 unless affirmatively extended by Congress[11] (at the end of 2010, Congress adopted a two-year extension for these rates[12]).

The 2001 Act did not change the maximum rates applicable to most net long-term capital gains.

2003 Capital Gains Tax Rate Decreases and Dividends Tax Rate Decreases

The Jobs and Growth Reconciliation Tax Act of 2003 retained a multistep formula for calculating an individual's taxes when that individual had net long-term capital gains. However, the 2003

---

8 Omnibus Budget Reconciliation Act of 1993, Pub.L.No.103-66, 107 Stat. 312, § 13201(a).

9 Taxpayer Relief Act of 1997, Pub.L.No.105-34, 111 Stat 788, § 311.

10 Economic Growth and Tax Relief Reconciliation Act of 2001, Pub.L.No.107-16, 115 Stat. 38, § 101(a).

11 Economic Growth and Tax Relief Reconciliation Act of 2001, Pub.L.No.107-16, 115 Stat. 38, § 901.

12 Tax Relief, Unemployment Insurance Reauthorization, and Job Creation Act of 2010, Pub.L.No.111-312, 124 Stat. 3296, § 101(a)(1).

Act decreased the maximum rate for most long-term capital gains from 20 percent to 15 percent. Prior 28 percent and 25 percent rates for selected kinds of capital gains remained.[13] The 2003 Act also allowed qualified dividends to be taxed the same as net long-term capital gains, with a maximum rate of 15 percent.[14] For most individuals, these changes were effective in 2003, but like the 2001 changes, would expire at the end of 2010 unless affirmatively extended by Congress[15] (at the end of 2010, Congress adopted a two-year extension for these rates).[16]

2012 Fiscal Cliff Tax Compromise

At the end of 2012, Congress reached a tax compromise that permanently extended the 2001 and 2003 tax changes for most individuals, but reinstated prior rates for individual incomes exceeding designated threshold amounts.[17] Starting in 2013, the 2012 fiscal cliff tax compromise raised the maximum tax rates on ordinary income to 39.6 percent and on long-term capital gains to 20 percent for individuals whose income exceeds a threshold amount (e.g., $400,000 for a single individual).

---

[13] Jobs and Growth Tax Relief Reconciliation Act of 2003, Pub.L.No.108-27, 117 Stat. 752, § 301(a)(1).

[14] Jobs and Growth Tax Relief Reconciliation Act of 2003, Pub.L.No.108-27, 117 Stat. 752, § 302(a).

[15] Jobs and Growth Tax Relief Reconciliation Act of 2003, Pub.L.No.108-27, 117 Stat. 752, § 301(c), § 302(f) [as amended by the Working Families Tax Relief Act of 2004, Pub.L.No.108-311, 118 Stat. 1166, § 402(a)(6)], and § 303 [as amended by the Tax Increase Prevention and Reconciliation Act of 2005, Pub.L.No.109-222, 120 Stat. 345, § 102].

[16] Tax Relief, Unemployment Insurance Reauthorization, and Job Creation Act of 2010, Pub.L.No.111-312, 124 Stat. 3296, § 102(a).

[17] American Taxpayer Relief Act of 2012, Pub.L.No. 112-240, 126 Stat. 2313, § 101.

Appendix 10C

———◆•◆•◆———

Individual income tax, comparing tax-rate changes to annual receipts from the individual income tax

Purpose: To reveal in a general way from historic data whether and to what extent tax-rate changes affect receipts from the individual income tax.

Comments

The table and two figures in this appendix provide data that address the question whether lower individual income tax rates increase economic activity so much that tax receipts from lower-rate taxes will actually increase.

Table 10C.1 shows the receipts from the individual income tax in each federal fiscal year from 1981 to 2012 in both current and constant dollars. The receipts in constant dollars remove the effects of inflation on the receipts. In addition, both sets of receipts are shown per person as a way to remove the effect on increased economic activity and, therefore, tax receipts caused solely by an expanded population.

Figure 10C.1 compares total receipts from the individual income tax in constant dollars to the timing of the four broad sets of tax-rate changes that occurred during 1981 to 2012 (1981 decreases, 1986 decreases, 1993 increases, and 2001 decreases). The receipts in this figure include increases that are caused solely by an expanded population.

Figure 10C.2 has the same format as figure 10C.1, but compares tax receipts in constant dollars per person in the United States to the timing of the four broad sets of tax-rate changes. These data remove the increases in tax receipts that are caused solely by an expanded population.

Looking at total tax receipts in constant dollars, the historic maximum occurred in fiscal year 2000. After the most recent broad tax decreases, which were adopted in 2001, total tax receipts initially declined, then rebounded, but at their peak in fiscal year 2007 before the Great Recession, still reached only 95 percent of their level in fiscal year 2000. In fiscal year

2010 during the Great Recession, total tax receipts from the individual income tax were just 70 percent of their level in fiscal year 2000.

After the broad tax decreases that were adopted in 2001, fiscal year tax receipts per person show a pattern similar to the pattern that occurred for total tax receipts from the individual income tax. However, the initial decline was larger, and the rebound was less large. Their peak in fiscal year 2007 before the Great Recession reached only 89 percent of their level in fiscal year 2000. In fiscal year 2010 during the Great Recession, tax receipts per person from the individual income tax were just 64 percent of their level in fiscal year 2000.

Data source:

Budget of the U.S. Government, Fiscal Year 2014, Historical Tables, Tables 1.3, 2.1; *Population Estimates, National* (US Census Bureau, 2013).

Table 10C.1. Individual income tax, receipts from the individual income tax in current and constant (FY 2005) dollars, 1981–2012

Federal fiscal year (1)	Receipts from individual income tax in current dollars (billions) (2)	Receipts from individual income tax in constant (FY 2005) dollars (billions) (3)	Composite deflator for constant (FY 2005) dollars (4)	United States resident population at July 1 (millions) (5)	Receipts in current dollars per U.S. resident person (6)	Receipts in constant dollars per U.S. resident person (7)
1981	286	597	0.4790	229	1,249	2,607
1982	298	580	0.5137	232	1,284	2,500
1983	289	536	0.5394	234	1,235	2,290
1984	298	525	0.5677	236	1,263	2,224
1985	335	571	0.5870	238	1,408	2,398
1986	349	580	0.6022	240	1,454	2,415
1987	393	633	0.6213	242	1,624	2,614
1988	401	627	0.6400	244	1,643	2,568
1989	446	672	0.6637	247	1,806	2,721
1990	467	683	0.6842	250	1,868	2,730
1991	468	653	0.7165	253	1,850	2,582
1992	476	640	0.7439	257	1,852	2,490
1993	510	668	0.7640	260	1,962	2,567
1994	543	698	0.7782	263	2,065	2,653
1995	590	738	0.7995	266	2,218	2,774
1996	656	801	0.8187	269	2,439	2,979
1997	737	882	0.8360	273	2,700	3,229
1998	829	982	0.8439	276	3,004	3,559
1999	879	1,027	0.8558	279	3,151	3,681
2000	1,004	1,145	0.8770	282	3,560	4,060
2001	994	1,105	0.8992	285	3,488	3,879
2002	858	939	0.9138	288	2,979	3,260
2003	794	847	0.9378	290	2,738	2,920
2004	809	839	0.9645	293	2,761	2,863
2005	927	927	1.0000	296	3,132	3,132
2006	1,044	1,008	1.0354	299	3,492	3,372
2007	1,163	1,093	1.0642	302	3,851	3,619
2008	1,146	1,039	1.1031	304	3,770	3,417
2009	915	826	1.1073	307	2,980	2,692
2010	899	802	1.1211	309	2,909	2,595
2011	1,091	954	1.1439	312	3,497	3,057
2012	1,132	967	1.1704	314	3,605	3,080

Figure 10C.1. Comparing broad tax-rate changes to receipts from the individual income tax in constant (FY 2005) dollars, 1981–2012

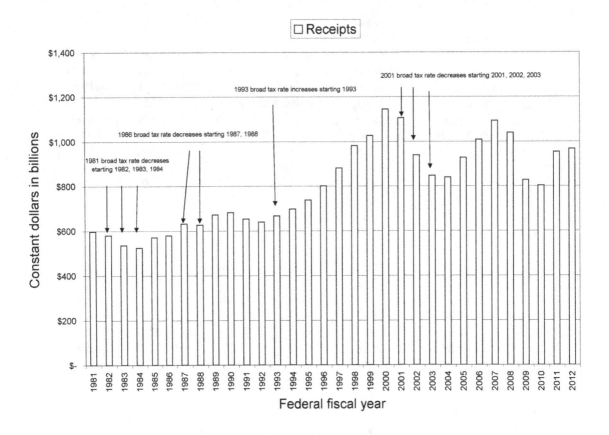

Figure 10C.2. Comparing broad tax-rate changes to receipts from the individual income tax per resident person in constant (FY 2005) dollars, 1981–2012

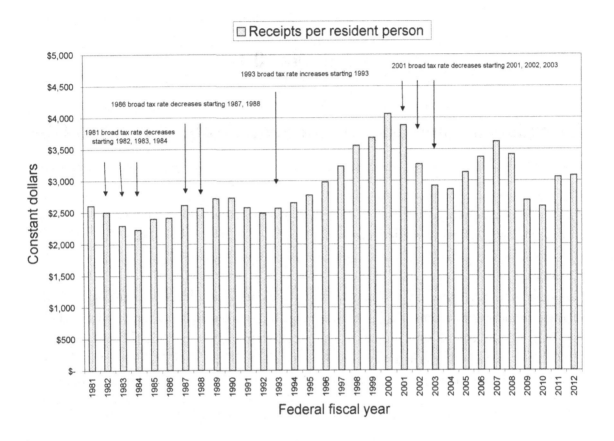

Appendix 10D

◆·◆·◆

Individual income tax, comparing tax-rate changes to GDP

Purpose: To reveal in a general way from historic data whether and to what extent individual income tax rate changes may affect economic activity, as measured by GDP.

Comments

The table and four figures in this appendix provide data that address the question whether changes in individual income tax rates also change economic activity as measured by GDP.

Table 10D.1 shows the GDP in each federal fiscal year from 1981 to 2012. This table also shows the GDP in constant dollars as a way to remove the effects of inflation. In addition, both sets of data are shown per person in the United States. These are the base data reflected in the figures.

The first two figures examine the potential effects of the four broad tax-rate changes that occurred between 1981 and 2012 (1981 decreases, 1986 decreases, 1993 increases, and 2001 decreases). Figure 10D.1 compares GDP in constant dollars to the timing of these four sets of tax-rate changes. The data in this figure include increases that are caused solely by an expanded population. Figure 10D.2 has the same format as figure 10D.1, but compares GDP in constant dollars per person in the United States to the timing of these four sets of tax-rate changes. These data remove the increases in GDP that are caused solely by an expanded population.

Whether broad tax-rate changes within the range of changes that were adopted from 1981 to 2012 have had a significant effect on GDP is not discernible from these data. Although GDP per person generally increased over time and after broad tax decreases (e.g., fiscal years 2003–07 and 1988–90), it also decreased in times when broad tax decreases were in effect (e.g., 1991–92) and increased after broad tax increases (e.g., 1993–96). This uneven correlation suggests that other factors are more important in affecting GDP. For example, technological advances may increase GDP per person, whereas an economic recession unrelated to tax policy may decrease GDP per person.

The second two figures examine potential effects of the four changes in the maximum tax rates for long-term capital gains that occurred from 1981 to 2012 (1982 new base, 1987 increase, 1997 decrease, 2003 decrease). Figure 10D.3 compares GDP in constant dollars to the timing of these changes. Figure 10D.4 has the same format as figure 10D.3, but compares GDP in constant dollars per person to the timing of these changes. As with the figures showing broad tax-rate changes, neither figure here shows any definitive correlation between GDP per person and the changes in the maximum long-term capital gains tax rate.

Data source:
  Budget of the U.S. Government, Fiscal Year 2014, Historical Tables, Table 1.3;
  Population Estimates, National (US Census Bureau, 2013).

Table 10D.1. Individual income tax, base data for comparing tax-rate changes to GDP, 1981–2012

Federal fiscal year (1)	GDP in current dollars (billions) (2)	GDP in constant (FY 2005) dollars (billions) (3)	United States resident population at July 1 (millions) (4)	GDP in current dollars per resident person (5)	GDP in constant (FY 2005) dollars per resident person (6)
1981	3,056	6,383	229	13,345	27,873
1982	3,219	6,266	232	13,875	27,009
1983	3,434	6,366	234	14,675	27,205
1984	3,850	6,780	236	16,314	28,729
1985	4,147	7,062	238	17,424	29,672
1986	4,394	7,297	240	18,308	30,404
1987	4,641	7,473	242	19,178	30,880
1988	4,995	7,802	244	20,471	31,975
1989	5,386	8,114	247	21,806	32,850
1990	5,733	8,378	250	22,932	33,512
1991	5,927	8,270	253	23,427	32,688
1992	6,234	8,383	257	24,257	32,619
1993	6,594	8,629	260	25,362	33,188
1994	6,994	8,989	263	26,593	34,179
1995	7,348	9,190	266	27,624	34,549
1996	7,729	9,441	269	28,732	35,097
1997	8,224	9,839	273	30,125	36,040
1998	8,653	10,256	276	31,351	37,159
1999	9,227	10,783	279	33,072	38,649
2000	9,830	11,209	282	34,858	39,748
2001	10,210	11,354	285	35,825	39,839
2002	10,528	11,523	288	36,556	40,010
2003	11,000	11,728	290	37,931	40,441
2004	11,677	12,106	293	39,853	41,317
2005	12,451	12,451	296	42,064	42,064
2006	13,225	12,775	299	44,231	42,726
2007	13,881	13,043	302	45,964	43,189
2008	14,341	13,000	304	47,174	42,763
2009	13,940	12,576	307	45,407	40,964
2010	14,325	12,768	309	46,359	41,320
2011	14,955	12,974	312	47,933	41,583
2012	15,506	13,247	314	49,382	42,188

Figure 10D.1. Comparing broad individual income tax rate changes to GDP in constant (FY 2005) dollars, 1981–2012

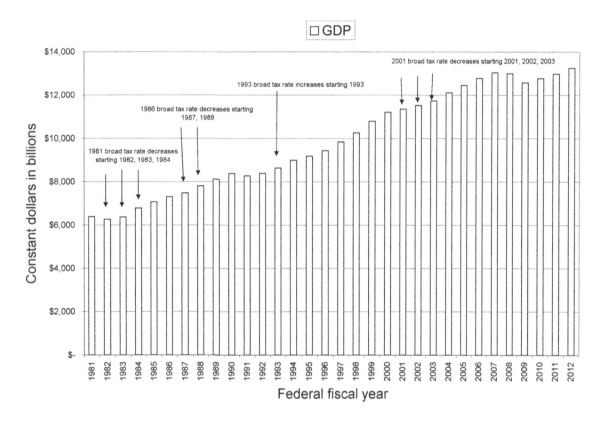

Figure 10D.2. Comparing broad individual income tax rate changes to GDP per resident person in constant (FY 2005) dollars, 1981–2012

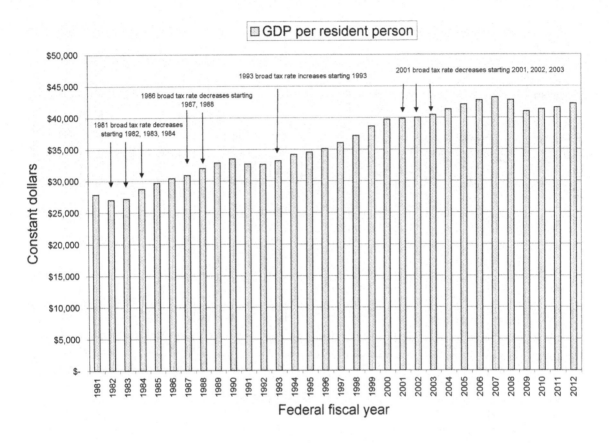

Figure 10D.3. Comparing long-term capital gains tax-rate changes to GDP in constant (FY 2005) dollars, 1981–2012

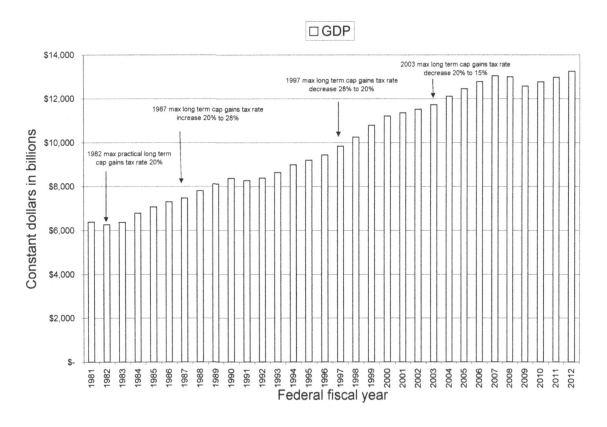

Figure 10D.4. Comparing long-term capital gains tax-rate changes to GDP per resident person in constant (FY 2005) dollars, 1981–2012

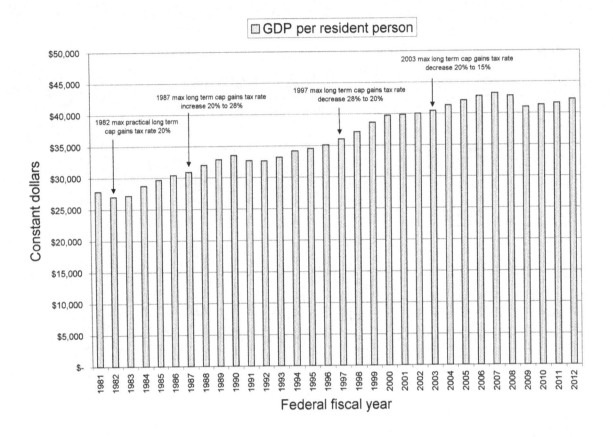

Appendix 10E

———◆•◆•◆———

Individual income tax, comparing marginal total federal tax rates under 2010 tax law

Purpose: To show by example how individuals with larger incomes can pay lower marginal total federal tax rates than individuals with smaller incomes under "current law" (2010) and to identify the highest marginal total federal tax rates in each filing category.

Comments

A marginal total federal tax rate is the sum of income, Social Security, and Medicare taxes applicable to the last dollar of income at a particular income level. This is the real out-of-pocket tax obligation an individual faces for that last dollar.

Each of the following examples compares the marginal total federal tax rates applicable to four different incomes of individuals in the same filing category. The chosen incomes are close to where marginal total federal tax rates increase:

(1) Near but above the amount where the income tax rate begins that applies to the last amount of income that is subject to the Social Security tax

(2) Near the Social Security tax cutoff (below or above) and below the amount where the income tax rate first increases from the rate in (1)

(3) Above the Social Security tax cutoff and in the next income tax rate bracket above the rate bracket in (1)

(4) In the highest income tax bracket

These examples assume that all of the income of each individual is earned income and that 2010 federal tax law applies, with its graduated tax rates, a $106,800 Social Security tax cutoff, and above-the-line reduction from income for one-half the self-employment tax (Social

Security and Medicare taxes) on self-employment income. This appendix uses 2010 tax law rather than 2009 tax law (used as a reference elsewhere in this book) because exemptions were not diminished for individuals with large incomes in 2010 tax law (simplifies showing the calculations for the large-income examples).

The examples consider these filing and income fact scenarios:

Example 1. A single individual whose income is wages only.

Example 2. A single individual whose income is self-employment income only.

Example 3. A married couple filing jointly whose incomes are wages only.

Example 4. A married couple filing jointly whose incomes are self-employment income only.

Example 5. A married couple filing separately whose incomes are equal and wages only.

Example 6. A married couple filing separately whose incomes are equal and self-employment income only.

Example 7. A head of household whose income is wages only.

Example 8. A head of household whose income is self-employment income only.

These examples show that the highest marginal total federal tax rate in 2010 was 40.15 percent (except for peculiar and rare circumstances for married individuals that can affect less than $4,000 of earned income, see Examples 4 and 6). That 40.15 percent rate applied to self-employed individuals whose earned incomes were as low as $78,000 (Example 6) and up to $115,647 (Example 2), depending upon filing category.

10E.1. Example 1

(single individual, wages income only, 2010 tax law)

This example assumes that each individual has wages income only and uses the standard deduction and one exemption to calculate taxable income. The respective wages incomes are $92,000 (Wages S1), $108,000 (Wages S2), $182,000 (Wages S3), and $400,000 (Wages S4).

Table 10E.1. Marginal total federal tax rates, single individual, wages income only, 2010 tax law

	Wages S1	Wages S2	Wages S3	Wages S4
Income				
Earned income	$ 92,000	$ 108,000	$ 182,000	$ 400,000
Less standard deduction	$ (5,700)	$ (5,700)	$ (5,700)	$ (5,700)
Less one exemption	$ (3,650)	$ (3,650)	$ (3,650)	$ (3,650)
Taxable income	$ 82,650	$ 98,650	$ 172,650	$ 390,650
Marginal tax rates				
Income tax rate	28.00%	28.00%	33.00%	35.00%
Social Security tax rate	6.20%	0.00%	0.00%	0.00%
Medicare tax rate	1.45%	1.45%	1.45%	1.45%
Marginal total tax rate	35.65%	29.45%	34.45%	36.45%

For a single employee in this scenario, the above marginal total tax rate for Wages S1 will be applicable to all wages between $91,750 (taxable income at $82,400, the beginning of the 28 percent rate that continues to $171,850) and $106,800 (wages earned income where the Social Security tax ends). In this scenario, the 28 percent income tax rate continues on earned income above $106,800 up to $181,200 ($171,850 taxable income plus $9,350 reductions above). In this scenario, the total tax rate for Wages S4 begins at wages of $383,000 ($373,650, the beginning of the 35 percent rate, plus $9,350 reductions above).

10E.2. Example 2

(single individual, self-employment income only, 2010 tax law)

This example assumes that each individual has self-employment income only and uses the standard deduction and one exemption to calculate taxable income. The respective self-employment incomes are $92,000 (Self S11), $116,000 (Self S12), $182,000 (Self S13), and $400,000 (Self S14).

Table 10E.2. Marginal total federal tax rates, single individual, self-employment income only, 2010 tax law

	Self S11	Self S12	Self S13	Self S14
Income				
Earned income	$ 92,000	$ 116,000	$ 182,000	$ 400,000
Less standard deduction	$ (5,700)	$ (5,700)	$ (5,700)	$ (5,700)
Less one exemption	$ (3,650)	$ (3,650)	$ (3,650)	$ (3,650)
Taxable income	$ 82,650	$ 106,650	$ 172,650	$ 390,650
Marginal tax rates				
Income tax rate	28.00%	28.00%	33.00%	35.00%
Social Security tax rate **	11.45%	0.00%	0.00%	0.00%
Medicare tax rate **	2.68%	2.68%	2.68%	2.68%
Deduct ½ Soc Sec/Med tax *	-1.98%	-0.38%	-0.44%	-0.47%
Marginal total tax rate	40.15%	30.30%	35.24%	37.21%

** Full rates of 12.4 percent (Social Security) and 2.9 percent (Medicare) times 0.9235.
* Social Security plus Medicare tax rates above times 0.28, 0.28, 0.33, or 0.35.

For a single, self-employed individual in this scenario, the above marginal total tax rate for Self S11 will be applicable to all self-employment income between $91,750 (taxable income at $82,400, the beginning of the 28 percent rate that continues to $171,850) and $115,647 (result from dividing 0.9235 into $106,800, which is where the self-employment Social Security tax ends). In this scenario, the 28 percent income tax rate continues on earned income above

$115,647 up to $181,200 ($171,850 taxable income plus $9,350 reductions above). In this scenario, the total tax rate for Self S14 begins at wages of $383,000 ($373,650 plus $9,350 reductions above).

10E.3. Example 3

(married couple filing jointly, wages income only, 2010 tax law)

This example assumes that each individual in the married couple has wages income only, that both wages are less than $106,800 if their total is less than $213,600, and that the couple uses the standard deduction and two exemptions to calculate taxable income. The respective total wages incomes are $158,000 (Wages MJ1), $214,000 (Wages MJ2), $230,000 (Wages MJ3) and $400,000 (Wages MJ4).

Table 10E.3. Marginal total federal tax rates, married couple filing jointly, wages income only, 2010 tax law

	Wages MJ1	Wages MJ2	Wages MJ3	Wages MJ4
Income				
Earned income	$ 158,000	$ 214,000	$ 230,000	$ 400,000
Less standard deduction	$ (11,400)	$ (11,400)	$ (11,400)	$ (11,400)
Less one exemption	$ (7,300)	$ (7,300)	$ (7,300)	$ (7,300)
Taxable income	$ 139,300	$ 195,300	$ 211,300	$ 381,300
Marginal tax rates				
Income tax rate	28.00%	28.00%	33.00%	35.00%
Social Security tax rate	6.20%	0.00%	0.00%	0.00%
Medicare tax rate	1.45%	1.45%	1.45%	1.45%
Marginal total tax rate	35.65%	29.45%	34.45%	36.45%

For a married couple filing jointly in this scenario, the above marginal total tax rate for Wages MJ1 will be applicable to all total wages between $156,000 (taxable income at $137,300, the beginning of the 28 percent rate that continues to $209,250) and $213,600 (twice the individual earned income of $106,800, where the Social Security tax ends). In this scenario, the 28 percent income tax rate continues on earned income above $213,600 up to $227,950 ($209,250 taxable income plus $18,700 reductions above). In this scenario, the total tax rate for Wages MJ4 begins at wages of $392,350 ($373,650, the beginning of the 35 percent rate, plus $18,700 reductions above).

10E.4. Example 4

(married couple filing jointly, self-employment income only, 2010 tax law)

This example assumes that each individual in the married couple has self-employment income only, that both of those incomes are less than $115,647 if their total is less than $231,294, and that the couple uses the standard deduction and two exemptions to calculate taxable income. The respective total self-employment incomes are $158,000 (Self MJ11), $226,000 (Self MJ12), $232,000 (Self MJ13), and $400,000 (Self MJ14).

Table 10E.4. Marginal total federal tax rates, married couple filing jointly, self-employment income only, 2010 tax law

	Self MJ11	Self MJ12	Self MJ13	Self MJ14
Income				
Earned income	$ 158,000	$ 226,000	$ 232,000	$ 400,000
Less standard deduction	$ (11,400)	$ (11,400)	$ (11,400)	$ (11,400)
Less one exemption	$ (7,300)	$ (7,300)	$ (7,300)	$ (7,300)
Taxable income	$ 139,300	$ 207,300	$ 213,300	$ 381,300
Marginal tax rates				
Income tax rate	28.00%	28.00%	33.00%	35.00%
Social Security tax rate **	11.45%	11.45%	0.00%	0.00%
Medicare tax rate **	2.68%	2.68%	2.68%	2.68%
Deduct ½ Soc Sec/Med tax *	-1.98%	-1.98%	-0.44%	-0.47%
Marginal total tax rate	40.15%	40.15%	35.24%	37.21%

** Full rates of 12.4 percent (Social Security) and 2.9 percent (Medicare) times 0.9235.
* Social Security plus Medicare tax rates above times 0.28, 0.28, 0.33, or 0.35.

For a married couple filing jointly in this scenario, the above marginal total tax rate for Self MJ11 will be applicable to all total self-employment incomes between $156,000 (taxable income at $137,300, the beginning of the 28 percent rate that continues to $209,250) and $227,950 ($209,250 taxable income plus $18,700 reductions above). In this scenario, the Social Security tax rate continues on self-employment income above $227,950 to $231,294 (result from dividing 0.9235 into $213,600, which is twice the individual self-employment income of $106,800 where the self-employment Social Security tax ends). An even higher marginal total tax rate of 44.80 percent thus exists for that rare and small slice of $3,344 income from $227,950 to $231,294 in this scenario (33% + 11.45% + 2.68% - 2.33% = 44.80%). In this scenario, the total tax rate for Self MJ14 begins at wages of $392,350 ($373,650 plus $18,700 reductions above).

10E.5. Example 5

(married couple filing separately, wages income only, 2010 tax law)

This example assumes that each individual in the married couple has wages income only, that those incomes are equal, and that each individual uses the standard deduction and one exemption to calculate taxable income. The respective wages incomes are $80,000 (Wages MS1), $108,000 (Wages MS2), $114,000 (Wages MS3), and $400,000 (Wages MS4).

Table 10E.5. Marginal total federal tax rates, married couple filing separately, wages income only, 2010 tax law

	Wages MS1	Wages MS2	Wages MS3	Wages MS4
Income				
Earned income	$ 80,000	$ 108,000	$ 114,000	$ 400,000
Less standard deduction	$ (5,700)	$ (5,700)	$ (5,700)	$ (5,700)
Less one exemption	$ (3,650)	$ (3,650)	$ (3,650)	$ (3,650)
Taxable income	$ 70,650	$ 98,650	$ 104,650	$ 390,650
Marginal tax rates				
Income tax rate	28.00%	28.00%	33.00%	35.00%
Social Security tax rate	6.20%	0.00%	0.00%	0.00%
Medicare tax rate	1.45%	1.45%	1.45%	1.45%
Marginal total tax rate	35.65%	29.45%	34.45%	36.45%

For a married couple filing separately in this scenario, the above marginal total tax rate for Wages MS1 will be applicable to all wages between $78,000 (taxable income at $68,650, the beginning of the 28 percent rate that continues to $104,625) and $106,800 (wages earned income where the Social Security tax ends). In this scenario, the 28 percent income tax rate continues on earned income above $106,800 up to $113,975 ($104,625 taxable income plus $9,350 reductions above). In this scenario, the total tax rate for Wages MS4 begins at wages of $196,175 ($186,825, the beginning of the 35 percent rate, plus $9,350 reductions above).

10E.6. Example 6

(married couple filing separately, self-employment income only, 2010 tax law)
This example assumes that each individual in the married couple has self-employment income only, that those incomes are equal, and that each individual uses the standard deduction and one exemption to calculate taxable income. The respective total self-employment incomes are $80,000 (Self MS11), $112,000 (Self MS12), $116,000 (Self MS13), and $400,000 (Self MS14).

Table 10E.6. Marginal total federal tax rates, married couple filing separately, self-employment income only, 2010 tax law

	Self MS11	Self MS12	Self MS13	Self MS14
Income				
Earned income	$ 80,000	$ 112,000	$ 116,000	$ 400,000
Less standard deduction	$ (5,700)	$ (5,700)	$ (5,700)	$ (5,700)
Less one exemption	$ (3,650)	$ (3,650)	$ (3,650)	$ (3,650)
Taxable income	$ 70,650	$ 102,650	$ 106,650	$ 390,650
Marginal tax rates				
Income tax rate	28.00%	28.00%	33.00%	35.00%
Social Security tax rate **	11.45%	11.45%	0.00%	0.00%
Medicare tax rate **	2.68%	2.68%	2.68%	2.68%
Deduct ½ Soc Sec/Med tax *	-1.98%	-1.98%	-0.44%	-0.47%
Marginal total tax rate	40.15%	40.15%	35.24%	37.21%

** Full rates of 12.4 percent (Social Security) and 2.9 percent (Medicare) times 0.9235.
* Social Security plus Medicare tax rates above times 0.28, 0.28, 0.33, or 0.35.

For a married couple filing separately in this scenario, the above marginal total tax rate for Self MS11 will be applicable to all self-employment income between $78,000 (taxable income at $68,650, the beginning of the 28 percent rate that continues to $104,625) and $113,975 ($104,625 taxable income plus $9,350 reductions above). In this scenario, the Social Security tax rate continues on self-employment income above $113,975 up to $115,647 (result from dividing 0.9235 into $106,800, which is where the self-employment Social Security tax ends). An even higher marginal total tax rate of 44.80 percent thus exists for that small slice of $1,672 income from $113,975 up to $115,647 in this scenario (33% + 11.45% + 2.68% - 2.33% = 44.80%). In this scenario, the total tax rate for Self MS14 begins at self-employment income of $196,175 ($186,825 plus $9,350 reductions above).

10E.7. Example 7
(head of household, wages income only, 2010 tax law)

This example assumes that the head of household has wages income only and uses the standard deduction and one exemption to calculate taxable income. The respective wages incomes are $58,000 (Wages HH1), $108,000 (Wages HH2), $130,000 (Wages HH3), and $400,000 (Wages HH4).

Table 10E.7. Marginal total federal tax rates, head of household, wages income only, 2010 tax law

	Wages HH1	Wages HH2	Wages HH3	Wages HH4
Income				
Earned income	$ 58,000	$ 108,000	$ 130,000	$ 400,000
Less standard deduction	$ (8,400)	$ (8,400)	$ (8,400)	$ (8,400)
Less one exemption	$ (3,650)	$ (3,650)	$ (3,650)	$ (3,650)
Taxable income	$ 45,950	$ 95,950	$ 117,950	$ 387,950
Marginal tax rates				
Income tax rate	25.00%	25.00%	28.00%	35.00%
Social Security tax rate	6.20%	0.00%	0.00%	0.00%
Medicare tax rate	1.45%	1.45%	1.45%	1.45%
Marginal total tax rate	32.65%	26.45%	29.45%	36.45%

For a head of household in this scenario, the above marginal total tax rate for Wages HH1 will be applicable to all wages between $57,600 (taxable income at $45,550, the beginning of the 25 percent rate that continues to $117,650) and $106,800 (wages earned income where the Social Security tax ends). In this scenario, the 25 percent income tax rate continues on earned income above $106,800 up to $129,700 ($117,650 taxable income plus $12,050 reductions above). In this scenario, the total tax rate for Wages HH4 begins at wages of $385,700 ($373,650, the beginning of the 35 percent rate, plus $12,050 reductions above).

10E.8. Example 8

(head of household, self-employment income only, 2010 tax law)
This example assumes that the head of household has self-employment income only and uses the standard deduction and one exemption to calculate taxable income. The respective self-employment incomes are $58,000 (Self HH11), $116,000 (Self HH12), $130,000 (Self HH13), and $400,000 (Self HH14).

Table 10E.8. Marginal total federal tax rates, head of household, self-employment income only, 2010 tax law

	Self HH11	Self HH12	Self HH13	Self HH14
Income				
Earned income	$ 58,000	$ 116,000	$ 130,000	$ 400,000
Less standard deduction	$ (8,400)	$ (8,400)	$ (8,400)	$ (8,400)
Less one exemption	$ (3,650)	$ (3,650)	$ (3,650)	$ (3,650)
Taxable income	$ 45,950	$ 103,950	$ 117,950	$ 387,950
Marginal tax rates				
Income tax rate	25.00%	25.00%	28.00%	35.00%
Social Security tax rate **	11.45%	0.00%	0.00%	0.00%
Medicare tax rate **	2.68%	2.68%	2.68%	2.68%
Deduct ½ Soc Sec/Med tax *	-1.77%	-0.34%	-0.38%	-0.47%
Marginal total tax rate	37.36%	27.34%	30.30%	37.21%

** Full rates of 12.4 percent (Social Security) and 2.9 percent (Medicare) times 0.9235.
* Social Security plus Medicare tax rates above times 0.25, 0.25, 0.28, or 0.35.

For a self-employed head of household in this scenario, the above marginal total tax rate for Self HH11 will be applicable to all self-employment income between $57,600 (taxable income at $45,550, the beginning of the 25 percent rate that continues to $117,650) and $115,647 (result from dividing 0.9235 into $106,800, which is where the self-employment Social Security tax ends). In this scenario, the 25 percent income tax rate continues on earned income above $115,647 up to $129,700 ($117,650 taxable income plus $12,050 reductions above). In this scenario, the total tax rate for Self HH14 begins at wages of $385,700 ($373,650 plus $12,050 reductions above).

Appendix 10F

———•◆•◆•◆•———

Individual income tax, comparing marginal total federal tax rates under alternative tax-rate approaches

Purpose: To show by example the differences in effective marginal total federal tax rates between different income levels under alternative individual income tax rate approaches (2009 law with its graduated income tax rates, the FAST Plan, and flat-tax proposals).

Comments

A marginal total federal tax rate is the sum of income, Social Security, and Medicare taxes applicable to the last dollar of income at a particular income level. This is the real out-of-pocket tax obligation an individual faces for that last dollar.

As noted in chapters 10 and 11 of this book, marginal total tax rates vary in surprising ways under current federal tax law because of the interplay between graduated income tax rates and the Social Security and Medicare taxes as add-ons. The FAST Plan greatly reduces this variation and ends the discriminatory rate favoritism now given to long-term capital gains and qualified dividends. Flat-tax proposals also reduce the variation in marginal total tax rates under current law, but they create total rates that are higher at small-income levels than at large-income levels. Flat-tax proposals also typically provide for zero tax on all capital-based income (capital gains, dividends, and interest), which historically has been a greater portion of large incomes than small incomes.

This appendix has two sets of three figures that provide visual comparisons between the marginal total federal tax rates under current law (2009 tax law with its graduated income tax rates), the FAST Plan, and typical flat-tax proposals.

The most important part of these comparisons is the pattern of discrimination in marginal total tax rates between different income levels that occurs under each tax-rate approach, not the value of the total tax rate in comparison with the other tax-rate approaches. This is so because the standard rate used in the FAST Plan example is an initial estimated value (see appendix 10A) and the rate used in the flat-tax example is just one of many possible flat-tax rates. The 2009 tax-law example, of course, is based on real rates and tax calculation rules.

Common Facts for the Examples

All of the six comparative examples reflected in the figures in this appendix are based on these common facts:

(1) The individual taxpayer is single (single-filer income tax rates apply under the 2009 law example).
(2) The only reductions from income to reach taxable income are the standard deduction and one exemption (total of $9,350).
(3) Marginal total tax rates are based on all of the income being the kind of income identified for the line in the figure (e.g., actual wages for the top line in figure 10F.1).

Employee Examples

The first set of three figures portrays the marginal total tax rates applicable to an employee with wages income only or with long-term capital gains and qualified dividends income only (figures 10F.1, 10F.2, and 10F.3). These latter rates are included in the figures to illustrate their discriminatory character compared to rates applicable to wages under current law and under flat-tax proposals, but not under the FAST Plan. The lines in the FAST Plan figure, figure 10F.2, deserve some explanation.

The apparent gap between the total tax rates applied to wages income and to long-term capital gains and qualified dividends income in figure 10F.2 is caused by using current actual wages for comparison rather than wages income as redefined under the FAST Plan. That is, under the FAST Plan, the standard rate (29 percent used here) applies to all wages income as defined in the FAST Plan and to all capital gains and dividends income. With wages so defined, the marginal total tax rates figure for wages would look the same as figure 10F.5 below. However, to compare tax rates paid on current actual wages received by the individual, the FAST Plan adjustments described in chapter 11 are taken into account in figure 10F.2. Those adjustments are (1) an increase for income tax purposes in actual wages equal to the amount of the employer's payment of Social Security and Medicare taxes and (2) an income tax credit of that same amount. These adjustments result in a comparative total tax rate on *current actual* wages received by the employee that is less than 29 percent. In the example of figure 10F.2, these adjustments reduce the 29 percent rate by 5.43 percentage points up to the Social Security tax cutoff of $106,800 and by 1.03 percentage points thereafter.

Self-Employed Examples

The second set of three figures portrays the marginal total federal tax rates applicable to a single individual with self-employment income only or with long-term capital gains and qualified dividends income only (figures 10F.4, 10F.5, and 10F.6). As with the figures for employees, these latter rates are included in the figures to illustrate their discriminatory character compared to rates applicable to self-employment income under current law and under flat tax proposals, but not under the FAST Plan. These latter rates are the same as those portrayed in figures 10F.1, 10F.2, and 10F.3 because they apply the same whether an individual is classified as an employee or a self-employed individual in the fact examples used. As demonstrated in appendix 10E, the marginal total federal tax rates for self-employed individuals are the highest total rates under current law (meaning 2003–12 law) (see figure 10F.4). The lines in the FAST Plan figure, figure 10F.5, also deserve some explanation.

The higher total rate for long-term capital gains and qualified dividends income between $9,350 and about $18,000 in figure 10F.5 (29 percent—the standard rate used here) is effectively a mathematical catch-up rate that results in the total amount of tax being the same for earned income and for capital gains and dividends income from about $18,000 onward. This catch-up occurs because (1) Social Security and Medicare taxes begin on earned income over just $400, whereas the standard-rate income tax on all income does not begin until income reaches $9,350 in this example and (2) the payment of Social Security and Medicare taxes is credited to income tax beginning after $9,350 in this example. This same feature is also present in figure 10F.2, which represents wages income.

Other Application

Although the examples reflected in the figures in this appendix are for a single individual only, the marginal total federal tax rates of individuals filing as married jointly, married separately, or head of household will follow similar patterns.

Figure 10F.1. Marginal total federal tax rates, 2009 tax law, single individual employee with wages income only or with long-term capital gains and qualified dividends income only

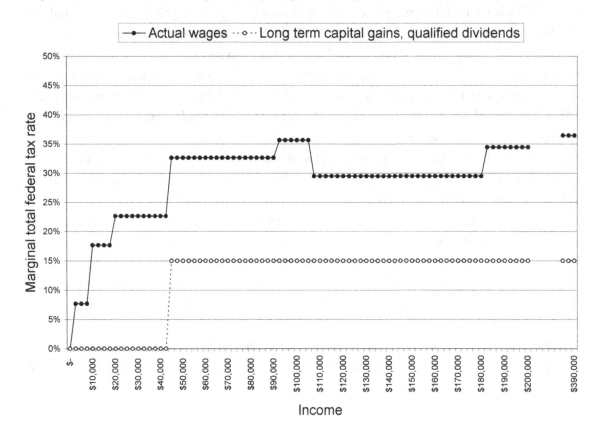

Figure 10F.2. Marginal total federal tax rates, FAST Plan (at 29%), single individual employee with wages income only or with long-term capital gains and qualified dividends income only

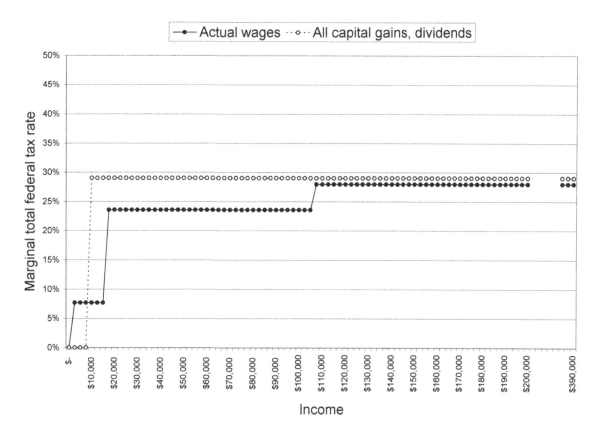

Figure 10F.3. Marginal total federal tax rates, flat-tax proposal (at 25%), single individual employee with wages income only or with long-term capital gains and qualified dividends income only

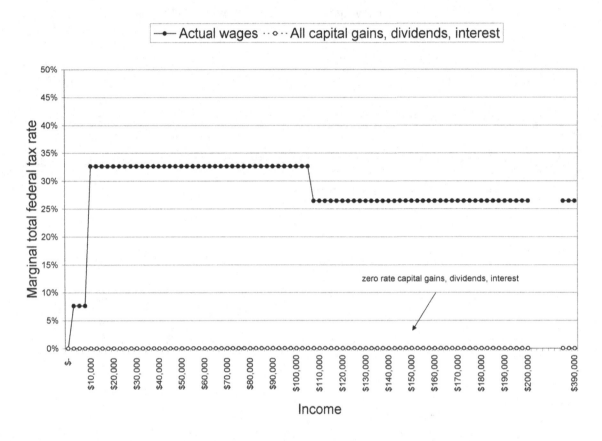

Figure 10F.4. Marginal total federal tax rates, 2009 tax law, single individual with self-employment income only or with long-term capital gains and qualified dividends income only

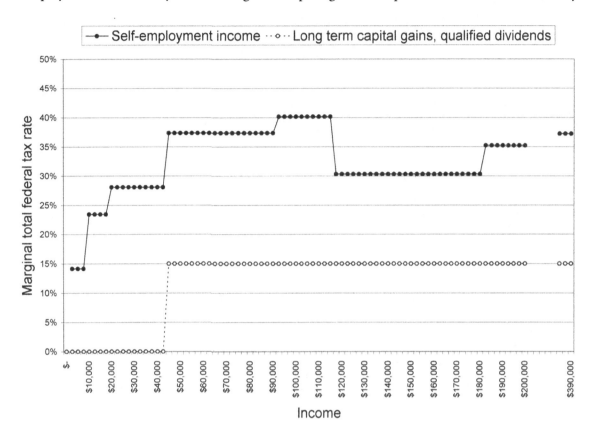

Figure 10F.5. Marginal total federal tax rates, FAST Plan (at 29%), single individual with self-employment income only or with long-term capital gains and qualified dividends income only

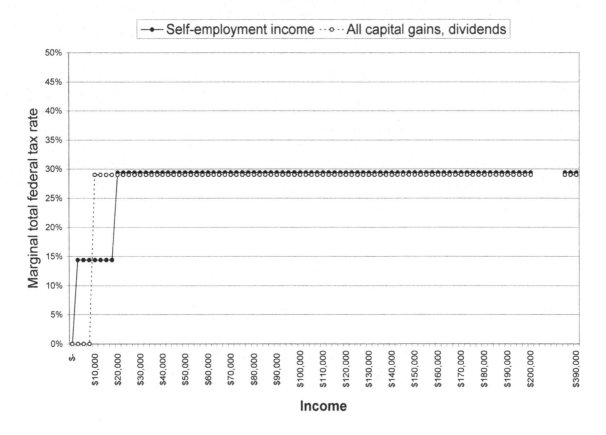

Figure 10F.6. Marginal total federal tax rates, flat-tax proposal (at 25%), single individual with self-employment income only or with long-term capital gains and qualified dividends income only

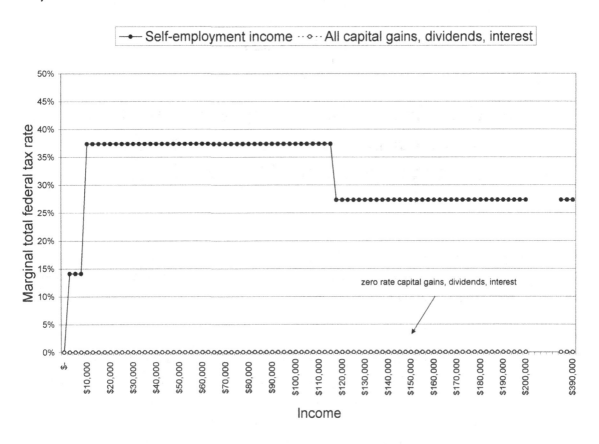

Appendix 11A

————◆•◆•◆————

Individual income tax, example marginal total tax-rate comparisons under one standard rate and no other 2009 tax-law changes

Purpose: To show by example how individuals with larger incomes will pay lower marginal total federal tax rates than individuals with smaller incomes if a standard-rate income tax is adopted with no other changes in 2009 federal tax law.

Comments

The following two examples illustrate what would occur under a standard-rate income tax on all income if that rate replaced the 2009 graduated income tax rates but all other 2009 tax law remained unchanged. The examples compare an individual whose earned income is below but near the Social Security tax cutoff to an individual whose earned income is above the Social Security tax cutoff. These examples assume that (1) all of the income of each individual is earned income, (2) the standard rate is 25 percent, and (3) all other 2009 tax law applies, including the $106,800 Social Security tax cutoff and above-the-line reduction from income for one-half the self-employment tax (Social Security and Medicare taxes) on self-employment income (incomes chosen are below the threshold for diminishing exemptions).

The examples show how a person whose earned income is below the Social Security tax cutoff would have a higher marginal total federal tax rate on *all* taxable income than the marginal total federal tax rate of a person whose income is above the Social Security tax cutoff.

11A.1. Example 1

The simplest example compares employee E and employee F, each of whom is single, with respective wages incomes of $106,800 (E) and $160,000 (F).

Table 11A.1. Marginal total federal tax rates, single individual, wages income only, standard rate (at 25%) within 2009 tax law

	Wages E	Wages F
Income		
Earned income	$ 106,800	$ 160,000
Less standard deduction	$ (5,700)	$ (5,700)
Less one exemption	$ (3,650)	$ (3,650)
Taxable income	$ 97,450	$ 150,650
Marginal tax rates		
Income tax rate	25.00%	25.00%
Social Security tax rate	6.20%	0.00%
Medicare tax rate	1.45%	1.45%
Marginal total tax rate	32.65%	26.45%

11A.2. Example 2

A more complex example but with greater disparity compares self-employed G and self-employed H, each of whom is single, with respective self-employed business net profits of $106,800 (G) and $160,000 (H).

Table 11A.2. Marginal total federal tax rates, single individual, self-employment income only, standard rate (at 25%) within 2009 tax law

	Self G	Self H
Income		
Earned income	$ 106,800	$ 160,000
Less standard deduction	$ (5,700)	$ (5,700)
Less one exemption	$ (3,650)	$ (3,650)
Taxable income	$ 97,450	$ 150,650
Marginal tax rates		
Income tax rate	25.00%	25.00%
Social Security tax rate **	11.45%	0.00%
Medicare tax rate **	2.68%	2.68%
Deduct ½ Soc Sec/Med tax *	-1.77%	-0.34%
Marginal total tax rate	37.36%	27.34%

** Full rates of 12.4 percent (Social Security) and 2.9 percent (Medicare) times 0.9235.
* Social Security plus Medicare tax rates above times 0.25.

Appendix 11B

---◆•◆•◆---

Social Security and Medicare taxes, determining the self-employment-tax multiplier

Purpose: To provide the numeric analysis that supports the FAST Plan's use of a 0.9290 self-employment-tax multiplier.

Comments

The FAST Plan proposes using a standard-rate income tax on individual income. Chapter 11 addresses the dilemma caused by Social Security and Medicare taxes when using a standard-rate income tax (these taxes are add-ons, and they apply differently to employees and self-employed individuals). The FAST Plan solves this dilemma by allowing the payments of Social Security and Medicare taxes as nonrefundable credits against an individual's income tax. Chapter 11 considers changes that will allow employees and self-employed individuals to have comparable income tax credits for their payment of Social Security and Medicare taxes. One of those changes is to modify the current self-employment-tax multiplier from 0.9235 to 0.9290, which is a factor derived from the effective tax rate calculated from proposed accounting changes to the Social Security and Medicare taxes on employees. This appendix provides the arguments used in deciding to use the new 0.9290 factor.

Arguments Regarding the Self-Employment-Tax Multiplier

Current law uses a 0.9235 factor against business net profit to calculate a self-employed individual's earned income that is subject to the self-employment tax (Social Security and Medicare taxes). Mathematically, this is the same as multiplying the full Social Security and Medicare tax rates of 15.3 percent by 0.9235 to create an effective rate of 14.13 percent for these taxes to be applied against business net profit. Multiplying the full Social Security and Medicare

347

tax rates of 15.3 percent by a different factor of 0.9290 gives an effective rate of 14.21 percent for these taxes under accounting changes proposed in the FAST Plan for the Social Security and Medicare taxes on employees.

Which factor should be used to try to make the Social Security and Medicare tax rates paid by self-employed individuals and employees the same or nearly the same?

Both factors represent compromises for mathematical simplicity. This is so because both factors are derived only from Social Security taxes and Medicare taxes on wages or net profit that are within the amount of the Social Security tax cutoff. For example, historically, the 0.9235 factor has been applied to all business net profit, including net profit that is above the Social Security tax cutoff. This application gives a small effective subtraction for Social Security taxes that have not actually been paid on net profit above the cutoff.

Let's consider the new 0.9290 factor first. As demonstrated in chapter 11, this factor derives from the accounting adjustment for employees that gives increased total income from wages by designating Social Security and Medicare taxes paid by the employer as income to the employee (for wages up to the Social Security tax cutoff). This increased income from wages for employees can be considered to be the equivalent of a self-employed individual's business net profit. Using the 0.9290 factor has the advantage of tying the factor to the accounting adjustments that are needed for employees to achieve credits for their Social Security and Medicare tax payments that are close to the credits that would be allowed to self-employed individuals.

Now let's consider the 0.9235 factor. This factor conceptually represents the fiction that a self-employed individual is his or her own employee. This fiction has led to the rule that allows one-half the Social Security and Medicare taxes paid by a self-employed individual as a subtraction from gross income in determining the income that is subject to the income tax.[18]

Retaining this subtraction would give a self-employed individual an income tax advantage over an employee with the same real income, where real incomes are, respectively, (a) business net profit and (b) increased total income from wages that includes the employer's payment of Social Security and Medicare taxes. This tax advantage would occur because the subtraction makes the taxable income of the self-employed individual less than the taxable income of the employee.[19] This is a particularly odd result when the method for equalizing the payment of Social Security and Medicare taxes for self-employed individuals and employees includes

---

[18] 26 U.S.C. § 164(f) (2009).

[19] In effect, retaining the subtraction from income for payment of the self-employment tax (Social Security and Medicare taxes) by self-employed individuals while also allowing Social Security and Medicare taxes to be credits against the income tax would give self-employed individuals *two* credits. One credit would be equal to the self-employment tax paid. The other credit would be equal to the standard income tax rate times the amount of the self-employment tax allowed as a subtraction from gross income in determining taxable income.

increased income attributed to the employee. For the employee and the self-employed individual to have the same total federal tax on the same amount of income, this subtraction should be eliminated.

When this subtraction is eliminated, the fiction of a self-employed individual being his or her own employee also dissolves. The self-employed individual's net profit then becomes exactly the equivalent of an employee's increased total income from wages. Accordingly, to achieve parity between wage earners and self-employed individuals, the 0.9290 factor should be used, rather than the 0.9235 factor, when calculating a self-employed individual's earned income that is subject to the self-employment tax (Social Security and Medicare taxes).

Appendix 12A

Individual income and tax data, identifying kinds of individual income and reductions to reach taxable income using sample years

Purpose: To provide data from which to assess the importance of different kinds of individual income for tax receipts and data from which to calculate a standard-rate individual income tax.

Comments

Appendix 12A contains three tables that have information derived from Form 1040 filed by individual taxpayers in three tax years. The tables show the major different kinds of income reported, the amount of income reported for each kind, and the amount of that kind of income as a percentage of total reported income. The tables also show the four major types of reductions from income used by individuals in calculating taxable income.

The tax years chosen are 2007, 2000, and 1993. The tax year 2007 is the last normal year before the Great Recession (table 12A.1). The tax year 2000 is the year before the broad tax decreases that were adopted in 2001 (table 12A.2). These decreases are reflected in the data for 2007 in table 12A.1. See 26 U.S.C. § 1(h) (2009). The tax year 1993 is the year that broad tax increases were first effective (table 12A.3). See 26 U.S.C. § 1(a)-(e) (2009) and Omnibus Budget Reconciliation Act of 1993, Pub.L.No. 103-66, 107 Stat 312., § 13201(a). These broad tax increases are also reflected in the data for 2000, although the 2000 data include the additional effects of decreased capital gains tax rates that began in 1997.

The data shown in table 12.1 in the main text combine the net gain or income and net loss figures in table 12A.1 for three kinds of income: taxable net gain (capital gains), partnership and S corporation net income, and business or profession net income (personal business income).

Data source:
   Publication 1304, *Individual Income Tax Returns*, IRS Statistics of Income, Table 1.4, tax years 2007, 2000, 1993.

Table 12A.1. Individual income and tax data, all returns, kinds of individual income and reductions types in current dollars, tax year 2007

Kind of income or reduction type All returns tax year 2007 (1)	Number of returns (2)	Income reported in current dollars, all returns (billions) (3)	% of total gross income (4)
Income reported			
Total gross income Note 1	142,978,806	$ 8,811	100.0%
Statutory adjustments to reach adjusted gross income	36,050,434	$ 123	1.4%
Adjusted gross income less deficit	142,978,806	$ 8,688	98.6%
Kind of income			
Salaries and wages	120,844,802	$ 5,842	66.3%
Taxable interest	64,505,131	$ 268	3.0%
(Tax exempt interest = $79 billion)	6,321,596		
Ordinary dividends	32,006,152	$ 237	2.7%
(Qualified dividends = $156 billion)	27,145,274		
Business or profession net income	16,932,476	$ 335	3.8%
Business or profession net loss	5,696,992	$ (55)	-0.6%
Taxable net gain (from Schedule D)	14,585,572	$ 912	10.4%
Taxable net loss (from Schedule D)	7,558,240	$ (17)	-0.2%
Taxable IRA distributions	10,683,225	$ 148	1.7%
Taxable pensions and annuities	25,180,637	$ 491	5.6%
Partnership and S corporation net income	5,146,366	$ 547	6.2%
Partnership and S corporation net loss	2,798,624	$ (133)	-1.5%
Social Security benefits taxable	15,011,961	$ 167	1.9%
All other income sources	varies	$ 69	0.8%
Total gross income		$ 8,811	100.0%
Unadjusted reductions to reach taxable income			
Basic standard deduction	90,510,904	$ 636	7.2%
Additional standard deduction	11,703,100	$ 18	0.2%
Total unadjusted itemized deductions	50,544,470	$ 1,333	15.1%
Unadjusted exemptions	282,613,371	$ 943	10.7%
Total unadjusted reductions		$ 2,930	33.3%
Taxable income	110,533,209	$ 6,063	68.8%
Tax			
Alternative minimum tax	4,108,964	$ 24	0.3%
Income tax before credits	110,547,229	$ 1,180	13.4%

Note 1: Calculated from data in data source.

Table 12A.2. Individual income and tax data, all returns, kinds of individual income and reductions types in current dollars, tax year 2000

Kind of income or reduction type All returns tax year 2000 (1)	Number of returns (2)	Income reported in current dollars, all returns (billions) (3)	% of total gross income (4)
Income reported			
Total gross income *Note 1*	129,373,500	$ 6,424	100.0%
Statutory adjustments to reach adjusted gross income	23,197,425	$ 59	0.9%
Adjusted gross income less deficit	129,373,500	$ 6,365	99.1%
Kind of income			
Salaries and wages	110,168,714	$ 4,456	69.4%
Taxable interest	68,046,458	$ 199	3.1%
(Tax exempt interest = $54 billion)	4,658,345		
Ordinary dividends	34,140,605	$ 147	2.3%
(Qualified dividends = not applicable in 2000)			
Business or profession net income	13,312,586	$ 245	3.8%
Business or profession net loss	4,287,423	$ (31)	-0.5%
Taxable net gain (from Schedule D)	16,000,423	$ 628	9.8%
Taxable net loss (from Schedule D)	6,875,037	$ (14)	-0.2%
Taxable IRA distributions	8,732,290	$ 99	1.5%
Taxable pensions and annuities	21,765,212	$ 326	5.1%
Partnership and S corporation net income	4,179,537	$ 285	4.4%
Partnership and S corporation net loss	2,120,784	$ (73)	-1.1%
Social Security benefits taxable	10,608,571	$ 90	1.4%
All other income sources	varies	$ 67	1.0%
Total income		$ 6,424	100.0%
Unadjusted reductions to reach taxable income			
Basic standard deduction	85,670,504	$ 456	7.1%
Additional standard deduction	11,330,554	$ 15	0.2%
Total unadjusted itemized deductions	42,534,320	$ 822	12.8%
Unadjusted exemptions	252,332,427	$ 630	9.8%
Total unadjusted reductions		$ 1,923	29.9%
Taxable income	105,259,292	$ 4,544	70.7%
Tax			
Alternative minimum tax (not in data)			
Income tax before credits	105,277,967	$ 1,018	15.8%

Note 1: Calculated from data in data source.

Table 12A.3. Individual income and tax data, all returns, kinds of individual income and reductions types in current dollars, tax year 1993

Kind of income or reduction type All returns tax year 1993 (1)	Number of returns (2)	Income reported in current dollars, all returns (billions) (3)	% of total gross income (4)
Income reported			
Total gross income Note 1	114,601,819	$ 3,760	100.0%
Statutory adjustments to reach adjusted gross income	17,179,519	$ 37	1.0%
Adjusted gross income less deficit	114,601,819	$ 3,723	99.0%
Kind of income			
Salaries and wages	98,003,356	$ 2,892	76.9%
Taxable interest	65,233,312	$ 131	3.5%
(Tax exempt interest = $46 billion)			
Ordinary dividends	24,690,816	$ 80	2.1%
(Qualified dividends = not applicable in 1993)			
Business or profession net income	11,864,976	$ 176	4.7%
Business or profession net loss	3,768,073	$ (21)	-0.6%
Taxable net gain (from Schedule D)	10,258,819	$ 150	4.0%
Taxable net loss (from Schedule D)	4,206,780	$ (8)	-0.2%
Taxable IRA distributions	4,382,772	$ 27	0.7%
Taxable pensions and annuities	17,441,114	$ 194	5.2%
Partnership and S corporation net income	3,385,545	$ 133	3.5%
Partnership and S corporation net loss	2,128,339	$ (41)	-1.1%
Social Security benefits taxable	5,688,191	$ 25	0.7%
All other income sources	varies	$ 22	0.6%
Total gross income		$ 3,760	100.0%
Unadjusted reductions to reach taxable income			
Basic standard deduction	80,840,916	$ 371	9.9%
Additional standard deduction	10,547,983	$ 11	0.3%
Total unadjusted itemized deductions	32,821,464	$ 490	13.0%
Unadjusted exemptions	232,920,023	$ 541	14.4%
Total unadjusted reductions		$ 1,413	37.6%
Taxable income	90,831,069	$ 2,454	65.3%
Tax			
Alternative minimum tax (not in data)			
Income tax before credits	90,754,509	$ 509	13.5%

Note 1: Calculated from data in data source.

Appendix 14A

------◆-●-◆------

Individual income and tax data, identifying which individual income groups have what kinds of income using sample years

Purpose: To show by example how those individuals who have smaller or larger adjusted gross incomes have very different kinds of income, especially comparing salaries and wages to income based on or generated by capital.

Comments

Which individual income groups have what kinds of income?

This question is important in the context of federal tax reform because current law provides special low tax rates for some kinds of income. Some tax-reform proposals would reduce or eliminate even these low rates and would extend special treatment to other kinds of income.

The Internal Revenue Service answers this important question with data that are collected from all individual tax returns. In IRS's "Table 1," all returns are divided into categories according to the total adjusted gross income reported on the return. In this IRS table, the income reported for each kind of income is added together for all returns in each category.[20] This massive table for the tax year 2007 shows nineteen categories of adjusted gross income and fifty-nine sources (kinds) of income. In this IRS table, the total of all adjusted gross incomes is called "adjusted gross income less deficit" because in some returns, the allowed statutory adjustments that were subtracted from gross income to determine adjusted gross income exceeded the gross income, giving a "deficit."[21]

The tables in this appendix use data from IRS Table 1, respectively, for the tax years 2007 and 2000 to compare four kinds of income received by individuals with smaller and much-larger adjusted

---

20 *SOI Tax Stats—Individual Income Tax Returns*, Internal Revenue Service, Table 1 (multiple tax years).

21 *Publication 1304, Individual Income Tax Returns*, IRS Statistics of Income, tax year 2007, Section 4, Explanation of Terms, 133–135.

gross incomes. The kinds of income selected are salaries and wages, taxable interest, dividends, and capital gains. The latter three kinds of income are all based on or generated from capital.

All of the tables in this appendix consolidate into one category the smaller adjusted gross income categories from IRS Table 1. For the tables that cover tax year 2000, that category comprises all returns with adjusted gross incomes under $75,000. For the tables that cover tax year 2007, that category comprises all returns with adjusted gross incomes under $100,000, which is approximately the inflation-adjusted equivalent of $75,000 used in the tables for tax year 2000.

Four tables are presented for each of the two tax years covered in this appendix.

(1) The first table divides income groups by inclusive amounts of adjusted gross income, designated as "categories" in the table (table 14A.1 for 2007, table 14A.5 for 2000). This table shows the amounts of each kind of income. For example, table 14A.1 shows that individuals in the "$500,000 under $1,000,000" income category reported $212 billion in salaries and wages income in 2007.

(2) The second table divides income groups by amounts of adjusted gross income that exceed selected amounts (table 14A.2 for 2007, table 14A.6 for 2000). This table also shows the amounts of each kind of income. As an example, table 14A.2 shows that individuals in the "$500,000 or more" group reported $580 billion in salaries and wages income in 2007.

(3) The third table also divides income groups by amounts of adjusted gross income that exceed selected amounts, but shows income data for each kind of income as a percentage of all income reported for that kind of income. These data reveal which income groups had most of a particular kind of income in the tax year covered. For example, in 2007, the income group "$500,000 or more" reported 73 percent of all capital gains income (net gains) that were reported that year (table 14A.3).

(4) The fourth table also divides income groups by amounts of adjusted gross income that exceed selected amounts, but shows income data for each kind of income as a percentage of all income reported by that income group. These data reveal the mix of kinds of income for each income group and, thus, which kinds of income are most important for that group. As an example, in 2007, for the income group "$500,000 or more," 36 percent of all income reported by that group was capital gains income (net gains) (table 14A.4).

Data source:
SOI Tax Stats—Individual Income Tax Returns, Table 1, tax years 2007, 2000.

Table 14A.1. Kinds of income by individual income category in current dollars, tax year 2007

		Total adjusted gross income less deficit in current dollars (billions)	Kind of income: salaries and wages in current dollars (billions)	↓ Income based on capital ↓				
				Kind of income: taxable interest in current dollars (billions)	Kind of income: ordinary dividends in current dollars (billions)	Kind of income: taxable net gain from Schedule D minus net loss in current dollars (billions)	Kind of income: all other in current dollars (billions)	*Columns (5), (6), and (7) combined in current dollars (billions)*
Adjusted gross income category All returns tax year 2007 (1)	Number of returns (2)	(3)	(4)	(5)	(6)	(7)	(8)	*(9)*
All returns	142,978,806	8,688	5,842	268	237	896	1,445	*1,401*
$ 0 under $100,000	124,985,308	4,047	3,320	99	55	66	507	*220*
$100,000 under $200,000	13,457,876	1,793	1,331	42	40	70	310	*152*
$200,000 under $500,000	3,492,353	1,005	611	33	38	103	220	*174*
$500,000 under $1,000,000	651,049	441	212	17	21	81	110	*119*
$1,000,000 under $1,500,000	166,362	201	79	9	10	47	56	*66*
$1,500,000 under $2,000,000	70,733	122	43	6	6	33	34	*45*
$2,000,000 under $5,000,000	108,641	325	104	16	18	104	83	*138*
$5,000,000 under $10,000,000	28,090	192	52	10	12	78	40	*100*
$10,000,000 or more	18,394	562	90	36	37	314	85	*387*

Table 14A.2. Kinds of income by individual income group in current dollars, tax year 2007

				↓ Income based on capital ↓				
Adjusted gross income group All returns tax year 2007 (1)	Number of returns (2)	Total adjusted gross income less deficit in current dollars (billions) (3)	Kind of income: salaries and wages in current dollars (billions) (4)	Kind of income: taxable interest in current dollars (billions) (5)	Kind of income: ordinary dividends in current dollars (billions) (6)	Kind of income: taxable net gain from Schedule D minus net loss in current dollars (billions) (7)	Kind of income: all other in current dollars (billions) (8)	Columns (5), (6), and (7) combined in current dollars (billions) (9)
All returns	142,978,806	8,688	5,842	268	237	896	1,445	1,401
Less than $100,000	124,985,308	4,047	3,320	99	55	66	507	220
$100,000 or more	17,993,498	4,641	2,522	169	182	830	938	1,181
$200,000 or more	4,535,622	2,848	1,191	127	142	760	628	1,029
$500,000 or more	1,043,269	1,843	580	94	104	657	408	855
$1,000,000 or more	392,220	1,402	368	77	83	576	298	736
$10,000,000 or more	18,394	562	90	36	37	314	85	387

Table 14A.3. Kinds of income by individual income group shown as % of all income for that kind, tax year 2007

| | | | | | ↓ Income based on capital ↓ | | | |
Adjusted gross income group All returns tax year 2007 (1)	Number of returns (2)	Total adjusted gross income less deficit (% of income kind) (3)	Kind of income: salaries and wages (% of income kind) (4)	Kind of income: taxable interest (% of income kind) (5)	Kind of income: ordinary dividends (% of income kind) (6)	Kind of income: taxable net gain from Schedule D minus net loss (% of income kind) (7)	Kind of income: all other (% of income kind) (8)	Columns (5,) (6), and (7) combined (% of income kind) (9)
All returns	142,978,806	100%	100%	100%	100%	100%	100%	100%
Less than $100,000	124,985,308	47%	57%	37%	23%	7%	35%	16%
$100,000 or more	17,993,498	53%	43%	63%	77%	93%	65%	84%
$200,000 or more	4,535,622	33%	20%	47%	60%	85%	43%	73%
$500,000 or more	1,043,269	21%	10%	35%	44%	73%	28%	61%
$1,000,000 or more	392,220	16%	6%	29%	35%	64%	21%	53%
$10,000,000 or more	18,394	6%	2%	13%	16%	35%	6%	28%

Table 14A.4. Kinds of income by individual income group shown as % of all income for the group, tax year 2007

| | | | | | ↓ Income based on capital ↓ | | | |
| | | Total adjusted gross income less deficit (% of income group) | Kind of income: salaries and wages (% of income group) | Kind of income: taxable interest (% of income group) | Kind of income: ordinary dividends (% of income group) | Kind of income: taxable net gain from Schedule D minus net loss (% of income group) | Kind of income: all other (% of income group) | Columns (5,) (6), and (7) combined (% of income group) |
Adjusted gross income group All returns tax year 2007 (1)	Number of returns (2)	(3)	(4)	(5)	(6)	(7)	(8)	(9)
All returns	142,978,806	100%	67%	3%	3%	10%	17%	16%
Less than $100,000	124,985,308	100%	82%	2%	1%	2%	13%	5%
$100,000 or more	17,993,498	100%	54%	4%	4%	18%	20%	25%
$200,000 or more	4,535,622	100%	42%	4%	5%	27%	22%	36%
$500,000 or more	1,043,269	100%	31%	5%	6%	36%	22%	46%
$1,000,000 or more	392,220	100%	26%	5%	6%	41%	21%	52%
$10,000,000 or more	18,394	100%	16%	6%	7%	56%	15%	69%

Table 14A.5. Kinds of income by individual income category in current dollars, tax year 2000

				↓ Income based on capital ↓			
Adjusted gross income category All returns tax year 2000 (1)	Number of returns (2)	Total adjusted gross income less deficit in current dollars (billions) (3)	Kind of income: salaries and wages in current dollars (billions) (4)	Kind of income: taxable interest in current dollars (billions) (5)	Kind of income: ordinary dividends in current dollars (billions) (6)	Kind of income: taxable net gain from Schedule D minus net loss in current dollars (billions) (7)	Kind of income: all other in current dollars (billions) (8)	Columns (5), (6), and (7) combined in current dollars (billions) (9)
All returns	129,373,500	6,365	4,456	199	147	615	948	961
$ 0 under $75,000	109,921,146	2,866	2,345	85	42	52	342	179
$75,000 under $100,000	8,597,328	738	581	18	13	20	106	51
$100,000 under $200,000	8,083,447	1,066	770	30	27	62	177	119
$200,000 under $500,000	2,135,763	614	358	21	23	79	133	123
$500,000 under $1,000,000	396,131	263	131	11	11	55	55	77
$1,000,000 under $1,500,000	99,510	121	50	5	5	31	30	41
$1,500,000 under $2,000,000	44,582	77	30	3	3	22	19	28
$2,000,000 under $5,000,000	66,768	199	75	9	8	69	38	86
$5,000,000 under $10,000,000	17,610	121	41	5	5	50	20	60
$10,000,000 or more	11,215	300	75	12	10	175	28	197

Table 14A.6. Kinds of income by individual income group in current dollars, tax year 2000

					↓ Income based on capital ↓		
Adjusted gross income group All returns tax year 2000 (1)	Number of returns (2)	Total adjusted gross income less deficit in current dollars (billions) (3)	Kind of income: salaries and wages in current dollars (billions) (4)	Kind of income: taxable interest in current dollars (billions) (5)	Kind of income: ordinary dividends in current dollars (billions) (6)	Kind of income: taxable net gain from Schedule D minus net loss in current dollars (billions) (7)	Kind of income: all other in current dollars (billions) (8)	Columns (5), (6), and (7) combined in current dollars (billions) (9)
All returns	129,373,500	6,365	4,456	199	147	615	948	961
Less than $75,000	109,921,146	2,866	2,345	85	42	52	342	179
$75,000 or more	19,452,354	3,499	2,111	114	105	563	606	782
$100,000 or more	10,855,026	2,761	1,530	96	92	543	500	731
$200,000 or more	2,771,579	1,695	760	66	65	481	323	612
$500,000 or more	635,816	1,081	402	45	42	402	190	489
$1,000,000 or more	239,685	818	271	34	31	347	135	412
$10,000,000 or more	11,215	300	75	12	10	175	28	197

Table 14A.7. Kinds of income by individual income group shown as % of all income for that kind, tax year 2000

				↓ Income based on capital ↓				
Adjusted gross income group All returns tax year 2000 (1)	Number of returns (2)	Total adjusted gross income less deficit (% of income kind) (3)	Kind of income: salaries and wages (% of income kind) (4)	Kind of income: taxable interest (% of income kind) (5)	Kind of income: ordinary dividends (% of income kind) (6)	Kind of income: taxable net gain from Schedule D minus net loss (% of income kind) (7)	Kind of income: all other (% of income kind) (8)	*Columns (5,) (6), and (7) combined (% of income kind) (9)*
All returns	129,373,500	100%	100%	100%	100%	100%	100%	100%
Less than $75,000	109,921,146	45%	53%	43%	29%	8%	36%	19%
$75,000 or more	19,452,354	55%	47%	57%	71%	92%	64%	81%
$100,000 or more	10,855,026	43%	34%	48%	63%	88%	53%	76%
$200,000 or more	2,771,579	27%	17%	33%	44%	78%	34%	64%
$500,000 or more	635,816	17%	9%	23%	29%	65%	20%	51%
$1,000,000 or more	239,685	13%	6%	17%	21%	56%	14%	43%
$10,000,000 or more	11,215	5%	2%	6%	7%	28%	3%	20%

Table 14A.8. Kinds of income by individual income group shown as % of all income for the group, tax year 2000

| | | | | ↓ Income based on capital ↓ | | | | |
Adjusted gross income group All returns tax year 2000 (1)	Number of returns (2)	Total adjusted gross income less deficit (% of income group) (3)	Kind of income: salaries and wages (% of income group) (4)	Kind of income: taxable interest (% of income group) (5)	Kind of income: ordinary dividends (% of income group) (6)	Kind of income: taxable net gain from Schedule D minus net loss (% of income group) (7)	Kind of income: all other (% of income group) (8)	Columns (5,) (6), and (7) combined (% of income group) (9)
All returns	129,373,500	100%	70%	3%	2%	10%	15%	15%
Less than $75,000	109,921,146	100%	82%	3%	1%	2%	12%	6%
$75,000 or more	19,452,354	100%	60%	3%	3%	16%	17%	22%
$100,000 or more	10,855,026	100%	55%	3%	3%	20%	18%	26%
$200,000 or more	2,771,579	100%	45%	4%	4%	28%	19%	36%
$500,000 or more	635,816	100%	37%	4%	4%	37%	18%	45%
$1,000,000 or more	239,685	100%	33%	4%	4%	42%	17%	50%
$10,000,000 or more	11,215	100%	25%	4%	3%	58%	9%	66%

Appendix 14B

———————◆•◆•◆———————

Individual income and tax data, comparing effective tax rates on all income paid by individuals in different income categories using sample years

Purpose: To identify the amount of income taxes paid by all individuals in different income categories, to show in a general way the effective tax rates paid by those individuals, and to provide data to assess the relative fairness of those tax payments.

Comments

Some individuals do not file income tax returns because their incomes are so small that they do not meet the threshold for filing a return. Other individuals file returns but have no income tax because allowed reductions from income create no taxable income or allowed credits fully offset any income tax that might otherwise be due. The number of these "nontaxable" returns is large. In 2007, more than 46 million returns were nontaxable out of a total of 143 million returns that were filed. The nontaxable returns, however, accounted for only 7 percent of all reported adjusted gross income ($615 billion out of $8,688 billion total).

The two tables in this appendix show the amount of income taxes paid by all individuals in different adjusted gross income categories and, in a general way, the effective income tax rates paid by those individuals. The two tables use as examples the tax year 2007, the last year before the Great Recession, and the tax year 2000, the last year before the 2001 broad tax decreases that became effective by stages in 2001, 2002, and 2003.

Column 10 in each table shows the effective income tax rates for different income categories as calculated from taxable income. Two factors cause the differences in those rates. The first factor is the application of graduated tax rates to different levels (segments) of taxable income. The second factor is the application of lower tax rates to some kinds of income, such as long-term capital gains, which are more prevalent among the largest-income categories. The lower rates and increased proportions of these kinds of income in the two largest-income categories probably account for the effective tax rates dropping in those two categories.

Column 11 of each table shows the effective income tax rates for different income categories as calculated from adjusted gross income. The differences in those rates reflect an additional third factor, namely, the different impacts of reductions from income used to determine taxable income. For example, the standard deductions and exemptions used by most individuals are fixed numbers that have a greater percentage effect for small incomes than for large incomes in reducing adjusted gross income to reach taxable income. On returns with small incomes, the adjusted gross income will thus be proportionally larger compared to taxable income than on returns with large incomes. This means that returns with small incomes will show an effective tax rate calculated as a percentage of adjusted gross income that is considerably lower than an effective tax rate calculated as a percentage of taxable income. The rates shown in columns 9 and 11 reflect this result.

The data in these two tables also allow one to calculate one measure of tax fairness, namely, who pays the most income taxes that support federal on-budget expenditures. For example, in 2007, the returns that reported adjusted gross incomes of $200,000 or more comprised 3.17 percent of all filed returns, paid 54.5 percent of all federal individual income taxes, but also had 32.6 percent of all reported adjusted gross income (income *before* reductions for exemptions and standard or itemized deductions). These numbers are derived simply by adding up the percentages for each income category of $100,000 and above, with the above-cited percentages shown respectively in columns 3, 9, and 5.

Data source:

Publication 1304, Individual Income Tax Returns, IRS Statistics of Income, Table 1.1, tax years 2007, 2000.

Note 1: This IRS table is different than the IRS table used as the data source for appendix 14A, so the adjusted gross income figures in appendix 14B do not exactly match the adjusted gross income figures in appendix 14A.

Note 2: The percentages in the tables in appendix 14B are taken from the data source. They are not calculated from the rounded numbers shown in the tables.

Table 14B.1. Income tax by individual income category in current dollars, tax year 2007

Adjusted gross income category All returns tax year 2007 (1)	Number of returns (2)	Number of returns as % of all returns (3)	Total adjusted gross income less deficit in current dollars (billions) (4)	Total adjusted gross income as % of total adjusted gross income for all returns (5)	Total taxable income in current dollars (billions) (6)	Total taxable income as % of total taxable income for all taxable returns (7)	Total income tax after credits in current dollars (billions) (8)	Total income tax as % of total income tax for all taxable returns (9)	Total income tax as % of taxable income (10)	Total income tax as % of adjusted gross income less deficit (11)
All returns	142,978,806	100.00%	8,688	100.0%						
All nontaxable returns	46,705,849	32.67%	615	7.1%						
All taxable returns	96,272,957	67.33%	8,073	92.9%	5,943	100.0%	1,116	100.0%		
No adjusted gross income	5,582									
$1 under $75,000	66,797,487	46.72%	2,456	28.3%	1,497	25.2%	183	16.4%	12.2%	7.5%
$75,000 under $100,000	11,559,682	8.08%	999	11.5%	689	11.6%	94	8.4%	13.6%	9.4%
$100,000 under $200,000	13,385,837	9.36%	1,784	20.5%	1,311	22.1%	229	20.5%	17.4%	12.8%
$200,000 under $500,000	3,483,706	2.44%	1,002	11.5%	819	13.8%	196	17.6%	24.0%	19.6%
$500,000 under $1,000,000	649,403	0.45%	440	5.1%	383	6.4%	103	9.2%	26.9%	23.4%
$1,000,000 under $1,500,000	165,970	0.12%	200	2.3%	178	3.0%	48	4.3%	27.2%	24.1%
$1,500,000 under $2,000,000	70,556	0.05%	121	1.4%	108	1.8%	29	2.6%	27.1%	24.2%
$2,000,000 under $5,000,000	108,357	0.08%	324	3.7%	290	4.9%	78	7.0%	26.7%	24.0%
$5,000,000 under $10,000,000	28,014	0.02%	192	2.2%	172	2.9%	44	3.9%	25.5%	22.9%
$10,000,000 or more	18,362	0.01%	559	6.4%	496	8.3%	111	9.9%	22.4%	19.8%

Table 14B.2. Income tax by individual income category in current dollars, tax year 2000

Adjusted gross income category / All returns tax year 2000 (1)	Number of returns (2)	Number of returns as % of all returns (3)	Total adjusted gross income less deficit in current dollars (billions) (4)	Total adjusted gross income as % of total adjusted gross income for all returns (5)	Total taxable income in current dollars (billions) (6)	Total taxable income as % of total taxable income for all taxable returns (7)	Total income tax after credits in current dollars (billions) (8)	Total income tax as % of total income tax for all taxable returns (9)	Total income tax as % of taxable income (10)	Total income tax as % of adjusted gross income less deficit (11)
All returns	129,373,500	100.00%	6,365	100.0%						
All nontaxable returns	32,557,706	25.17%	282	4.4%						
All taxable returns	96,815,794	74.83%	6,083	95.6%	4,503	100.0%	980	100.0%		
No adjusted gross income	5,608									
$1 under $75,000	77,384,050	59.81%	2,589	40.7%	1,644	36.5%	248	25.3%	15.1%	9.6%
$75,000 under $100,000	8,580,510	6.63%	736	11.6%	537	11.9%	100	10.2%	18.6%	13.6%
$100,000 under $200,000	8,076,542	6.24%	1,066	16.7%	822	18.3%	184	18.8%	22.4%	17.3%
$200,000 under $500,000	2,133,889	1.65%	613	9.6%	522	11.6%	146	14.9%	28.1%	23.9%
$500,000 under $1,000,000	395,754	0.31%	269	4.2%	239	5.3%	76	7.8%	31.8%	28.3%
$1,000,000 under $1,500,000	99,414	0.08%	120	1.9%	109	2.4%	35	3.6%	32.3%	29.2%
$1,500,000 under $2,000,000	44,543	0.03%	77	1.2%	70	1.6%	23	2.3%	32.4%	29.4%
$2,000,000 under $5,000,000	66,690	0.05%	199	3.1%	182	4.0%	58	5.9%	32.0%	29.2%
$5,000,000 under $10,000,000	17,591	0.01%	120	1.9%	110	2.4%	34	3.5%	31.2%	28.5%
$10,000,000 or more	11,202	0.01%	300	4.7%	269	6.0%	76	7.8%	28.3%	25.4%

Appendix 14C

Individual income tax, capital gains, example showing tax-payment effect of special capital gains tax rates under 2009 tax law

Purpose: To show by example the large difference in total tax payments that can occur under 2009 tax law based solely on the different kinds of income that two individuals have.

Comments

The two examples in this appendix illustrate how federal tax payments can be very different for two individuals who have the same amount of income but whose income is classified differently under current federal tax law. These examples are simplified by assuming that both individuals are single and use only the standard deduction and exemptions as reductions from gross income to determine taxable income.

14C.1. Example 1: Surgeon S, Total Federal Tax Payments

Surgeon S performed numerous difficult surgeries in 2009. She earned a solid income from those surgeries, which resulted in gross cash income of $300,000, all being from personal services. She was single and self-employed, and used the standard deduction. Her federal taxes under 2009 law are shown in table 14C.1 (using the tax calculation from 2009 Form 1040 Instructions):

Table 14C.1. Calculation of federal taxes owed by Surgeon S under 2009 tax law

	Surgeon S
Income tax calculation	
Gross income (all earned income)	$ 300,000
Less ½ self-employment tax	$ (10,639)
Adjusted gross income	$ 289,361
Less standard deduction	$ (5,700)
Less one reduced exemption	$ (2,577)
Taxable income	$ 281,084
Income tax *(1)*	$ 77,900
Self-employment tax calculation	
Self-employment income	$ 300,000
Net earnings from self-employment *(2)*	$ 277,050
Self-employment tax Social Security *(3)*	$ 13,243
Self-employment tax Medicare *(4)*	$ 8,034
Self-employment tax	$ 21,277
Total federal tax	$ 99,177

Note (1): $281,084 x 0.33 less $14,858
Note (2): $300,000 x 0.9235
Note (3): $106,800 maximum x 0.124
Note (4): $277,050 x 0.029

14C.2. Example 2: Investor I, Total Federal Tax Payments

Investor I bought stocks of five companies in 2008, spent significant time monitoring their performance, and selected a date exactly 367 days after their purchase to sell them in 2009 because they had all increased in value. In these sales, the difference between the total sales prices and total purchase prices was large enough that his gross income was also $300,000, all being from long-term capital gains. He was single and self-employed, and used the standard deduction. His federal taxes under 2009 law are shown in table 14C.2 (using the tax calculation from 2009 Form 1040 Instructions):

Table 14C.2. Calculation of federal taxes owed by Investor I under 2009 tax law

	Investor I
Income tax calculation	
Gross income (all net capital gains)	$ 300,000
Less ½ self-employment tax	$ -0-
Adjusted gross income	$ 300,000
Less standard deduction	$ (5,700)
Less one reduced exemption	$ (2,433)
Taxable income (net gains)	$ 291,867
Income tax *(1)*	$ 38,688
Self-employment tax calculation	
Self-employment income	$ none
Net earnings from self-employment	$ none
Self-employment tax Social Security	$ none
Self-employment tax Medicare	$ none
Self-employment tax	$ -0-
Total federal tax	$ 38,688

Note (1): From Schedule D tax worksheet (Form 1040)

In these examples, Surgeon S would pay $77,900 in federal income taxes, but Investor I would pay only $38,688 in federal income taxes. The difference is $39,212, with Surgeon S's income tax being more than double Investor I's income tax.

The disparity in total federal taxes owed between Surgeon S and Investor I is even greater because Surgeon S is required to pay Social Security and Medicare taxes, but Investor I is not. Surgeon S's total federal tax would be $99,177, which is $60,489 greater than and over two and a half times Investor I's total federal tax liability of $38,688. Of course, Investor I would not be building up Social Security credits for Social Security benefits upon retirement, although he would get Medicare benefits provided that he paid Medicare taxes on earned income for a total of at least ten years before reaching the age of sixty-five.

Appendix 14D

• • ◆ • •

Individual income tax, capital gains, comparing capital gains tax-rate changes to jobs

Purpose: To discern in a general way from historic data whether and to what extent changes in tax rates for capital gains may affect jobs in the United States.

Comments

The table and two figures in this appendix address the question whether and to what extent changes in the capital gains tax rates affect jobs in the United States. This question is relevant to proposed tax changes because some people assert that decreased tax rates for capital gains increase investment, which in turn creates more jobs.

Table 14D.1 shows the average number of nonfarm employees in the private sector in each calendar year from 1981 to 2012. These particular jobs are probably the most likely to be affected by increased (or decreased) overall investment. This table also shows the number of these employees as a percentage of US population as a way to remove job increases that are caused solely by an expanded population with its expanded demand for goods and services.

Figure 14D.1 compares the number of nonfarm employees to the timing of changes in capital gains tax rates from 1981 to 2012 (1982 new base, 1987 increase, 1997 decrease, 2003 decrease). The data in this figure include increases that are caused solely by an expanded population.

Figure 14D.2 has the same format as figure 14D.1, but compares the number of nonfarm employees as a percentage of US population to the timing of changes in capital gains tax rates from 1981 to 2011. These data remove the increases in jobs that are caused solely by an expanded population.

These data are inconclusive on the question whether decreasing (or increasing) capital gains tax rates has a significant effect on jobs. Although the number of employees per population

372

increased slightly after capital gains tax decreases in 2003 and more significantly after capital gains tax decreases in 1997, the job increases appear to be part of unrelated trends. The trend of job increases that occurred after 1997 up to 2000 is a continuation of the trend that occurred from 1992 to 1996, when a maximum 28 percent capital gains tax rate was in effect. The slight increases in jobs that occurred after 2003 may or may not have been influenced by the decrease in long-term capital gains tax rates, because 2003 also marked the beginning of the full broad tax decreases adopted in 2001 and the end of the mild recession that began in 2001. The number of employees per population also showed *decreases* in each of the time periods when the maximum long-term capital gains tax rate remained constant (1990 to 1991 under a 28 percent maximum rate; 2002 to 2003 under a 20 percent maximum rate; 2007 to 2010 under a 15 percent maximum rate).

The trend of job *increases* that occurred from 1983 to 1986, when an effective maximum 20 percent tax rate on long-term capital gains was in effect, continued up to 1989 even after the maximum tax rate on long-term capital gains increased to 28 percent in 1987. That increase in the long-term capital gains tax rate does not appear to have adversely affected jobs growth.

Like the comparisons of tax-rate changes to GDP, these data on jobs suggest that tax rates on capital gains are far less important in affecting jobs growth or loss than other factors (see appendix 10D).

Data source:

Current Employment Statistics, Historical (Bureau of Labor Statistics, US Department of Labor, 2012), Table B-1;

Population Estimates, National (US Census Bureau, 2013).

Table 14D.1. Individual income tax, capital gains, data used to compare nonfarm employee jobs (private sector) to capital gains tax-rate changes, 1981–2012

Calendar year (1)	Employees on nonfarm payrolls annual average (private sector) (millions) (2)	United States resident population at July 1 (millions) (3)	Nonfarm employees (private sector) as % of resident population (4)	Calendar year (1)	Employees on nonfarm payrolls annual average (private sector) (millions) (2)	United States resident population at July 1 (millions) (3)	Nonfarm employees (private sector) as % of resident population (4)
1981	75	229	32.8%	1997	103	273	37.7%
1982	74	232	31.9%	1998	106	276	38.4%
1983	74	234	31.6%	1999	109	279	39.1%
1984	78	236	33.1%	2000	111	282	39.4%
1985	81	238	34.0%	2001	111	285	38.9%
1986	83	240	34.6%	2002	109	288	37.8%
1987	85	242	35.1%	2003	109	290	37.6%
1988	88	244	36.1%	2004	110	293	37.5%
1989	90	247	36.4%	2005	112	296	37.8%
1990	91	250	36.4%	2006	114	299	38.1%
1991	90	253	35.6%	2007	115	302	38.1%
1992	90	257	35.0%	2008	114	304	37.5%
1993	92	260	35.4%	2009	108	307	35.2%
1994	95	263	36.1%	2010	107	309	34.6%
1995	98	266	36.8%	2011	109	312	34.9%
1996	100	269	37.2%	2012	112	314	35.7%

Figure 14D.1. Comparing nonfarm employee jobs (private sector) to changes in long-term capital gains tax rates, 1981–2012

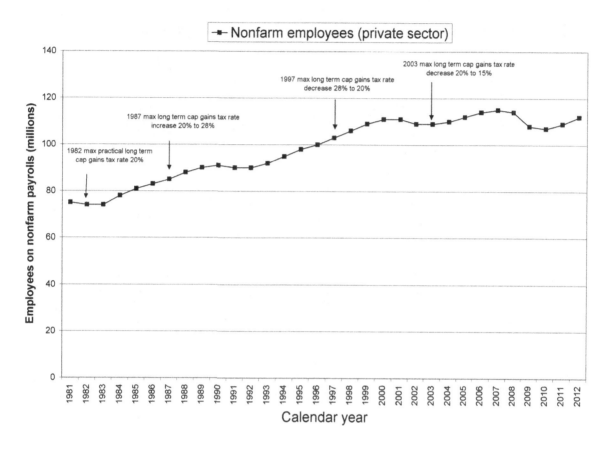

Figure 14D.2. Comparing nonfarm employee jobs (private sector) per US resident population to changes in long-term capital gains tax rates, 1981–2012

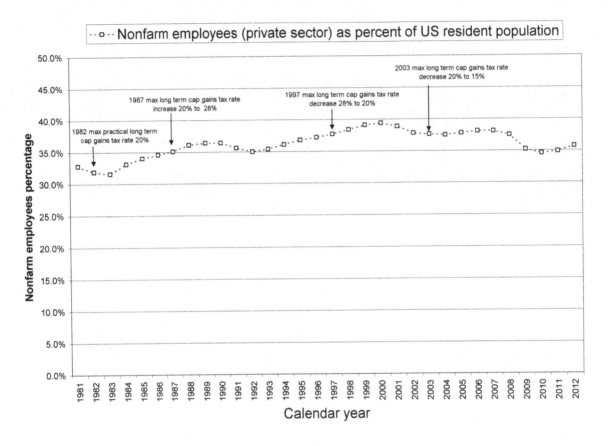

Appendix 14E

———◆•◆•◆———

Individual income tax, capital gains, comparing capital gains tax-rate changes to reported net capital gains

Purpose: To discern in a general way from historic data whether and to what extent changes in tax rates for capital gains may decrease "lock-in" of capital assets.

Comments

The table and two figures in this appendix address the question whether and to what extent changes in capital gains tax rates decrease "lock-in" of capital assets, at least within the range of changes that have occurred historically. Some economic theorists assert that taxation of capital gains tends to "lock in" the ownership of capital assets because these taxes make owners less willing to sell their capital assets to new owners, who might make more efficient economic use of them.

Since 1987, Congress has twice decreased the long-term capital gains tax rates. The 1997 decrease from a maximum rate of 28 percent to 20 percent occurred independent of other broad tax changes. In contrast, the 2003 decrease from a maximum rate of 20 percent to 15 percent occurred the same year that the 2001 broad decreases in individual income tax rates became fully effective. Neither decrease gave the zero tax rate that some economists assert would be needed to fully avoid "lock-in" effects. Despite these limitations, comparing the capital gains tax-rate changes to variations in reported net capital gains potentially provides insight into whether capital-asset sales are greatly encouraged by lower capital gains tax rates.

Table 14E.1 shows the net capital gains reported by individuals in each tax year from 1993 to 2008 in both current and constant dollars. Net capital gains is the figure that is reported before subtracting net capital losses. Reported net capital gains provide one measure of activity in capital sales. The net capital gains in constant dollars remove the effects of inflation. This table also shows net capital gains as a percentage of total adjusted gross income reported by all individuals as a way to remove the effects of general increased or decreased individual income over time.

Figure 14E.1 compares the reported net capital gains in constant dollars to the timing of changes in long-term capital gains tax rates from 1993 to 2008. The data in this figure remove increases that are caused solely by inflation.

Figure 14E.2 has the same format as figure 14E.1, but compares the timing of changes in long-term capital gains tax rates from 1993 to 2008 to the reported net capital gains as a percentage of total reported adjusted gross income. These data remove the changes in net capital gains that are caused solely by generally changed incomes.

These data are inconclusive on the question whether lower capital gains tax rates cause significantly increased sales of capital assets.

To be sure, net capital gains as a percentage of total adjusted gross income increased after both long-term capital gains tax decreases. However, the increases after the 1997 change from a maximum rate of 28 percent to 20 percent, the only test of a rate change by itself, appear to be part of a trend of increases that began several years earlier from a small base. The increased net capital gains did not continue, as shown by significantly smaller net gains in 2001 and 2002.

Net capital gains as a percentage of total adjusted gross income also increased after the 2003 change from a maximum rate of 20 percent to 15 percent, but that tax rate change occurred along with other broad tax changes. Thus, the effects of the 2003 capital gains tax-rate decrease cannot be discerned independently from the other 2003 changes.

Significant fluctuations in net capital gains over time, with lower levels occurring both before and after capital gains tax-rate decreases, suggest that other factors are mostly responsible for the observed fluctuations and periodic increases.

Data source:

Publication 1304, Individual Income Tax Returns, IRS Statistics of Income, Table 1.4, 1993–2008;
Budget of the U.S. Government, Fiscal Year 2014, Historical Tables, Table 1.3.

Table 14E.1. Individual income tax, capital gains, reported net capital gains in current and constant (FY 2005) dollars, 1993–2008

Federal fiscal year (1)	Total adjusted gross income in current dollars (billions) (2)	Taxable net gain Schedule D in current dollars (billions) (3)	Composite deflator for constant (FY 2005) dollars (4)	Taxable net gain Schedule D in constant (FY 2005) dollars (billions) (5)	Taxable net gain Schedule D as % total adjusted gross income (6)
1993	3,723	150	0.7640	196	4.0%
1994	3,908	150	0.7782	193	3.8%
1995	4,189	176	0.7995	220	4.2%
1996	4,536	255	0.8187	311	5.6%
1997	4,970	365	0.8360	437	7.3%
1998	5,516	455	0.8439	539	8.2%
1999	5,855	541	0.8558	632	9.2%
2000	6,365	628	0.8770	716	9.9%
2001	6,171	348	0.8992	387	5.6%
2002	6,034	268	0.9138	293	4.4%
2003	6,207	323	0.9378	344	5.2%
2004	6,789	497	0.9645	515	7.3%
2005	7,422	685	1.0000	685	9.2%
2006	8,031	790	1.0354	763	9.8%
2007	8,688	912	1.0642	857	10.5%
2008	8,263	495	1.1031	449	6.0%

Figure 14E.1. Comparing changes in long-term capital gains tax rates to reported net capital gains in constant (FY 2005) dollars, 1993–2008

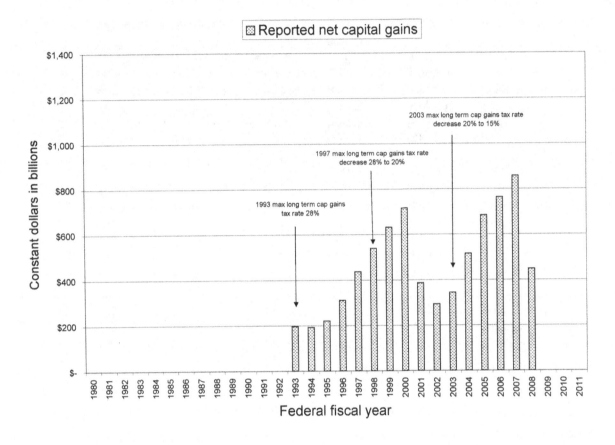

Figure 14E.2. Comparing changes in long-term capital gains tax rates to reported net capital gains as a percentage of total adjusted gross income, 1993–2008

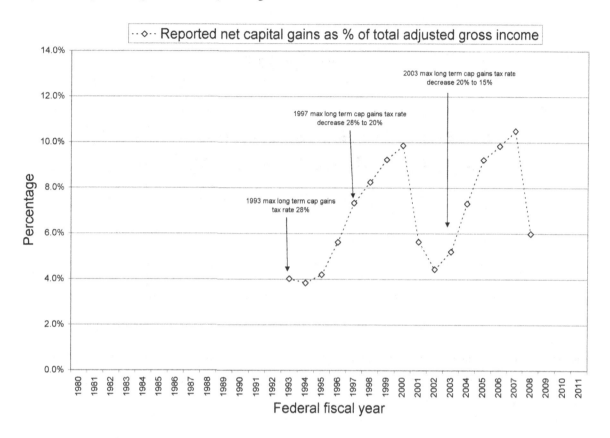

Appendix 14F

◆·◆·◆·◆

Individual income tax, capital gains, evaluating Congress's "Reasons for Change" for decreasing capital gains tax rates in 1997

Purpose: To provide a summary of the primary rationales used to support lower tax rates for capital gains than for other income so that those reasons can be judged by historic data.

Comments

In 1997, Congress decreased the maximum long-term capital gains tax rate from 28 percent to 20 percent, along with other changes in capital gains tax rates. Its "Reasons for Change" for these decreases are quoted in full in this appendix. They provide a partial template against which to judge whether the anticipated results from the decreases actually occurred. Congress decreased the maximum long-term capital gains rate again in 2003, from 20 percent to 15 percent.

In terms of benefits to all Americans, the Reasons for Change identify three potential results from lower tax rates on capital gains: (1) increased growth in GDP, (2) increased tax revenues from the taxation of increased wages and business profits that will offset losses from lower capital gains tax rates (that is, no loss in tax revenues), and (3) overall higher wages, resulting from greater productivity.

The question whether increased growth in GDP has occurred as a result of decreased capital gains tax rates is addressed in appendix 10D.

The question whether tax revenues have increased after decreases in capital gains tax rates is addressed in appendix 10C.

The question whether overall higher wages occurred after decreases in capital gains tax rates is addressed by table 14F.1 in this appendix. This table shows that even before the Great Recession, the average American had little real wage or income increase after 1997. As a group, women did better than men during this time period, but their median wages still remained far below those of men. All of the numbers shown in table 14F.1 for 2007 were less in 2008, 2009, and 2010, when the Great Recession impacted incomes in the United States. "Median" data are used in table 14F.1 because the median better reflects how all Americans are faring than the mean (average) number.

Data source:

   Measuring America—People, Places, and Our Economy, People and Households, Income (US Census Bureau, 2013).

Table 14F.1. Comparing median incomes in 1998 to median incomes in 2007 in constant (FY 2010) dollars

Description	1998	2007
Median household income (1)	$51,944	$52,823
Median income per person (2)	$26,654	$27,998
Median earnings for people with earnings (3)	$30,265	$32,694
Median wage and salary earnings male (4)	$38,749	$38,687
Median wage and salary earnings female (4)	$23,705	$27,458

Note (1): Data are from data source Table H-8.
Note (2): Data are from data source Table P-10.
Note (3): Data are from data source Table P-43.
Note (4): Data are from data source Table P-53.

House Report No. 105-148, 105th Cong. (1997), 340–341

Reasons for Change

The Committee believes it is important that tax policy be conducive to economic growth. Economic growth cannot occur without saving, investment, and the willingness of individuals to take risks and exploit new market opportunities. The greater the pool of savings, the greater the monies available for business investment in equipment and research. It is through such investment in equipment and new products and services that the United States economy can increase output and productivity. It is through increases in productivity that workers earn higher real wages. Hence, greater saving is necessary for all Americans to benefit through a higher standard of living.

The net personal saving rate in the United States has averaged less than 5 percent of gross domestic product for the past 15 years. The Committee believes such saving is inadequate to finance the investment that is needed to equip the country's businesses with the equipment and research dollars necessary to create the higher productivity that results in higher real wages for working Americans. A reduction in the taxation of capital gains increases the rate of return on household saving. Testimony by many economists before the Committee generally concluded that increasing the after-tax return to saving should increase the saving rate of American households.

American technological leadership has been enhanced by the willingness of individuals to take the risk of pursuing new businesses exploiting new technologies. Risk taking is stifled if the taxation of any resulting gain is high and the ability to claim losses is limited. The Committee believes it is important to encourage risk taking and believes a reduction in the taxation of capital gains will have that effect.

Reduction in the taxation of capital gains also should improve the efficiency of the capital markets. The taxation of capital gains upon realization encourages investors who have accrued past gains to keep their monies "locked in" to such investments even when better investment opportunities present themselves. All economists that testified before the Committee agreed that reducing the rate of taxation of capital gains would encourage investors to unlock many of these gains. This unlocking will permit more monies to flow to new, highly valued uses in the economy. When monies flow freely, the efficiency of the capital market is improved.

The unlocking effect also has the short-term and long-term effect of increasing revenues to the Federal Government. The current revenue estimating methods employed by the Congress account for this long-term behavioral response. Nevertheless, current Congressional estimates project that revenue losses to the Federal Government will arise from the reduction in the tax rate on capital gains. The Committee observes, however, that the conservative approach embodied in such estimates does not attempt to account for the potential for increased growth in GDP that can result from increased saving and risk taking. Many macroeconomists have concluded that reductions in the taxation of capital gains may increase GDP and wage growth sufficiently that future tax revenues from the taxation of wages and business profits will offset the losses forecast from the sale of capital assets. The potential for future growth and its benefits both for all United States citizens and for future Federal revenues were important considerations for the Committee.

The Committee rejects the narrow view that reductions in the taxation of capital gains benefit primarily high-income Americans. Taking a longer view, the Committee sees a reduction in the taxation of capital gains as providing potential benefits to all individuals. Most importantly, the Committee stresses that economic growth benefits all Americans. Increased investment leads to greater productivity and leads to higher wages. Traditional attempts to measure the benefit or burden of a tax change do not account for this critical outcome.

Appendix 16A

◆·◆·◆·◆·◆

Individual income tax, new approach to taxation of Social Security benefits

Purpose: To provide a simplified way to determine whether an individual's Social Security benefits are taxable income, and if so, what portion of those benefits is taxable.

Comments

At present, a portion of the Social Security benefits paid to individuals with large-enough adjusted gross incomes is considered to be taxable income. So long as Congress continues this general policy, some method will be needed to determine whether an individual's Social Security benefits are taxable income, and if so, what portion of those benefits should be taxable.

This appendix has one proposal, one new figure, and one IRS worksheet. Proposal 16A.1 suggests a specific rewrite of the current statute that treats a portion of Social Security benefits as taxable [26 U.S.C. § 86 (2009)].

Figure 16A.1 is an example of a simplified worksheet that can be used to determine taxable Social Security benefits if the statutory changes in Proposal 16A.1 are adopted. Both the proposal and this new worksheet provide simple structures that are flexible enough to accommodate different visions about whose Social Security benefits should be taxable income and what portion of those benefits should be taxable.

As a contrast to the proposal and new worksheet, figure 16A.2 is a copy of the 2009 Social Security Benefits Worksheet from the 2009 Form 1040 Forms and Instructions. This worksheet is based on the 2009 version of 26 U.S.C. § 86.

Proposal 16A.1

New Approach to Taxation of Social Security Benefits
Modified 26 U.S.C. § 86

Replace 26 U.S.C. § 86 (a), (b), and (c) with this language:

(a) IN GENERAL—
Social Security benefits are tax exempt income except as follows:

(1) A taxpayer shall report as taxable income that portion of the total Social Security benefits received during the taxable year that is equal to 50 percent of the taxpayer's modified adjusted gross income above the base income amount stated in (2), but not exceeding 50 percent of the total Social Security benefits received.

(2) Base income amount

(a) For taxpayers filing a joint return, the base income amount is ten times the joint taxpayers' standard deduction allowed in the tax year.

(b) For all other taxpayers, the base amount is ten times the taxpayer's standard deduction allowed in the tax year.

(b) MODIFIED ADJUSTED GROSS INCOME—
For purposes of this section, the term "modified adjusted gross income" means adjusted gross income—

(1) determined without regard to this section and sections 135, 137, 199, 221, 222, 911, 931, and 933, and

(2) increased by the amount of interest received or accrued by the taxpayer during the taxable year which is exempt from tax.

Note 1: This proposal is written in a way that the fixed percentage (50 percent) and the base income amount (ten times the applicable standard deduction) can easily be modified, while maintaining the simple structure of the statutory change.

Note 2: (b) is the same language as current §86(b)(2) (2009).

Figure 16A.1. New approach to taxation of Social Security benefits: simplified Social Security benefits worksheet to determine taxable benefits (using 2009 Form 1040 as reference)

Taxable Social Security benefits

1. Enter the total of the amounts from Form 1040, lines 7, 8a, 9a, 10 through 14, 15b, 16b, 17 through 19, and 21 . . . .   1. _____

2. Enter the amount, if any, from Form 1040, line 8b [tax-exempt interest]   . . . .   2. _____

3. Add lines 1 and 2 . . . .   3. _____

4. If you are
   • Married filing jointly, enter $114,000
        [ten times 2009 standard deduction]
   • Head of household, enter $83,500
        [ten times 2009 standard deduction]
   • All others, enter $57,000
        [ten times 2009 standard deduction] . . . .   4. _____

5. Subtract line 4 from line 3   . . . .   5. _____

6. Multiply line 5 by 0.50 . . . .   6. _____

7. Enter the total amount from box 5 of all of your Forms SSA-1099 and Forms RRB-1099. Also, enter this amount on Form 1040, line 20a   . . . .   7. _____

8. Multiply line 7 by 0.50   . . . .   8. _____

9. **Taxable Social Security benefits**. Enter the smaller of line 6 or line 8. Also enter this amount on Form 1040, line 20b   . . .   9. _____

The FAST Plan for Tax Reform

Figure 16A.2. 2009 Form 1040 Social Security benefits worksheet to determine taxable benefits

Form 1040—Lines 20a and 20b

Social Security Benefits Worksheet—Lines 20a and 20b   *Keep for Your Records*

Before you begin:
√ Complete Form 1040, lines 21 and 23 through 32, if they apply to you.
√ Figure any write-in adjustments to be entered on the dotted line next to line 36 (see the instructions for line 36 on page 35).
√ If you are married filing separately and you lived apart from your spouse for all of 2009, enter "D" to the right of the word "benefits" on line 20a. If you do not, you may get a math error notice from the IRS.
√ Be sure you have read the **Exception** on page 27 to see if you can use this worksheet instead of a publication to find out if any of your benefits are taxable.

1. Enter the total amount from **box 5** of **all** your **Forms SSA-1099** and **Forms RRB-1099.** Also, enter this amount on Form 1040, line 20a...... **1.** _____
2. Enter one-half of line 1 .... **2.** _____
3. Enter the total of the amounts from Form 1040, lines 7, 8a, 9a, 10 through 14, 15b, 16b, 17 through 19, and 21 .... **3.** _____
4. Enter the amount, if any, from Form 1040, line 8b .... **4.** _____
5. Add lines 2, 3, and 4 .... **5.** _____
6. Enter the total of the amounts from Form 1040, lines 23 through 32, plus any write-in adjustments you entered on the dotted line next to line 36 .... **6.** _____
7. Is the amount on line 6 less than the amount on line 5?
   ☐ **No.** (STOP) None of your social security benefits are taxable. Enter -0- on Form 1040, line 20b.
   ☐ **Yes.** Subtract line 6 from line 5 .... **7.** _____
8. If you are:
   • Married filing jointly, enter $32,000
   • Single, head of household, qualifying widow(er), or married filing separately and you **lived apart** from your spouse for all of 2009, enter $25,000
   • Married filing separately and you lived with your spouse at any time in 2009, skip lines 8 through 15; multiply line 7 by 85% (.85) and enter the result on line 16. Then go to line 17
   .... **8.** _____
9. Is the amount on line 8 less than the amount on line 7?
   ☐ **No.** (STOP) None of your social security benefits are taxable. Enter -0- on Form 1040, line 20b. If you are married filing separately and you **lived apart** from your spouse for all of 2009, be sure you entered "D" to the right of the word "benefits" on line 20a.
   ☐ **Yes.** Subtract line 8 from line 7 .... **9.** _____
10. Enter: $12,000 if married filing jointly; $9,000 if single, head of household, qualifying widow(er), or married filing separately and you **lived apart** from your spouse for all of 2009 .. **10.** _____
11. Subtract line 10 from line 9. If zero or less, enter -0- .... **11.** _____
12. Enter the **smaller** of line 9 or line 10 .... **12.** _____
13. Enter one-half of line 12 .... **13.** _____
14. Enter the **smaller** of line 2 or line 13 .... **14.** _____
15. Multiply line 11 by 85% (.85). If line 11 is zero, enter -0- .... **15.** _____
16. Add lines 14 and 15.. **16.** _____
17. Multiply line 1 by 85% (.85) .... **17.** _____
18. **Taxable social security benefits.** Enter the **smaller** of line 16 or line 17. Also enter this amount on Form 1040, line 20b .... **18.** _____

(TIP) *If any of your benefits are taxable for 2009 **and** they include a lump-sum benefit payment that was for an earlier year, you may be able to reduce the taxable amount. See Pub. 915 for details.*

Appendix 25A

---•◆•◆•◆•---

Individual income tax, can refundable tax credits for payments of Social Security and Medicare taxes achieve the goals of the Earned Income Credit?

Purpose: To determine whether refundable tax credits for payments of Social Security and Medicare taxes can achieve the goals of the Earned Income Credit.

Comments

Chapter 25 examines the current Earned Income Credit available to low-income individuals. That chapter shows that part of the EIC is intended to reimburse an individual's payment of Social Security and Medicare taxes. A potential suggestion to accomplish this EIC goal in a simpler way in the context of the FAST Plan would be to allow an individual's payment of Social Security and Medicare taxes as a refundable tax credit rather than a nonrefundable tax credit as provided in the FAST Plan.

Would this work?

Evaluation
Can Refundable Tax Credits Achieve the Same Result as the Current EIC?

As shown in chapter 25, a portion of the Earned Income Credit now refunds Social Security and Medicare taxes paid by an eligible low-income individual.

Designating the FAST Plan's nonrefundable tax credit for payment of Social Security and Medicare taxes as refundable will *not* achieve the same result because the income tax credit for Social Security and Medicare taxes is nearly double the refundable credit for these taxes found in the current EIC for the same amount of earned income. This credit cannot arbitrarily be changed because it is based on other FAST Plan changes in the Internal Revenue Code.

In addition, making the FAST Plan's credit for Social Security and Medicare taxes a refundable credit will also create income triggers for payback of these taxes that are more variable and potentially much larger than the income triggers for paybacks under the EIC. Many people who are not now considered to be individuals with small incomes could then be eligible for a cash refund.

How this would occur is a multistep process:

- A payback would be triggered anytime an individual's calculated income taxes are less than his or her credit for Social Security and Medicare taxes.
- Income taxes are calculated against taxable income, which in turn reflects reductions based on both the standard deduction and variable reductions for exemptions and medical expenses. These reductions can effectively insulate a variable and relatively large amount of earned income from the income tax.
- The tax credit for payment of Social Security and Medicare taxes, however, is based on the full amount of earned income. This dichotomy increases the likelihood that a refundable credit for payment of Social Security and Medicare taxes will exceed the calculated income tax, even for relatively large earned incomes. This excess will trigger a payback of some of the Social Security and Medicare taxes even for relatively large earned incomes.

Appendix 28A

─────◆─◆─◆─────

Individual income tax, identifying tax subsidies targeted by the Alternative Minimum Tax in 2009 tax law

Purpose: To show the tax subsidies that current law targets for reduction via the Alternative Minimum Tax.

Comments

Figure 28A.1 of this appendix consists of the first page of the Alternative Minimum Tax form for the tax year 2009 (Form 6251). Lines 2 through 28 show the many reductions from income that normally are allowed in determining taxable income, but that Congress has targeted with the Alternative Minimum Tax. That is, Congress has decided that individuals should not be able to use these particular reductions in a combined way that permits the individual's taxable income to be so low that the effective rate of tax on the individual's unreduced income is less than a minimum rate defined by Congress.

Figure 28A.1. First page of 2009 Form 6251 showing tax preferences targeted by the Alternative Minimum Tax

Form **6251**	**Alternative Minimum Tax—Individuals**	OMB No. 1545-0074
Department of the Treasury Internal Revenue Service (99)	▶ See separate instructions. ▶ Attach to Form 1040 or Form 1040NR.	20**09** Attachment Sequence No. **32**
Name(s) shown on Form 1040 or Form 1040NR		Your social security number

Part I   Alternative Minimum Taxable Income (See instructions for how to complete each line.)

1	If filing Schedule A (Form 1040), enter the amount from Form 1040, line 41 (minus any amount on Form 8914, line 6), and go to line 2. Otherwise, enter the amount from Form 1040, line 38 (minus any amount on Form 8914, line 6), and go to line 7. (If less than zero, enter as a negative amount.)	1		
2	Medical and dental. Enter the **smaller** of Schedule A (Form 1040), line 4, **or** 2.5% (.025) of Form 1040, line 38. If zero or less, enter -0-	2		
3	Taxes from Schedule A (Form 1040), lines 5, 6, and 8	3		
4	Enter the home mortgage interest adjustment, if any, from line 6 of the worksheet on page 2 of the instructions	4		
5	Miscellaneous deductions from Schedule A (Form 1040), line 27	5		
6	If Form 1040, line 38, is over $166,800 (over $83,400 if married filing separately), enter the amount from line 11 of the **Itemized Deductions Worksheet** on page A-11 of the instructions for Schedule A (Form 1040)	6	(	)
7	If filing Schedule L (Form 1040A or 1040), enter as a negative amount the sum of lines 6 and 20 from that schedule	7	(	)
8	Tax refund from Form 1040, line 10 or line 21	8	(	)
9	Investment interest expense (difference between regular tax and AMT)	9		
10	Depletion (difference between regular tax and AMT)	10		
11	Net operating loss deduction from Form 1040, line 21. Enter as a positive amount	11		
12	Alternative tax net operating loss deduction	12	(	)
13	Interest from specified private activity bonds exempt from the regular tax	13		
14	Qualified small business stock (7% of gain excluded under section 1202)	14		
15	Exercise of incentive stock options (excess of AMT income over regular tax income)	15		
16	Estates and trusts (amount from Schedule K-1 (Form 1041), box 12, code A)	16		
17	Electing large partnerships (amount from Schedule K-1 (Form 1065-B), box 6)	17		
18	Disposition of property (difference between AMT and regular tax gain or loss)	18		
19	Depreciation on assets placed in service after 1986 (difference between regular tax and AMT)	19		
20	Passive activities (difference between AMT and regular tax income or loss)	20		
21	Loss limitations (difference between AMT and regular tax income or loss)	21		
22	Circulation costs (difference between regular tax and AMT)	22		
23	Long-term contracts (difference between AMT and regular tax income)	23		
24	Mining costs (difference between regular tax and AMT)	24		
25	Research and experimental costs (difference between regular tax and AMT)	25		
26	Income from certain installment sales before January 1, 1987.	26	(	)
27	Intangible drilling costs preference	27		
28	Other adjustments, including income-based related adjustments	28		
29	**Alternative minimum taxable income.** Combine lines 1 through 28. (If married filing separately and line 29 is more than $216,900, see page 8 of the instructions.)	29		

Part II   Alternative Minimum Tax (AMT)

30 Exemption. (If you were under age 24 at the end of 2009, see page 8 of the instructions.)

IF your filing status is . . .	AND line 29 is not over . . .	THEN enter on line 30 . . .		
Single or head of household	$112,500.	$46,700		
Married filing jointly or qualifying widow(er)	150,000	70,950	}	
Married filing separately.	75,000	35,475		30

If line 29 is **over** the amount shown above for your filing status, see page 8 of the instructions.

31	Subtract line 30 from line 29. If more than zero, go to line 32. If zero or less, enter -0- here and on lines 34 and 36 and skip the rest of Part II.	31	
32	• If you are filing Form 2555 or 2555-EZ, see page 9 of the instructions for the amount to enter. • If you reported capital gain distributions directly on Form 1040, line 13; you reported qualified dividends on Form 1040, line 9b; **or** you had a gain on both lines 15 and 16 of Schedule D (Form 1040) (as refigured for the AMT, if necessary), complete Part III on the back and enter the amount from line 55 here. • **All others:** If line 31 is $175,000 or less ($87,500 or less if married filing separately), multiply line 31 by 26% (.26). Otherwise, multiply line 31 by 28% (.28) and subtract $3,500 ($1,750 if married filing separately) from the result.	32	
33	Alternative minimum tax foreign tax credit (see page 9 of the instructions)	33	
34	Tentative minimum tax. Subtract line 33 from line 32	34	
35	Tax from Form 1040, line 44 (minus any tax from Form 4972 and any foreign tax credit from Form 1040, line 47). If you used Schedule J to figure your tax, the amount from line 44 of Form 1040 must be refigured without using Schedule J (see page 11 of the instructions)	35	
36	**AMT.** Subtract line 35 from line 34. If zero or less, enter -0-. Enter here and on Form 1040, line 45	36	

For Paperwork Reduction Act Notice, see page 12 of the instructions.   Cat. No. 13600G   Form **6251** (2009)

Appendix 29A

———————•◦●◦•———————

Corporation income tax, calculation of a standard rate for a corporation revenue tax

Purpose: To provide a realistic calculation of a standard rate for a corporation revenue tax that will be required to produce the same total corporation income tax receipts as occurred historically under the corporation earnings (net profit) tax.

Comments

An initial standard rate for a corporation revenue tax should be tax receipts–neutral. That is, the standard rate should produce the same total corporation income tax receipts as would have been produced under "current law," which uses a corporation earnings (net profit) tax. This approach is desirable so that the proposal to replace the current corporation net profit tax with a corporation revenue tax will not be viewed as an excuse to increase or decrease the total amount of money received by the United States from a corporation income tax.

Table 29A.1 uses data from the last five tax years before the Great Recession to calculate a standard rate for a corporation revenue tax that is tax receipts–neutral. The "status quo" method of table 29A.1 calculates rates using two alternative figures for each year in the numerator: total actual income tax before credits (column 6) and total actual income tax after credits (column 7). The denominator in these rate calculations is the corporation receipts (revenues) from all returns (column 2) because the corporation revenue tax would apply to the revenues of all corporations, not just those reporting net profit. The simulated tax rates each year are then shown in columns 8 and 9, including their five-year averages.

Which five-year average rate is the proper rate for a new corporation revenue tax that is tax receipts–neutral? For two reasons, the answer is the approximate 1.5 percent rate shown at the bottom of column 8, because only that rate will achieve the target tax receipts of column 7 (actual income tax after credits).

First, recall that the FAST Plan's corporation revenue tax applies only to revenues derived from US operations. With this tax, no foreign tax credits will be allowed under the FAST Plan because foreign-based income is not taxed (whether earnings or revenues). These two facts affect rate calculations using data in table 29A.1 in a three-part analysis.

(1) The corporation receipts (revenues) data in column 2 include some receipts derived from foreign operations. This is so because the IRS 2007 Corporation Income Tax Returns report states that the data estimates "encompass corporate business activities in the United States, as well as certain foreign activities as reported on returns of domestic corporations, and foreign corporations with U.S. business activities" (see page 4 of the report).

(2) Foreign tax credits comprise most of the credits that reduce the "total actual income tax before credits" in column 6 to the "total actual income tax after credits" figure in column 7. Because foreign tax credits cannot be used to reduce US tax liability on US-sourced income, their amount in proportion to total income tax before credits roughly represents the proportion of foreign-based income in the corporation receipts (revenue) figure of column 2 (especially to the extent that the effective foreign taxes on income are comparable to US corporation income taxes). (See IRS 2007 Corporation Income Tax Returns report, p. 283.)

(3) Using the larger figures in column 6 to calculate the revenue tax rate rather than the smaller after-credits figures in column 7 has the same mathematical effect as using reduced revenue figures to reflect US income in column 2. Those reduced revenue figures are the base for the corporation revenue tax.

Second, table 29A.1 shows that many credits are available to corporations that reduce the total income tax each year by about one-third to obtain the income tax paid. This book does not address the many credits other than foreign tax credits that are available to corporations. Whether these other credits are tax subsidies or something else, their continued existence is assumed in the calculation of a receipts-neutral standard rate for a corporation revenue tax. If we used the revenue tax rate in column 9 as the standard rate for a receipts-neutral corporation revenue tax, those credits would be counted twice. Thus, the "calculated standard revenue tax rate based on total income tax before credits" in column 8 is the proper target rate for a standard-rate revenue tax. That rate is approximately 1.5 percent, calculated as an average for tax years 2003 through 2007.

Data source:
Corporation Income Tax Returns, IRS Statistics of Income, Corporation Returns—Basic Tables, Table 1 (tax years 2003, 2004, 2005, 2006, 2007).

Table 29A.1. Calculation of a standard rate for a corporation revenue tax

Tax year (1)	Total actual receipts (revenues) all returns in current dollars (billions) (2)	Total actual receipts (revenues) returns with net income in current dollars (bilions) (3)	Total actual net income in current dollars (billions) (4)	Total actual income subject to tax in current dollars (billions) (5)	Total actual income tax before credits in current dollars (billions) (6)	Total actual income tax after credits in current dollars (billions) (7)	Calculated standard revenue tax rate based on total income tax before credits (8)	Calculated standard revenue tax rate based on total income tax after credits (9)
2003	20,690	15,691	1,176	699	244	178	1.18%	0.86%
2004	22,712	18,274	1,456	857	300	224	1.32%	0.99%
2005	25,505	21,858	2,235	1,201	419	312	1.64%	1.22%
2006	27,402	23,280	2,240	1,291	453	353	1.65%	1.29%
2007	28,763	24,008	2,253	1,248	437	331	1.52%	1.15%

2003 Rate difference before v. after credits	-0.32%
2004 Rate difference before v. after credits	-0.33%
2005 Rate difference before v. after credits	-0.42%
2006 Rate difference before v. after credits	-0.36%
2007 Rate difference before v. after credits	-0.37%

5 year average calculated standard rate 2003-2007	1.46%	1.10%

Note: Rates are calculated using as the denominator "Total actual receipts (revenues) all returns" in column 2.

Appendix 33A

——◆•◆•◆——

Individual income tax, examples comparing tax payments under 2009 tax law to tax payments under the FAST Plan standard-rate approach: married wage earners filing jointly

Purpose: To show by examples how the total tax payments of married wage earners filing jointly will be different under the proposed standard-rate approach of the FAST Plan as compared to 2009 federal tax law.

Comments

This appendix compares the total federal tax liability of eight examples of married wage earners as calculated under 2009 federal tax law and under the standard-rate income tax approach of the FAST Plan, using 29 percent as the standard rate (possibly too low, as discussed in chapter 10). In one set of four examples, the married wage earners have no children. In the other set of four examples, they have two children. In all examples, the married individuals file jointly.

Total federal tax liability is the sum of income, Social Security, and Medicare taxes. For the examples in this appendix, these simplifying assumptions apply: (1) the only income is wages, (2) both spouses have the same wages, (3) the only reductions from income to determine taxable income are the standard deduction and personal exemptions, and (4) no tax subsidies exist, such as the Earned Income Credit under 2009 law or a potential comparable tax subsidy under the standard-rate approach.

The results of the calculations are stated first, followed by the formulas used to reach these results. The 2009 tax payment is based on the tax calculation from 2009 Form 1040 ES Instructions (estimated tax payments) as the correct 2009 tax law.

33A.1. Example Set 1A

Married filing jointly: no children.

    All income is wages.

    Spouses have equal incomes.

    No tax subsidies.

    Amounts are total federal taxes paid.

Table 33A.1. Example Set 1A taxes comparison between 2009 law and 29% standard rate

	2009 law	**29% standard rate**
Total income is $25,000.	$ 2,543	$ 1,913
Total income is $50,000.	$ 7,685	$ 6,362
Total income is $100,000.	$ 20,350	$ 18,147
Total income is $200,000.	$ 54,328	$ 41,717

33A.2. Example Set 2A

Married filing jointly: two dependent children.

    All income is wages.

    Spouses have equal incomes.

    No tax subsidies.

    Amounts are total federal taxes paid.

Table 33A.2. Example Set 2A taxes comparison between 2009 law and 29% standard rate

	2009 law	**29% standard rate**
Total income is $25,000.	$ 1,913	$ 1,913
Total income is $50,000.	$ 6,590	$ 4,245
Total income is $100,000.	$ 18,525	$ 16,030
Total income is $200,000.	$ 52,284	$ 39,600

33A.1c. Example Set 1A Calculations

• 33A.1c.1. Example Set 1A formulas for both 2009 law and a standard rate

Married filing jointly: no children.

Standard deduction = $11,400

Two exemptions (2 x $3,650) = $7,300

Total income reductions = $18,700

Income and tax assumptions:

All income is wages.

Spouses have equal incomes.

No tax subsidies.

I is total income of both spouses.

Formulas are valid for total income up to $213,600 (two equal incomes up to the Social Security tax cutoff; these incomes are below the threshold for diminishing exemptions).

• 33A.1c.2. Example Set 1A simplified formulas for 2009 law

Note 1: The first number in each formula is the tax on the amount of taxable income shown as the last number in the parentheses. That last number is the amount of taxable income where the rate applied against the figures in the parentheses begins. For example, "9,350" is the tax on taxable income of "67,900" that results from applying the 2009 graduated tax rates on the segments of that amount of taxable income.

Note 2: The income tax portion is first; the Social Security and Medicare tax portion (0.0765I) is last.

Formula for Income over -0-, but not over $35,400

Total tax = 0 + 0.10(I − 18,700) + 0.0765I

Formula for Income over $35,400, but not over $86,600

Total tax = 1,670 + 0.15(I − 18,700 − 16,700) + 0.0765I

Formula for Income over $86,600, but not over $155,750

Total tax = 9,350 + 0.25(I − 18,700 − 67,900) + 0.0765I

Formula for Income over $155,750, but not over $213,600

Total tax = 26,638 + 0.28(I − 18,700 − 137,050) + 0.0765I

• 33A.1c.3. Example Set 1A simplified formulas for a 29% standard rate

Note 1: The formula here is used only to allow calculation comparisons to 2009 law. In practice, the calculation will be much simpler because of the way that wages will be reported.

Note 2: In these calculations, the credit for payment of Social Security and Medicare taxes (– 0.153I) cannot exceed the calculated income tax (becomes zero if the income tax portion is calculated as a negative number).

Note 3: The income tax portion is first; the Social Security and Medicare tax portion (0.0765I) is last.

General formula

Total tax = 0.29(I – 18,700 + 0.0765I) – 0.153I + 0.0765I

Where the income tax portion is -0- if a negative number

Under this formula,

Formula for income over -0-, but not over $34,107

Total tax = 0.0765I

Formula for income over $34,107, but not over $213,600

Total tax = 0.29(I – 18,700) – 0.0543I

33A.2c. Example Set 2A Calculations

33A.2c.1. Example Set 2A formulas for both 2009 law and a standard rate

Married filing jointly: two dependent children.

Standard deduction = $11,400

Four exemptions (4 x $3,650) = $14,600

Total income reductions = $26,000

Income and tax assumptions:

All income is wages.

Spouses have equal incomes.

No tax subsidies.

I is total income of both spouses.

Formulas are valid for total income up to $213,600 (two equal incomes up to the Social Security tax cutoff; these incomes are below the threshold for diminishing exemptions).

• 33A.2c.2. Example Set 2A simplified formulas for 2009 law

Note 1: The first number in each formula is the tax on the amount of taxable income shown as the last number in the parentheses. That last number is the amount of taxable income where the rate applied against the figures in the parentheses begins. For example, "9,350" is the tax on taxable income of "67,900" that results from applying the 2009 graduated tax rates on the segments of that amount of taxable income.

Note 2: The income tax portion is first; the Social Security and Medicare tax portion (0.0765I) is last.

Formula for Income over -0-, but not over $42,700

Total tax = 0 + 0.10(I − 26,000) + 0.0765I

Formula for Income over $42,700, but not over $93,900

Total tax = 1,670 + 0.15(I − 26,000 − 16,700) + 0.0765I

Formula for Income over $93,900, but not over $163,050

Total tax = 9,350 + 0.25(I − 26,000 − 67,900) + 0.0765I

Formula for Income over $163,050, but not over $213,600

Total tax = 26,638 + 0.28(I − 26,000 − 137,050) + 0.0765I

• *33A.2c.3. Example Set 2A simplified formulas for a 29% standard rate*

Note 1: The formula here is used only to allow calculation comparisons to 2009 law. In practice, the calculation will be much simpler because of the way that wages will be reported.

Note 2: In these calculations, the credit for payment of Social Security and Medicare taxes (− 0.153I) cannot exceed the calculated income tax (becomes zero if the income tax portion is calculated as a negative number).

Note 3: The income tax portion is first; the Social Security and Medicare tax portion (0.0765I) is last.)

General formula

Total tax = 0.29(I −26,000 + 0.0765I) − 0.153I + 0.0765I

Where the income tax portion is -0- if a negative number

Under this formula,

Formula for income over -0-, but not over $47,421

Total tax = 0.0765I

Formula for income over $47,421, but not over $213,600

Total tax = 0.29(I − 26,000) − 0.0543I

Appendix 33B

Individual income tax, examples comparing tax payments under 2009 tax law to tax payments under the FAST Plan standard-rate approach: married self-employed individuals filing jointly

Purpose: To show by examples how the total tax payments of married self-employed individuals filing jointly will be different under the proposed standard rate of the FAST Plan as compared to 2009 federal tax law.

Comments

This appendix compares the total federal tax liability of eight examples of married self-employed individuals as calculated under 2009 federal tax law and under the standard-rate income tax approach of the FAST Plan, using 29 percent as the standard rate (possibly too low, as discussed in chapter 10). In one set of four examples, the married individuals have no children. In the other set of four examples, they have two children. In all examples, the married individuals file jointly.

Total federal tax liability is the sum of income, Social Security, and Medicare taxes. For the examples in this appendix, these simplifying assumptions apply: (1) the only income is self-employed business income, (2) both spouses have the same income, (3) the only reductions from income to determine taxable income are the standard deduction and personal exemptions, and (4) no tax subsidies exist, such as the Earned Income Credit under 2009 law or a potential comparable tax subsidy under the standard-rate approach.

The results of the calculations are stated first, followed by the formulas used to reach these results. The 2009 tax payment is based on the tax calculation from 2009 Form 1040 ES Instructions (estimated tax payments) as the correct 2009 tax law.

The total federal taxes paid directly by married self-employed individuals will be more than the total federal taxes paid directly by married wage earners with the same total income (see previous appendix) because the wage earner's employer pays one-half of a wage earner's Social Security and Medicare taxes. The full payment of these taxes by self-employed individuals affects the total amount of tax paid before the nonrefundable credit for payment of Social Security and Medicare taxes can be used against income tax owed.

33B.1. Example Set 1B

Married filing jointly: no children.

    All income is self-employed business income.

    Spouses have equal incomes.

    No tax subsidies.

    Amounts are total federal taxes paid.

Table 33B.1. Example Set 1B taxes comparison between 2009 law and 29% standard rate

	2009 law	**29% standard rate**
Total income is $25,000.	$ 3,987	$ 3,553
Total income is $50,000.	$ 10,396	$ 9,077
Total income is $100,000.	$ 25,065	$ 23,577
Total income is $200,000.	$ 63,334	$ 52,577

33B.2. Example Set 2B

Married filing jointly: two dependent children.

    All income is self-employed business income.

    Spouses have equal incomes.

    No tax subsidies.

    Amounts are total federal taxes paid.

Table 33B.2. Example Set 2B taxes comparison between 2009 law and 29% standard rate

	2009 law	**29% standard rate**
Total income is $25,000.	$ 3,533	$ 3,553
Total income is $50,000.	$ 9,301	$ 7,105
Total income is $100,000.	$ 23,336	$ 21,460
Total income is $200,000.	$ 61,290	$ 50,460

33B.1c. Example Set 1B Calculations

• 33B.1c.1. Example Set 1B formulas for both 2009 law and a standard rate

Married filing jointly: no children.

Standard deduction = $11,400

Two exemptions (2 x $3,650) = $7,300

Total income reductions = $18,700

Income and tax assumptions:

All income is self-employed business income.

Spouses have equal incomes.

No tax subsidies.

I is total income of both spouses.

Formulas are valid for total income up to $234,294 (two equal incomes up to the Social Security tax cutoff using the 2009 tax law 0.9235 factor; these incomes are below the threshold for diminishing exemptions).

• 33B.1c.2. Example Set 1B simplified formulas for 2009 law

Note 1: Income is reduced by one-half the self-employment tax (Social Security and Medicare taxes) on earned income, which is $(0.153)(0.5)(0.9235)(I) = 0.0706I$.

Note 2: For the self-employment tax portion (Social Security and Medicare taxes), the tax is $(0.153)(0.9235)(I) = 0.1413I$.

Note 3: The first number in each formula is the tax on the amount of taxable income shown as the last plain number (number without an I multiplier) in the parentheses. That last plain number is the amount of taxable income where the rate applied against the figures in the parentheses begins. For example, "9,350" is the tax on taxable income of "67,900" that results from applying the 2009 graduated tax rates on the segments of that amount of taxable income.

Note 4: The income tax portion is first; the self-employment tax portion (Social Security and Medicare taxes) $(0.1413I)$ is last.

Formula for Income over -0-, but not over $38,089

Total tax = $0 + 0.10(I - 18,700 - 0.0706I) + 0.1413I$

Formula for Income over $38,089, but not over $93,178

Total tax = $1,670 + 0.15(I - 18,700 - 16,700 - 0.0706I) + 0.1413I$

Formula for Income over $93,178, but not over $167,581

Total tax = $9,350 + 0.25(I - 18,700 - 67,900 - 0.0706I) + 0.1413I$

Formula for Income over $167,581, but not over $231,294

Total tax = $26,638 + 0.28(I - 18,700 - 137,050 - 0.0706I) + 0.1413I$

• **33B.1c.3. Example Set 1B simplified formulas for a 29% standard rate**

Note 1: In these calculations, the credit for payment of Social Security and Medicare taxes cannot exceed the calculated income tax (becomes zero if the income tax portion is calculated as a negative number).

Note 2: For the Social Security/Medicare tax portion, using the new 0.9290 factor against income, the tax is $(0.153)(0.9290)(I) = 0.1421I$.

Note 3: The income tax portion is first; the Social Security and Medicare tax portion $(0.1421I)$ is last.

General formula

Total tax = $0.29(I - 18,700) - 0.1421I + 0.1421I$

Where the income tax portion is -0- if a negative number

Under this formula,

Formula for income over -0-, but not over $36,667

Total tax = $0.1421I$

Formula for income over $36,667

Total tax = $0.29(I - 18,700)$

33B.2c. Example Set 2B Calculations

• **33B.2c.1. Example Set 2B formulas for both 2009 law and a standard rate**

Married filing jointly: two dependent children.

Standard deduction = $11,400

Four exemptions (4 x $3,650) = $14,600

Total income reductions = $26,000

Income and tax assumptions:

All income is self-employed business income.

Spouses have equal incomes.

No tax subsidies.

I is total income of both spouses.

Formulas are valid for total income up to $234,294 (two equal incomes up to the Social Security tax cutoff using the 2009 tax law 0.9235 factor; these incomes are below the threshold for diminishing exemptions).

• **33B2c.2. Example Set 2B simplified formulas for 2009 law**

Note 1: Income is reduced by one-half the self-employment tax (Social Security and Medicare taxes) on earned income, which is $(0.153)(0.5)(0.9235)(I) = 0.0706I$.

Note 2: For the self-employment tax portion (Social Security and Medicare taxes), the tax is (0.153)(0.9235)(I) = 0.1413I.

Note 3: The first number in each formula is the tax on the amount of taxable income shown as the last plain number (number without an I multiplier) in the parentheses. That last plain number is the amount of taxable income where the rate applied against the figures in the parentheses begins. For example, "9,350" is the tax on taxable income of "67,900" that results from applying the 2009 graduated tax rates on the segments of that amount of taxable income.

Note 4: The income tax portion is first; the self-employment tax portion (Social Security and Medicare taxes) (0.1413I) is last.

Formula for Income over -0-, but not over $45,944

Total tax = 0 + 0.10(I − 26,000 − 0.0706I) + 0.1413I

Formula for Income over $45,944, but not over $101,033

Total tax = 1,670 + 0.15(I − 26,000 − 16,700 − 0.0706I) + 0.1413I

Formula for Income over $101,033, but not over $175,436

Total tax = 9,350 + 0.25(I − 26,000 − 67,900 − 0.0706I) + 0.1413I

Formula for Income over $175,436, but not over $231,294

Total tax = 26,638 + 0.28(I − 26,000 − 137,050 − 0.0706I) + 0.1413I

• *33B.2c.3. Example Set 2B simplified formulas for a 29% standard rate*

Note 1: In these calculations, the credit for payment of Social Security and Medicare taxes cannot exceed the calculated income tax (becomes zero if the income tax portion is calculated as a negative number).

Note 2: For the Social Security/Medicare tax portion, using the new 0.9290 factor against income, the tax is 0.153(0.9290)(I) = 0.1421I.

Note 3: The income tax portion is first; the Social Security and Medicare tax portion (0.1421I) is last.)

General formula

Total tax = 0.29(I − 26,000) − 0.1421I + 0.1421I

Where the income tax portion is -0- if a negative number

Under this formula,

Formula for income over -0-, but not over $50,980

Total tax = 0.1421I

Formula for income over $50,980

Total tax = 0.29(I − 26,000)

Notes

Introduction

1. Economic Growth and Tax Relief Reconciliation Act of 2001, Pub.L.No. 107-16, 115 Stat. 38, § 901(a)-(b); Jobs and Growth Tax Relief Reconciliation Act of 2003, Pub.L.No. 108-27, 117 Stat. 752, § 303.

2. Tax Relief, Unemployment Insurance Reauthorization, and Job Creation Act of 2010, Pub.L.No. 111-312, 124 Stat. 3296, § 101(a).

3. National Commission on Fiscal Responsibility and Reform, *The Moment of Truth* (Washington, DC: The White House, 2010), 15. The report is available online at http:// www.fiscalcommission.gov/sites/fiscalcommission.gov/files/documents/TheMomentof Truth12_1_2010.pdf. The Fiscal Commission did not formally recommend the plan in the report because fewer than fourteen of the eighteen commission members endorsed the plan as required by the president's February 18, 2010 executive order that established the commission.

4. American Taxpayer Relief Act of 2012, Pub.L.No. 112-240, 126 Stat. 2313, §§ 101–102.

Chapter 1

5. *Budget of the U.S. Government, Fiscal Year 2014* (Washington, DC: The White House, 2012), Historical Tables, Tables 3.1, 3.2, and 1.4.

6. See appendix 1B (data for 1981 to 2012).

7. Scott Bittle and Jean Johnson, *Where Does the Money Go?* (New York: Harper/Collins, 2008); Addison Wiggin and Kate Incontrera, *I.O.U.S.A.* (Hoboken, NJ: John Wiley & Sons, 2008).

8. *Budget of the U.S. Government, Fiscal Year 2014*, Historical Tables, Table 7.1.

9. *Budget of the U.S. Government, Fiscal Year 2014*, Historical Tables, Table 1.4.

10. *Budget of the U.S. Government, Fiscal Year 2014*, Historical Tables, Table 1.1.

11. For a more exacting description of the parts of the national debt, see *Budget of the U.S. Government, Fiscal Year 2014*, Analytical Perspectives, 61–76 ("5. Federal Borrowing and Debt").

12. *Budget of the U.S. Government, Fiscal Year 2014*, Historical Tables, Introduction, pp. 4–5 (terms are derived from those descriptions).

13. *Budget of the U.S. Government, Fiscal Year 2014*, Historical Tables, Introduction, 4, and Table 13.1 (Social Security trust funds, Medicare hospital insurance trust fund, and highway trust fund); see 26 U.S.C. § 9503 (2009) (highway trust fund).

14. *Budget of the U.S. Government, Fiscal Year 2014*, Historical Tables, Tables 1.1, 1.4, 7.1, 13.1. Calculations were made from data in those tables. What I call the "true discretionary deficit" is labeled the "Surplus or Deficit (-)—Federal Funds" in Historical Table 1.4. See appendixes 2A and 2B in this book (data for 1981 to 2012).

15. See appendix 1B for federal tax receipts data. The annual federal deficit has sometimes been compared to total outlays rather than tax receipts. This comparison diminishes the apparent size of the deficit. To illustrate the different ways that annual deficits can be characterized, appendix 2C compares the federal deficit, on-budget deficit, and true discretionary deficit to (1) total federal outlays, (2) total federal receipts, and (3) total federal receipts without social insurance and retirement receipts (mostly Social Security and Medicare tax receipts) (data for 1981 to 2012).

16. *Budget of the U.S. Government, Fiscal Year 2014*, Historical Tables, Table 7.1. See appendix 2D in this book (data for 1981 to 2012). Appendix 2D also contains a table and figure that show national debt increases since 1981 (the figure also shows the presidential administrations since 1981).

17. American Recovery and Reinvestment Act of 2009, Pub.L.No. 111-5, 123 Stat. 115.

18. *Budget of the U.S. Government, Fiscal Year 2014*, Historical Tables, Tables 1.1, 1.2; see appendixes 1B and 1C for tables with the data from which the numbers in this paragraph were derived.

19. Expressed in current dollars, total federal receipts were $2,568 billion in fiscal year 2007 and just $2,105 billion in fiscal year 2009 ($463 billion decrease). Federal "on-budget" receipts (excluding receipts from the Social Security tax) were $1,933 billion in fiscal year 2007 and just $1,451 billion in fiscal year 2009 ($482 billion decrease). *Budget of the U.S. Government, Fiscal Year 2014*, Historical Tables, Table 1.1. See federal receipts data in appendixes 1B and 1C.

20. See appendix 2E for federal national debt interest obligations (data for 1981 to 2012).

21. *Budget of the U.S. Government, Fiscal Year 2014*, Historical Tables, Table 3.1. See, e.g., *1040 Forms and Instructions 2009, Package 1040-10* (Internal Revenue Service, 2009), 100.

22. *Budget of the U.S. Government, Fiscal Year 2014*, Historical Tables, Tables 1.1, 2.1, 3.1. See appendixes 2C and 2E in this book (data for 1981 to 2012).

23. Perhaps surprisingly, the fiscal year 2008 figures that compare (1) the public debt net interest payments and the national debt gross interest obligations to (2) total tax receipts other than social insurance and retirement tax receipts were not the largest such figures in the last thirty years.

    These figures for 2008 were 15.6 percent (public debt net interest) and 27.8 percent (national debt gross interest).

    The largest percentage figures for these comparisons in the last thirty years occurred in fiscal years 1991 and 1992 (1991 being 29.5 percent for public debt net interest and 43.3 percent for national debt gross interest; 1992 being 29.4 percent for public debt net interest and 43.1 percent for national debt gross interest).

    In 1991 and 1992, however, the interest rates paid on treasury securities were higher than in 2008. If the 1991 approximate average treasury securities rate of 8.0 percent had been paid in 2008, rather than the 4.7 percent that was paid, the figures for 2008 would have been similar to those in 1991 and 1992, at 26.6 percent for public debt net interest and 47.3 percent for national debt gross interest.

    Comparable figures for fiscal year 2009 would be even larger.

    See appendixes 2E and 2F (data for 1981 to 2012).

24. *Budget of the U.S. Government, Fiscal Year 2014*, Analytic Perspectives, 68.

25. *Budget of the U.S. Government, Fiscal Year 2014*, Historical Tables, Tables 3.1, 3.2, 7.1; see data in appendix 2E.

26. See appendix 2F for a calculation of approximate average annual interest rates on the public debt annually from 1981 to 2012. *Budget of the U.S. Government, Fiscal Year 2014*, Historical Tables, Tables 3.1, 7.1.

27. A policy by the Federal Reserve to avoid inflation also makes paying down the national debt more difficult because inflated dollars will not be available to retire larger portions of older fixed-dollar debt.

28. *Budget of the U.S. Government, Fiscal Year 2014*, Historical Tables, Table 7.1. Comparative figures for the public debt's percentage of gross domestic product are: 2012 = 72.6 percent; 1991 to 1997 = minimum of 45.3 percent and maximum of 49.3 percent; other years after 1951 ranged from a low of 23.9 percent (1974) to a high of 61.6 percent (1952). See also appendix 2D (data for 1981 to 2012).

29. National Commission on Fiscal Responsibility and Reform, *The Moment of Truth*, 11.

Chapter 3

30. A brief summary about federal trust funds is found in the 2014 United States Budget documents:

    > The largest trust funds are for retirement and social insurance (e.g., civil service and military retirement, Social Security, Medicare, and unemployment benefits). They are financed largely by social insurance taxes and contributions and payments from the general fund (the main component of Federal funds). However, there are also major trust funds for transportation (highway and airport and airways) and for other programs financed in whole or in part by beneficiary-based, dedicated taxes. *Budget of the U.S. Government, Fiscal Year 2014*, Historical Tables, Introduction, 4.

31. See *Budget of the U.S. Government, Fiscal Year 2014*, Historical Tables, Table 13.1.

32. The 2009 tax rate for Social Security was 12.4 percent of an individual's earned income up to $106,800. A self-employed individual paid the full rate of 12.4 percent. 26 U.S.C.

§ 1401(a) (2009). An employee paid one-half this rate (6.2 percent), with the employee's employer paying the other half. 26 U.S.C. §§ 3103(a), 3111(a) (2009). *Budget of the U.S. Government, Fiscal Year 2014*, Historical Tables, Table 13.1.

33. See discussion in chapter 11 under the topic "Important Features of Social Security and Medicare Taxes."

34. The 2009 tax rate for Medicare was 2.9 percent of an individual's earned income without limit. A self-employed individual paid the full rate of 2.9 percent. 26 U.S.C. § 1401(b) (2009). An employee paid one-half this rate (1.45 percent), with the employee's employer paying the other half. 26 U.S.C. §§ 3103(b), 3111(b) (2009). *Budget of the U.S. Government, Fiscal Year 2014*, Historical Tables, Table 13.1.

35. *Budget of the U.S. Government, Fiscal Year 2014*, Historical Tables, Table 13.1. Borrowings from the Social Security trust funds are the sum of the "invested balances" in the old age and survivors trust fund and the disability insurance trust fund (end fiscal year 1999 = $855 billion; end fiscal year 2009 = $2,504 billion). The United States debt to all federal government accounts at the end of fiscal year 2009 was $4,331 billion. See appendix 3A (data for 1981 to 2012).

36. *Budget of the U.S. Government, Fiscal Year 2014*, Historical Tables, Table 13.1. Borrowings from the Medicare hospital insurance trust fund are the "invested balances" (end fiscal year 1999 = $154 billion; end fiscal year 2009 = $310 billion).

37. National Commission on Fiscal Responsibility and Reform, *The Moment of Truth*, 48.

38. *Budget of the U.S. Government, Fiscal Year 2014*, Historical Tables, Table 13.1.

39. Matt Sedensky, "Leaning Hard on Social Security," *Denver Post*, August 9, 2010, sec. A.

40. National Commission on Fiscal Responsibility and Reform, *The Moment of Truth*, 48.

41. *Budget of the U.S. Government, Fiscal Year 2014*, Historical Tables, Tables 7.1, 13.1. See appendix 3A in this book (data for 1981 to 2012). Borrowings from the Social Security, Medicare, and federal employee retirement trust funds are estimated to account for 93 percent of all borrowings from federal government accounts by the end of fiscal year 2014. *Budget of the U.S. Government, Fiscal Year 2014*, Analytic Perspectives, 70.

42. *Budget of the U.S. Government, Fiscal Year 2014*, Historical Tables, Introduction, 4.

43. The 8 percent figure for Social Security tax receipts being diverted to general governmental expenditures during 2000 to 2009 is calculated by (1) subtracting total cash outgo from the Social Security trust funds ($5,221 billion) from total Social Security tax receipts into those trust funds ($5,695 billion), then (2) dividing that difference ($474 billion) by the total Social Security tax receipts ($5,695 billion). This process assumes that only current-year Social Security tax receipts are available to pay Social Security benefits (no interest income on borrowings from the Social Security trust funds). *Budget of the U.S. Government, Fiscal Year 2014*, Historical Tables, Table 13.1.

44. The percentage of cash income to the Social Security trust funds that was diverted to general governmental expenditures during 2000 to 2009 (24 percent) is calculated by (1) subtracting total cash outgo from the Social Security trust funds ($5,221 billion) from total cash income into those trust funds, including interest on prior borrowings that was not in fact paid ($6,870 billion), then (2) dividing that difference ($1,649 billion) by the total Social Security trust funds cash income ($6,870 billion). *Budget of the U.S. Government, Fiscal Year 2014*, Historical Tables, Table 13.1.

45. For 2001: Economic Growth and Tax Relief Reconciliation Act of 2001, Pub.L.No.107-16, 115 Stat. 38.

   For 2003: Jobs and Growth Tax Relief Reconciliation Act of 2003, Pub.L.No.108-27, 117 Stat. 752.

   As expressed in the House Report on the 2001 Act, a major reason supporting the 2001 tax decreases was the projection of budget surpluses of $5,000 billion over the ten-year period from fiscal years 2001 to 2010. H.R.Rep.No. 107-7, 107th Cong. (2001), 6. Instead, those projected surpluses turned into federal *deficits* of $4,357 from the end of fiscal year 2000 to the end of fiscal year 2008 (figure based on the increase in the national debt during that time period). See appendix 2D for national debt data.

46. I say that excess Social Security tax money was "initially paid" by or on behalf of every individual who had earned income above minuscule amounts because many individuals with small incomes did not end up paying all of their Social Security taxes. This is so because the Earned Income Credit that was and is available to eligible individuals with small incomes provided a credit that could return some or even all Social Security and Medicare taxes paid by those people. 26 U.S.C. § 32(b). See also chapter 25 on current individual income tax credits.

Chapter 4

47. 26 U.S.C. § 68 (2009). See "Deduction for Exemptions Worksheet—Line 42" in the *1040 Forms and Instructions 2009, Package 1040-10* (Internal Revenue Service, 2009).

48. The Internal Revenue Service conducted a National Research Program for the Tax Year 2001. From that research, the IRS estimated $345 billion as the 2001 tax gap for receipts from the individual income tax. Successful enforcement actions reduced this amount to a net tax gap of $290 billion. Fully closing this net tax gap would have increased by 31 percent the $934 billion of individual income taxes reported on all filed returns in tax year 2001 (before credits).

     Although greater simplicity in federal taxes can help to close the tax gap, at least one IRS researcher has concluded that "nonmatchable" income is also a major cause of the tax gap. Nonmatchable income is that income for which there is no cross-check available to the IRS on its existence or accuracy (e.g., income from some self-employed businesses).

     "IRS Updates Tax Gap Estimates," *IRS newsroom article IR-2006-28* (2006); *Publication 1304, Individual Income Tax Returns*, IRS Statistics of Income, Table 1.4, Tax Year 2001; Kim M. Bloomquist, "Trends as Change in Variance: The Case of Tax Noncompliance," *2003 IRS Research Conference*, 2003.

Chapter 5

49. *Budget of the U.S. Government, Fiscal Year 2014*, Historical Tables, Tables 2.1, 2.4. See appendix 9A in this book for these data and other receipts data used in this chapter. The 91 percent for fiscal year 2008 is the rounded sum of 45.4 percent (individual income tax), 12.0 percent (corporation income tax), 26.1 percent (Social Security tax), and 7.7 percent (Medicare tax).

50. Joseph Bankman and David A. Weisbach, *The Superiority of an Ideal Consumption Tax over an Ideal Income Tax* (Chicago: University of Chicago Law School, John M. Olin Law & Economics Working Paper Series, Working Paper No. 251; and Stanford, CA: Stanford Law School, John M. Olin Program in Law and Economics, Working Paper No. 310, 2005).

51. Edward J. McCaffery, *Fair Not Flat: How to Make the Tax System Better and Simpler* (Chicago: University of Chicago Press, 2002), 15.

52. See appendix 9A, table 9A.1.

53. See appendix 14B and table 14B.1.

54. See calculation in appendix 5A.

55. McCaffery, *Fair Not Flat*, 97.

56. 26 U.S.C. § 2001 (2009).

57. 26 U.S.C. §§ 2501–2502 (2009).

58. 26 U.S.C. § 9503 (2009).

59. 26 U.S.C. §§ 4261–4282, § 9502 (2009).

60. 26 U.S.C. §§ 4251–4254 (2009).

61. 26 U.S.C. §§ 5701–5763 (tobacco); 26 U.S.C. §§ 5001–5418 (distilled spirits, wines, and beer) (2009).

62. 26 U.S.C. §§ 4001–4003 (luxury passenger automobiles); 26 U.S.C. §§ 4401–4405 (wagers); 26 U.S.C. §§ 4161–4162 (sport fishing equipment and bows and arrows) (2009).

63. See the 2010/2012 platform of the Constitution Party, especially the section entitled "Taxes," found at http://www.constitutionparty.com.

64. Neal Boortz and John Linder, *The Fair Tax Book: Saying Goodbye to the Income Tax and the IRS* (New York: Regan Books, 2005).

65. Duard Lawley, *Common Sense Tax Reform* (Bloomington, IN: AuthorHouse, 2005), ch. 2.

66. McCaffery, *Fair Not Flat*, p. 6 and ch. 6.

67. *Budget of the U.S. Government, Fiscal Year 2014*, Historical Tables, Tables 2.1, 2.5. See appendix 9A in this book for these data and the other receipts data used in this chapter (data for 2008 and 2001).

68. See, for example, "From Freedom to Fascism," a video presentation shown on some Public Broadcasting System channels in early 2009.

69. See endnote 67 for data.

70. The heavy reliance of the Constitution Party's platform on tariffs and excise taxes to fund federal government spending does not specify how these taxes can even come close to covering funding just for national defense, leaving nothing for clearly constitutional governmental operations like operating the federal courts system. See its platform at www.constitutionparty.com.

Chapter 6

71. *Webster's New Universal Unabridged Dictionary* (n.p.: Barnes & Noble Publishing, 2003), 1896.

72. 26 U.S.C. § 163(h) (2009).

73. 26 U.S.C. § 170 (2009).

74. 26 U.S.C. § 23 (2009)

75. National Commission on Fiscal Responsibility and Reform, *The Moment of Truth*, 28.

Chapter 7

76. In fiscal year 2008, federal tax receipts came from four categories of sources, as follows (with percent of total receipts of $2,524 billion):

    (1) Taxes on individual income [income tax, Social Security tax, Medicare tax, and a few other taxes] ($2,046 billion) (81.1 percent).
    (2) Taxes on corporation net profit ($304 billion) (12.0 percent).
    (3) Excise taxes ($67 billion) (2.7 percent).
    (4) Other ($106 billion) (4.2 percent). The "other" category includes the taxes on estates and gifts ($29 billion) (1.1 percent).

    Budget of the U.S. Government, Fiscal Year 2014, Historical Tables, Tables 2.1, 2.5. See appendix 9A.

77. The 2001 and 2003 tax reforms contained the one-year provisions. The December 2010 tax compromise is the Tax Relief, Unemployment Insurance Reauthorization, and Job Creation Act of 2010, Pub.L.No.111-312, 124 Stat. 3296, § 101(a); the 2012 fiscal cliff tax compromise is the American Taxpayer Relief Act of 2012, Pub.L.No. 112-240, 126 Stat. 2313, § 101.

78.   26 U.S.C. § 1(a)–(d), (i) (2009).

79.   26 U.S.C. § 1(h) (2009).

80.   26 U.S.C. § 1(h)(11) (2009).

81.   For example, twenty-one Worksheets are present in the *1040 Forms and Instructions 2009, Package 1040-10* (Internal Revenue Service, 2009), not including the tax computation worksheet.

82.   26 U.S.C. § 68 (2009). The 2001 Tax Act adopted a stepwise schedule over time for decreasing the limits on itemized deductions for individuals with large incomes. By 2010, there were no limits on itemized deductions. 26 U.S.C. § 68(f)–(g) (2009).

83.   "Itemized Deductions Worksheet—Line 29" in the *1040 Forms and Instructions 2009, Package 1040-10* (Internal Revenue Service, 2009).

84.   "Social Security Benefits Worksheet—Lines 20a and 20b" in the *1040 Forms and Instructions 2009*, Package 1040-10 (Internal Revenue Service, 2009); 26 U.S.C. § 86 (2009).

85.   See 2009 Form 1040 Schedule A, lines 10, 21, and 26.

86.   See 2009 Form 1040, lines 49 and 52 (Form 8839) respectively; 26 U.S.C. §§ 25A, 23 (2009).

87.   Revenue Act of 1978, Pub.L.No. 95-600, 92 Stat 2763, § 421(a); S.Rep.No.95-1263, 95th Cong. (1978), 200-205; 26 U.S.C. §§ 55–59 (2009).

88.   The Internal Revenue Code uses the terms "earnings" or "earnings and profits" rather than "net profit" in connection with corporation taxable income. See, e.g., 26 U.S.C. §§ 312, 531, 535 (2009).

89.   26 U.S.C. § 11 (tax on corporations); § 1 (tax on individuals) (2009).

90.   26 U.S.C. §§ 611–617 (2009).

91.   26 U.S.C. §§ 2501–2502 (2009).

92.   26 U.S.C. §§ 2001(c), 2210 (2009).

Chapter 8

93. The Internal Revenue Code is huge. One printed version of the code uses more than 5,000 pages for income, estate, gift, and employment taxes, including statutory historic notes. Federal excise taxes occupy nearly 600 additional pages. And these numbers do not include regulations issued by the Internal Revenue Service or case law interpreting the tax statutes. *Internal Revenue Code, Winter 2009 Ed.* (Chicago: CCH, 2009).

94. In fiscal year 2008, total federal receipts were $2,524 billion. Receipts from the five groups of taxes covered in this chapter were $2,331 billion (92 percent of total receipts). By tax group, they were:

    (1) Individual income ($1,146 billion).
    (2) Social Security ($658 billion).
    (3) Medicare ($194 billion).
    (4) Corporation net profit ($304 billion).
    (5) Estates and gifts ($29 billion).

    Budget of the U.S. Government, Fiscal Year 2014, Historical Tables, Tables 2.1, 2.4, 2.5. See also appendix 9A.

Chapter 9

95. Some people assert that the Sixteenth Amendment is invalid. Federal court cases disagree. *Brushaber v. Union Pacific Railroad Co.*, 240 U.S. 1 (1916); *United States v. Foster*, 789 F.2d 457, 462-463 (7th Circuit 1986).

    Other people assert that filing income tax returns and paying income taxes is "voluntary." As shown in appendix 9B, these assertions are false.

96. In fiscal year 2008, Social Security tax receipts were $658 billion and Medicare tax receipts were $194 billion, for a total of $852 billion. This $852 billion is 34 percent of the total federal receipts of $2,524 billion in that fiscal year. *Budget of the U.S. Government, Fiscal Year 2014*, Historical Tables, Tables 2.1, 2.4. See appendix 9A in this book.

97. *Budget of the U.S. Government, Fiscal Year 2014*, Historical Tables, Table 13.1. Receipts from the Medicare tax are allocated to the Medicare hospital insurance trust fund, not to general Medicare outlays.

98. In fiscal year 2008, individual income tax receipts were $1,146 billion, while total federal receipts were $2,524 billion and all federal receipts other than Social Security and Medicare tax receipts were $1,671 billion. The individual income tax receipts were respectively 45 percent and 69 percent of those total figures. *Budget of the U.S. Government, Fiscal Year 2014*, Historical Tables, Table 2.1. See appendix 9A in this book.

99. 26 U.S.C. § 61 (2009).

100. 26 U.S.C. §§ 101–139 (2009)

101. 26 U.S.C. §§ 1(a)–(d), (i) (2009).

102. American Taxpayer Relief Act of 2012, Pub.L.No. 112-240, 126 Stat. 2313, §101.

103. 26 U.S.C. § 1(h) (2009). The general sets of rates on most long-term capital gains and all qualified dividends income have a maximum 15 percent rate no matter how large this income (2009 law).

Chapter 10

104. See, e.g., *1040 Forms and Instructions 2009, Package 1040-10* (Internal Revenue Service, 2009), 89. 26 U.S.C. § 1(a)–(d) (2009).

105. See calculations in appendix 10E for all four filing categories (single, married filing jointly, married filing separately, and head of household). Peculiar and rare circumstances exist for married individuals with self-employment income where the marginal total federal tax rate is even larger at 44.80 percent, but this total rate can be applicable only to a small slice of income that is less than $4,000.

106. See calculations in appendix 10E.

107. Using the methodology of appendix 10E, the calculation of the 41.75 percent marginal tax rate is:
    Income tax rate = 39.6 percent
    Add effective Medicare tax rate = 2.68 percent
    Subtract allowed deduction = 0.53 percent
    Result = 41.75 percent

108. The highest marginal tax rate for wage earners is simply obtained by adding their maximum income tax rate (39.6 percent) and their Medicare tax rate (1.45 percent) (equals 41.05 percent).

109. Appendix 10F shows by example the pattern of marginal total federal tax rates that occurs for different income levels under 2009 tax law with its graduated income tax rates. Appendix 10F also compares that pattern to the pattern of marginal total federal tax rates that would occur under the FAST Plan and under a typical flat-tax proposal.

110. National Commission on Fiscal Responsibility and Reform, *The Moment of Truth*, 28.

111. Steve Forbes of *Forbes* magazine fame and a former presidential candidate has long advocated a flat tax, but one that ignores the total tax effect of the flat income tax rate combined with Social Security and Medicare tax rates. His flat-tax proposal features zero tax on capital gains, interest, and dividends. Steve Forbes, *Flat Tax Revolution: Using a Postcard to Abolish the IRS* (Washington, DC: Regnery Publishing, 2005), 60–63.

112. For full data, see appendix 14A, tables 14A.2 and 14A.4.

113. Calculations for a standard income tax rate on individuals are found in appendix 10A.

114. Tax Reform Act of 1986, Pub.L.No. 99-514, 100 Stat. 2085, §§ 101(a) and 302. I say "nominal" graduated income tax rates of 15 percent and 28 percent because other provisions in the Tax Reform Act of 1986 effectively increased the tax on larger incomes by phasing out the 15 percent rate on the initial amounts of those larger incomes. See H.R.Rep.No. 99-841, 99th Cong., (1986), II-1 to II-6 (Conf.Rep.).

115. Increases in the national debt in 1988 and later years are shown in appendix 2D. Receipts from the individual income tax for the same time period are shown in appendix 10C.

116. See appendix 2C, table 2C.1.

117. See appendix 2C, table 2C.1.

118. See appendix 1C for on-budget outlays and appendix 2A for total and on-budget deficits (data for 1981 to 2012).

119. The 34.4 percent standard rate is calculated by adding $342 billion to the $2,000 billion target shown in line 14 of table 10A.1 in appendix 10A and dividing that total by the estimated taxable income of $6,807 billion in line 11 of table 10A.1.

120. For an example of the contention that lower tax rates will actually increase tax receipts, see Forbes, *Flat Tax Revolution*, 71.

121. See appendix 10B (summary of significant tax rate changes 1981–2012).

122. See Kevin A. Hassett and Kathryn Newmark, "Taxation and Business Behavior: A Review of the Recent Literature" in *Fundamental Tax Reform—Issues, Choices and Implications*, ed. John W. Diamond and George R. Zodrow (Cambridge, MA: MIT Press, 2008), 202.

123. The increase of $3,322 billion in the national debt from 2001 to 2007 is determined by subtracting the national debt at the end of fiscal year 2007 ($8,951 billion) from the national debt at the end of fiscal year 2000 (beginning of fiscal year 2001) ($5,629 billion). See appendix 2D (data for 1981 to 2012).

124. In constant dollars, individual income tax receipts were $826 billion in fiscal year 2009 and $802 billion in fiscal year 2010, as compared to $1,093 billion in fiscal year 2007 and $1,145 billion in fiscal year 2000. *Budget of the U.S. Government, Fiscal Year 2014*, Historical Tables, Tables 1.3, 2.1. See appendix 10C, table 10C.1.

Chapter 11

125. *Social Security tax*: 26 U.S.C. §§ 1401(a), 1402, 3101(a), 3111(a), 3121 (2009). If you search for the "Social Security tax" in some versions of the United States Code, you may not find it. What we all know as the Social Security tax is found in two places:

    (1) In a chapter entitled "tax on self-employment income," under "rate of tax" for "old-age, survivors, and disability insurance" [§ 1401(a)]; and
    (2) In a chapter entitled "Federal Insurance Contributions Act"(hence the familiar "**FICA**" on wage statements), also under "rate of tax" for "old-age, survivors, and disability insurance" [§§ 3101(a), 3111(a)].

    Medicare tax: 26 U.S.C. §§ 1401(b), 1402, 3101(b), 3111(b), 3121 (2009). As with the Social Security tax, if you search for the "Medicare tax" in some versions of the United States Code, you may not find it. Like the Social Security tax, what we all know as the Medicare tax is found in two places:

    (1) In a chapter entitled "tax on self-employment income," under "rate of tax" for "hospital insurance" [§ 1401(b)]; and
    (2) In a chapter entitled "Federal Insurance Contributions Act," also under rate of tax" for "hospital insurance" [§§ 3101(b), 3111(b)].

    When first enacted effective in 1966, the Medicare tax also ended at the Social Security tax cutoff. Social Security Amendments of 1965, Pub.L.No. 89-97, 79 Stat. 286, § 321.

Congress adopted the current approach effective in 1994. 26 U.S.C. §§ 1402(b)(1), 3121(b)(1) (2009); Omnibus Budget Reconciliation Act of 1993, Pub.L.No.103-66, 107 Stat. 312, §13207.

126. 26 U.S.C. §§ 1402(b)(2) [$400], 3121(x) [$1,000] (2009).

127. Social Security tax rates are found at 26 U.S.C. § 1401(a) (self-employment income) and §§ 3101(a) and 3111(a) (wages) (2009). The official parlance in the Social Security Act for the maximum amount subject to the Social Security tax is the "**contribution and benefit base**." 42 U.S.C. § 430 (2009); see also 26 U.S.C. §§ 1402(b)(2) and 3121(a)(1) (2009) and 2009 Form 1040, Schedule SE.

128. 26 U.S.C. §§ 1401(b), 3101(a) (2009).

129. 26 U.S.C. §§ 1402(b)(1), 3121(a)(1) (2009).

130. 26 U.S.C. §§ 3101, 3102, 3111 (2009).

131. 26 U.S.C. §§ 3101, 3102, 3111 (2009).

132. Tax Relief, Unemployment Insurance Reauthorization, and Job Creation Act of 2010, Pub.L.No.111-312, 124 Stat. 3296, § 601(a) [percentage reductions in Social Security tax], § 601(e) [transfers from the general fund to cover lost Social Security tax receipts].

133. Temporary Payroll Tax Cut Continuation Act of 2011, Pub.L.No. 112-78, 125 Stat. 1281–1282.

134. See Charles Krauthammer, "Cliffjumping with Barack," *The Denver Post*, November 30, 2012, sec. A. We can roughly calculate what Social Security tax receipts would have been in fiscal year 2012 without the 2.0 percentage-point rate reduction. The ratio between the normal 12.4 percent rate and the lower 10.4 percent rate is 1.2. Multiplying actual Social Security tax receipts ($570 billion) by 1.2 gives $684 billion, which is much closer to the $762 billion paid for benefits than actual Social Security tax receipts. *Budget of the U.S. Government, Fiscal Year 2014*, Historical Tables, Table 13.1.

135. American Taxpayer Relief Act of 2012, Pub.L.No. 112-240, 126 Stat. 2313.

136. 26 U.S.C. § 1401 (2009).

137. Tax Relief, Unemployment Insurance Reauthorization, and Job Creation Act of 2010, Pub.L.No.111-312, 124 Stat. 3296, § 601(a) [% reductions in Social Security tax], § 601(e) [transfers from general fund to cover lost Social Security tax receipts].

138. Temporary Payroll Tax Cut Continuation Act of 2011, Pub.L.No. 112-78, 125 Stat. 1281–1282.

139. American Taxpayer Relief Act of 2012, Pub.L.No. 112-240, 126 Stat. 2313.

140. 26 U.S.C. § 1402(a)(12) (2009). The rule that allows a self-employed individual to subtract the sum of one-half the Social Security and Medicare tax rates applied against business net profit in calculating earned income that is subject to the self-employment tax is "in lieu" of deducting one-half the self-employment taxes as a trade or business deduction under 26 U.S.C. § 164(f) (2009).

141. 26 U.S.C. § 164(f)(1) (2009).

142. *Budget of the U.S. Government, Fiscal Year 2014*, Historical Tables, Table 13.1.

143. See Matt Sedensky, "Leaning Hard on Social Security," *The Denver Post*, August 9, 2010, sec. A.

144. The 2.9 percent rate Medicare tax alone provided enough money for payment of hospital insurance benefits in nearly all years in the last thirty years up to fiscal year 2003. Beginning in fiscal year 2003, the payment of benefits required use of some other income owed to the hospital insurance trust fund, such as the payment of interest on US borrowings from this trust fund. *Budget of the U.S. Government, Fiscal Year 2014*, Historical Tables, Table 13.1.

145. Patient Protection and Affordable Care Act, Pub.L.No.111-148, 124 Stat. 119 (2010), § 9015.

146. 26 U.S.C. § 164(f) (2009).

147. See calculations in appendix 10E, example 1.

148. See calculations in appendix 10E, example 2.

149. Under a standard-rate income tax within current law, all employees would still pay the Medicare tax of 1.45 percent, which would add to the standard rate.

150. Appendix 11A shows the calculations of the marginal total federal tax rates for employees and self-employed individuals using a standard-rate income tax but otherwise no changes in 2009 federal tax law.

151. Using the Social Security tax as the example, the effective tax rate for self-employed individuals is 11.45 percent (calculated as 0.9235 times 12.4 percent), which is 1.85 times the effective tax rate of 6.2 percent for employees.

152. Under the accounting adjustment, increased total taxable wages income includes the amount of Social Security and Medicare taxes paid by the employer on the original wages. For wages less than the Social Security tax cutoff, a straightforward formula can be used for calculating the effective rates for Social Security and Medicare taxes on the increased total taxable wages. The formula and its calculation steps are shown below. In this formula,

- **W** represents the original wages.
- (**W + 0.0765W**) represents the increased total wages.
- 15.3 percent represents the full combined Social Security and Medicare taxes rate on the original wages **W.**
- **R** represents the equivalent combined Social Security and Medicare taxes rate on the increased total wages (**W + 0.0765W**).

The formula in calculation steps is:

(1) R (W + 0.0765W) = 0.153 W
(2) R = 0.153/1.0765 = 0.14213
(3) R as a percent of the 15.3% combined rate
    = 0.14213/0.153 = 0.9290 = 92.90%

Chapter 12

153. US Constitution, Amendment XVI (1913).

154. *Webster's New Universal Unabridged Dictionary* (n.p.: Barnes & Noble Publishing, 2003), 967.

155. 26 U.S.C. § 61 (2009). The fifteen listed items of income are: (1) Compensation for services, including fees, commissions, fringe benefits, and similar items; (2) Gross income derived from business; (3) Gains derived from dealings in property; (4) Interest; (5)

Rents; (6) Royalties; (7) Dividends; (8) Alimony and separate maintenance payments; (9) Annuities; (10) Income from life insurance and endowment contracts; (11) Pensions; (12) Income from discharge of indebtedness; (13) Distributive share of partnership gross income; (14) Income in respect of a decedent; and (15) Income from an interest in an estate or trust. (In the original, these numbered items are on separate lines.)

156. The Internal Revenue Code has at least one exception to the general statement that income does not exist unless an event occurs in which a person receives money or other new value. Under 26 U.S.C. § 1256 (2009), certain market-related contracts held by the taxpayer are treated as if they were sold for their fair market value on the last business day of the taxable year even if they were not, in fact, sold.

157. McCaffery, *Fair Not Flat*, p. 6 and ch. 6.
McCaffery's "Basic Plan" is stated on page 6 of his book:

- Change the inconsistent income tax to a consistent spending tax by granting an unlimited deduction for savings and making other logical corrections.
- Repeal the so-called death tax.
- Keep tax rates progressive.
- Reduce the paperwork burden that most Americans now face.

McCaffery's four simple steps to converting the current income tax to a true consumption tax are stated on page 97 of his book:

1. Include borrowing as income.
2. Allow unlimited deductions for contributions to savings accounts; tax withdrawals from such accounts.
3. Repeal the special capital gains rate.
4. Repeal the gift and estate tax.

In these proposals, the term "savings accounts" is meant broadly to include all savings and investments. McCaffery proposes a three-level progressive-rate tax on income as generally defined, with the above modifications (thereby creating a consumption rather than income tax). The first level would be zero or very low tax on spending on life's necessities; the second level would be a second, higher-rate tax on spending on ordinary consumer items; and a third level would be an even higher rate on spending on luxuries.

158. 26 U.S.C. § 102 (gifts and inheritances) and § 117 (qualified scholarships) (2009).

159. 26 U.S.C. § 103 (2009).

160. See data in appendix 12A, table 12A.1.

Chapter 13

161. U.S.C. § 61(a)(1) (2009). This section does not use the term "wages," but describes this kind of income as "Compensation for services, including fees, commissions, fringe benefits, and similar items."

162. *Publication 1304, Individual Income Tax Returns*, IRS Statistics of Income, Table 1.4, tax year 2007. See appendix 12A in this book.

163. 26 U.S.C. § 3402 (2009).

164. 26 U.S.C. § 274(a) (2009).

165. 26 U.S.C. § 106(a) (2009).

166. Free use of a Cadillac sedan would not be a "qualified transportation fringe" that is excluded from a wage earner's gross income under 26 U.S.C. § 132 (2009). Vehicle fringe benefits can also be wages on which income tax withholding may be required. See 26 U.S.C. § 3402(s) (2009).

167. 26 U.S.C. § 119 (2009).

168. 26 U.S.C. § 61(a)(2) (2009).

169. 26 U.S.C. § 63(a) (2009).

170. 26 U.S.C. § 162(a) (2009). Section 62 of 26 U.S.C. reinforces the deduction for trade and business expenses found in § 162(a) by defining an individual's "adjusted gross income" as being gross income minus "deductions allowed by this chapter (...) which are attributable to a trade or business carried on by the taxpayer, if such trade or business does not consist of the performance of services by the taxpayer as an employee."

171. 26 U.S.C. § 701 (2009).

172. 26 U.S.C. § 702(a), 703(a) (2009).

173. 26 U.S.C. § 61(a)(13) (2009).

174. 26 U.S.C. §§ 1361–1363 (2009).

175. 26 U.S.C. § 1366 (2009).

176. 26 U.S.C. § 61(a)(4) (2009).

177. Paul Ryan, *A Roadmap for America's Future* (Washington, DC: January 2010).

178. In tax year 2007, the group of taxpayers who reported adjusted gross incomes of $100,000 or more accounted for 63 percent of all taxable interest income, as compared to 93 percent of taxable net capital gains and 77 percent of ordinary dividends. That same group accounted for only 53 percent of all reported gross income. Taxable interest comprised only 3 percent of all reported gross income for all taxpayers in 2007. *SOI Tax Stats—Individual Tax Returns*, Internal Revenue Service, Table 1, tax year 2007. See appendix 14A, tables 14A.3 and 14A.4.

179. 26 U.S.C. § 103 (2009).

180. See 2009 Form 1040, line 8b.

181. Respectively 26 U.S.C. § 61(a)(5), (6), (15) and § 74 (2009).

182. 26 U.S.C. § 61(a)(12) (2009).

183. 26 U.S.C. § 117 (2009).

Chapter 14

184. U.S.C. § 1221(a) (2009).

185. 26 U.S.C. § 1001 (2009).

186. 26 U.S.C. § 1012 (2009). For example, if an individual gave an antique car rather than cash as the price for buying a real estate lot, the basis of the lot would be the value of the car.

187. 26 U.S.C. § 1016 (2009).

188. 26 U.S.C. § 1001 (2009).

189. 26 U.S.C. § 1222 (2009).

190. 26 U.S.C. § 1(h) (2009). Before 2003, the maximum rate for long-term capital gains was 20 percent. See Jobs and Growth Tax Relief Reconciliation Act of 2003, Pub.L.No.108-27, 117 Stat. 752, § 301(a)(2). Maximum rates were also higher historically, at 28 percent, after the Tax Reform Act of 1986. See H.R.Rep.No.105-148, 105th Cong. 1339–1342 (1997), relating to the Taxpayer Relief Act of 1997, Pub.L.No.105-34, 111 Stat 788, §311(a), which changed the 28 percent rate to the 20 percent rate.

191. 26 U.S.C. § 1(h) (2009).

192. American Taxpayer Relief Act of 2012, Pub.L.No. 112-240, 126 Stat. 2313, § 102.

193. E.g., 26 U.S.C. § 1256 (2009) (long-term capital gain treatment applies to 60 percent of the gain or loss with respect to certain contracts, such as regulated futures contracts).

194. As an example of how current tax law on capital gains fails the simplicity test, look at the Schedule D Tax Worksheet in the 2009 Form 1040 Instructions.

195. *SOI Tax Stats—Individual Tax Returns*, Internal Revenue Service, Table 1, tax year 2007 and tax year 2000. See appendix 14A (data for tax years 2007 and 2000). In the IRS data, "net capital gains" is the sum of both short-term and long-term capital gains and losses. *Publication 1304, Individual Income Tax Returns*, IRS Statistics of Income, Section 4, Explanation of Terms, Sale of Capital Assets—Net Gain or Loss, tax year 2007.

196. See the data in appendix 14A, tables 14A.3 and 14A.4.

197. See the data in appendix 14A, tables 14A.3, 14A.4, 14A.7, and 14A.8 and in appendix 14B, table 14B.1.

198. The calculations in this example of federal income taxes owed by Surgeon S and Investor I are shown in appendix 14C.

199. See Medicare Eligibility Tool at http://www.medicare.gov/MedicareEligibility/home.asp ?dest=NAVHomeGeneralEnrollment#TabTop.

200. All data discussed in this paragraph and the following paragraphs are found in appendix 14B (data for tax years 2007 and 2000). *Publication 1304, Individual Income Tax Returns*, IRS Statistics of Income, Table 1.1, tax years 2007 and 2000.

201. See data in appendix 14B.

202. 26 U.S.C. §1(a)-(d) (2009).

203. 26 U.S.C. § 1202 (2009).

204. The Fiscal Commission's 2010 report recommends that capital gains be taxed the same as ordinary income, although it also suggests an alternative approach where a portion of capital gains is excluded from income, thereby effectively reducing the maximum tax rate on that income. *The Moment of Truth*, 31. This alternative approach is what existed before the Tax Reform Act of 1986. See appendix 10B. Because the Fiscal Commission report still assumes **progressive tax rates**, the problem of bunched capital gains income will remain under its recommendation. That problem will lead to pressure again to have lower actual or effective tax rates for long-term capital gains. Any such rates would again increase complexity in the tax code.

205. H.R.Rep.No. 108-94, 108th Cong. (2003), 29, relating to the Jobs and Growth Tax Relief Reconciliation Act of 2003, Pub.L.No. 108-27, 117 Stat. 752.

206. H.R.Rep.No. 105-148, 105th Cong. (1997), 340–341 relating to the Taxpayer Relief Act of 1997, Pub.L.No.105-34, 111 Stat. 788. Appendix 14F of this book contains the full text of the "Reasons for Change" in the 1997 House Report that gives reasons for decreasing the maximum tax rate on long-term capital gains from 28 percent to 20 percent.

207. William A. Klein, Joseph Bankman, and Daniel N. Shaviro, *Federal Income Taxation, Thirteenth Edition* (New York: Aspen, 2003), 642-643. See also H.R.Rep.No. 105-148, 105th Cong. (1997), 340–341.

208. Measuring the "lock-in" caused by a tax on capital gains is at best an uncertain exercise. Appendix 14E looks at one potential measurement by comparing recent changes in the capital gains tax rates to net capital gains reported by taxpayers. In my opinion, these data are inconclusive in showing whether or not decreases in those rates diminish lock-in of capital assets.

209. 26 U.S.C. § 1222 (2009). This section not only defines short-term and long-term capital gains and losses, but also defines seven different combinations of short-term and long-term capital gains and losses. These combinations allow some losses to offset gains, thereby reducing the taxable gains. Under a standard tax rate for all capital gains, only capital gains and losses would remain. Just two combinations of capital gains and losses would be necessary—net capital gains and net capital losses.

210. 42 U.S.C. § 430 (2009).

211. In a recession, indexing could also *decrease* the adjusted basis. Decreased value is what occurred in the Great Recession for many recently purchased houses.

212. Another asset of an individual that might increase greatly in value over time is the individual's retirement account. Most likely the money placed in the retirement account was subtracted from gross income or contributed by an employer. In either case, the money distributed from the account will be taxable as ordinary income, even though most of that money may have resulted from capital gains on corporate shares or other investments held in the account.

213. 26 U.S.C. § 121 (2009).

214. Before 1997, Congress allowed a homeowner to buy another principal residence of equal or greater value within two years after the first was sold without having to pay any tax on a capital gain from the first residence. The adjusted basis of the first residence was carried over to the second residence. 26 U.S.C. § 1034 (repealed in 1997). This rule allowed a homeowner to move to a different place without having to pay a capital gains tax that would reduce the amount of money available to buy a comparable residence.

Chapter 15

215. 26 U.S.C. § 1(h)(11) (2009); Jobs and Growth Tax Relief Reconciliation Act of 2003, Pub.L.No. 108-27, 117 Stat. 752, § 302(a).

216. H.R.Rep.No.1337, 83rd Cong. (1954), citation found in United States Code Congressional and Administrative News, 83rd Congress—Second Session, 1954, Volume 3, p. 4030.

217. David L. Brumbaugh, "Federal Business Taxation: The Current System, Its Effects, and Options for Reform" in *Taxation and Tax Policy Issues*, ed. Brian L. Yashov (New York: Nova Science, 2007), 51–52, 55.
    The March 2013 Fiscal Year 2014 Budget Resolution of the United States House of Representatives appears to adopt this idea that all business income is the same no matter the legal form in which it is obtained (available at http://www.budget.house.gov/uploadedfiles/fy14budget.pdf). That resolution describes the current total tax on dividends income as 55 percent (p. 23). Presumably the 55 percent figure is the sum of the maximum 35 percent corporation tax on taxable earnings and the maximum 20 percent individual income tax on qualified dividends. This broad 55 percent figure assumes (1) that all dividends come only from corporation earnings that are actually taxed at 35 percent and

(2) that corporations are solely conduits of business income to their shareholders without any separate tax obligations, even though they are "persons" for most legal purposes (see chapter 29).

218. Generally, the amount paid for repurchase of corporate stock is not a business expense deduction and so the amount comes out of earnings, thereby reducing the earnings available for dividends. 26 U.S.C. § 162(k) (2009).

    A study on how oil and gas corporations were spending their unexpectedly large profits from a rapid surge in petroleum prices during 2008 showed that half of the profits were used to buy back stock. See "Big Oil Cash Goes to Stock Buybacks," *Rocky Mountain News*, July 22, 2008. These purchases increase the value of each share of the remaining stock because there is less total stock in the market. Cynics could assert that this is a way for corporate executives with stock options to increase their compensations by later selling their optioned stock at the increased value.

219. 26 U.S.C. § 172 (2009) (allowing carryover and carryback of losses); see also 26 U.S.C. § 382 (2009).

    The 2010 annual report of General Electric provides an example of circumstances where no federal corporation income tax is likely to be owed, yet $5.2 billion in dividends were paid to shareholders. General Electric Corp. *2010 Annual Report*, 33 (dividends) and 101 (Note 14 to financial statements showing income tax *benefits* exceeding GE's US tax expense).

220. *SOI Tax Stats—Individual Tax Returns*, Internal Revenue Service, Table 1, tax year 2007. See appendix 14A in this book, table 14A.3.

221. The Fiscal Commission's 2010 report recommends that dividends be taxed the same as ordinary income, although it also suggests an alternative approach where a portion of dividends is excluded from income, thereby effectively reducing the maximum tax rate on that income. *The Moment of Truth*, 31. This alternative approach would increase complexity in the tax code.

Chapter 16

222. 26 U.S.C. §§ 1401(a), 3101(a), and 3111(a) (2009).

223. In this chapter, I refer only to Social Security benefits (and the Social Security tax). Railroad retirement benefits are generally treated also as Social Security benefits. The Social Security analysis is equally applicable to those benefits.

224. See, e.g., "Point/Counterpoint," *Denver Post*, May 18, 2010, sec. B.

225. Social Security Amendments of 1983, Pub.L.No. 98-21, 97 Stat. 65, § 121; 26 U.S.C. § 86 (2009).

226. S.Rep.No. 98-23, 98th Cong. (1978), 25–26.

227. The Senate Report that relates to the Social Security Amendments of 1983, Pub.L.No. 98-21, 97 Stat. 65, contains a concise summary of the basic approach used to determine what portion of an individual's Social Security benefits would be included in gross income:

> Social Security benefits that will be included in the gross income of a taxpayer for a taxable year will be limited to the lesser of (1) one-half of the Social Security benefits received, or (2) one-half of the excess of the sum of the taxpayer's adjusted gross income, interest on obligations exempt from tax, and one-half of the Social Security benefits received, over the appropriate base amount.

S.Rep.No. 98-23, 98th Cong. (1983), 27.

228. S.Rep.No. 98-23, 98th Cong. (1983), 28–29.

229. H.R.Rep.No. 103-111, 103rd Cong. (1993) relating to the Omnibus Budget Reconciliation Act of 1993, Pub.L.No. 103-66, 107 Stat. 312.

230. Omnibus Budget Reconciliation Act of 1993, Pub.L.No.103-66, 107 Stat. 312, § 13215, especially subsections (a)(2) and (c)(2). See 26 U.S.C. § 86(a)(2) and (c)(2) (2009).

231. H.R.Rep.No. 103-111, 103rd Cong. (1993), 654.

232. H.R.Rep.No. 103-213, 103rd Cong. (1993), 594–595 (Conf.Rep.).

233. See "Social Security Benefit Worksheet—Lines 20a and 20b" in the *1040 Forms and Instructions 2009, Package 1040-10* (Internal Revenue Service, 2009). A copy of this worksheet is found in appendix 16A.

234. The inflation adjustment in the text for $32,000 in 1984 up to 2009 is calculated from the "Composite Deflator" found in Table 1.3 of the Historical Tables, *Budget of the U.S. Government, Fiscal Year 2014*. That number is used in Table 1.3 to convert annual current dollars into Constant (FY 2005) Dollars (the "Deflator" for 2005 being 1.0000). The adjustment calculation is first to calculate the ratio between the Composite Deflator of

the later year and the Composite Deflator of the initial year; then apply that ratio to the dollar amount in the initial year. Here are the numbers:

> 1984 Composite Deflator = 0.5677
> 2009 Composite Deflator = 1.1073
> Ratio, 2009 over 1984: = 1.1073/0.5677 = 1.9505
> Ratio applied: = 1.9505 x $32,000 = $62,420 (rounded to ten)

235. Using the Composite Deflator method of the previous note, the inflation adjustment for $44,000 in 1994 up to 2009 is:

> 1994 Composite Deflator = 0.7782
> 2009 Composite Deflator = 1.1073
> Ratio, 2009 over 1994: = 1.1073/0.7782 = 1.4229
> Ratio applied: = 1.4229 x $44,000 = $62,610 (rounded to ten)

236. *Publication 1304, Individual Income Tax Returns*, IRS Statistics of Income, Table 1.4, tax year 2007, tax year 2000, and tax year 1993. See appendix 12A in this book (data for tax years 2007, 2000, and 1993).

Chapter 17

237. 26 U.S.C. §§ 3101 and 3111 (2009) (wages subject to Social Security and Medicare taxes); 26 U.S.C. §§ 1401 and 1402 (2009) (self-employment earned income subject to Social Security and Medicare taxes).

238. 26 U.S.C. § 3121(a)(5) (2009).

239. 26 U.S.C. § 3121(a)(5) (2009).

240. 26 U.S.C. §§ 1402(a) and 162 (2009); see 26 U.S.C. § 219 (2009).

Chapter 18

241. 26 U.S.C. §§ 101–140 (2009).

242. 26 U.S.C. § 102 (2009).

243. 26 U.S.C. § 109 (2009).

244. 26 U.S.C. § 117 (2009).

245. 26 U.S.C. § 105 (2009).

246. 26 U.S.C. § 106 (2009).

247. 26 U.S.C. § 129 (2009).

248. See 26 U.S.C. § 6051(a)(8) (2009). *Instructions for Forms W-2 and W-3* (Internal Revenue Service, 2009), 9.

249. 26 U.S.C. § 3121(a)(5) (2009).

250. 26 U.S.C. § 103 (2009).

251. 26 U.S.C. § 121 (2009) (qualifying rules exist that allow limited capital gains from the sale of a principal residence to be excluded from taxable income).

252. 26 U.S.C. § 131 (2009).

253. US Constitution, Amendment X (1791):

    The powers not delegated to the United States by the Constitution, nor prohibited by it to the States, are reserved to the States respectively, or to the people.

254. National Commission on Fiscal Responsibility and Reform, *The Moment of Truth*, 31.

255. *Publication 1304, Individual Income Tax Returns*, IRS Statistics of Income, Table 1.4, tax year 2007.

Chapter 19

256. See 2009 Form 1040, lines 23–37; 26 U.S.C. § 62 (2009).

257. See *Publication 1304, Individual Income Tax Returns*, IRS Statistics of Income, Table 1.1, tax year 2007.

258. 26 U.S.C. § 68 (2009); Economic Growth and Tax Relief Reconciliation Act of 2001, Pub.L.No.107-16, 115 Stat. 38, § 901.

259. 26 U.S.C. § 68 (2009); Omnibus Budget Reconciliation Act of 1990, Pub.L.No.101-508, 104 Stat. 1388, §11103.

260. 26 U.S.C. § 151(d) (2009); Omnibus Budget Reconciliation Act of 1990, Pub.L.No.101-508, 104 Stat 1388, § 11104 (initially scheduled to expire at the beginning of 1996).

261. 26 U.S.C. §§ 68(f), (g), 151(d) (2009).

262. Economic Growth and Tax Relief Reconciliation Act of 2001, Pub.L.No. 107-16, 115 Stat. 38, § 901 (a)–(b) (original expiration); Tax Relief, Unemployment Insurance Reauthorization, and Job Creation Act of 2010, Pub.L.No. 111-312, 124 Stat. 3296, § 101(a)(1) (inserting December 31, 2012 in § 901).

263. American Taxpayer Relief Act of 2012, Pub.L.No. 112-240, 126 Stat. 2313, § 101.

Chapter 20

264. 26 U.S.C. §§ 61, 63, and 162 (2009).

265. 2009 Form 1040, line 23; 26 U.S.C. § 62(a)(2)(D) (2009).

266. 2009 Form 1040, line 24; 26 U.S.C. § 62(a)(2)(B), 162 (2009).

267. 2009 Form 1040, line 26; 26 U.S.C. §§ 62(a)(15), 217 (2009).

268. 2009 Form 1040, line 35; 26 U.S.C. § 199 (2009). Effective in 2010, the reduction from income for domestic production activities is 9 percent of qualified production income, which is defined broadly to include such items as a qualified film produced by the taxpayer and construction of real property in the United States. Transition rates are 3 percent in 2005 and 2006 and 6 percent in 2007, 2008, and 2009.

269. 26 U.S.C. § 62(a)(6) and (7) (2009).

270. 26 U.S.C. § 219 and 408 (2009).

271. See *Publication 560, Retirement Plans for Small Business* (Internal Revenue Service, 2008).

272. *Instructions for Forms W-2 and W-3* (Internal Revenue Service, 2009), 9; 26 U.S.C. § 3121(a)(5) (2009).

273. See 26 U.S.C. § 501(a) (2009).

274. 26 U.S.C. § 61(a)(9) and (11) (2009) (annuities and pensions); 26 U.S.C. § 408(d) (2009) (IRA distributions).

275. Rules exist to determine the proportion of a distribution that is taxable where some payments into the retirement plan were not used to reduce taxable income. See *Publication 939, General Rules for Pensions and Annuities* (Internal Revenue Service, 2003) and 26 U.S.C. § 72(c) (2009).

276. See *Publication 590, Individual Retirement Arrangements (IRAs)* (Internal Revenue Service, 2009) for both early withdrawal penalties and required distributions.

277. 26 U.S.C. § 61(a)(8) (2009).

278. 26 U.S.C. § 215 (2009).

Chapter 21

279. 2009 Form 1040, showing the result of adjustments for inflation per 26 U.S.C. § 151(d)(4) (2009).

280. 26 U.S.C. § 151 (2009).

281. 26 U.S.C. § 151(d)(3) (2009). The phase-out rule for exemptions ended for 2010. It would have returned under the automatic reversion to pre-2001 law at the end of 2010 (pre-2010 law had a phase-out rule), but Congress extended automatic reversion to the end of 2012 as part of the December 2010 tax compromise. The 2012 fiscal cliff tax compromise reinstated a version of a phase-out rule beginning in 2013. Economic Growth and Tax Relief Reconciliation Act of 2001, Pub.L.No.107-16, 115 Stat 38, § 901 (a)–(b) (original expiration); Tax Relief, Unemployment Insurance Reauthorization, and Job Creation Act of 2010, Pub.L.No.111-312, 124 Stat 3296, § 101(a)(1) (inserting December 31, 2012 in § 901). American Taxpayer Relief Act of 2012, Pub.L.No. 112-240, 126 Stat. 2313, §101.

282. 2009 Form 1040 (Internal Revenue Service, 2009); 26 U.S.C. § 63(c) (2009). Adjustments for inflation are required by 26 U.S.C. § 63(c)(4) (2009).

283. 26 U.S.C. § 63(c)(3) and (f) (2009).

284. Patient Protection and Affordable Care Act, Pub.L.No.111-148, 124 Stat 119 (2010). Among the provisions of this Act that alter 2009 tax law relating to medical expenses are:

   (1) An excise tax on an "excess benefit" from an employer-provided health insurance plan (§ 9001).

(2) An increase from 7.5 percent to 10 percent of adjusted gross income as the threshold for allowing an itemized deduction for medical expenses (§ 9013).

(3) A 0.5 percent surcharge Medicare tax on individual incomes that exceed $250,000 (joint returns) or $200,000 (all other returns) (§ 9015).

285. 26 U.S.C. § 106(a) (2009) (the benefit of employer-provided medical insurance or medical services is not gross income subject to the individual income tax). This benefit also is *not* considered to be wages subject to Social Security and Medicare taxes. 26 U.S.C. §§ 3101, 3121(a) (2009).

286. 26 U.S.C. § 213 (2009).

287. 26 U.S.C. §§ 223, 220 (2009).

288. 26 U.S.C. § 213 (itemized deductions for medical expenses) and § 162(l) (reductions for payments for medical insurance established under a business) (2009). Payments for medical insurance are not allowed as a business expense of a self-employed individual when calculating self-employment earned income subject to the Social Security and Medicare taxes. 26 U.S.C. § 162(l)(4) (2009).

289. 26 U.S.C. §§ 223, 220 (2009).

290. 26 U.S.C. § 213 (2009).

291. 26 U.S.C. § 223 (2009).

292. 26 U.S.C. § 223 (c) (2009).

293. 26 U.S.C. § 223(d)(2) (2009).

294. 26 U.S.C. § 162(l) (2009); 2009 Form 1040, line 29 Instructions.

295. 26 U.S.C. § 213(d)(9) (2009).

296. 26 U.S.C. §223 (Health Savings Accounts) and §220 (Archer MSAs) (2009).

Chapter 22

297. 26 U.S.C. § 170 (2009).

298. 26 U.S.C. § 170(b) (2009).

299. 26 U.S.C. § 68 (2009). In 2009, the amount that ceased to be allowed could not exceed 26.7 percent of the otherwise allowed itemized deductions. Thus, at least 73.3 percent of the dollar amount of gifts to charity was allowed as an itemized deduction no matter how large an individual's adjusted gross income. The 26.7 percent figure is calculated by taking ⅓ of 80 percent, which is subsection (f) of § 68 (the ⅓) applied to subsection (a) (the 80 percent).

300. 26 U.S.C. § 68(g) (2009).

Chapter 23

301. For basic state taxation information, see the annual publication *Martindale-Hubbel Law Digest,* published by Lexis-Nexis.

302. 26 U.S.C. § 164(b) (2009). See 2009 Form 1040 Schedule A, line 5, and Instructions (Internal Revenue Service, 2009). The term "deduction" is used in the discussion of state and local taxes because these reductions have historically occurred below the line that calculates adjusted gross income and are called itemized "deductions" in current tax forms.

303. 26 U.S.C. § 164(a) (2009). See 2009 Form 1040 Schedule A, line 5 Instructions (Internal Revenue Service, 2009).

304. 26 U.S.C. § 164(f); § 1401 (2009) (self-employment taxes imposed for Social Security and Medicare).

305. 26 U.S.C. § 165 (2009).

306. 26 U.S.C. § 165(c) (2009).

307. 26 U.S.C. § 165(f), (g) (2009).

308. 26 U.S.C. § 165(l) (2009).

309. 26 U.S.C. § 165(a) (2009).

310. 26 U.S.C. § 165(h) (2009). Net losses are the excess of all casualty and theft losses over all casualty and theft gains (as defined in this section). A casualty gain is possible if property has been converted to higher value as the result of fire or storm (e.g., fire destroys a dilapidated wooden structure that was scheduled to be razed to permit other use of the property on which it was located).

Chapter 24

311. 26 U.S.C. §§ 21–26; also §§ 27–30D (2009), although these latter credits are not labeled as "nonrefundable."

312. 26 U.S.C. § 23 (adoption expenses) and § 22 (elderly or disabled) (2009).

313. 26 U.S.C. §§ 31–37 (2009).

314. 26 U.S.C. § 31 (taxes withheld), §§ 37 and 6401 (overpayments), and § 6315 (estimated tax) (2009).

315. 26 U.S.C. § 32 (2009).

316. 26 U.S.C. § 36 (homebuyer) and § 35 (health insurance cost) (2009).

317. See Form 1040 and its Schedule A (Internal Revenue Service, 2009).

Chapter 25

318. 26 U.S.C. § 32(d) (2009).

319. *1040 Forms and Instructions 2009, Package 1040-10* (Internal Revenue Service, 2009).

320. 26 U.S.C. § 32(b) (2009).

321. 26 U.S.C. § 32(b) (2009).

322. 26 U.S.C. § 24 (2009).

323. *Publication 1304, Individual Income Tax Returns*, IRS Statistics of Income, Table 2.5, tax year 2007.

324. 26 U.S.C. § 38(a)–(b) (2009).

325. 26 U.S.C. § 38(c)(1) (2009) states:

> The credit allowed under subsection (a) for any taxable year shall not exceed the excess (if any) of the taxpayer's net income tax over the greater of—
>   (A) the tentative minimum tax for the taxable year, or
>   (B) 25 percent of so much of the taxpayer's net regular tax liability as exceeds $25,000.

326. 26 U.S.C. § 44 (2009).

327. 26 U.S.C. § 45C (2009).

328. 26 U.S.C. § 45J (2009).

Chapter 26

329. 26 U.S.C. § 1402(a) (2009).

330. "Net earnings from self-employment" is the language used to identify the earned income of self-employed individuals that is subject to Social Security and Medicare taxes. That definition specifically excludes rentals from property, dividends, bonds interest, and capital gains. 26 U.S.C. § 1402(a) (2009).

331. 26 U.S.C. §§ 1402(a), 3121(a) (2009).

332. See *Publication 590, Individual Retirement Arrangements (IRAs)* (Internal Revenue Service, 2008).

Chapter 27

333. 26 U.S.C. § 1(a)–(d) (2009).

334. 26 U.S.C. § 1(f)(8) (2009).

335. Klein, Bankman, and Shaviro, *Federal Income Taxation, Thirteenth Edition*, 14–16, 581–583.

336. 26 U.S.C. § 1(b) (2009).

337. Compare 26 U.S.C. § 1(d) to § 1(c) (2009).

338. In 2009, a single head of household could use an $8,350 standard deduction compared to a $5,700 standard deduction for a single person. 2009 Form 1040 (Internal Revenue Service, 2009).

Chapter 28

339. Revenue Act of 1978, Pub.L.No. 95-600, 92 Stat. 2763, §§ 421–422; S.Rep.No. 95-1263, 95th Cong. (1978), 200–205 (1978); 26 U.S.C. §§ 55–59 (2009).

340. *Publication 1304, Individual Income Tax Returns*, IRS Statistics of Income, Table 1.4, tax years 2002, 2007. The numbers of returns that included the Alternative Minimum Tax were 1,910,789 in tax year 2002 and 4,108,964 in tax year 2007.

341. 26 U.S.C. §§ 55-59 (2009).

342. Klein, Bankman, and Shaviro, *Federal Income Taxation, Thirteenth Edition*, 559.

343. 26 U.S.C. § 55(b)(2), (d) (2009).

344. 26 U.S.C. § 55(d)(3) (2009).

345. 26 U.S.C. § 55(b)(3); § 1(h) (2009); American Taxpayer Relief Act of 2012, Pub.L.No. 112-240, 126 Stat. 2313, § 102.

346. 26 U.S.C. § 55(b)(2); §§ 56 and 58 (adjustments); § 57 (tax preferences) (2009).

347. 26 U.S.C. § 56(b)(1)(A), (B) (2009). In 2009, only medical expenses that exceeded 10 percent of adjusted gross income were allowed in calculating alternative minimum taxable income. In contrast, medical expenses that exceeded 7.5 percent of adjusted gross income were allowed in calculating regular taxable income (a larger itemized deduction gives a smaller taxable income).

348. 26 U.S.C. § 56(b)(1)(C) (2009). The "home" mortgage means a mortgage on a qualified dwelling, which includes a house, apartment, condominium, or "mobile home not used on a transient basis" (see 2009 Instructions for Form 6251 (Internal Revenue Service, 2009), 2). Current law limits the amount of indebtedness that can qualify, but not the amount of interest that can be deducted. 26 U.S.C. § 163(h)(3)(B)(ii) (2009) (e.g., one limit is $1,000,000 indebtedness for acquisition of a qualified residence).

349. 26 U.S.C. § 56(b)(1)(E) (2009).

350. Lines 9–28 of 2009 Form 6251 (Internal Revenue Service, 2009) are found on the first page of that form, which is reproduced here in appendix 28A.

Chapter 29

351. In fiscal year 2008, corporation income tax receipts were 12.0 percent of all federal receipts ($304 billion divided by $2,523 billion). They were 18.2 percent of all federal receipts other than Social Security and Medicare tax receipts ($304 billion divided by $1,671 billion). *Budget of the U.S. Government, Fiscal Year 2014*, Historical Tables, Tables 2.1, 2.4. See appendix 9A for fiscal year 2008 data, table 9A.1.

352. 26 U.S.C. § 11 (2009).

353. 26 U.S.C. §§ 61, 63 (2009).

354. 26 U.S.C. § 162 (2009).

355. See, e.g., 26 U.S.C. §§ 312, 531, 535 (2009).

356. 26 U.S.C. § 11 (2009).

357. Economics theory also treats all business income the same way. As stated by one author:

> Corporations are not people; they are economic entities (firms) taking a particular legal form (incorporation). Thus, corporations cannot bear the burden of the corporate income tax in any real sense; it ultimately is borne by individuals. In the short run—that is, before economic actors have had a chance to adjust to the tax—the tax is thought to be borne by corporate stockholders.

Brumbaugh, "Federal Business Taxation," 51–52.

358. 26 U.S.C. §§ 211–224, see § 213 (2009) (medical expenses).

359. 26 U.S.C. §§ 241–249, see § 248 (2009) (organizational expenses).

360. 26 U.S.C. § 179C (2009) (expensing certain refineries).

361. Robert S. McIntyre, Matthew Gardner, Rebecca J. Wilkins, and Richard Phillips, *Corporate Taxpayers & Corporate Tax Dodgers 2008–10* (Washington, DC: Citizens for Tax Justice and Institute on Taxation and Economic Policy, 2011). See also *Big No-Tax Corps Just Keep on Dodging* (Washington, DC: Citizens for Tax Justice, April 9, 2012).

362. 26 U.S.C. § 61 (2009).

363. Payments to qualified retirement accounts are also common reductions, but these reductions postpone rather than avoid taxation on the amounts paid into these accounts.

364. 26 U.S.C. § 61 (2009).

365. National Commission on Fiscal Responsibility and Reform, *The Moment of Truth*, 28, 33.

366. Greg Griffin, "Keeping It," *Denver Post*, April 13, 2010, sec. B.

367. See, e.g., 26 U.S.C. § 382 and its regulations in the Code of Federal Regulations (2009).

368. See, e.g., 26 U.S.C. § 382 and its regulations in the Code of Federal Regulations (2009).

369. National Commission on Fiscal Responsibility and Reform, *The Moment of Truth*, 33.

370. The grocery business is often cited as an example of a low-margin type of business. A study of supermarket operations many years ago cited low profit margins of less than 3 percent before applying the corporate earnings tax. Ralph Cassady Jr., *Competition and Price Making in Food Retailing—The Anatomy of Supermarket Operations* (New York: Ronald Press, 1962), 267–268. In this type of business, a small corporation revenue tax will act much like a small excise tax, where the tax will be passed on to the customers of the business because all corporations will pay the same tax.

    Is this a bad result? The answer is no if you think that consumers should pay for the true costs of what they buy. At present, the protections and benefits that these low-margin corporations now enjoy in the United States are being subsidized by other taxpayers who are the customers of other corporations that have larger profit margins than these low-margin corporations.

371. National Commission on Fiscal Responsibility and Reform, *The Moment of Truth*, 33.

372. 26 U.S.C. §§ 1361–1362 (2009).

373. 26 U.S.C. § 1363 (2009).

374. 26 U.S.C. § 1366 (2009).

375. See appendix 29A for the calculation of a standard rate for a corporation revenue tax.

376. See discussion in chapter 25 on revisiting current business-related income tax credits.

377. 26 U.S.C. § 38(c)(1) (2009).

378. National Commission on Fiscal Responsibility and Reform, *The Moment of Truth*, 32–33.

Chapter 30

379. Some states levy taxes only on inheritances (e.g., Texas), some only on estates (e.g., California), and some on neither (e.g., Wyoming). *Martindale-Hubbel Law Digest* (n.p. Lexis-Nexis, 2006).

380. 26 U.S.C. § 102(a) (2009).

381. 26 U.S.C. § 2001 (2009).

382. 26 U.S.C. §§ 2051–2058 (2009).

383. 26 U.S.C. § 2031 (2009).

384. 26 U.S.C. § 2001 (2009).

385. 26 U.S.C. § 1 (2009).

386. 26 U.S.C. § 2210 (estate tax does not apply to estates after December 31, 2009), §§ 2501–2502 (gift tax still applies in 2010) (2009).

387. Sunset provisions for the 2001 Tax Act are found in §§ 901(a)(1) and (b) of the Act. Economic Growth and Tax Relief Reconciliation Act of 2001, Pub.L.No. 107-16, 115 Stat. 76.

388. Tax Relief, Unemployment Insurance Reauthorization, and Job Creation Act of 2010, Pub.L.No. 111-312, 124 Stat. 3296, § 302(a)(2).

389. American Taxpayer Relief Act of 2012, Pub.L.No. 112-240, 126 Stat. 2313, § 101.

390. 26 U.S.C. § 1014 (2009). The tax provisions relating to estates use the term "property," not "capital asset."

391. 26 U.S.C. §§ 1014(f) and 1022 (2009), both added by the Economic Growth and Tax Relief Reconciliation Act of 2001, Pub.L.No. 107-16, 115 Stat. 76, §§ 541 and 542.

392. 26 U.S.C. § 1015 (2009). The basis of property received by gift can also be increased by the amount of any gift tax paid on the property.

393. 26 U.S.C. § 1022 (2009) (fair market value limit is at § 1022(d)(2)).

394. Tax Relief, Unemployment Insurance Reauthorization, and Job Creation Act of 2010, Pub.L.No. 111-312, 124 Stat. 3296, § 301(a) (rescinding the 2001 Tax Act changes that eliminated the stepped-up basis rule starting 2010) and § 304 (applying to the new 2010 estate tax the sunset provisions of the 2001 Tax Act (§ 901), as amended to December 31, 2012).

395. American Taxpayer Relief Act of 2012, Pub.L.No. 112-240, 126 Stat. 2313, § 101.

396. Authority for the IRS to create a form that reports the adjusted bases of a deceased's property is found in 26 U.S.C. § 1022(d)(3) and § 6018 (2009).

397. "After-tax" cash and the basis of property purchased with "after-tax" cash fit the scenario that taxes have already been paid (assuming no tax subsidies when the cash was received). However, no taxes have been paid on embedded capital gains when property gets a stepped-up basis upon death.

398. 26 U.S.C. § 2055 (2009). The reduction is the fair market value to the extent that fair market value is included in the total value of the estate.

399. Congress already has attempted to accommodate the "family farm" style of business owned by a decedent by reducing the estate value of property used as a farm for farming purposes. 26 U.S.C. § 2032A (2009).

400. *Budget of the U.S. Government, Fiscal Year 2014*, Historical Tables, Tables 2.1, 2.5. See also appendix 9A in this book.

Chapter 32

401. 26 U.S.C. § 1(h)(11) (2009); Jobs and Growth Tax Relief Reconciliation Act of 2003, Pub.L.No. 108-27, 117 Stat. 752, § 301(a).

Chapter 33

402. Two simple formulas can be used to compare an individual's after-tax net dividend income from a corporation under current law and under the FAST Plan (assuming that all available earnings are taxable and paid out as dividends).

$ Current law formula
Earnings per share
minus Earnings tax per share
equals Dividend per share
times (1 minus current dividend tax rate)
equals After-tax dividend income per share

$ FAST Plan formula
Earnings per share
minus Revenue tax per share
equals Dividend per share
times (1 minus standard tax rate)
equals After-tax dividend income per share

Glossary

above the line. For an individual, entries that precede the adjusted gross income figure in tax-reporting forms.

accountability. As used in this book for taxes, the ability to ascertain easily the total monetary impacts on federal tax receipts of every federal tax provision.

adjusted basis. As used in the Internal Revenue Code, the basis of a capital asset as increased or decreased by certain allowed actions relating to the capital asset (e.g., installing a new roof on a building).

adjusted gross income. For an individual, a midpoint calculation in the determination of taxable income wherein gross income is reduced by limited allowed reductions known as "statutory adjustments."

Alternative Minimum Tax (AMT). A taxing scheme that exists alongside the regular individual income tax, with a different set of rates and a smaller set of allowed tax subsidies.

amount realized. The amount received from the sale of a capital asset.

annual deficit. See federal deficit.

basis. As used in the Internal Revenue Code, the cost of a capital asset.

below the line. For an individual, entries that follow the adjusted gross income figure in tax-reporting forms.

capital asset. As defined in the Internal Revenue Code, "property held by the taxpayer (whether or not connected with his trade or business), but does not include— [followed by a list of exceptions, such as business inventory]."

capital gain. As used in the Internal Revenue Code, the difference between the amount realized from the sale or other disposition of a capital asset and its adjusted basis. In this book, one of the three major forms of income based on capital.

consumption tax. A tax on spending for goods and services.

contribution and benefit base. The term applied in the Social Security Act for the maximum amount of earned income that is subject to the Social Security tax.

deficit. See federal deficit.

deficit spending. The common term applied to the circumstance when the US government spends more money in a fiscal year than it receives from all federal taxes and other revenue sources.

direct subsidy. As used in this book, a tax provision that *can* require the United States to pay an individual or entity money that is not otherwise held by the United States on behalf of the individual.

dividend. A pro rata distribution of money (or additional stock) to a shareholder of a corporation by the corporation. In this book, one of the three major forms of income based on capital.

earned income. Income that is subject to Social Security and Medicare taxes, summarily described as wages of employees and net earnings from self-employment by self-employed individuals.

earnings or **earnings and profits.** Terms used in the Internal Revenue Code and many public reports for the net profit of a corporation. The two terms are synonymous.

embedded capital gain. As used in this book, the gain in the value of property in an estate that preceded the decedent's death and that a stepped-up basis rule excludes from a later determination of capital gain.

estate. All property, including money, that a deceased person owned at the time of death.

excise tax. A tax on the manufacture, sale, or use of a commodity or on identified activities.

exemption. A specific dollar amount allowed as a reduction from income in the determination of taxable income for an individual and the individual's spouse, children, and others who are dependent upon the individual.

fair tax. A term used by its proponents for a national sales tax.

fairness. As used in this book, fairness for taxes on income means that individuals who receive the same cash or cash-equivalent benefits in a year should owe the same total amount of federal taxes before the calculation of defined and accountable federal subsidies that may be applicable.

FAST Plan. All of the tax reform proposals in this book. Acronym for **F**air, **A**ccountable, and **S**imple **T**ax Plan.

federal accounts interest. Money credited to all government accounts (mostly trust funds) as interest on treasury securities held by those accounts (historically usually money credited rather than actually paid to those accounts).

federal deficit. The difference between the total amount of money spent (outlays) and the total amount of money received by (receipts of) the US government in a fiscal year when outlays exceed receipts. Also called the "total" deficit, the "annual" deficit, or just the "deficit."

federal fiscal year. October 1 through September 30.

federal funds deficit. The difference between federal funds outlays and federal funds receipts in a fiscal year when those outlays exceed receipts. Synonymous with true discretionary deficit.

federal funds outlays. All federal outlays other than those allocated to federal trust funds.

federal funds receipts. All federal receipts other than those allocated to federal trust funds.

federal government accounts debt. See government accounts debt.

federal outlays. Money spent (paid out) by the US government, usually meaning the money spent in a federal fiscal year.

federal receipts. The sum of receipts from all federal taxes and all other income sources, usually meaning the receipts in a federal fiscal year.

federal surplus. The difference between the total receipts and the total outlays of the US government in a fiscal year when receipts exceed outlays. Also called the "total" surplus.

FICA. Federal Insurance Contributions Act, the formal name of the statute that imposes Social Security and Medicare taxes on employees and employers.

filing category. For individuals who file federal income tax returns, one of four designations under current law that have different sets of graduated tax rates. The IRS refers to these as "single," "married filing jointly" (or "qualified widow(er)"), "married filing separately," and "head of household."

flat tax. An income tax that uses one rate for all taxable ordinary income, usually accompanied by a zero rate for capital gains, dividends, and interest.

GDP. Acronym for gross domestic product.

government accounts debt. That portion of the national debt held by federal government accounts, such as the Social Security trust funds, generally resulting from borrowing money from trust funds for non-trust fund purposes.

graduated tax rates. Tax rates that apply a different percentage rate to different segments of taxable income, with a lower rate being applied to the first amount of taxable income received in a tax year, a higher rate being applied to the second amount of taxable income, and so on until a maximum rate is reached that applies to all taxable income above a certain amount.

gross domestic product (GDP). One measure of the size of the US economy.

gross income. As used in the Internal Revenue Code, "all income from whatever source derived, including (but not limited to) the following items— [followed by a list of fifteen different kinds of income]." 26 U.S.C. §61 (2009).

gross interest. The sum of the net interest and government accounts interest.

inheritance. The property, including money, that a person receives from an estate (excluding earnings from the estate).

interest. Money paid by a borrower to a lender for the use of the lender's money. In this book, one of the three major forms of income based on capital.

itemized deduction. One of a group of reductions from income that are allowed in place of but not in addition to the standard deduction in the determination of taxable income.

marginal tax rate. The rate applied to the last additional dollar of income that is subject to a tax.

marginal total federal tax rate. For an individual, the effective rate that results from applying income, Social Security, and Medicare taxes on the last dollar earned by the individual.

marriage bonus. A term applied to the circumstance that occurs when a married couple's income tax owed per individual is less than the income tax owed by a similarly situated single individual with the same taxable income per individual.

marriage penalty. A term applied to the circumstance that occurs when a married couple's income tax owed per individual is more than the income tax owed by a similarly situated single individual with the same taxable income per individual.

Medicare. The US government program of health insurance for elderly individuals.

Medicare trust funds. Two trust funds that pay Medicare benefits and expenses. The two funds are the "hospital insurance trust fund" (the fund into which receipts from the Medicare tax are paid) and the "supplementary medical insurance trust fund" (the fund that receives its money from premiums and other sources).

national debt. At a given point in time, the sum of all of the US treasury securities issued over time that have not been paid back.

net interest. Money paid as interest on the public debt portion of the national debt (generally money actually paid out from federal tax receipts).

nonrefundable tax credit. A credit against income tax owed that cannot exceed the amount of the income tax owed and, therefore, cannot generate a payment from the United States to the taxpayer.

off-budget outlays. Money paid out by the US government for the Social Security program and for the United States Postal Service.

off-budget receipts. Money received by the US government from the Social Security program (Social Security taxes and other receipts) and from the United States Postal Service.

on-budget deficit. The difference between on-budget outlays and on-budget receipts in a fiscal year when outlays exceed receipts.

on-budget outlays. All money paid out by the US government except for off-budget outlays.

on-budget receipts. All money received by the US government except off-budget receipts.

ordinary income. Income that is fully subject to the individual income tax rates.

outlays (federal). See federal outlays.

personal property. All property other than real property.

progressive tax rates. See graduated tax rates.

public debt. That portion of the national debt held by the public, namely all of the national debt other than the debt held by federal government accounts.

real property. Land and all structures attached to the land.

receipts (federal). See federal receipts.

reductions from income. The term applied in this book for all subtractions from an individual's gross income that are allowed in the determination of taxable income.

refundable tax credit. A credit against income tax owed that can exceed the amount of the income tax owed and, therefore, can generate a payment from the United States to the taxpayer.

sales tax. A tax on the sale of goods or services.

self-employment tax. The tax on self-employed individuals for "old-age, survivors, and disability insurance" (Social Security) and for "hospital insurance" (Medicare hospital insurance).

simplicity. As a criterion in this book for taxes, simplicity means that tax calculations are mathematically easy, few calculations are needed to determine the amount of taxes owed, and the policies that underlie the calculations are readily apparent and understandable.

Social Security. The US government program of retirement and disability benefits for qualified individuals, also known as "old-age, survivors, and disability insurance."

Social Security benefits. Funds paid to qualified individuals from the Social Security trust funds.

Social Security trust funds. Two trust funds into which Social Security tax receipts and other receipts are paid and from which Social Security benefits and expenses are paid. The two funds are the "old age and survivors insurance fund" (retirement trust fund) and the "disability insurance trust fund."

standard deduction. A specific dollar amount that is allowed for each filing category as a reduction from income in the determination of taxable income.

standard-rate tax. As used generally in this book, a tax that uses a single rate for all taxable amounts. As proposed in the FAST Plan, a tax that uses one rate for all income, including capital gains, dividends, and interest; and for an individual, also characterized by allowing a tax credit for the individual's payment of Social Security and Medicare taxes.

statutory adjustments. A term used by the Internal Revenue Service to characterize all reductions from gross income that are allowed in the determination of adjusted gross income.

stepped-up basis. The basis of property in an estate that has been increased to the fair market value of the property at the time the decedent died when that fair market value exceeds the adjusted basis of the property at the time of death.

surplus. See federal surplus.

tariff. A tax on the import or export of an item.

tax bracket. In a graduated-tax rate system, a segment of income to which a particular tax rate applies. When used to identify an individual's tax bracket, usually meaning the segment of an individual's income that is subject to the highest income tax rate.

tax subsidy. As used in this book, when compared to a standard taxpayer who pays the maximum total tax on all income received, any tax provision that allows a greater reduction of a taxpayer's income before taxes apply, a monetary credit against taxes otherwise due, or a lower or zero tax rate on certain kinds of income. As used in this book, "tax subsidy" does not include a tax provision that fits an overall policy not to tax income necessary for the healthy life of an individual or the individual's dependents.

taxable income. For an individual, the individual's gross income less all reductions from income allowed by law, such as the standard deduction. For a corporation, under current law the corporation's earnings (net profit), calculated as revenues less all reductions from revenues allowed by law, such as trade or business expenses.

treasury security. An evidence of debt issued by the US government for money received.

true discretionary deficit. A term used here to describe the difference between federal funds outlays and federal funds receipts in a fiscal year when outlays exceed receipts. Synonymous with federal funds deficit.

trust fund. As used for federal receipts and outlays, a fund into which the receipts from taxes dedicated to specific purposes are allocated and from which outlays are to be made only for those purposes.

value-added tax. A tax on the market value added to a consumer item at each stage of its creation and distribution.

Bibliography

Nongovernmental Materials

Bankman, Joseph, and David A. Weisbach. *The Superiority of an Ideal Consumption Tax over an Ideal Income Tax*. Chicago: University of Chicago Law School, John M. Olin Law & Economics Working Paper Series, Working Paper No. 251; and Stanford, CA: Stanford Law School, John M. Olin Program in Law and Economics, Working Paper No. 310, 2005. http://ssrn.com/abstract=758645.

"Big No-Tax Corps Just Keep on Dodging." Washington, DC: Citizens for Tax Justice. April 9, 2012. http://www.ctj.org/ctjreports/2012/04/big_no-tax_corps_just_keep_on_dodging.php.

Bittle, Scott, and Jean Johnson. *Where Does the Money Go?* New York: HarperCollins, 2008.

Boortz, Neal, and John Linder. *The Fair Tax Book: Saying Goodbye to the Income Tax and the IRS*. New York: Regan Books, 2005.

Brumbaugh, David L. "Federal Business Taxation: The Current System, Its Effects, and Options for Reform." In *Taxation and Tax Policy Issues*, edited by Brian L. Yashov, 40–62. New York: Nova Science, 2007.

Cassady, Ralph Jr. *Competition and Price Making in Food Retailing: The Anatomy of Supermarket Operations*. New York: Ronald Press, 1962.

Constitution Party, 2012 platform. http://www.constitutionparty.com/OurPrinciples/2012 Platform.

Forbes, Steve. *Flat Tax Revolution—Using a Postcard to Abolish the IRS*. Washington, DC: Regnery, 2005.

"From Freedom to Fascism," a video presentation shown on some Public Broadcasting System channels in early 2009. The video appears to have been selected from the film *America:*

Freedom to Fascism, directed by Aaron Russo and produced by Aaron Russo and Richard Whitley, 2006.

General Electric Corp. *2010 Annual Report*.

Griffin, Greg. "Keeping It." *The Denver Post*, April 13, 2010, sec. B.

Hassett, Kevin A., and Kathryn Newmark. "Taxation and Business Behavior: A Review of the Recent Literature." In *Fundamental Tax Reform—Issues, Choices and Implications*, edited by John W. Diamond and George R. Zodrow, 191–202. Cambridge, MA: MIT Press, 2008.

Klein, William A., Joseph Bankman, and Daniel N. Shaviro. *Federal Income Taxation, Thirteenth Edition*. New York: Aspen, 2003.

Krauthammer, Charles, "Cliffjumping with Barack," *The Denver Post*, November 30, 2012, sec. A.

Lawley, Duard. *Common Sense Tax Reform*. Bloomington, IN: AuthorHouse, 2005.

Martindale-Hubbel Law Digest. N.p. Lexis-Nexis, 2006.

McCaffery, Edward J. *Fair Not Flat: How to Make the Tax System Better and Simpler*. Chicago: University of Chicago Press, 2002.

McIntyre, Robert S., Matthew Gardner, Rebecca J. Wilkins, and Richard Phillips. *Corporate Taxpayers & Corporate Tax Dodgers 2008–10*. Washington, DC: Citizens for Tax Justice and Institute on Taxation and Economic Policy, 2011. http://www.ctj.org/corporatetaxdodgers/ CorporateTaxDodgersReport.pdf.

"Point/Counterpoint." *The Denver Post*, May 18, 2010, sec. B.

Porretto, John. "Big Oil Cash Goes to Stock Buybacks." *Rocky Mountain News*, July 22, 2008.

Ryan, Paul. *A Roadmap for America's Future—Version 2.0*. Washington, DC: January 2010. http://roadmap.republicans.budget.house.gov/uploadedfiles/roadmap2final2.pdf.

Sedensky, Matt. "Leaning Hard on Social Security." *The Denver Post*, August 9, 2010, sec. A.

Webster's New Universal Unabridged Dictionary. N.p. Barnes & Noble Publishing, 2003.

Wiggin, Addison, and Kate Incontrera. *I.O.U.S.A.* Hoboken, NJ: John Wiley & Sons, 2008.

Governmental Materials

1040 Forms and Instructions 2009, Package 1040-10. Internal Revenue Service, 2009.

Bloomquist, Kim M. "Trends as Changes in Variance: The Case of Tax Noncompliance." *2003 IRS Research Conference*, 2003. http://www.irs.gov/pub/irs-soi/bloomquist.pdf.

Budget of the U.S. Government, Fiscal Year 2014. Washington, DC: The White House, 2013. http://www.whitehouse.gov/omb/budget.

Budget Resolution, US House of Representatives, March 2013. http://www.budget.house.gov/uploadedfiles/fy14budget.pdf.

Corporation Income Tax Returns. Internal Revenue Service, Statistics of Income—2007. Washington, DC (same report for 2003, 2004, 2005, and 2006). http://www.irs.gov/uac/SOI-Tax-Stats-Corporation-Complete-Report.

Current Employment Statistics, Historical. Bureau of Labor Statistics, US Dept. of Labor. http://data.bls.gov/pdq/SurveyOutputServlet (this table shows employees on nonfarm payrolls, total private, not seasonally adjusted).
The URL is correct, but the document cannot be retrieved directly. The specific table was retrieved by searching www.bls.gov in this sequence: Tools (bottom of page) > Databases & Tables (becomes Databases, Tables & Calculators by Subject) > More Sources of Data (becomes BLS Information) > Subject Areas: Employment > National Employment (becomes Current Employment Statistics—CES (National)) > Browse CES: CES Databases > CES Data Access Tips: Access to historical data for the "B" tables of the Employment Situation News Release > 1. Employees on nonfarm payrolls by industry sector and selected industry detail (becomes Data Retrieval: Employment, Hours, and Earnings (CES)) > Table B-1: Total private (Not seasonally adjusted) > Retrieve data.

Instructions for Forms W-2 and W-3. Internal Revenue Service, 2009.

Internal Revenue Code, Winter 2009 Ed. Chicago: CCH, 2008.

"IRS Updates Tax Gap Estimates," *IRS newsroom article IR-2006-28 (2006).* http://www.irs.gov/uac/IRS-Updates-Tax-Gap-Estimates.

Measuring America—People, Places, and Our Economy, People and Households, Income. US Census Bureau. http://www.census.gov/hhes/www/income/data/historical.

Medicare Eligibility Tool at http://www.medicare.gov/MedicareEligibility/home.asp?dest=NA
VHomeGeneralEnrollment#TabTop.

National Commission on Fiscal Responsibility and Reform. *The Moment of Truth*. Washington,
DC: The White House, 2010. http://www.fiscalcommission.gov/sites/fiscalcommission.gov/
files/documents/TheMomentofTruth12_1_2010.pdf.

Population Estimates, National. U.S. Census Bureau, 2013.
For 1981–2009 data:
Statistical Abstract of the United States: 2012, Table 2. Population: 1960 to 2009. http://
www.census.gov/compendia/statab/2012/tables/12s0002.pdf.
The URL is correct, but the document may not be retrievable directly. The specific table
was retrieved by the following process. First by searching "statistical abstract" in www.
census.gov. That search found "The 2012 Statistical Abstract—U.S. Census Bureau."
This document was opened. Then the specific table was retrieved by searching in this
sequence: Population > National Estimates and Projections: 2—Population.
For 2010–2012 data:
Current Estimates Data, National Totals, Vintage 2012, Table 1. Monthly Population
Estimates for the United States: April 1, 2012 to April 1, 2013. http://www.census.gov/
popest/data/national/totals/2012/index.html.
The URL is correct, but the document may not be retrievable directly. The specific
table was retrieved by searching www.census.gov in this sequence: People (top of page)
> Population Estimates > Current Estimates Data > Nation: Total population: V2012
> Tables: Monthly Population Estimates: Monthly Population Estimates for the United
States.

Publication 560, Retirement Plans for Small Business. Internal Revenue Service, 2008.

Publication 590, Individual Retirement Arrangements (IRAs). Internal Revenue Service, 2008.

Publication 939, General Rules for Pensions and Annuities. Internal Revenue Service, 2003.

Publication 1304, Individual Income Tax Returns. Internal Revenue Service, Statistics of
Income—2007. Washington, DC (same publication for 2000 and 1993). http://www.
irs.gov/uac/SOI-Tax-Stats-Individual-Income-Tax-Returns-Publication-1304-(Complete-
Report).

SOI Tax Stats—Individual Income Tax Returns. Internal Revenue Service, 2007 and 2003.
http://www.irs.gov/uac/SOI-Tax-Stats-Individual-Income-Tax-Returns.

Public Laws, Legislative History, and Case Law

(chronological sequence)

US Constitution, Amendment X (1791).

US Constitution, Amendment XVI (1913).

Brushaber v. Union Pacific Railroad Co., 240 U.S. 1 (1916).

H.R.Rep.No. 1337, 83rd Cong. (1954), citation found in US Code Congressional and Administrative News, 83rd Congress—Second Session, 1954, Volume 3, p. 4030.

Social Security Amendments of 1965, Pub.L.No. 89-97, 79 Stat. 286.

Revenue Act of 1978, Pub.L.No. 95-600, 92 Stat. 2763.

S.Rep.No. 95-1263, 95th Cong. (1978).

Economic Recovery Act of 1981, Pub.L.No. 97-34, 95 Stat. 172.

S.Rep.No. 97-144, 97th Cong. (1981).

Social Security Amendments of 1983, Pub.L.No. 98-21, 97 Stat. 65.

S.Rep.No. 98-23, 98th Cong. (1983).

Tax Reform Act of 1986, Pub.L.No. 99-514, 100 Stat. 2085.

H.R.Rep.No. 99-841, 99th Cong. (1986) (Conf.Rep.).

United States v. Foster, 789 F.2d 457 (7th Circuit 1986).

Omnibus Budget Reconciliation Act of 1990, Pub.L.No. 101-508, 104 Stat. 1388.

Omnibus Budget Reconciliation Act of 1993, Pub.L.No. 103-66, 107 Stat. 312.

H.R.Rep.No. 103-111, 103rd Cong. (1993).

H.R.Rep.No. 103-213, 103rd Cong. (1993) (Conf.Rep.).

Taxpayer Relief Act of 1997, Pub.L.No. 105-34, 111 Stat. 788.

H.R.Rep.No. 105-148, 105th Cong. (1997).

Economic Growth and Tax Relief Reconciliation Act of 2001, Pub.L.No. 107-16, 115 Stat. 38.

H.R.Rep.No. 107-7, 107th Cong. (2001).

Jobs and Growth Tax Relief Reconciliation Act of 2003, Pub.L.No. 108-27, 117 Stat. 752.

H.R.Rep.No. 108-94, 108th Cong. (2003).

Working Families Tax Relief Act of 2004, Pub.L.No. 108-311, 118 Stat. 1166.

Tax Increase Prevention and Reconciliation Act of 2005, Pub.L.No. 109-222, 120 Stat. 345.

American Recovery and Reinvestment Act of 2009, Pub.L.No. 111-5, 123 Stat. 115.

26 U.S.C. (2009).

42 U.S.C. (2009).

Patient Protection and Affordable Care Act, Pub.L.No. 111-148, 124 Stat. 119 (2010).

Tax Relief, Unemployment Insurance Reauthorization, and Job Creation Act of 2010, Pub.L.No. 111-312, 124 Stat. 3296.

Temporary Payroll Tax Cut Continuation Act of 2011, Pub.L.No. 112-78, 125 Stat.

American Taxpayer Relief Act of 2012, Pub.L.No. 112-240, 126 Stat. 2313.

Index

A

above the line. *See under* reductions from income
accountability
    applied to capital gains tax rates, 103–104
    applied to corporation income tax, 51
    applied to EIC, 163
    applied to FAST Plan elements, 157, 160, 165
    applied to reductions from income, 130–131, 147–148
    applied to tax-exempt income, 127–128
    as a criterion, 2, 27–28, 207
    definition, 28, 207, 449
adjusted basis. *See under* basis
adjusted gross income
    accountability problems, 131
    calculation of, 129, 136, 147, 449
    generally, 62, 135, 136–140, 147
    importance of, 136
    principles for determining, 136
alimony, 139
Alternative Minimum Tax (ATM)
    generally, 50, 176–178, 449
    subsidies targeted by, 177–178, 392–393
Amendment X, US Constitution, 127
Amendment XVI, US Constitution, 61, 88
amount realized, 99–100, 449
annual deficit. *See* deficit, annual
anti-dynasty tax. *See under* estate tax
Archer Medical Savings Account, 143, 145
ATM (Alternative Minimum Tax). *See* Alternative Minimum Tax (ATM)

assets
    business losses as assets (*see* business losses as assets)
    capital asset (*see* capital asset)

B

balanced budget goal, 70–71
barriers to reform. *See* reform barriers
basis
    adjusted, 99–100, 109, 196, 198, 449
    definition, 99, 449
    stepped-up (*see* stepped-up basis)
below the line. *See under* reductions from income
bigger is better, 186
business entities
    corporations (*see* corporations)
    noncorporate entities, 190–192
business expenses, 34, 51, 76, 134, 137, 182–183
business income
    individual vs. corporation, 182–185, 189
    self-employed individual business, 90, 94, 96, 137, 182–185
    taxation of, 94, 113–114, 182–184
business losses as assets, 187
business reductions. *See under* reductions from income
business-related tax credits. *See under* tax credits

C

capital asset, 99–100, 107–110, 195, 197, 211–212, 377, 449
capital-based income
    definition, 67, 90, 335

who has most, 68

zero tax on (*see under* zero tax)

capital gains income

    definition, 99, 196, 449

    FAST Plan taxation of, 55, 67, 69, 107–108, 206–207, 240

    embedded capital gain (*see* embedded capital gain)

    importance, 90

    inflation, effect on, 109-111

    long-term, 100

    principal residence sale, 111

    short-term, 100

    taxation of generally, 48, 63, 65, 67, 70, 100, 177, 211–212

    who has most, 67–68, 101–104, 354–363

    zero tax on. *See under* zero tax

capital gains tax

    Congress's 1997 reasons for rate decrease, 382–385

    rate changes effect on GDP, 106, 314–315, 319–320

    rate changes effect on jobs, 106, 372–376

    rate changes effect on median incomes, 382–384

    rate changes effect on net capital gains, 377–381

    rates, 100

    rationales for and against, 104–108

    tax-payment effect of special rates, 102–103, 368–371

casualty insurance. *See* insurance for losses

casualty losses. *See* reductions from income: losses

child, qualifying for Earned Income Credit. *See* qualifying child for Earned Income Credit

Child Tax Credit, 159–160, 163–164

complexity

    of corporation income tax, 50–51

    of estate tax, 51–52, 200

    of federal taxes generally, 1–2, 4, 29, 47–52, 54

    of individual income tax generally, 47–50

consumption tax, 31–32, 34, 36–37, 39, 89, 426n157, 449

contribution and benefit base, 423n127, 449

contribution base, 148

corporation earnings (net profit)

    corporation tax on, 182

    definition, 51, 182, 450

    flaws as tax base, 184

corporation earnings tax. *See* corporation income tax

corporation income. *See* corporation earnings (net profit)

corporation income tax

    flaws, 184

    generally, 34, 39, 50–51, 181–184

    rates, 182

    proposed reform of, 3, 54, 57, 185–187

    receipts from, 39, 181, 290–294

    taxable corporation income, 34, 39, 50–51, 182

    territorial tax, 185, 188–189

    treaties, 188

corporation net profit. *See* corporation earnings (net profit)

corporation net profit tax. *See* corporation income tax

corporation revenue tax

    advantages, 186–187

    calculated standard rate, 189–190, 394–396

    effect on different corporations, 188, 444n370

    proposal for, 3, 54, 57, 115, 185–187, 206, 208, 245

    proposal for with rationale, 185–189

    territorial tax, 185, 188–189

corporations

    characteristics of, 183, 185, 191–192

    compared to personal business, 182–184

    foreign, 186–187

    foreign taxes paid by, 188–189

    nonprofit (*see* tax-exempt nonprofit corporations)

D

death tax. *See* estate tax

debt, national. *See* national debt

December 2010 tax compromise, 3, 48, 77, 133, 195, 197, 308

dedicated taxes. *See* trust funds: dedicated taxes for generally

deductions, itemized. *See* reductions from income: itemized deductions generally

deferred compensation, 122, 139

deficit, annual
 2014 Budget description, 273n1
 comparisons to federal amounts, 13, 265–271
 deficit spending, 10–21, 450
 federal deficit (total deficit), 10–15, 70–71, 259–
  261, 262–264, 450
 federal funds component, 13, 262–264, 265–
  271, 451
 off-budget component, 259–261
 on-budget component, 12–15, 24, 70–71, 207,
  259–261, 265–267, 270, 452
 total deficit (federal deficit), 10–15, 70–71, 259–
  261, 262–264, 450
 true discretionary deficit, 13, 263, 265, 410n14,
  454
 trust funds component, 12–14, 21, 262–264
deficit spending. *See* deficit, annual
depletion allowance, 51, 178
dilemma, Social Security and Medicare taxes, 74–87
diminished reductions from income. *See under*
  reductions from income
direct subsidy
 definition, 43, 450
 effect on standard rate, 70
 generally, 43–45, 57, 156–158, 160
discrimination, tax. *See* tax discrimination
dividends
 corporation revenue tax, effect on, 217–218, 447n402
 definition, 450
 FAST Plan taxation of, 55, 115–116, 169, 187–
  188, 212, 240
 taxation of , 48, 63, 67, 113–116, 184
domestic production activities, 138, 436n268

E

earned income
 definition, 61, 75, 450
 exclusions from, 166–170, 244
 self-employment tax base, 78–79, 85–86, 207,
  347–349
 Social Security and Medicare tax base, 47, 55,
  61–62, 67, 69, 75–76, 79, 123, 163, 174,
  238–239, 244

Earned Income Credit (EIC), 158, 162–164, 244,
  390–391
earnings, corporation. *See* corporation earnings (net
  profit)
educator expenses, 137
EIC (Earned Income Credit). *See* Earned Income
  Credit (EIC)
elective payments (tax subsidies)
 definition, 49, 147
 examples, 49–50, 134, 147–149, 211
embedded capital gain, 196–199, 216, 450
employees
 Medicare tax, 76–77
 Social Security tax, 76–77
employers
 Medicare tax, 76–77
 Social Security tax, 76–77
estate
 definition, 194, 450
 gross estate, 195
estate tax
 anti-dynasty tax, 199
 arguments against and for, 199–200
 embedded capital gain (*see* embedded capital
  gain)
 generally, 34, 39, 51–52, 194–201, 213–214, 216
 gift tax, 35, 51–52, 194, 214
 history of, 194–195
 proposed reform of, 57, 197–201, 213–214, 246
 proposed reform of with rationale, 197–201
 rates, 195
 receipts from, 39, 200–201, 291–294
 stepped-up basis (*see* stepped-up basis)
excise taxes
 example taxes, 35
 generally, 35, 39, 41, 417n70, 450
exemptions. *See under* reductions from income
expenditures, federal. *See* outlays, federal

F

fairness
 applied to individual income tax generally,
  33–34, 47–48

applied to reductions from income generally, 129–133

applied to special capital gains tax rates, 103–104, 109

applied to tax-exempt income, 127

as a criterion, 2, 27–28, 207

definition, 27–28, 450

fair tax. *See* sales tax: potential federal (fair tax)

FAST Plan

bottom line, 53–58

name derivation, 2, 450

needed grand compromise, 220

standard rate for individuals (*see* standard-rate income tax)

summaries, 53–58, 205–208, 237–246

tax payments compared to current law, 216–218, 397–407

federal accounts interest. *See under* interest on national debt

federal deficit (total deficit). *See under* deficit, annual

federal expenditures. *See* outlays, federal

federal fiscal year, 8, 450

federal funds deficit component. *See under* deficit, annual

federal funds outlays. *See under* outlays, federal

federal funds receipts. *See under* receipts, federal

federal outlays. *See* outlays, federal

federal receipts. *See* receipts, federal

federal surplus. *See* surplus, federal

federal tax compliance

costs of, 1, 29, 215–216

decreased costs of, 215–216

federal tax receipts. *See* receipts, federal

federal taxes purpose, 7–8

FICA. *See under* Social Security tax; *see also under* Medicare tax

filing categories

generally, 63, 64–65, 67, 171, 297, 321–322, 451

history of, 171–173

structural flaws, 173–174

fiscal cliff tax compromise, 3–4, 48, 62, 66, 77, 100, 133, 195, 197, 308, 417n77, 437n281

Fiscal Commission

debt warning, 20

December 2010 report, 3–4, 24–25, 45, 67, 127, 188, 190, 409n3, 430n204

tax expenditures, 45

flat tax

description, 67, 335, 451

flaws, 67–68

foreign corporations. *See under* corporations

foreign taxes paid by corporations. *See under* corporations

G

GDP (gross domestic product)

comparing tax rate changes to, 72, 106, 314–320

description, 451

use of GDP data, 19, 272, 274

gifts to charity. *See under* reductions from income

gift tax. *See under* estate tax

government accounts debt, 12–14, 20–21, 25, 272–275, 284–285, 413n41, 451

graduated tax rates

definition, 42–43, 62, 451

historic effects of, 64–66, 133, 156, 171–174, 364–367

use of, 48, 62–63, 220

Great Recession

effect on federal receipts, 15, 24, 72, 79, 247–252

identified, 13

gross domestic product. *See* GDP (gross domestic product)

gross income

corporations, 182, 185, 451

individuals, 62, 88–89, 94, 125, 129, 185, 194, 451

gross interest. *See under* interest on national debt

H

health insurance, 93, 143–144, 208

Health Savings Account, 143–145

healthy life, 126. *See also* reductions from income: healthy life payments

High Deductible Health Plan, 144

I

incentive. *See* tax subsidy

income
- bunching, 104–105
- corporation (*see* corporation earnings (net profit))
- definition, 88–89
- individual (*see* individual income)
- taxable corporation income (*see under* corporation income tax)
- taxable individual income (*see under* individual income tax)
- tax-exempt (*see* tax-exempt income generally)

individual income
- kinds for different income groups, 101–102, 354–363
- major kinds overall, 88–91, 350–353
- miscellaneous income (*see* miscellaneous income)
- ordinary income, 92–98, 452
- specific kinds (*see specific kind of income in the index*)

individual income tax
- calculation of, 62–63, 129–130
- comparing capital gains rate changes to jobs, 372–376
- comparing capital gains rate changes to median incomes, 382–384
- comparing capital gains rate changes to net capital gains, 377–381
- comparing rate changes to GDP, 72, 314–320
- comparing rate changes to receipts, 72, 309–313
- comparing taxes paid by different income groups, 33, 68, 103, 364–367
- comparing taxes paid, capital gains vs. ordinary income, 102, 368–371
- effective rates, 102–104, 364–367
- fairness, 33–34, 47–48, 103–104
- generally, 32–34, 38–39, 43, 62–63,
- historic rate changes, 305–308
- proposed reform of (*see* FAST Plan: summaries)
- rates, 62–63
- rates, effective on all income, 102–104, 364–367
- receipts from, 62, 72, 309–313

taxable individual income, 62, 129–130

individual income tax returns, filing, 295–297

individual retirement arrangements (IRAs). *See* IRAs (individual retirement arrangements)

inflation adjustment
- capital gains, 109–111
- exemptions, 141
- standard deduction, 142

inheritance, 194, 451

insurance for losses, 154

interest income
- description, 95, 452
- from state and local bonds, 89, 96, 126–128
- taxation of, 95–96, 126–128

interest on national debt
- compared to federal amounts, 16–18, 277–281
- federal accounts interest, 16–17, 20–21, 277–281, 450
- gross interest, 16–17, 277–281, 451
- net interest, 16–20, 277–281, 452
- rates, 18–19, 282–283

Internal Revenue Code
- generally, 1–2, 53–54, 113
- recent tax law history, 305–308
- references to (*see specific topic in the index*)
- size, 1–2, 419n93

investors
- definition, 166
- investment income, 167, 169–170
- investor's option. *See under* Social Security tax; *see also under* Medicare tax
- special circumstances, 166–168

IRAs (individual retirement arrangements)
- payments into, 138–139
- taxation of withdrawals, 122, 168–169

itemized deductions. *See under* reductions from income

J

jobs, comparing tax rate changes to, 106, 372–376

joint tax return, 172–174

joint ventures, 192

L

local bonds interest. *See* interest income, from state and local bonds

local taxes. *See* reductions from income: local tax payments

losses. *See under* reductions from income

M

maintenance to ex-spouse, 139

marginal tax rate
    current law features, 49–50, 65–66, 130, 172, 218, 321–334
    definition, 43, 452
    examples, 65–66, 80–82, 104, 211, 321–334
    example total rates: alternative tax approaches for individuals, 335–343
    example total rates: current law for individuals, 65–66, 80–82, 321–334, 335–338, 341
    example total rates: standard rate within current law for individuals, 82, 344–346
    highest, 65–66, 322

marginal total federal tax rate for individuals
    definition, 65, 74, 209–210, 452
    examples, 65–68, 72, 74, 80–83, 86, 166, 209–210, 321–334, 335–343, 344–346
    highest, 65–66, 322

marriage bonus, 64–65, 171–174, 452

marriage penalty, 64–65, 171–174, 452

median incomes, 384

medical expenses. *See under* reductions from income

Medicare hospital insurance trust fund, 13, 22–24, 79–80, 119, 121, 168, 262, 265, 413n36

Medicare tax
    earned income (*see* earned income)
    FICA, 422n125, 451
    generally, 22–23, 26, 34, 47, 61–62, 75–79, 102, 143, 153
    history of, 22–23, 75–80
    investor's option, 167–168
    pension, 168–169
    proposed payment as tax credit, 55, 68–70, 72–73, 74–86, 166, 174, 206–207, 209–210, 238–239, 347–349
    proposed payment as tax credit with rationale, 68–69, 74–75
    rates, 76–80
    receipts from, 23, 31–32, 61, 290–294
    retirement plans, 122–123
    retirement plans distributions, 168–169

Medicare trust funds, 22–24, 452. *See also* Medicare hospital insurance trust fund

miscellaneous income
    examples, 96–97
    taxation of, 96–97

money transfers
    properly above the line, 136, 138–139
    reduction from income for, 138–139

mortgage interest payments. *See under* reductions from income

moving expenses. *See under* reductions from income

municipal bonds interest. *See* interest income: from state and local bonds

N

National Commission on Fiscal Responsibility and Reform. *See* Fiscal Commission

national debt
    compared to GDP, 19
    debt to Medicare trust funds, 23, 284–285
    debt to Social Security trust funds, 23, 284–285
    description, 11–12, 452
    generally, 11–21, 22–23, 70, 77, 412n27, 452
    government accounts debt, 12–14, 20–21, 272–276, 451
    increases in, 14–15, 72, 223, 272–276, 414n45, 422n123
    interest on (*see* interest on national debt)
    public debt, 11–15, 18–20, 272–276, 453

net capital gains, comparing tax rate changes to, 377–381

net interest. *See under* interest on national debt

net profit
    corporation (*see* corporation earnings (net profit))
    self-employed individual business (*see under* business income)

noncorporate entities. *See under* business entities

nondiscrimination, 28, 164, 213

nonelective payments
    definition, 150
    examples, 134, 150–155
nonprofit corporations. *See* tax-exempt nonprofit
    corporations
nonrefundable tax credit. *See under* tax credits
nontaxable returns, 364

O

Obamacare. *See* Patient Protection and Affordable
    Care Act
off-budget deficit. *See* deficit, annual: off-budget
    component
off-budget outlays. *See under* outlays, federal
off-budget receipts. *See under* receipts, federal
on-budget deficit. *See* deficit, annual: on-budget
    component
on-budget outlays. *See under* outlays, federal
on-budget receipts. *See under* receipts, federal
ordinary income. *See under* individual income
outlays, federal
    definition, 8
    federal funds outlays, 12–13, 262–264, 451
    major components, 8–9
    off-budget outlays, 253–258, 277, 452
    on-budget outlays, 12, 253–258, 452
    total outlays (federal outlays), 8–17, 247–252,
        259–261, 265, 451

P

parity challenge, employees and self-employed
    individuals, 83–86
partnership income
    description, 95
    taxation of, 95
partnerships
    generally, 95
    when a corporation, 190–192
Patient Protection and Affordable Care Act, 79–80,
    142, 437n284
pension payments
    description, 122
    taxation of, 122–123, 168–169

performing artist expenses, 137
personal business
    compared to corporation, 182–184
    earned income from, 47
    taxable income from, 94, 137
personal property, 37, 40–41, 452
personal property tax. *See* property tax
phasing out and phasing in taxes and reductions, 29,
    48–50, 132–133, 141–142, 149, 177, 212–213
principal residence, 111, 126, 431n214
production activities. *See* domestic production
    activities
progressive tax rates. *See* graduated tax rates
property tax
    generally, 37, 39, 150
    potential federal, 37, 40–41
public debt. *See under* national debt

Q

qualifying child for Earned Income Credit, 163

R

real property, 37, 453
real property tax
    generally, 37, 150
    itemized deduction for, 151
    potential federal, 37, 40
receipts, federal
    comparing tax rate changes to, 72, 106, 309–313
    federal funds receipts, 13, 451
    from corporation income tax, 181, 290–294,
        394–396
    from estate tax, 39, 200–201
    from individual income tax, 62, 290–294
    from Medicare tax, 23, 79, 290–294
    from Social Security tax, 22–26, 77, 79,
        290–294
    major sources of, 31–32, 54, 61–62, 290–294
    off-budget receipts, 253–258, 452
    on-budget receipts, 12–15, 253–258, 452
    total receipts (federal receipts), 9, 10–18, 247–
        252, 290–294, 451

reduced federal taxes, effects of, 72, 106, 309–313, 314–320

reductions from income
  above the line, 129–131, 136–140, 147–148, 153, 299, 449
  accountability applied to, 130–131
  below the line, 129–130, 145, 147–148, 449
  business expenses (*see also* business expenses), 94, 134, 137
  business reductions, 134, 137–138
  categories, 134–135
  diminished reductions from income, 132–133
  effect on state governments, 131–132
  elective payments (*see* elective payments (tax subsidies))
  exemptions, 29, 44, 70, 130, 132–133, 141–142, 450
  generally, 129–135, 453
  gifts to charity, 148–149
  healthy life payments, 28, 44, 134, 141–146
  itemized deductions generally, 44, 49–50, 129–133, 142, 148, 452
  local tax payments, 150–153
  losses, 134, 154–155
  major kinds overall, 350–353
  medical expenses, 44, 131, 142–144, 177, 210, 217, 299
  mortgage interest payments, 44, 49, 148, 159, 216, 442n348
  moving expenses, 49, 137, 159
  nonelective payments (*see* nonelective payments)
  payments to IRAs, 138–139
  self-employment tax payment, 79–80, 86, 137, 153
  standard deduction (*see* standard deduction)
  state tax payments, 150–153
  statutory adjustments (*see* above the line *under this heading*)
  structural flaws, 130–131
reform barriers, 1–2
reform criteria. *See* taxes: criteria for judging
refundable tax credit. *See under* tax credits
residence, principal. *See* principal residence

retirees
  description of, 166, 169
  investment income of, 114–116, 168–170
  temporary tax subsidy for, 168–170
retirement plans
  distributions from, 122, 168–169
  generally, 122–123, 138–139, 168–169
  payments into, 122–123, 138–139
  taxation of distributions from, 122–124, 168–170

S

sales tax
  description, 36, 42, 453
  itemized deduction for, 151, 153, 177
  potential federal (fair tax), 30, 32, 36–37, 40, 450
  state, 150
savings. *See* consumption tax
S corporation
  description, 95, 189
  taxation of, 95, 189
Section 86. *See* Social Security benefits: taxation of
self-employed individual
  business income (*see under* business income)
  compared to corporation (*see* business income: individual vs. corporation)
  self-employment tax on (*see* self-employment tax)
self-employment tax
  description, 77–79, 453
  multiplier for earned income, 78–79, 347–349
  payment as reduction from income, 79, 86, 137, 153, 155, 243
  payment as tax credit, 68–69, 72–73, 74, 85–86, 174, 207, 239
  rates, 78–79
simplicity
  as a criterion, 1–2, 27–30, 206–207
  benefits of, 29, 215–216
  definition, 28–29, 453
sin taxes, 35
Social Security benefits
  compared to Social Security tax receipts, 22–25, 68–69, 71, 77, 79

generally, 117, 453

taxation of, 49, 117–121, 386–389

Social Security generally, 117, 453

Social Security tax

  earned income (*see* earned income)

  FICA, 422n125, 451

  generally, 22–23, 26, 34, 47, 61–62, 75–79, 102, 143, 153

  history of, 22–23, 75–80

  investor's option, 167–168

  pension, 168–169

  proposed payment as tax credit, 55, 68–70, 72–73, 74–86, 166, 174, 206–207, 209–210, 238–239, 347–349

  proposed payment as tax credit with rationale, 68–69, 74–75

  rates, 76–80

  receipts from, 22–23, 26, 31–32, 61, 290–294

  retirement plans, 122–123

  retirement plans distributions, 168–169

  self-employment tax (*see* self-employment tax)

spending, federal. *See* outlays, federal

Social Security trust funds

  borrowings from, 21, 23–26, 68–69, 259–261, 284–285

  description, 22, 453

  "runs out" meaning, 23–25

standard deduction

  current law usage, 49, 129–130, 142, 174, 177, 185, 453

  FAST Plan approach, 44, 54, 56, 70, 144, 208, 210, 242, 299

  purposes, 142, 144, 149, 153

standard-rate tax generally, 42, 453

standard-rate income tax

  calculating a rate, 69–71, 298–304

  description, 67

  effect on marriage penalty and bonus, 174

  proposal for, 3, 54–55, 67–70, 206–207, 238–239

  proposal for with rationale, 67–70

  rate comparisons, 216

  total federal tax rate under FAST Plan, 54, 83, 335–337, 339, 342

total federal tax rate within current law, 82, 344–346

  transition to, 209–212

state bonds interest. *See* interest income: from state and local bonds

state taxes. *See* reductions from income: state tax payments

statutory adjustments, 129, 354, 453

stepped-up basis

  description, 196, 453

  embedded capital gain feature (*see* embedded capital gain)

  history of, 196–197

  proposed elimination of, 57, 197–198, 200–201, 206, 208, 213, 246

  proposed elimination of with rationale, 196–198

  proposed option to obtain, 198–199

stock trades, 183

subsidies

  direct (*see* direct subsidy)

  tax (*see* tax subsidy)

surplus, federal, 10–12, 451

T

target tax receipts. *See* tax receipts, target

tariffs, 35–36, 39, 454

taxable income

  generally, 89, 454

  taxable corporation income (*see under* corporation income tax)

  taxable individual income (*see under* individual income tax)

tax alternatives, 31–41

taxation

  purposes of, 7–8

  varieties of, 31–41

tax bracket

  definition, 42, 62, 454

  generally, 42–43, 62–63

tax complexity. *See* complexity

tax compliance, federal. *See* federal tax compliance

tax compromise, December 2010. *See* December 2010 tax compromise tax compromise, fiscal cliff. *See* fiscal cliff tax compromise

tax concepts, 42–46

tax credits

    as preferred subsidy method, 3, 54, 56–57, 135, 148, 156–161, 206, 208, 213, 243

    as preferred subsidy method with rationale, 156–160

    business-related, 164–165

    categories, 157–158

    corporation credits, 190

    for payments of Social Security and Medicare taxes, 55, 68–70, 74, 83, 166, 206–207, 209–210, 238–239

    for payment of Social Security and Medicare taxes with rationale, 68–69, 74–75

    generally, 63, 156–161

    nonrefundable, 148, 157, 178, 452

    refundable, 43, 157, 453

tax discrimination, 48, 65, 102–103, 108, 127, 162, 335

taxes

    criteria for judging, 2, 27–30, 219–220

    on individual income. *See* individual income tax; *see* Medicare tax; *see* Social Security tax

    potential choices, 31–41

tax-exempt income generally, 125–128

tax-exempt nonprofit corporations, 189

tax expenditures. *See under* Fiscal Commission

tax gap, 29, 415n48

tax incentive. *See* tax subsidy

tax rates

    corporation income tax (*see* corporation income tax: rates)

    different rates for different kinds of income, 48

    effect of reduced rates, 72, 309–313, 314–320

    estate tax (*see* estate tax: rates)

    graduated (*see* graduated tax rates)

    history, 72, 305–308

    individual income tax (*see* individual income tax: rates)

    marginal tax rate (*see* marginal tax rate)

    Medicare tax (*see* Medicare tax: rates)

    Social Security tax (*see* Social Security tax: rates)

    progressive (*see* graduated tax rates)

tax receipts. *See* receipts, federal

tax receipts, target, 69–71, 298

Tax Reform Act of 1986, 69–70, 216, 306

Tax Relief Reconciliation Act of 2001, 3, 307

tax reform criteria. *See* taxes: criteria for judging

tax return, joint. *See* joint tax return

tax returns, filing. *See* individual income tax returns, filing

tax subsidy

    business-related, 137–138, 164–165, 178

    definition, 43–45, 51, 208, 454

    depletion allowance, 51

    effect on standard rate, 70, 299

    elective payments, 44–45, 49–50, 147–149

    generally, 43–45, 89, 106, 126, 156–157

    uncompensated losses, 154–155

tax withholding. *See* withholding

tax worksheets, 48, 119

territorial tax. *See under* corporation income tax; *see also under* corporation revenue tax

theft losses. *See* reductions from income: losses

thicket, tax, 2, 4, 46, 53–54, 219–220

top income group, taxes paid, 33, 286–289

total deficit. *See under* deficit, annual

total federal tax, individual

    description, 53–54, 65, 67, 217

    example: capital gains income, 102, 368, 370–371

    examples: ordinary income, 102, 217, 368–369

    paid by top income group (*see* top income group, taxes paid)

total tax rate. *See* marginal tax rate: example total rates; *see also* marginal total federal tax rate for individuals

trade and business expenses. *See* business expenses

transfers, money. *See* money transfers

transition

    to corporation revenue tax, 188–190, 212–213

    to FAST Plan, 209–214

    to standard-rate income tax, 209–212

    to standard-rate income tax on capital gains, 211–212

treasury securities, 11, 15–16, 18–20, 24, 272–273, 277–278, 454

treaties. *See* corporation income tax

true discretionary deficit. *See under* deficit, annual

trust funds

    borrowings from generally, 12–14, 20–21, 22, 262–264, 272–275, 277–278, 413n41

    dedicated taxes for generally, 12, 21, 22, 262, 412n30, 454

    laws concerning, 25, 454

    Medicare hospital insurance (*see* Medicare hospital insurance trust fund)

    Social Security (*see* Social Security trust funds)

U

uncompensated losses. *See* reductions from income: losses

V

value-added tax, 32, 37–38, 41, 454

voluntary tax return filing. *See* individual income tax returns, filing

W

wages

    as earned income (*see* earned income: definition)

    as percent of all income, 90

    individual income taxation of generally, 92–94, 126, 139

withholding, 92–93

worksheets. *See* tax worksheets

Z

zero tax

    beneficiaries of proposed, 67–68

    capital-based income, zero tax on, 67, 96, 335

    capital gains, zero tax on, 67, 107, 335, 337

    flat-tax feature, 67, 70, 451